PAUL

THE APOSTLE

PAUL

THE APOSTLE

The Illustrated Handbook
on His Life and Travels

Robert T. Boyd

WORLD
Bible Publishers, Inc.
Iowa Falls, IA 50126 U.S.A.

To
Curvin and Darlene
Stambaugh

Good
friends
in the Lord

who
know all
my faults

but
love me
anyhow!

CONTENTS

ILLUSTRATIONS

FOREWORD

For the past thirty-two years Bob Boyd has served four pastorates
and has ministered as an evangelist and Bible-conference speaker.
His ministry has been a vital contribution to many.
I pray that this volume will instruct many
for God's glory.

Andrew Telford, D.D.
Veteran Bible-conference Speaker

ACKNOWLEDGEMENTS

*The author wishes to express his appreciation to the following
for their help, suggestions, and encouragement
in making this volume possible:*

*Peggy, my wife,
who down through the years
has been a motivating factor in our ministry;*

*Nate Taylor,
who discipled me as a babe in Christ;*

*Ethel Goatley and Katie Hooker,
who helped in proofreading;*

*Drs.
Karl Keefer,
Andy Telford,
and George Miles.*

SAUL: NOW THE APOSTLE PAUL

The conversion of Saul of Tarsus took place possibly within two years after the crucifixion of Christ (about A.D. 35). His was an about-face conversion. He went from a desire to stamp out Christianity to a passion to build it to its greatest heights. His conversion had an impact on history second only to the birth of Jesus Christ. His ministry, which followed, changed the course of Christianity and with it the course of the so-called religious world, especially Judaism.

He stands above all others in Christian leadership. Even though the Roman Catholic church claims that Peter is second to Christ and remembers him through a Pope (the Vicar of Christ, supposedly Peter's successor), it is Paul to whom the Christian church looks in matters of doctrine and practical godly living. Although Peter is very prominent in the earthly ministry of Christ and the early church in Jerusalem, even writing two epistles contained in the New Testament, no early church saint surpassed Paul in preaching, in establishing churches in Asia and Europe, and in writing. His writings comprise more than a third of our New Testament.

By land and by sea he traveled two continents, determined to know nothing among his hearers "save Jesus Christ and him crucified" (1 Corinthians 2:2). On his four missionary journeys, plus his journey to Rome, he traveled close to 19, 970 miles. This distance is nothing today, but in the first century journeys of the type that Paul undertook lasted for several years.

There have been a few great religious leaders known to the world down through the centuries, but none have made the impact on the hearts and spiritual needs of humanity as Paul has. Most other religious leaders, such as Confucius, who founded an ethical system based on ancestral and weak moral worship, and Mohammed, who founded the Muslim religion and authored the Koran, satisfied needs in a specific geographical location only. Moses is revered universally, but he is confined mostly to the Jewish religion. Thanks, however, to the link between the Old and New Testaments and the fulfillment of prophecy by Christ, Moses is also a part of Christianity. Only Paul stands tall in religious circles throughout the world, particularly in the Christian faith.

The life and ministry of Paul have so intensely influenced every successive generation that they must be studied anew. The length, breadth, width, and depth of his character cannot be limited to the period in which he lived and died. Before he entered the picture, his task had already begun. In a study of his life one soon gets the impression that he was expressly sent into the world for that moment. In Galatians 1:15 and 16 Paul says: "It pleased God, who separated me from my mother's womb and called me by his grace, to reveal his Son in me, that I might preach him among the heathen [Gentiles]." God, who knows the end from the beginning and whose foreknowledge enables Him to bring everything to pass at the right moment according to the good pleasure of His will, saw to it that Paul appeared on the horizon when Christianity needed a genius who would incorporate in his teachings the world's need for all that Christ is. As Christ was born at just the right moment (in the fullness of God's time, Galatians 4:4–5) to be our Redeemer, so God engineered circumstances to accommodate His purposes through Paul. As James Stalker put it: "They [Christ and Paul] seemed likely to have totally diverse careers. Yet, by the mysterious arrangement of Providence, these two lives, like streams flowing from opposite watersheds, were one day, as river and tributary, to mingle together."[1]

God gave the apostle Paul to Christianity in its infancy for a very specific purpose. Even though leaders and preachers such as

Peter and Philip were able to preach the gospel in their native areas of Jerusalem, Judaea, Samaria, and Galilee, there was the uttermost parts of the world. And Rome and Greece needed a man whose qualifications would enable him to be all things to all men that he might win some; a man who knew what Jews thought when Christ was presented to them as Messiah; a man who knew Roman law and could face proud magistrates and governors and kings without fear of embarrassment; a man who could stay one step ahead of the philosophers in their desire of learning; a man who knew how to travel on both land and sea while coping with situations and customs in large cities; a man who always knew how to be content in whatsoever state he found himself.

Paul certainly would have been a distinguished man in Judaism but his becoming a Christian changed that. The other apostles probably would have been nameless in life and death if it had not been for Christianity. They were unlettered men; Paul was educated. This did not make Paul better than they, but he was much better qualified to show the world the whole force of Christianity—the deeper meaning of Christ's death, burial, and resurrection.

Paul could not content himself with being "just another Christian." He was not content just to believe that Christ died for our sins; he had to find out why His death alone could take away humanity's sin. He became the church's greatest thinker and the one who raised the Christ of the Cross to His greatest heights in a largely pagan world. He transcends the limits of time and speaks to all ages. His personality seems to lie in his humanity. As human as Peter was, Paul was equally, if not more, human.

That he was in many ways the ablest and the greatest, the most creative mind, the boldest originator personage in the whole apostolic circle—will be admitted by most readers. That he was the most clever and most brilliant of the apostles everyone must admit.

With all the charm he possessed, these attributes are not what makes a man really interesting. The clever man is, on the whole, unattractive to the mass of mankind. But Paul's secret was that with all his qualifications, he was most intently human—he was a "man's man." The career of Paul can easily and truthfully be described as a series of brilliant and marvelous successes, but it was not through this that he seized upon the hearts of men. It is because behind the achievements we can see his trials and his failures. To others his life might seem like the triumphal progress of a conqueror, but the record we find in the Word of God enables us to look through his eyes and see his toil and stress; we can see him on the point of failure, always guarding against the ceaseless dangers that threatened him, "troubled on every side, yet not distressed; perplexed but not in despair; persecuted but not forsaken; cast down but not destroyed, always bearing about in [his] body the dying of the Lord Jesus" (2 Corinthians 4:8–10).

"We follow his fortunes with the keenest interest because we feel that he was thoroughly representative of the eager, strenuous, toiling man, and his ministry was full of situations and difficulties such as the ordinary man has to face in the world every day. His life, as it stands before us in his letters and his biography, was one constant struggle against difficult circumstances. He was always suspected, always misunderstood by some; but he always found a friend to stand by him in those difficulties, to believe in him in spite of appearances, and to be his champion and guarantee. This is the daily lot of men who work amidst difficulties to find a friend, such as Paul. This is what every man hopes for, and seeing this in the life of Paul, makes it easy to relate to him. In Paul we see the life of *man*, and thus his story never grows old, nor does it ever lose its fascination."[2]

Paul often referred to himself (as we note in his testimony) but only to show either what Christ had done for him or what he was going through to proclaim the unsearchable riches of Christ. Just as he had sold out to Satan before his conversion, so he sold out to the Lord after his conversion. His thorn (see chapter 4), the "messenger of Satan" to buffet him, took its toll on a once-strapping young man. He mentioned to those at Corinth that he was weak, but when one reads what he went through in his determination to "know nothing save Jesus Christ and Him crucified," one can see why his physical being, racked with pain, was weak. Yet, in his weakness, he testified that God's strength was made perfect (1 Corinthians 2:2; 2 Corinthians 11:21, 29; 12:9–10). Even as he came to the close of his ministry, his faith, his fight, and his fundamental uncompromising position in matters of truth were a challenge to all who knew him. By then in his sixties, he had, for some twenty years, traveled and preached, often while working at his trade of tentmaking, with apparent superhuman activity. While his Savior seemed often to avoid the larger cities for the hill country and lake shores, Paul was relentless in his moving from one metropolis to another, over sea and land, from one continent to another. The words of Jesus were common to the area in which He taught, illustrative of farmers (sower), sheep, flowers, sparrows, salt, light, a door, food and water, fish, coins, and so forth. Christ's ministry was accepted more by the common people who heard Him gladly (Mark 12:37). Paul's presentation was theological as he met with religious leaders, philosophers, governors, kings, and other Gentiles in the Graeco-Roman culture of the Roman empire.

Paul's epistles, as they relate to his total dedication and separation to Christlikeness, rank next to the words of Christ in power. He could be kind and warm: "But we were gentle among you, even as a nurse cherishes her children: So being affectionately desirous of you, we were willing to have imparted unto you, not the Gospel of God only, but also our own souls, because you were dear unto us" (1 Thessalonians 2:7–8; cf. to Christ's words in Matthew 11:28–29 and 23:37). He could also give vent to his "righteous indignation," such as in Galatians 5:12 where Paul berates Jews who had led the Galatians astray: "I would that they who are besetting you would even have themselves mutilated" (cf., with Christ's scathing denunciation of the Pharisees in Matthew 23).

As personal as Paul was in his epistles, he was profoundly a theologian. Theologians are supposed to be very dry—hard to understand by the average layman—yet Paul is easy to understand in many instances, such as his reasoning that "all have sinned and come short of the glory of God" (Romans 3:23). Peter, however, said that those who are unlearned and unstable—those who do not take the time to study the Word of God, thereby wresting the Scriptures (or distorting it) to their own destruction (2 Peter 3:15–16), find Paul hard to understand.

Even though there are believers who find some verses of Scripture difficult to grasp at first, much study in comparing Scripture with Scripture often brings one to a revelation of intended truth in that particular portion. Paul's writings in general not only present problems but also give us solutions to our problems. He is always putting in little words or phrases that connect what he has said previously to what is to follow. His thought is like a train—Christ is the Engine and many cars follow, but there is no caboose. His thoughts about Christ as our solution never end; we go from one car to another. Some of his wonderful transitional phrases or words are *therefore*, *wherefore*, and *if*. A good example is found in Romans 3–5; in chapter 3, we see ourselves as sinners, hopelessly lost and undone; in chapter 4, we find there is forgiveness for the vilest of sinners—our salvation is dependent on Christ and not on works: then, in 5:1, we find a *therefore* to let us know that guilty sinners, who have been forgiven, now have "peace with God." How simple, yet how deep and unfathomable this truth. It is no wonder that God used Paul to write almost half of the New Testament.

After a life of total dedication, having spent himself in the service of his Master, Paul comes to the end of life's road. With bent body, face marked with lines of hard living and premature old age, and snow-white hair, there are no signs of his quitting or even slowing down to semiretirement. His spirit and will still display his fervor to preach Christ and preserve truth. In his closing words to Timothy he says in effect, "the Word of God is not bound even though I am in bonds;" "be not ashamed of the Gospel;" "preach the Word in season and out of season" (2 Timothy 1:8; 2:9; 4:2). What an encouragement this must have been to a young preacher, especially coming from a man "who had been there." Paul now refers to himself as "Paul the aged" (Philemon 9). Possibly as he awaited execution, and reminisced about his having stayed on course, his mind went back to the day he consented to the martyrdom of Stephen. Here, too, was a man who had stayed on course, kept the faith, and fought a good fight. Now Paul was about to experience his "gain" or entrance into glory by forfeiting his life for Christ the same as had Stephen.

As he looked back to the old days of his persecution of the church and with Stephen's face ever in his mind's eye, he probably thought over and over the truth he proclaimed to the Galatians: "Whatsoever a man soweth, that shall he also reap" (6:7). Throughout his ministry, from his conversion at Damascus to the end of his life, Paul reaped manifold what he had sown in his hatred of Christ and His followers. But as the one who had labored more abundantly than they all (1 Corinthians 15:10), as the one who gloried in his infirmities because God's grace was sufficient (2 Corinthians 12:9), he knew that when he stood before his Savior to give account of his life's work (2 Corinthians 5:10) that he would hear Him say: "Well done, thou good and faithful servant" (Matthew 25:21). Paul closes his ministry by saying: "For I am now ready to be offered, and the time of my departure is at hand. I have fought a good fight, I have finished my course, I have kept the faith: henceforth there is laid up for me a crown of righteousness, which the Lord, the righteous

Judge, shall give me in that day" (2 Timothy 4:6-8). His testimony here reflects the song writer's thought: "It will be worth it all when we see Jesus." When his final moment came, he closed his eyes only to awaken and find himself on the shores of heaven in the presence of the One who had laid down His life for him.

In this book, *Paul the Apostle: The Illustrated Handbook on His Life and Travels,* we will give an account of his life from birth to his death based as much as possible on the Word of God. We will see him as one who was determined to wipe out Christianity; then as one who was determined to tell the whole world the claims of the Christ of Christianity. What do we really know about this "persecutor of the church" turned missionary? Who was he? How did he come upon the scene of history? Webster's dictionary devotes a few lines to him; the Encyclopedia Britannica devotes over eight-and-a-half pages to him, but the Bible gives the details that are necessary for us to know his ministry. With all we know about him from the Bible, however, there is much the Bible does not say about his life, thoughts, and ways. Where the Scripture is silent, for example about how soon after his conversion he went to Arabia, where he went in Arabia, and how long he stayed there, we must use our "sanctified imaginations" within, of course, the bounds of spiritual reasoning.

HOW TO READ THIS BOOK

Come with me as we take a journey with Paul from his birth in Tarsus of Cilicia (ancient Asia Minor, now Turkey, Acts 21:39), to Jerusalem and Damascus as the "persecutor of the church" (1 Corinthians 15:9), to his being the "ringleader of the Nazarenes" (or followers of Jesus of Nazareth, Acts 24:5), through all his persecutions and sufferings, and to his death in Rome (2 Timothy 4:6–8). For best results, keep your Bible open and read the references as you travel with this saint of God, joining in with him as he meets with and witnesses to those who need Jesus Christ as their own personal Savior. Check the maps of each journey. The Table of Contents may also be used as an index. The name *Paul* will be used throughout except where *Saul* or *Saul of Tarsus* is practical.

Chapter One

PAUL BEFORE CONVERSION

The Jews who had been scattered over the world and lived outside Palestine were called "Jews of the Dispersion." There were more Jews living outside Judaea than were living within its boundaries, as today there are more Jews in various parts of the world than there are in Israel.

PAUL'S FAMILY After the Babylonian exile many Jews did not return to their homeland but settled in Babylon, Persia, Egypt, Asia Minor, and some even in Rome on the European continent. We learn from Luke that "Jews, devout men, out of every nation under heaven" were in Jerusalem for the feast of Pentecost. They came from Persia, Mesopotamia, Asia, Rome, and so forth (Acts 2:5, 9–11).

His Father

Paul's ancestors had migrated to Asia Minor and settled in Tarsus of Cilicia. Paul was of the tribe of Benjamin (Philippians 3:5), which had originated with Benjamin, one of Jacob's sons (Genesis 49:1, 27). When Israel was divided after Solomon's death, the tribe of Benjamin remained true to God and became a part of the southern kingdom of Judah under the reign of Solomon's son, Rehoboam (1 Kings 12:16–21). After the Babylonian captivity some of the tribe of Benjamin returned to Jerusalem (Nehemiah 11:7–9, 31–36), but, as noted above, Paul's ancestors chose to settle in Tarsus in Asia Minor. In addition to his being from the tribe of Benjamin, Paul was a Pharisee (Acts 23:6) and a Roman citizen (Acts 22:25–28).

His Mother

Paul's mother was Jewish, but we know little else of her background. Paul alludes to his father's being the "son of a Pharisee" (Acts 23:6). The only time he mentions his mother is in Galatians 1:15: "It pleased God, who separated me from my mother's womb." We know nothing else about her, though we do find notices about his sister and nephew and about distant relatives (Romans 16:7, 11, 21). Paul tells of his instructor Gamaliel, but nothing of his mother, no doubt his earliest teacher. Did she pass away in Paul's youth, leaving his father to raise him and teach him what a Jewish mother ordinarily taught her children? Or, did she live to mourn and grieve his apostasy from Pharisaism? Did she die unreconciled to the obedience of Christ? Or, did she believe and obey the Savior of her son? These are questions we cannot answer. If we wish to visualize the earliest infancy of Paul, we must be content with the simple picture of a Jewish mother and her child, such as the picture presented to us in the short history of John the Baptist and his mother, Elizabeth (Luke 1:5–25).

His Sister and Nephew

Paul had an unnamed sister and nephew in Jerusalem (Acts 23:16) who looked after his well-being. After Paul was taken by the Roman soldiers for protection from the Jews, his nephew learned of a plot to take his life. He informed the authorities about it, which necessitated Paul's being transferred to Caesarea to be under the jurisdiction of Felix. The nephew was instrumental in saving Paul's life (Acts 23:12–24).

His Relatives

Paul also had kinsmen living in Rome (Romans 16:7, 11, 21). Andronicus and Junia evidently had lived in Jerusalem before moving to Rome since they were so well acquainted with the apostles. They both had come to know Christ as their own personal Savior before Paul, and possibly witnessed to him before his own conversion. Paul refers to them as his fellow prisoners. As Paul was in prison often, it is likely these two shared the honor with him on some occasions, or were possibly in prison for their own testimony's sake.

PAUL'S CHILDHOOD   Paul was born in Tarsus (see map 1, p. 442), "a city in Cilicia [Asia Minor, now Turkey], a citizen of no mean [a significant] city" (Acts 21:39) about the time of, or soon after, the birth of Christ. When Jesus was a boy playing in the streets of Nazareth, Paul probably was playing in the streets of Tarsus.

Birthplace

Tarsus, a city of considerable importance, was almost one thousand years old when Paul was born. The city is mentioned on an inscription made during the time of the Assyrian captivity of Cilicia (about 883 B.C.). In New Testament times it was a commercial center, located on the river Cyndus, not far from the coast. Ships from distant lands docked, bringing goods for local trade. Sailors, merchants, and citizens of Tarsus mingled daily with one another as well as with the populace of central Asia Minor who came to Tarsus through the Cilician Gates to do business. (Timber and goat hair were the major commodities and made transport trade possible. The timber, of course, was used in building and the long goat hair was used for cloth and tent material.) The majority of Tarsus' citizens were native civilians; however, the wealthiest were Greeks. Tarsus, a rival of the city of Rome, was at one time the capital of all Cilicia and was one of the three principal university cities of its time, competing with Alexandria and Athens in arts and sciences. The inhabitants in the time of Julius Caesar (100–44 B.C.), having shown themselves friendly to the Romans, were accorded and endowed with all the privileges of Roman citizens, including the rare privilege of self-government. What a place for Paul to be born and raised; a place where he would mingle with men of every description; a place where he would see firsthand many practices and customs of both Romans and Greeks. All this would help prepare him for a city-to-city ministry as the Apostle to the Gentiles. Of all the great patriots of Tarsus, graduates from its universities of science and arts, none has ever achieved the greatness of Paul; none are remembered except him. In fact, Tarsus itself would be forgotten if it were not for Paul.

Name

Paul's parents named him *Saul*, a Jewish name meaning "asked for, he asked, sought, inquired." They probably gave him this Jewish name after King Saul, who was the first king of Israel and also of the tribe of Benjamin (1 Samuel 9:1–2, 21). It was not until Saul and Barnabas were on their first missionary journey that Saul's name was changed to Paul (Acts 13:9). This was appropriate for him because of his Roman citizenship. *Paul* (*Paulus*) is Latin, and it means "little." For one called to go to the Gentiles, this name was acceptable to both the Romans and the Greeks. In Hebrew it means "extraordinary, wonderful, one who stands tall" (not necessarily in height), "strong willed." He could have been small of stature but not weak physically. Acts 8:1–3 indicates that he had to be strong to drag Christians out of their homes and to beat them (Acts 22:19). He admitted to weakness in 2 Corinthians 10:10, but this was after years of physical suffering that had taken its toll on his body (2 Corinthians 11:23–33). Considering his ability to confound the Jews with the Old Testament, he was extraordinary, wonderful, and mighty in ability. The name *Paul* was also acceptable to the Jews because of its Hebrew connotation—a person of determination with a strong will.

Jewish Heritage

Scripture records Paul as being a Jew. According to Philippians 3:5, Paul was circumcised the eighth day as were all Jewish boys (proselytes were circumcised when they embraced Judaism, Genesis 17:9–13). Philippians 3:5 also declares that Paul was "of the stock of Israel." This expression denotes that he was not a proselyte who had embraced the Jewish religion. He was born a Jew.

Paul was from the tribe of Benjamin (Philippians 3:5). When Jacob blessed his sons, who were to make up the twelve tribes of Israel, he said, "Benjamin shall ravin [rend in pieces] as a wolf; in the morning he shall devour the prey, and at night he shall divide the spoil" (Genesis 49:27). In examining the methods and techniques of Saul of Tarsus in seeking to make "havoc of the church, entering into every house" (Acts 8:3) or, in essence, rending in pieces and devouring Christians, we see that the family trait as recorded in Genesis was probably the source of his meanness.

As one reads the last three chapters of Judges, one receives insight into the "preying and devouring" of the Benjamites on others. A good example is King Saul, of Benjamin's tribe, who lived up to the characteristics of a wolf. He was jealous of David, whom he thought to be his competitor (1 Samuel 18:8; 19:1); Paul, King Saul's namesake, was jealous of the infringement of Christianity on the Jews' religion. King Saul was dishonest with Samuel in withholding the spoils of victory (1 Samuel 15:11–23); Paul was ignorantly dishonest in withholding the truth of Scriptures presenting error in the form of traditions (cf. Matthew 15:6 and Romans 10:2–3). King Saul was disobedient to the command of God (1 Samuel 15:13, 22–24); Paul was disobedient to the commandments of God, killing others and seeking to establish his own righteousness by his good works. King Saul was rebellious (1 Samuel 15:23); Paul rebelled against freedom of religion. King Saul was self-willed (1 Samuel 15:23); Paul was self-willed in his determination to stamp out the name of Christ.

Paul's Jewishness is further proved by the fact that he was a Hebrew of the Hebrews (Philippians 3:5; 2 Corinthians 11:22). As a true Israelite of the seed of Abraham, Paul was a pure-blooded Israelite because both sides of his family, father and mother, were Israelites (Romans 9:4–8).

Paul's last Jewish characteristic was his Pharisaism. From a youth up after the "straitest sect, I lived a Pharisee" of the Pharisees (Philippians 3:5; Acts 23:6; 26:4–5). His Pharisaism is discussed in detail under his education.

Roman Citizenship

In addition to being a Jew, Paul was a Roman citizen (Acts 22:25–29). We deduce from Paul's statement in Acts 22:28 that he was a Roman citizen because his father was and he had been born free. Neither history nor the Bible reveals how Paul's family became citizens of Rome (see illustration 1). Julius Caesar accorded favors to those who "advanced" the Roman Empire. Cilicia was under the jurisdiction of several Roman generals during the first century B.C., and possibly under one of these generals Paul's family was accorded citizenship.

Roman citizenship could be achieved (1) by being born free, as was the case of Paul; (2) by performing some favorable deed for Rome; (3) by a person of note—an honor; (4) by soldiers for bravery or upon their being honorably discharged; and (5) by being purchased (Acts 22:25–28). Illustration 1 shows a military

1—A certificate of Roman citizenship. *Courtesy of author.*

diploma that granted citizenship to honorably discharged soldiers and their wives. Their names are listed below the official declaration. However, in Paul's case, speculation as to how his father became a Roman citizen is the best that one can do. It is quite evident that Paul, who was freeborn, never would have appealed to his citizenship if he were not a Roman citizen. To fraudulently claim citizenship was punishable by death. Rome had a system whereby citizens could verify their citizenship by having registered the matter in court (before a magistrate) at birth, when it was bestowed on them, or when it was purchased. Upon registering, a certificate was issued, which they carried on their person (as an automobile driver must carry a license when driving). Nothing is said in Scripture about Paul's having any such identification, but it appears that the centurion who rescued Paul from the Jews had sufficient evidence to believe him (Acts 22:29).

No matter where a Roman citizen went throughout the Roman Empire, as a citizen he was entitled to all the rights and privileges that its law provided. As we study Paul's arrest in Jerusalem and the events that followed, we will note some of these privileges.

HIS OCCUPATION   Paul's occupation was tent making (see illustration 2), which he continued throughout his life as a missionary (Acts 18:1–3; 1 Corinthians 4:12; 1 Thessalonians 2:9). Tent making in those days was a good business among bedouins (or nomads). Sons usually followed the family trade, and since Roman soldiers needed tents, Paul's family could have been awarded citizenship because of their craftsmanship.

HIS EDUCATION   The Promised Land had been invaded by the Assyrians, the Babylonians, the Greeks, and the Romans. Numberless Jews had been taken captive to distant lands. Wherever they went, they took their Scriptures and relied on the Law of Moses as well as the traditions of their fathers. Throughout all these lands, synagogues had been established and the Jews were distinguished by their religion. Strabo, a great historian of the first century A.D., said, "It is hard to find a place in the habitable earth that has not admitted this tribe of man and is not possessed by it."[1] Scattered from Babylon in the East to Rome and Spain in the West, they were called dispersion Jews. Although they wore their own robes of righteousness and made their boast in the Law, they blasphemed the name of God among the heathen (Romans 2:23–24). They were "queer" to the world, but they made sure their children were raised according to their religion and customs.

Paul's parents were strict Jews. To have a son was a joyous occasion, and Paul, at birth, was dedicated to the service of God; dedicated to be brought up as a good Jew. From his infancy onward he heard, "Hear, O Israel: The LORD our God is one LORD: and thou shalt love the LORD thy God with all thine heart, and

2—An example of tentmaking—Paul's occupation. *Courtesy of the American Bible Society,* New York.

with all thy soul, and with all thy might" (Deuteronomy 6:4–5). He learned to pray in a kneeling position facing Jerusalem, where the holy temple was located and where Jehovah dwelt among His people. Until the age of four his mother taught him Bible stories. At an early age he was conscious that he belonged to a group of "God people," a God who blessed His own no matter where they lived. Whenever there were enough Jews in a given city they would build a synagogue in which to worship Jehovah on the Sabbath. They read the Law of Moses, and being true Jews, they had a synagogue school in which the Law of Moses, the Torah, was the textbook. When Paul was old enough, his mother took him to the synagogue to observe the Sabbath. At the age of five his father became his teacher and at six he was taken to the Rabbi's school. Here he had drilled into him the rudiments of the Law. He had to memorize it as the Rabbi repeated it. There were no crayons to draw pictures, no kool-aid, no recess, no blocks, no games—just rigid, disciplined study. There was a progression from the rudiments of the Law into the rituals, ceremonies, feasts, and so forth of the Mosaic teachings. His textbook was the Old Testament Scripture in Hebrew and the Greek Septuagint (the Hebrew Scriptures that had been translated into Greek about 175 B.C.). Paul likely knew several languages—Hebrew and Greek from studying; Aramaic since dispersion Jews kept in close contact with the Jews of Palestine, who spoke Aramaic; and Latin, the official language of the Roman Empire.

Synagogue-school training under the Rabbi typically continued until one was about thirty. This was likely the scenario for Paul since the universities in Tarsus were of the Hellenistic literary and philosophical type, and dispersion Jewish fathers followed the principle, "Cursed be he that shall teach Greek science to his son."[2]

Learning much as a lad in the Jews' religion in his home and the synagogue, Paul was about the age of fourteen or fifteen when he left home to enroll as a student for Rabbinical training in Jerusalem. In Jerusalem, he was "brought up at the feet of Gamaliel and taught according to the perfect manner of the law of our fathers and was zealous toward God" (Acts 22:3). So brilliant a student was he that he told those in Galatia, "I profited in the Jews' religion above many my equals in mine own nation, being more exceedingly zealous . . ." (Galatians 1:14). His Roman citizenship and the influence of Grecian culture never lessened his loyalty to his Jewish heritage. He was a zealous Jew who sought to establish his own righteousness, who was not willing to submit to the righteousness of God, and who bragged about his ancestry (Romans 10:1–3; Philippians 3:4–8).

His Jewish religious and moral education was by far the most important piece of "equipment" that he was to have for the work that would be set before him as a Christian. His experiences as a Tarsian and a Roman would also be indispensable to him since he would be the apostle to the Gentile world. Someone has said that the Old Testament is the New Testament concealed and the New Testament is the Old Testament revealed. The Old Testament is the prophecy and the New Testament is the fulfillment. God needed a man at a particular time whose mind was not only overflowing with Old Testament law and history but also so receptive to its fulfillment that he would be the master theologian of Christianity for all ages. Paul was destined to be that man and to became the principal writer of the New Testament. He wrote thirteen epistles (fourteen if he wrote Hebrews as some expositors believe).

PAUL'S PHARISAISM   Paul's father was a Pharisee (see illustration 3) and as a Pharisee he saw to it that his son was schooled in its teachings, especially as a youth.

3—How Pharisees might have looked. *Courtesy of author.*

Paul described himself as a "Pharisee, the son of a Pharisee" (Acts 23:6). The Pharisaism that Paul learned in his youth in Tarsus as the son of a Pharisee simply meant being loyal to the Law of Moses and to every precept and every interpretation that his Rabbi gave to the Law. It also meant arriving at a so-called true and satisfying righteousness. Giving heed to the Law meant not only the ceremonial law of Moses but also the thousand-and-one other rules added to it by the Jewish teachers. William Ramsey said: "The observance of these laws made life a purgatory to a tender conscience."[3] Being a good Pharisee, Paul was a man of conviction, one who would not compromise his beliefs. In his early training his thoughts were focused on the capital of Jewry—Jerusalem, and a good school there.

Having left home to further his education in Jerusalem, Paul soon began to realize that the Pharisaism of Palestine was vastly different from what he had been taught in Tarsus. The Greek word *Pharisee* comes from an Aramaic word *peras*, which means to "divide and separate" (see Daniel 5:28), the "separated one," or a "separatist." The word *Pharisee* was first used after the Maccabean revolt against Antiochus Epiphanes, the Syrian general who sought to force Grecian culture on the Jews. He forbade the circumcising of their male infants and offered a swine on the altar in the temple in Jerusalem. The Jewish revolt was successful and Israel was once again a self-ruling people (about 165 B.C.). A group called the Pharisees was formed, and their avowed purpose was to enforce the teachings of the Law, the Prophets, and the Psalms. Josephus wrote that the Pharisees "appear more religious than others, and seem to interpret the laws more accurately."[4] One advantage that the Pharisees had was having the Scribes, the learned men of the Law, the lawyers, in their camp. Another advantage that the Pharisees had was a following among the majority of the Jewish people.

In their zeal for the Law, the Pharisees had all but deified it and in so doing they became merely external, formal, and mechanical. In their role as custodians of the Law, they took it on themselves to be the sole interpreters of it; thus their interpretation of the Law became the law. According to Josephus, Pharisaism "pretended to have more exact knowledge of the law, as being the exactest sect of the Jews, and the most exact interpretation of the law."[5] In the Pharisees' interpretation of the Law, many oral laws were added, which later became known as the so-called traditions of their fathers. These traditions superseded the Scriptures and the Pharisees became legalistic in enforcing them.

In Christ's and Paul's day, there were two famous divinity and philosophical schools among the Jews; that of Shammai and that of Hillel. A classic example of their differences is seen in the question proposed to Jesus concerning divorce and remarriage. Hillel's followers were liberal in their view, believing a man could divorce his wife for any reason. Shammai's followers were more conservative, believing adultery to be the only reason for divorce. Both groups tried to trick Jesus into siding with their particular view, but Christ gave a biblical answer, not an oral interpretation as they certainly expected (Matthew 19:3–9). Hillel became the so-called spiritual leader among the Jews in Palestine (from about 30 B.C. to A.D. 10). He was a prince in the Sanhedrin and was known as Hillel the Elder. He was an authority on the interpretation of the added laws and helped to arrange or classify more than six hundred sections of them. In Gamaliel's school, Paul was taught the philosophy of both Hillel and Shammai. His beliefs and attitudes changed as he began to succumb to a Pharisaism that was new to him. He would soon learn that this Pharisaism had fallen from the high character, which marked it at its inception, to criminal depths.

By substituting the traditions of their fathers for the Scriptures (Matthew 15:3, 6; Mark 7:3, 8), the Pharisees' doctrine became like leaven—it permeated the whole, thus making their interpretation and teachings compatible to their own nature and thought. Being separatists and legalists, their strict observance of their own laws became a way of life—they were wedded to their interpretation of what they said the Law meant. This resulted in an outward exhibition of formalism and ritualism—a life of piety with no inward purity or righteousness. They lost the spirit of their institution and retained nothing but external regulations, or the letter of the law. They were exact in obeying all the washing and purifications ordained by the Law, but they paid no attention to inward cleansing that was necessary for godly righteousness. Little did they realize that outward purity availed nothing because inward holiness was lacking. The Pharisees became remarkably scrupulous in the performance of all the rites and ceremonies of the Jews' religion but totally neglected their own souls and spirits.

The more emphasis they put on outward observances, the more they walked by sight and not by faith. This led to their censuring the conduct of others rather than rectifying their own; to their desiring that everyone else regulate personal piety by theirs and embrace their particular customs and forms of devotion; and to their comparing themselves with other people so that they would have an opportunity to distinguish and exalt themselves.

It appeared that everything they did was an outward act to be seen of men. When they prayed, sometimes for as much as three hours, they would stand in the synagogue or on a street corner because if they knelt, they might not be seen (Matthew 6:5). In praying they would raise their voices and make it known that they were better than anyone else (Luke 18:11). When they fasted, it was noised abroad the number of times (Luke 18:21), and they would fake a long face to make others think they had gone a long time without food (Matthew 6:16). They engaged in superstitious fasts in order to have lucky dreams, to obtain interpretation of dreams, to avert the evil import of dreams, and to obtain things they wished for. They were also superstitious in the observance of the Sabbath, making it a crime to defend themselves on the Sabbath. (On one occasion this resulted in the defeat of Jerusalem when the Roman general, Pompey, attacked in A.D. 63.) When they sat at banquets, it was always in the prominent seats (Matthew 23:6). Being destitute of righteousness within, they endeavored to supply it by large lettered phylacteries and long fringes (Matthew 23:5). They demanded respectful greetings in the market place (Matthew 23:7). They condemned anyone who did not wash his hands or wipe his plate clean before eating (Luke 11:39). They took to task anyone who plucked corn on the Sabbath (Matthew 12:1–8); who ate with a sinner (Mark 2:16–17); or who left a fallen ox in a pit (Luke 14:5). They made public a woman taken in adultery (John 8:3–11). (Many more illustrations are to be found in the encounters Jesus had with them.)

The Pharisees were never satisfied unless they were emphasizing the minor and minimizing the major; straining at a gnat and swallowing a camel (Matthew 7:3–5; 23:24). The outward religion of the Pharisees led to a hardening of their hearts, resulting in their becoming antagonistic, bigoted, crafty, despisers of good, envious, fanatical, greedy, hypocritical, intolerant, judgmental, knavish, libelous, full of malice, narrow-minded, opinionated, prejudiced, quarrelsome, ritualistic, self-righteous, temperamental, unrepentant, vehement, willful, xanthic (yellow, cowardly), yammerers (complainers, clamorers, shouters, Acts 22:21–23), zelotypic (morbid, insane zeal), and last but not least, proud.

The above "alphabet soup" of outward acts that flow from any religiously hardened heart define the Pharisaical heart. Whatever they did outwardly was to the neglect of justice, mercy, and faith, showing that the righteousness they were seeking to establish was not of God (Romans 10:1–3). Being blind themselves, they blinded others by adding useless ceremonies that in reality had neither reason, expediency, nor revelation to countenance them. They were severe to others but very indulgent to themselves. Their intolerance and censorious spirit became their greatest curse. Their malice and envy worked overtime. They incessantly hunted their prey (such as their desire to trap and finally kill Christ, or like Saul of Tarsus in his desire to wreak havoc with the church). In their association with others, they considered it the equal to legal defilement to sit in the company of tax collectors and sinners (heathen). In their determination to exalt and enforce their traditions, they took away the key of knowledge. They were ever seeking but never coming to a knowledge of the truth. It was no longer thus saith the Lord, but thus saith the oral law or the interpretation of the law. By their traditions they took away the true interpretation of Scripture. They gave the wrong meaning to those portions of the Word that spoke of the kingdom of the Messiah, and they led people astray; thus hindering their entrance into the kingdom of God. They were blind leaders of the blind. They were concerned only with self-interests and had absolutely no concern for others (Luke 11:46).

Like all religious sects and parties, the Pharisees degenerated, having substituted the letter of the law for the spirit. They had a form of godliness that was ruled not by the Holy Spirit but by man-made rules. A Pharisee never felt himself indebted to the infinite mercy of God for the salvation of his own soul and cared less about the salvation of others. Pharisaism honored God with the lips but not with the heart (Mark 7:6). Christ said: "Do not ye after their works: for they say, and do not" (Matthew 23:3). There was no place in their thinking for further revealed truth; they had it all and gloated that all others were doomed heretics.

Pharisaism led otherwise good men to plot to take the lives of any who opposed them. Anyone who reproved them—Christ, Stephen, or Paul—was put on their so-called hit list. Those who sought Paul's life during his missionary journeys, are classic examples of this tragic aspect of Pharisaism (John 11:53; Acts 7:51–60; 8:1–3; 9:23–25). Their religion took them into a new battlefield. They sought to kill all who disagreed, to stamp out all religions that did not conform to their stated beliefs. Thus, they became fiercely intolerant toward anyone whose religious views were not in accord with theirs. They were so devoted to their earthly life and their prejudiced doctrines that they had little concern for the hereafter. They literally became murderers, nothing more than wolves in sheep's clothing seeking to devour all who crossed their paths. With the backing and support of the majority of the Jewish public and relying on the Scribes, or lawyers, to back them in every situation, the Pharisees were challenged and encouraged to be all the more fanatical in their ruthless opposition to any religion and to Christianity in particular. These biased religious bigots had a morbid zeal in the prosecution of their cause.

Josephus said there were as many as six thousand Pharisees at the peak of their history, which lasted from the time of the Maccabees (about 160 B.C.) to the time of Emperor Hadrian (about A.D. 135), a total of almost three hundred years.

PAUL'S EARLY MANHOOD   Paul must have left Jerusalem after his graduation from the Jewish seminary of Dr. Gamaliel. We do not know how old he was then, but like most new graduates, he knew everything and was out to set the world on fire and bring everyone under his sway and religious beliefs. He made mention of the zeal that all Jews had—a zeal without knowledge of God—and claimed it as his own (Romans 10:2–3). In all probability he went back to his home in Tarsus soon after his graduation because his path clearly would have crossed that of Jesus somewhere in and around Jerusalem had he stayed. Since there is no mention of this either in Acts or in Paul's epistles, it is quite possible that he never met Jesus until he was on the road to Damascus (Acts 9:3–6).

Paul could have been among those of Asia who had come to Jerusalem during Pentecost, the time of the descent of the Holy Spirit, and may even have heard Peter's sermon (Acts 2:1–40). Present in Jerusalem at that time were "Jews from every nation (v. 5), including Asia (v. 9), of which Tarsus of Cilicia was a part. If he had been in attendance on this day and remained in Jerusalem, he could have received his "boot training" in hatred,

THE PHARISEES

Description	Scripture
A sect of the Jews	Acts 15:5
Strict observers of Mosaic ritual	Acts 26:5
Zealous of the Law	Philippians 3:5
Zealous of tradition	Mark 7:3, 5–8; Galatians 1:14
Outwardly moral	Luke 18:1; Philippians 3:5–6
Active in proselytizing	Matthew 23:15
Self-righteous	Luke 16:15; 18:9
Fond of public salutations	Matthew 23:7
Boastful of their life of prayer and fasting	Luke 18:11–12
Fond of distinguished titles	Matthew 23:7–10
Cruel in persecuting	Acts 9:1–2
Outwardly religious	Matthew 23:5
Repulsed by John's baptism	Luke 7:30
Compared to whited sepulchers	Matthew 23:27
Blind leaders of the blind	Matthew 23:16
Put heavy burdens on others	Matthew 23:4
Strained at gnats and swallowed "camels"	Matthew 23:4
Tempted Christ	Matthew 16:1

THE PHARISEES

Description	Scripture
Imputed Christ's miracles to Satan's power	Matthew 9:34; 12:24
Often sought to destroy Christ	Matthew 12:14; Luke 4:28–30
Sent officers to apprehend Christ	John 7:32, 45
Totally rejected Christ. Even though they were told by the high priest, Caiaphas, that Jesus was the One who should die for them, they sought to kill him.	John 1:11; 11:47, 53
Falsely arrested and tried Christ	John 18:2–14, 19–40
Condemned Christ	Matthew 9:11; Luke 7:39; 15:1–2
Demanded Christ's life	Luke 23:21
Demanded that the guilty go free	Mark 15:7–15
Mocked Christ while He was dying	Matthew 27:41–43
Bribed Roman soldiers to say that Christ's body had been stolen by His disciples; thus denying His resurrection	Matthew 27:62–66; 28:11–15
Continued to persecute followers of Christ as we shall see throughout the book of Acts and in the life of Paul both before and after his conversion	Acts
Were denounced by Christ as hypocrites	Matthew 23:28

and during this early formation of Christianity and the church he could have been party to the persecution of the disciples (Acts 4:1–4, 21; 5:17–33). This would have helped him to his position as chief persecutor of the church, as we note at the time of Stephen's stoning. Although Paul is not mentioned by name, some from Cilicia of Asia opposed Stephen and by the time Stephen was killed, Paul was the ringleader of persecution (Acts 6:8–9; 7:57–8:1). If he was not present on the Day of Pentecost in Jerusalem, he came soon after and had a part in Stephen's death. All this shows that he had adopted the neo-Jerusalem Pharisaism, which meant that he was no longer a typical strict, orthodox, religious Jew of zealous Jewish parents. Now a bigoted Jew, he became cold and proud; a despiser of all who did not agree with him; narrow-minded in his sympathies, intolerant of others. He kept every little detail of the Law and traditions of his fathers but passed up soul-hungry multitudes. To paraphrase Jesus, he swallowed a camel and choked on a gnat (see Matthew 23:24).

He was fanatical, cruel, and violent in his opposition of those who held other religious beliefs. This led to his determination to stamp out Christianity, even if he had to kill all Christians to do it. He even labeled himself the chief persecutor of the church, one who profited or advanced in Judaism far above those his own age, being more exceedingly zealous of the traditions of his fathers (see Galatians 1:13–14). He admitted, as a Pharisee, that he was a blasphemous and injurious or violent man (1 Timothy 1:12–13). All this will become obvious in our study of him up to the time of his conversion to Christ.

Paul's brand of Pharisaism gave him a much clearer and wider outlook than the Palestinian Pharisees had. He could no longer act in agreement with them except in their destructive efforts against the Christians. According to Acts 8:1–3, Paul had consented to Stephen's death and was wreaking havoc on the church. So addictive was the hatred that this man bore for Christ and His followers that he delighted in their destruction. So blind was his heart with superstitious zeal that he thought he was doing God a service by offering Him the blood of his fellow creatures, those whose creed or beliefs he thought to be erroneous. Paul was actually pleased with his murderous work.

The word *havoc* in verse 3 signifies the act of ferocious animals seeking and devouring their prey, and means that, as a Benjamite (Genesis 49:27), Paul was set to destroy the church. This shows what zeal he had in pursuing harmless Christians and magnifies his one-sided, narrow-minded bigotry and his false and morbid zeal in the prosecution of his cause. His every breath was a threat to the disciples of Christ, and he must have been a strapping, strong young man to have been able to drag people out of their homes (Acts 9:1–3).

Prior to Paul's conversion, Caiaphas was the high priest in Jerusalem. He served from A.D. 18 to about the year after Paul was saved (A.D. 36). He was the high priest when Jesus was put to death (Matthew 16:3–5, 67–66). According to tradition, he was a politician of the highest degree and was known as the "sacred butcher." Although he predicted that Jesus was to die for Israel and other nations, he said it in such a sarcastic way that the Sanhedrin evidently took it to mean that since Jesus was to die anyhow they would go ahead and kill Him (John 11:47–53).

This same Caiaphas played an important role in Paul's life. The fact that Paul had close connections with him is evident. In fact, he had direct access to him. He "went unto the high priest and desired of him letters to go to Damascus" to arrest and bring back Christians to Jerusalem (Acts 9:1–2). Where did Paul get the privilege? To grant such a request, the Sanhedrin had to vote on the matter. According to Acts 26:10, Paul testified before King Agrippa that in arresting followers of Jesus of Nazareth he had given his voice against them, that he had received authority from the chief priests. The word *voice* in Greek means "vote," which definitely implies that Paul was a member of the Sanhedrin. He was party to the vote of the Sanhedrin to punish Christians. The Sanhedrin had the same power over Jews in foreign cities in regard to religious questions as they exercised in Jerusalem. Since the bulk of the early church consisted of converted Jews, the Sanhedrin held that it was their right to exterminate these Jews for apostatizing. Paul was the chosen henchman to do the job. With the yes vote, Caiaphas gladly complied with Paul's request, giving him the necessary letters to go to Damascus and live up to his Pharisaical expectations.

PAUL'S MARITAL STATUS While we are on the subject of Paul's early manhood, it is appropriate to consider his marital status. Was he a married man, a bachelor, or a widower? In speaking of marriage Paul said, "I say therefore to the unmarried and widows, it is good for them if they abide even as I" (1 Corinthians 7:8). This verse, taken as is, would seem to imply that Paul was a bachelor, that he had chosen what was called the divine life—celibacy. This resolution was expressed by Rabbi Asai, who took no wife, saying "My soul cleaves to the Law; let others see to the upbuilding of the world."[6] It is quite true that Scripture is silent as to the definiteness of his having a family, but in spite of 1 Corinthians 7:8, circumstantial evidence leans heavily toward his having been married and then having become a widower.

The pride and joy of every Jewish man was to be married and the proud father of sons. Jewish boys were expected to marry sometime before the age of twenty. If Paul married, he did so while he was a student in Jerusalem. Tradition says that a good Pharisee was a married man with a family. Strong circumstantial evidence, based on Paul's vote to harass believers, also puts him as a member of the Sanhedrin (Acts 26:10).

> One of the necessary qualifications of members of this Jewish ruling body was that they should be the father of children because such were supposed to be more likely to lean toward mercy. It was the rule when Stephen was tried, and if Paul was one of the judges, especially in the latter decision to arrest Christians in Damascus, then Paul must have been married at the time. It is probable that his wife and children did not long survive; for otherwise some notice of them would have occurred in the subsequent narrative or some allusion to them in his Epistles.[7]

The fact that Paul on his missionary journeys chose elders who were "the husband of one wife who ruled their houses well" (1 Timothy 3:4) supports the idea of a religious leader's being married, including Paul.

Since we cannot overlook Paul's statement in 1 Corinthians 7:8, which has led some to believe that he was never married, we must consider this verse in light of the Greek text. It does not imply that Paul was celibate, a bachelor, a single man. Rather, this verse seems to say: I say, therefore, to the married men who are now widowers and to the married women who are widows, it is good for them to abide even as I am a widower, who has not remarried. Paul knew from the Old Testament (and that was all he had to go on) that it was God's ordained plan for a man to marry a woman, leave his father and mother and cleave to his wife (Genesis 2:23–24). For him to advise the unmarried not to marry would go contrary to Scripture. In fact, on one occasion he rebuked religious leaders in the matter of forbidding others to marry (1 Timothy 4:3). To further substantiate his having been married was the question of his taking his wife on a long journey to preach, that is, if his wife were still living. Paul reminds those at Corinth that other apostles had taken their wives on journeys and as much as asked: Why couldn't I have done the same thing when mine was living? (see 1 Corinthians 9:5). As previously stated, there is much circumstantial evidence to support his having been married.

Paul was a privileged man. As Saul of Tarsus his parents bestowed on him a cherished freedom, Roman citizenship, which gave him the rights and privileges that less than two-thirds of the Roman Empire enjoyed. His parents were considerate of him, giving him the best that Jewry could afford in his home, in his synagogue school in Tarsus, and with his Rabbinical training in Jerusalem. Although his leadership was of an evil nature and his father and mother (if she was still living) probably disagreed with his methods of persecution, yet inside they no doubt were proud that their boy attained heights in Jewish circles. However, God's ways are not man's ways, and standing in the background, the God and Father of the Lord Jesus Christ had better and different plans for him.What a change God wrought in this man's life when he was converted. Whatever Paul had in mind to fully accomplish for Jewry, God had something more noble in mind for Paul to accomplish for Christianity.

TEST YOURSELF ON CHAPTER ONE

1. After the Babylonian captivity, many Jews did not return to their homeland. What comparison do you see between these Jews and many of today's Jews' not having a desire to go back to Israel?

2. Tell at least five things you learned about Paul's family.

3. Where was Paul born? Tell as much as you can about this city.

4. Give some highlights of Paul's childhood.

5. What was Paul's occupation?

6. How did Paul acquire his Roman citizenship? How could one become a Roman citizen? What were the advantages of being a Roman citizen?

7. How many languages do you believe Paul knew? Name them.

8. Do you believe Paul was married? Prove your answer.

9. What was the difference between being a Pharisee in Tarsus and being one in Jerusalem?

10. What do you know about Pharisaism per se?

11. In what ways did the Pharisees substitute the traditions of their fathers for the Scriptures?

12. Can a born-again believer of today have a Pharisaical heart? How?

Chapter Two

PAUL'S CONVERSION

Probably one of the reasons that the Jews, and in particular Paul the Pharisee, hated Christians with such a passion was because of their misconception of Christ as Messiah—their interpretation of Old Testament prophecies relating to His coming and His purpose.

> It was the universal belief of His people that the Messiah would only come to a nation keeping the Law, and it was even said that if one man kept it perfectly for a single day, his merit would bring to the earth the King for whom they were waiting. Paul's Rabbinical training, then, culminated in the desire to win this prize of righteousness and he left the halls of sacred learning with this as the purpose of his life.[1]

JEWISH HATRED OF CHRISTIANS To a Jew who saw vividly and keenly either the material or the spiritual position which was open to the Jews in the Roman Empire, the coming of Messiah meant the realization of that commanding position in the Roman world of which they dreamed and to which they looked forward. The Messiah was to make them the "lords over their conquerors." Messiah would help them plant their feet on the necks of their Roman enemies. However, it wasn't long after the One claiming to be Messiah came that the Jews began to take notice that Christ and kingdom were not the Messiah and kingdom they expected. The kingdom of God "is righteousness, and peace, and joy in the Holy Spirit" (Romans 14:17). The Jews thought they were establishing their own righteousness and having it made known at His trial before Pilate that His kingdom was not of this world (John 18:36), the death of Jesus was peculiarly offensive to all Jews.

Christ's death had turned His career into a hateful parody of their Messianic hopes. He had set before them a life of humility and poverty, finally being extinguished in ridicule and shame in a Roman crucifixion. They were set to worship Messiah, "King of the Jews," and now He was nothing more than an imposter. The more eagerly Paul had thought about the glory that lay before triumphant Judaism in the Roman Empire, the more intensely he must have detested this deceiver who had, as he thought, degraded him and his nation before the whole world.[2]

The intense bitterness with which Paul pursued the Christians was the necessary consequence of his anticipated desire to win the prize of righteousness. Messiah's establishment of a spiritual kingdom and His numberless converts in many parts of the Roman world had openly thwarted this plan. To Paul, Christ was a dead Christ, and his followers were impostors. To Paul, Jesus' followers were now the enemy; they were degrading Paul's ideal. Therefore they had to be destroyed, and he, Paul, had to renew his pursuit of his goal.

PAUL'S PERSECUTION OF THE CHURCH   Paul had become so fanatical an opponent of Jesus that he was determined to go throughout the whole Roman Empire (see map 1, p. 442), if necessary, to annihilate all Christians and bring Christianity to naught. He started his mission of slaughter in Jerusalem, the seat of both Pharisaism and Christianity. To the delight of the Jews, Stephen was stoned to death (see illustration 4), with Paul giving his consent (Acts 7:58–8:1). St. Stephen's Gate in Jerusalem is built over the reputed site of his stoning (see illustration 5). This so-called victory (Stephen's death) against Christianity caused Paul to act more boldly in his opposition against the followers of Christ, which resulted in his "breathing out threatenings and slaughter against the disciples of the Lord" (Acts 9:1). Not realizing at the time that the blood of the martyrs is the seed of the church and that Christians were being scattered because of persecution (Acts 8:1, 4), Paul probably wondered whether he should stay in Jerusalem and finish the job there, or move on.

4—The stoning of Stephen. *Courtesy of author.*

The Gospel was spreading throughout Judaea and Samaria. Already Paul was persecuting believers in strange cities, no doubt Pentecost believers who were being organized into groups (Acts 26:11). Having heard that Christians in Damascus were making that city a haven for other Christian refugees, Paul went to the high priest for letters of authority to beat, bind, and drag them out of their houses if necessary, and arrest those he found and return to Jerusalem (Acts 9:1–2; 22:5).

Paul wanted his reputation and fame as the persecutor of the church to go beyond the

5—St. Stephen's Gate, Jerusalem: site of Stephen's stoning. *Courtesy of author.*

PAUL'S PERSECUTION OF THE CHURCH   49

environs of Jerusalem. In his zeal he had it in his subconscious mind that God might someday speak to him as He had spoken to men of old. For a long time the Jews had refused to listen to God's voice. Paul knew that for some centuries God's favor had been turned from His people, His nation. History had revealed to him that this had happened to other nations who had flatly rejected the God of Israel, and he knew that sooner or later his kinsmen, the Jews, in their self-satisfaction, would also be rejected. By preparing educationally, by punctilious and strict obedience to the Law, and by tyrannical zeal in enforcing it on others, Paul felt that he might someday be in a state to hear the voice of God. Little did he realize that he would soon hear the voice of God as he made his way to Damascus.

The journey of about 160 miles from Jerusalem to Damascus took at least six days, which gave Paul plenty of time to think. Many thoughts must have come into his mind. His mentor, Gamaliel, had said that if Christianity was not of God it would come to naught (Acts 5:34–39). Given the growth of Christianity, Gamaliel's statement possibly preyed on his mind. Had Stephen been right when he preached before Paul, or had Paul been right when he gave his consent to Stephen's death? Damascus was to become the battleground between Paul and God—his heart and mind were being prepared for the head-on collision he was to have with the God of Israel: the Jesus he despised.

PAUL'S ARRIVAL God's encounter with Paul finally took place
IN DAMASCUS on the outskirts of Damascus. God always uses the unusual to confound the mighty; thus, Paul was blinded that he might see! Several things of interest took place during his encounter with the Christ he thought was dead (Acts 9:3–6).

First, this was Christ's first appearance to Paul (vv. 3–4).

Second, when he was blinded by the great light (see illustration 6) from heaven, Paul heard a voice speak to him saying, "Saul, Saul, why persecutest thou me?" (v. 4). Throughout history we have seen that when someone "touches" a child of God, he touches God. For example, when the children of Israel murmured against Moses and Aaron, Moses said, "Your murmurings are not against us, but against God" (Exodus 16:8). Although Paul's actions caused great physical pain to the Christians he persecuted, his behavior also hurt their Savior, "He being touched with the feelings of our infirmities" (Hebrews 4:15).

Third, when Paul asked, "Who art thou, Lord?" (v. 5), he did

6—Saul's conversion near Damascus. *Courtesy of author.*

not know to whom he was speaking. The expression literally means, "Who are you, Sir?" He simply accepted it as another man's voice, saying "Sir" out of respect.

Fourth, the voice informed Paul that He was none other than God Himself, incarnate in His Son Jesus, whom Paul was persecuting. Paul's dream of being spoken to by God had come to pass, but not in the way he had expected.

Fifth, in speaking to Paul, Jesus said, "It is hard for thee to kick against the pricks" (v. 5). Many ancient manuscripts do not have the expression *kick against the pricks* in this verse. However, Paul makes the same statement in his personal testimony before King Agrippa (Acts 26:14), so evidently the translators added this expression to Acts 9:5 without adding anything to Scripture.[3]

What does this expression mean? The word *pricks* literally means "a goad—an instrument with a point for prodding; a brier." A goad was often used by a farmer to prod an animal along while plowing, and kicking against it would cause a deep wound or cut. Figuratively *pricks* means opposition from an enemy. God told Israel that if she did not drive out the inhabitants of the land of Canaan, then those who remained in the land would haunt her. They would be "pricks in your eyes and thorns in your sides and [they] shall vex you" (Numbers 33:55). When God prophesied against Zidon, He said, "there shall be no more a pricking brier unto the house of Israel, nor any grieving thorn of all that are round about them that despised them; and they shall know that I am the Lord God" (Ezekiel 28:24). A prick could also mean fighting against God; a searing guilty conscience of wrongdoing.

Paul's "kicking against the pricks" meant a number of things due to this new battle that was going on in his mind concerning his part in persecuting the church of the living God—his part in persecuting Christ. In traveling the 160 miles from Jerusalem to Damascus, he had had at least six days to mull over in his mind his attitudes, actions, and Jewish beliefs taught in Tarsus versus the Pharisaism he had learned in Jerusalem. He had possibly even thought about the consequence of his evil way in breaking some of the Ten Commandments, such as, "Thou shalt not kill" (Exodus 20:13). Possibly the thought that Christ might really be alive haunted him. After all, he knew that believers all over the Roman Empire were willing to die for their risen Savior, rather than deny Him. Maybe he was beginning to see that Christ had not come to overthrow Rome but to establish a spiritual kingdom. With his mind being flooded with so many thoughts, it was becoming torture for him to even think. "Paul," said Jesus, "you are kicking against the pricks."

THE FALL OF SAUL, THE PHARISEE What were some of the pricks that Paul was kicking against? It is very possible that *one prick was a guilty conscience* that was the result of Paul's giving consent to Stephen's death, making him guilty of murder by association (Acts 8:1; 22:20).

Because Paul knew the Old Testament Scriptures, he also knew the Ten Commandments. He probably also knew that he was breaking some in his attitudes and actions against others and against the Word of God itself. The *prick of convicting sin* was getting to him. It is difficult to resist the power of God's Word. Paul had heard Stephen's sermon, and he had no defense against the Scripture that Stephen preached as he gave Israel's history and told how they, along with the fathers of old, resisted the Holy Spirit (Acts 7:1–53). Paul was experiencing the prick of the Word (Hebrews 4:12).

Paul was kicking against the *prick of the convicting power of the Holy Spirit,* who had been sent to convict any sinner of sin, of the righteousness of God, and of judgment to come (John 16:7–9). Paul had set about to establish his own righteousness, but one cannot do this without being prodded or pricked. Maybe he thought about what the prophet Isaiah had said: "all our righteousnesses are as filthy rags" (Isaiah 64:6).

In addition, there was the *prick of breathing out threatenings and slaughter* against innocent people (Acts 9:1–2, 13–14). He not only threatened them but also murdered and beat some (Acts 22:4, 19). Their only crime was trusting in Jesus Christ. This was a prick of decency against a blind, evil, overly zealous religionist.

Then there was the *prick of Gamaliel's statement,* "If it [Christianity] be of God ye cannot overthrow it, lest haply ye be found even to fight against God" (Acts 5:34–39). Paul knew that many religions had come to the forefront but had failed because they were not of God. He also knew that Christianity was growing by leaps and bounds, and he was conscious that the blood of martyrs only challenged others to believe. Gamaliel's statement was beginning to make Paul realize that he was fighting a losing battle.

There was the *prick of his warped Pharisaical mind* that was following the traditions of his fathers. But he knew full well that he was going contrary to all the true Law of Moses, the Prophets, and the Psalms. As James puts it, "For whosoever shall keep the whole law and yet offend in one point, he is guilty of all" (2:10). Paul was beginning to see that the whole of Scripture had been meaningless to him and that the sword of the Word was mightier than his wrestling against flesh and blood—that the whole Law was pulling down his strongholds.

There was the *prick of the character of a true child of God.* This makes a forceful impact on the mind of an unbeliever, and this prick would not allow Paul to erase from his mind the glow on Stephen's face as he fell asleep in Jesus (Acts 7:59–60). As well as seeing the joy on Stephen's face, Paul had seen joy on the faces of others he had persecuted.

Finally, there was the *prick of prayer.* One of the outstanding marks of the early Christians was their prayer life. "They continued steadfastly in . . . prayers" (Acts 2:42; 4:31). When persecution scattered believers you can be sure they prayed all the more, not only for themselves and other believers but also, being Christians who had a compassion for the lost, for their persecutors. Christians in those days prayed for needs, whether theirs or others, and for one another because they loved one another. Their lives exemplified their Savior to the point that, as sinners observed them, they had to admit that these people had been with Jesus (Acts 4:13). Their prayers were having an effect on others. Prayer is a prick against which one cannot escape. No doubt the name of Paul was on the top of their prayer list—not for God to strike him dead because of what he was doing to Christians and the cause of Christ but for his salvation. Paul had some relatives in Rome who had been saved before he was (Romans 16:7, 11), and with a knowledge of his reputation as the persecutor of the church, surely these kinsmen were praying for his salvation. We all pray for our lost loved ones to be saved regardless of how mean and sinful they might be. Prayer is one thing that will help bring about conviction in the heart of any unbeliever.

Perhaps we can learn a lesson from these early New Testament saints regarding prayer. Their example puts the church to shame today. We can become so hardened and calloused that many times our prayers are limited to just our unsaved loved ones. When we meet opposition from others, it is likely that we do not feel a burden for their particular needs and our prayers for them might be spiteful. In our day and times, many hearts are hardened toward those who would lift a finger against what we believe to be right.

Recent newspaper articles give us some good examples of opposition from our own government in the matter of church and state. Yes, we believe our government is wrong in a lot of areas when decisions are made against the church, and we should stand up and be heard, but we are to "pray for those in authority"; "pray for them who despitefully use you and persecute you," even to the point of blessing and loving them (1 Timothy 2:1–3; Matthew 5:44).

One pastor, who felt the sting of opposition when his state government ruled against him, said that for a right decision to be made, God would have to "convert them, restrain them, or kill them."[4] Another pastor who opposes abortion asked his congregation to pray for the death of a Supreme Court jurist who voted for abortion so he could be replaced by one who opposes it. He even had an airplane circle over the Supreme Court building trailing the message, "Pray for Death to the Baby Killer."[5] On one occasion when the U. S. State Department refused to grant a visa to a foreigner engaged to speak at a religious conference, the host was so angered at the Secretary of State that he labeled him "a monster in human flesh"; and called on God to "smite him hip and thigh, bone and marrow, heart and lungs . . . and destroy him quickly and utterly."[6] An educator asked God to damn the Supreme Court justices because of what he believed was a wrong judgment. Early saints knew there were wrong decisions being made against them, but even though they were the victims of wrong, they were people of prayer, and we see the effects of their prayers in the life of the apostle Paul. Maybe if we took to heart the truth that the "effectual fervent prayer of a righteous man availeth much" (James 5:16), our prayer life would be such that those who oppose us would find our prayer pricks hard to kick against. It seemed that regardless of which way Paul turned, these pricks were preparatory to bringing him to his knees before God. Finally, Jesus appeared to him (Acts 9:3–6). As Jesus revealed Himself, Paul must have begun to realize just how hard it really was for him to kick against the pricks, just how hard it was for him to fight against God. Meeting Jesus face-to-face will reveal to any sinner that salvation (the righteousness of God) is of the Lord (Jonah 2:9), and that God Himself will engineer circumstances in such a way that it will be brought about.

THE RISE OF SAUL, THE CHRISTIAN   Evidently, somewhere between verses 5 and 6 of the ninth chapter of Acts, Paul made a complete surrender to Christ. The prayers of persecuted saints, as well as the other pricks that Paul had experienced, had finally caught up with him. It appears that all the pricks we have mentioned made him so miserable that surrender to God was his only relief. He gave his heart to Jesus and was truly born again. When he asked, "Lord, what wilt thou have me to do?" (v. 6), he was not addressing just another person. Actually, he was saying "Lord," calling Jesus "God, Lord, Master." No man can call Jesus "Lord" but by the Holy Spirit (1 Corinthians 12:3). His fight against God had ended. Paul had lost his war, but he had won God's salvation through Christ; he had come to a true knowledge of God's righteousness. Satan had lost a powerful ally, the "chiefest of sinners," the main persecutor of the church (1 Timothy 1:15; Galatians 1:13). Paul had suddenly met Jesus in person, not dead but alive! He could not disbelieve; he saw, he heard, he knew. He said to those in Corinth, "have I not seen Jesus?" (1 Corinthians 9:1). God had won the heart of the one who would now sell out to him just as much, if not more, than he had sold out to the devil. He would now tell the world "for to me to live [now] is Christ" (Philippians 1:21). The persecutor of the church would now become the "ringleader of the sect of the Nazarenes" (Acts 24:5).

At his conversion, Paul was in darkness on the outside, but Jesus appeared to him as "the light" of the world, and Paul now had the "light of life" on the inside (John 8:12)! If Paul's conversion proves anything, it proves that salvation is in the person of Jesus and is instantaneous; it is not a dragged-out ritual looking to works, things, creeds, or churches. When Paul asked "what wilt thou have me to do?" Jesus answered, "arise and go into the city [of Damascus]. . . ." Paul had been going his way. Now he would be going God's way. The revelation of Christ to Paul exposed in a flash the bankruptcy of the law—that the law at best had been a schoolmaster that had led him to the Messiah (Galatians 3:24–25). Paul now knew that failure to recognize and receive

7—A street called Straight.
Courtesy of author.

Christ as Messiah was proof that the Jews had ceased to be the favored nation. Christ had come to his own and they had not received him (John 1:11). But God is now making a new nation who will bring forth fruit for his glory (Matthew 21:42–45). The redeemed church makes up this new nation and Paul had become a part of it.

During his three days of blindness in the house of Judas (see illustration 7) on the "street called Straight" (Acts 9:6–11), Paul experienced what he later wrote to the Corinthians, "If any man be in Christ Jesus he is a new creature [or creation]; old things pass away, behold all things become new" (2 Corinthians 5:17). All Christians at their new birth are put on the straight and narrow. The old life begins to fade away and all the things of God become new. Paul, in his mid-thirties, is no longer going about to establish his own righteousness; there is a new thirst and hunger in his heart for the "righteousness of God" (Matthew 5:6).

There are many who make professions of faith in Christ. Everything on the surface looks good—a testimony, vows, even a willingness to be baptized, join a church, and go to work for God (or the church's program), but their professions are shallow. Soon they have fallen by the wayside, as Jesus mentioned in the parable of the sower (Luke 8:4–15). Paul could not disbelieve what he had heard and whom he had seen. He had seen the Jesus whom he had fancied to be a dead imposter. He knew now that Christ was alive, and that He was God. There was no more to be said at this point. What remained was for him to act! From here on out he testified to this Damascus experience and backed it up with his life and the use of Scripture.

Paul's obedience in following Christ's command to go into the city shows that Paul meant business for his new Master. Having this new hunger and thirst for God's righteousness, God told Ananias to help this babe in Christ (Acts 9:10–17). God is always prepared to meet any emergency of ours. In spite of the fear Ananias had concerning Paul, the evil persecutor of Christians, God met that need in his heart by casting out his fear. Going to see Paul in obedience to the Lord, Ananias found a new friend who knew just what he needed for that moment. God never leaves His children alone, or without help, in the time of need. A new song has put it aptly, "He was [is] there all the time," and we should never, never underestimate God. There is no situation too big for Him; nothing is impossible with Him (Luke 1:37).

Ananias was the right person, raised up at the right time to help. His name means "one who bends or stoops [humbles himself] in kindness; one who favors; one who is merciful; one who makes supplications."[7] When fear left Ananias' heart, there was no hatred for Paul's crimes against his fellow believers; just open arms and a forgiving heart. This is exactly what Paul needed in this transition in his life. He was blind, hungry, and frightened because he knew what his former Jewish supporters might do to him now that he had experienced an about-face.

Ananias, living up to his name, visited Paul. Putting one's hands on someone in need will break down resistance and at the same time create fellowship and friendship. This Ananias did, speaking kindly, and assuring Paul that because of his new-found

Savior, he would be filled with the Holy Spirit and have his sight restored. When Paul's sight was restored, what a joy it must have been to look into the face of forgiveness, kindness, compassion, and love. Maybe Paul heard anew the words that fell from the lips of Christ when He was dying, "Father, forgive him for he knew not what he was doing" (author's paraphrase). When the Holy Spirit filled him as a new believer to begin his Christian life of service for the Lord, not only was his sight restored but also "forthwith . . . he was baptized" (Acts 9:17–18). Thus, the disciples were being obedient in following God's ordained plan: evangelize, baptize, and then teach the new converts to observe what Christ had commanded (Matthew 28:19–20). Paul was strengthened, welcomed, and fellowshipped with the Damascus disciples. He received a boldness to step out in faith and preach Christ, seeking to win others to Christ, the exact opposite of what he had been doing (Acts 9:6–20). Old things had passed away, all things were now new (2 Corinthians 5:17).

PAUL, A NEW CREATURE

Paul's life up to the moment of his conversion is now counted but dung (Philippians 3:4–8). He is now that new creation in Christ Jesus with new friends, a new outlook on life, and a new calling in the things of the Lord. Paul is no longer ignorant of God's righteousnesses that he so long sought and needed—he now has it in Christ Jesus (Romans 10:1–4; 2 Corinthians 5:21).

What were some of the old things that passed away from him?

1. His "natural" heart; that is, his zeal and ambition to make a name for himself as the persecutor of the church and to be the Pharisee of the Pharisees disappeared (Acts 9:1–2).

2. His "defiant" heart; that is, his determination to kill all Christians vanished.

3. The old enjoyment of persecuting Christians ceased to exist.

4. His old, bigoted friends departed.

5. His old religion vanished. Anytime people come to Christ, they lose their religion but gain God's gift of eternal life.

6. His own righteousness no longer existed. It had always

been as filthy rags (Isaiah 64:6), but Paul didn't know it until he experienced God's righteousness .

7. The traditions of his fathers now meant nothing.

8. Everything he had stood for became as dung (Philippians 3:4–9). Paul learned the hard way that God's way was the best way; that God's way was the right way.

What were some of the new things that came to him?

1. He received a humble heart; that is, submission to Christ; "What wilt Thou have me to do, Lord?" (Acts 9:6).

2. He gained an obedient heart; that is, a willingness to do anything his new master commanded of him (Acts 9:6–18).

3. He obtained a changed heart; that is, he immediately began to undo what he had set out to do. Instead of seeking to destroy the church, which at that time he had not realized was an impossibility (Matthew 16:18), he immediately began to preach Christ, thus building up the church (Acts 9:20).

4. He acquired a real Jesus, not an imposter.

5. He accepted the truth that Jesus was raised from the dead—is now alive in heaven.

6. He received the truth that Jesus is Lord, God, Master.

7. He secured the truth that Jesus dwells in His people on earth.

8. He accepted the fact that he was the "chief of sinners" for whom Jesus died.

9. He discovered the truth that the God he thought he was favoring was the One he was fighting against.

10. He secured the truth that the One who said "I am Jesus" was the long promised Messiah.

11. He realized the truth that it took God's mercy to forgive him.

12. He ignited a new light of truth in his heart.

13. He procured a new life (new birth) that began to satisfy.

14. He gained new friends who stood by him.

15. He accepted a new calling.

16. He gained a desire to serve instead of oppose Christ.

17. He acknowledged a new righteousness.

18. He received new insight into the riches of Scripture.

19. He acquired a new spirit, the Holy Spirit, to guide him. In Paul we see a "new man," a man who had been a ravenous wolf as a Benjamite (Genesis 49:27), who ceased his threatenings against the things of God and became a staunch defender of the faith, one who was now "determined to know nothing among men save Jesus Christ and Him crucified" (1 Corinthians 2:2).

Note the summary of Saul's conversion in Acts 9:

he was an enemy of Christ (vv. 1–2),

he was convicted by Christ (vv. 3–4),

he was called by Christ (vv. 4–5),

he called on Christ (v. 6),

he surrendered to Christ (vv. 6, 8), and

he witnessed for Christ (vv. 20–22).

We should notice one other thing in relation to his conversion. Galatians 6:7 reminds us that "Whatsoever a man soweth, that shall he also reap." Ananias was told that Paul would be shown what "great things he would suffer for my name's sake" (Acts 9:16). Some things he suffered are listed in chapter 4.

TEST YOURSELF ON CHAPTER TWO

1. Why did the Jews hate Christians?

2. What concept of Messiah did the Jews have?

3. Why was Paul so antagonistic toward Christians and what did he want to do to Christians?

4. What was Paul's purpose in going to Damascus?

5. Describe what happened to Paul on the outskirts of Damascus.

6. What does the expression *kicking against the pricks* mean?

7. What were the pricks Paul kicked against?

8. How did Paul recognize Christ at his conversion?

9. How did Paul address Christ once he knew who He was?

10. To whose house was the blinded Paul led, and who visited him?

11. What was Ananias' attitude toward Paul's conversion?

12. How did God overcome Ananias' attitude, and what was Ananias told to do when he met Paul?

13. What evidence do we have that Paul was truly converted, becoming a new creature in Christ?

14. What did Paul start doing that was opposite to what he set out to do in Damascus?

15. What was the reaction of those who heard him in the synagogues?

16. Give a summary of Paul's conversion as recorded in Acts 9.

Chapter Three

PAUL'S COMMISSION AND APOSTLESHIP

Following Paul's dramatic conversion on the road to Damascus, he was led to the house of Judas on the street called Straight where for three days, in blindness, he neither ate nor drank. Many things must have crossed his mind during this time. Having had normal sight and then suddenly losing it must have been devastating for Paul, especially with no foreknowledge that he would ever see again. He may have thought through many truths about Christ that he had heard by way of testimony from people he had persecuted. During this three-day period he may have struggled with the knowledge of his former beliefs, especially since much of his former Jewish religious teachings were in opposition to what he now believed. Many new converts have problems about former beliefs. Surely during this time the Lord must have enabled Paul to see enough about Christ to give him the assurance that no mistake had been made in his acceptance of God's Son, Jesus. During this time of blindness, Ananias was being briefed by the Lord that he should visit Paul and restore his sight. In the meantime, Judas had a vision from the Lord that Ananias would perform this miracle. Judas told Paul of Ananias' coming to lay hands on him that his sight might be restored, which would make any saint shout, "Amen, Hallelujah!" (Acts 9:6–18).

At the end of the three days, Judas' vision and Ananias' visiting his house came to pass. Upon arrival, Ananias laid hands on Paul and restored his sight; thus verifying the vision as having been from the Lord. The Holy Spirit filled Paul; he was baptized, and had a "good church supper" (Acts 9:10–19). The disciples and Paul must have had an old-fashioned testimony meeting, which lasted for several days. Scripture does not tell us the nature of their discussions, but in this brief babe-in-Christ stage, Paul must have been enlightened as he listened to these older, mature Christians unfold Old Testament prophecies relating to Christ, and their fulfillment in His finished work at Calvary. There must have been rapid growth in grace and in knowledge of this Jesus he had just met because after several days with the Christians in Damascus, straightway Paul preached Christ in the synagogues saying that "He is the Son of God" (Acts 9:20). Quite naturally all who heard him preach Christ were amazed, for they had known him as the man who was intent on destroying all followers who called on "this name" (Acts 9:20–21). Paul, however, was simply "on fire" for the Lord, and he could not refrain from preaching his new discovery of God's righteousness—God's way of salvation in Christ. It didn't take him long to learn that he was a debtor to all men, that the present is the accepted time to preach, and that he must preach "in season and out of season." He was not only ready to preach but not ashamed to proclaim the Gospel. He was not disobedient to his heavenly vision but began immediately to preach Christ in Damascus (Romans 1:14–16; Acts 26:19).

PAUL'S MESSAGE We must ever keep in mind that the only tools that Paul was able to use for preaching were the Old Testament Scripture and his testimony—the experience he had with Christ and what God had done in his heart and life. The Old Testament is full of Jesus Christ. When Paul preached Christ, he affirmed that the Gospel came from this portion of God's Word (1 Corinthians 15:3–4). When Philip preached to the Ethiopian eunuch from Isaiah 53, he preached Jesus to him and the eunuch confessed that Christ was the Son of God and the eunuch was baptized (Acts 8:26–38). On the Day of Pentecost, Peter used a portion from the book of Joel (cf. Joel 2:28–32 with Acts 2:14–21). Christ defeated Satan by using Old

Testament Scriptures (Matthew 4:1–10). The Gospel, God's Good News of man's deliverance from sin, was all the hope any Old Testament person had for salvation. Old Testament saints looked forward to the Cross through sacrifice (Isaiah 53; Acts 19:4). The Gospel is the only hope we have in this dispensation as we look back to the Cross (Acts 16:31; Ephesians 2:8–9), and it is also the only hope anyone will have in the Tribulation and the Millennium (Revelation 7:9–10, 14). Notice the Gospel of grace given in the Old Testament.

GOSPEL OF GRACE IN THE OLD TESTAMENT	
Messianic Promise	The promise is from Genesis (cf. Genesis 3:15 with Galatians 4:4–5).
Coat of Skin	This, necessitating a blood sacrifice of animals, was Adam's deliverance (Genesis 3:21).
Abel's Sacrifice	Abel offered a more excellent sacrifice, the first of his flock, obtaining witness that he was righteous (Genesis 4:4; Hebrews 11:4).
Noah's Faith	Noah's faith through sacrifice was counted unto him for righteousness (Genesis 8:20; Hebrews 11:7).
Gospel to Abraham	The Gospel was preached to Abraham. He saw Christ's day and rejoiced in it when he met Melchizedek (Genesis 14:18–20), and in his offering of Isaac when God said that He would provide Himself a lamb for a sacrifice (cf. John 8:56 with Genesis 22:8; Hebrews 11:17–19; see also Romans 4:1–4).

GOSPEL OF GRACE IN THE OLD TESTAMENT

Promise to Moses	There was the promise of Christ to Moses who chose to cast his lot with that promise even though it meant reproach as well as the loss of Egypt's riches (Deuteronomy 18:15; Hebrews 11:24–28).
The Passover Lamb	This act (the shedding of blood for the remission of sin) was a part of Israel's worship, pointing to Christ our Passover. This confirms Paul's statement that Christ was in the wilderness when the Gospel was preached to the children of Israel (note carefully Exodus 12:21–23; 1 Corinthians 5:7; 1 Corinthians 10:4, 9; Hebrews 4:2; and Hebrews 11:28).
Water from Rock Manna from Heaven	These both spoke of Christ to Israel (cf. Exodus 17:6 with I Corinthians 10:4; Exodus 1 6:14–15, 35; Nehemiah 9:20; and John 6:30–33).
Types and Shadows	The book of Hebrews lists a number of so-called types and shadows of good things to come, meaning Christ and His atoning work (cf. Hebrews 10:1 with 9:11–22).
Grace to David	David knew the blessedness of grace—the forgiveness of sin by faith (Psalms 51; 32; Romans 4:5–8).

GOSPEL OF GRACE IN THE OLD TESTAMENT

Heritage of Timothy's Family	Timothy's mother and grandmother used the Old Testament Scripture to show him the need for giving his heart to the Lord. These Scriptures made him "wise unto salvation through faith in Christ Jesus" (2 Timothy 3:15).
Old Testament Prophets	The Old Testament prophets had the Spirit of Christ in them when they inquired about salvation through Christ (1Peter 1:10–11).
Simeon and Anna	These two knew enough about Old Testament prophecy to recognize God's salvation in the person of Christ (Luke 2:25–38).
Paul's Preaching	Paul preached Christ's "Gospel of the kingdom of God" message, which was based on the Old Testament Scripture (Mark 1:14–15; Acts 19:8; 1 Corinthians 15:3–4; see also chapter 8. When Paul said he was determined to know nothing among people save Jesus Christ and Him crucified (see 1 Corinthians 2:2), he did so by reasoning with both Jew and Gentile alike out of the Old Testament Scripture those things concerning God's only begotten Son. Later, in a brief summary of each epistle that Paul wrote, the Old Testament references will be listed.

Chapter Three

PAUL'S JOURNEY TO ARABIA   Luke does not give us a complete chronological order of events in Acts 9, immediately following Paul's conversion. He makes no mention of his going to Arabia (see map 1 on p. 442) and returning to Damascus before going back to Jerusalem. We must piece together those events from Paul's own testimony and from some information he gave when he wrote his letter to the Galatian churches.

Many scholars are of the opinion that Paul went to Arabia after he first reasoned with the Damascus Jews that Jesus was the Son of God (Acts 9:20–21). This would make his visit to Arabia fall between verses 21 and 22 of Acts 9, which seems logical. The reasoning is that with his educational background Paul needed, in solitude, to attend the "School of God" and "unlearn" all he knew about the Jews' religion and his brand of Pharisaism. This would in turn enable him to understand the unsearchable riches of Christ in order to better preach the Gospel, something these scholars say was new to him. Paul did not need to be taught anew that Christ was the Son of God (Messiah) because, as we noted, "straightway [a few days after his conversion] he preached Christ . . . the Son of God" in the synagogues in Damascus (Acts 9:20). However, he needed in-depth study about the Messiah, and since he had just received a first-hand revelation of Christ, it appeared that the Holy Spirit led him to Arabia to instruct him in the who, what, and why of God's overall plan for humanity.

> It cannot but be wondered that he felt this to be a necessity. He had believed his former creed intensely and staked everything on it; to see it suddenly shattered in pieces must have shaken him severely. The new truth which had been flashed on him was so far-reaching and revolutionary that it could not be taken in at once in all its bearings. Paul was a born thinker; it was not enough for him to experience anything; he required to comprehend it and fit it into the structure of his convictions.[1]

Paul stated that after his conversion that he did not confer with flesh and blood; neither did he go up to Jerusalem to discuss the things of the Lord with Peter and John and the apostles, but went to Arabia (Galatians 1:15–17).

Arabia in Paul's day was known as the Nabatean kingdom, ruled by Aretas IV (9 B.C.–A.D. 40), who was known as the king of Petra. Arabia included the desert region east of Syria and stretched southward fifteen hundred miles to the Sinai peninsula. Damascus, at this time, was part of this region.

Since Arabia is desert, just where did Paul go? Possibly he went to Petra, an important city on the trade route from Syria to Egypt in the land of the Edomites in the mountains of Seir where people lived in the "clefts of the rocks" (Obadiah 3). He certainly had to go where there was food and water.

Obadiah tells us that the land of the Edomites was where the descendants of Ishmael and Esau settled. Knowing the breach that existed between these descendants and Isaac, maybe Paul wanted to preach Christ as Messiah to any who might be left in the region, supposing that their Messiah would heal their differences.

The Nabateans had also settled in Petra (see illustration 8). As pagans, they worshiped many Grecian gods, bowing before and burning incense at shrines as shown in illustration 9. On the first panel is a relief of the thunder god, carved in the form of Zeus. On the side is Tyche, the goddess of victory. With no Biblical (Old Testament Jewish) background, the Nabateans might have been of interest to Paul because of their need of Christ. Even with his Jewish background, he had a vast knowledge of humanity's ways

8—Petra: temples and houses carved in rock. *Courtesy of author.*

9—Shrine of Nabatean worship. *Courtesy of the Israel Department of Antiquities and Museums.*

and customs, and it would have been a challenge to him to reach these Gentiles.

If Paul did go to Petra, it is quite possible that he left and went south to the Sinai Peninsula. Paul knew that God would speak to him in Arabia, and what better place to be alone with God than at Horeb, "the mount of God," where God had spoken to Moses in the giving of the Law and to Elijah who had fled from Jezebel (Exodus 19:3, 18; 1 Kings 19:1–15). We cannot say for sure that he went to Mount Sinai (see illustration 10); however, in Galatians 1:17 he mentions his going to Arabia and in 4:25 he mentions Mount Sinai in Arabia.

Wherever he was in Arabia, he states that the Gospel he preached was not based on the information he received from the other disciples, "For I neither received it from man, neither was I taught it, but by the revelation of Jesus Christ" (Galatians 1:11–12). The revelation that Paul received unfolded many mysteries concerning Christ—His Person, His ministry on earth, His present intercessory ministry in heaven, the mystery of the church as the bride of Christ, His return, His future kingdom, and so forth. Being the thinker that he was, Paul must have learned why salvation was of the Lord, why man could not establish his

10—Mount Sinai. *Courtesy of the American Bible Society, New York.*

11—A Damascus wall like that over which Paul escaped. *Courtesy of author.*

own righteousness, why all Jews were lost even though they were the chosen people of God, why Christ was the only Way to the Father, and why Christ's death was necessary for Jew and Gentile alike. While in Arabia his knowledge of Christ was broadened and his desire to return to civilization to preach Christ was heightened. No one knows how long Paul stayed in Arabia. Just as God had encouraged Elijah at Mount Sinai and told him to go to Damascus (1 Kings 19:15a), He also told Paul to return to Damascus because that is where he went (Galatians 1:17; Acts 9:22–25).

PAUL'S RETURN TO DAMASCUS If Paul indeed did go to Arabia after Acts 9:21, whatever he received from the Lord so stirred him up and empowered him that on his return to Damascus (see map 1, p. 442) he had "increased the more in strength [ability] and confounded the Jews who dwelt in Damascus, proving that this is [the] very Christ [Messiah]" (Acts 9:22). So convincing and overwhelming was his argument in proving that Christ was the Messiah that those Jews were "obliged to blush for the weakness of their cause."[2] After many days, and on learning that their cause was lost, the Jews decided to kill Paul. Aretas, ruler of Arabia, was very friendly with the Jews. He had placed an "ethnarch" (governor) to rule in Damascus, and evidently the

12—Temple area of Jerusalem as seen today. *Courtesy of Matson Photo Service.*

Jews persuaded him to send a garrison to apprehend Paul. Paul, however, managed to escape through a window (see illustration 11), and at night was lowered over the wall in a basket (2 Corinthians 11:32–33; Acts 9:23–25). He escaped death because he had been befriended by fellow believers. It must be pointed out that Paul did not spend three years in Arabia as many seem to think. According to Galatians 1:17–18, after leaving Arabia to return to Damascus (see map 1, p. 442), Paul said, "Then, after three years [in Damascus] I went up to Jerusalem to see Peter" (read carefully Galatians 1:11–18).

PAUL'S FIRST VISIT TO JERUSALEM AFTER HIS CONVERSION After escaping from the Jews in Damascus, Paul made his first trip back to Jerusalem (Acts 9:1–2; 26–29). No one knows what was in his heart as he journeyed to the Holy City. Perhaps he wondered if he could win the high priest to the Lord. Perhaps he speculated as to whether the high priest and his henchmen would seek his life as he had once sought the lives of other believers and like the Jews at Damascus had sought his. (See illustration 12.) He had great reason to fear because he knew firsthand the hatred that the Jews had for Christians—especially since they no doubt looked on him as a traitor. Yet he knew that many believers were in the city, so he made his way there to find Peter. Upon arrival, Paul did find the disciples apprehensive, fearful, and suspicious of him (Acts 9:26). It is difficult for us to understand their fear because Paul, by then, had been saved at least four years. Surely some believers in Damascus had sent word back to the Jerusalem church that Saul of Tarsus was now preaching Christ; that he was no longer persecuting Christians. Maybe the Jerusalem believers thought that Paul was a phony, a fake, putting on a front before suddenly becoming more violent in his persecutions. Perhaps, like Thomas after Christ's resurrection (John 20:19–28), they followed the philosophy that "seeing is believing."

Befriended by Barnabas

Nevertheless, soon after Paul arrived in Jerusalem he was befriended by a man named Barnabas and soon the other believers' fears were put to rest, being assured that "he who persecuted us in times past now preaches the faith which once he destroyed" (Galatians 1:23). Barnabas, whose name means "consolation" and "exhortation," and who is first mentioned in Acts 4:36 in connection with the church in Jerusalem, was the son of a Levite, from the island of Cyprus. Barnabas was to be influential in Paul's life and ministry. Altogether, Barnabas is mentioned twenty-nine times in the New Testament. Tradition has it that he wrote an epistle; some early church fathers attributed the authorship of the book of Hebrews to him.

How fitting that a man like Barnabas was there to greet Paul. Barnabas took Paul under his wing, so to speak, and helped him become established in Jerusalem's Christian community. Barnabas was just the man Paul needed to console him at this time; to exhort the brethren to accept him as a brother in Christ (Acts 9:26–27). What a comfort (consolation) Barnabas' friendship must have been to Paul. At the outset of his Christian experience, Paul was learning that Christian brethren love one another. From the beginning he was learning that God truly supplies needs (Philippians 4:19).

Barnabas' character is typical of any Christian who loves the brethren and is in fellowship with the Lord. He was (1) cooperative, unselfish, and honest (Acts 4:36–37); (2) impartial and understanding (Acts 9:26–27); (3) an encourager; one of influence (Acts 11:22–23); (4) yielded, filled with the Holy Spirit (Acts 11:24); (5) a man of faith (Acts 11:24); (6) trustworthy (Acts 11:29–30); (7) obedient to God's calling (Acts 13:1–2); (8) considerate, willing to give one who failed a second opportunity (Acts 15:36–39); and (9) industrious (1 Corinthians 9:6).

Christ Second Appearance to Paul

While Paul was in Jerusalem at this time, Christ appeared to him, though no actual mention is made of it until later. In giving testimony before the Jews on his fourth and final visit to Jerusalem (Acts 22:1–21), Paul mentions that the Lord had appeared to him when he visited the city on another occasion. Looking at Christ's four appearances to Paul, we note that the first was when Paul was converted (Acts 9:3–6) and the third was when Paul was in Corinth (Acts 18:9–11). Christ's other appearances to Paul took place in Jerusalem. We know that Christ's fourth appearance to Paul took place after he was arrested on his final visit there (Acts 23:11). Paul had visited Jerusalem before he and Barnabas took an offering to the needy throughout Judaea (Acts 11:27–30; 12:25) and when they attended the Jerusalem Council (Acts 15:1–35). There are no recorded appearances of Christ during these two visits; thus the appearance mentioned in Acts 22:18–19 must have taken place during his first visit after his conversion. This second appearance of Christ to Paul took place while he was in the temple.

C. I. Scofield, Adam Clarke, and Lange are agreed that the account given in Acts 22:1–17 was Paul's first visit to Jerusalem after his conversion. Lange bases this conclusion on Paul's reply that, when Christ had appeared the second time to him, it had not been too long since he had persecuted the church (Acts 22:19–20). The whole of Paul's conversation and argument in Acts 22 had to do with his defense, involving his Jewish background (v. 3), his persecution of the church (vv. 4–5), his conversion (vv. 6–16), his first visit to Jerusalem (cf. v. 17 with Acts 9:26–29), Christ's second appearance to him (vv. 17–18), the stoning of Stephen (cf. v. 20 with Acts 7:58–8:1), and his call to preach to Gentiles (v. 21).

In giving his testimony, Paul is giving a chronological account of events that took place just a few years after his conversion. Verses 19 and 20 are not in the exact order of events but are illustrations to show how he persecuted believers. While he was on his first visit to Jerusalem he had remained true to his calling—preaching Christ (Acts 9:29), but even before he left the city, antagonistic Greeks had sought to destroy his ministry and take his life (Acts 9:29).

Paul's Warning from Christ

Before Paul left Jerusalem, Christ gave him two commandments. First, He commanded, "Make haste, and get thee quickly out of Jerusalem, for they will not receive thy testimony concerning Me" (Acts 22:18) and "Depart" (v. 21). The thought behind the expressions, *make haste* and *depart*, means to get out of town in as brief a time as possible—flee. Get out now! It was an emphatic warning for Paul to get out of the seat of Jewry and Pharisaical Jerusalem.

The warning that Christ gave did not necessarily mean that Paul could never go back to Jerusalem, but it is very clear that his calling, as noted, was not primarily to his kinsmen, the Jews. This warning implies that in spite of the burden he had to witness to the Jews at Jerusalem, his testimony would not be received there. Paul became aware that the Jews were not going to receive him during his first visit to the city (Acts 9:29). That this warning should have been taken seriously we note from Acts 21:8–12 when Paul was warned by the Holy Spirit through the prophet Agabus as well as the disciples at Tyre (Acts 21:1–6) not to go to Jerusalem. This will be discussed later.

Paul's Gentile Commission

Second, Christ told Paul to go and preach to Gentiles. "I will send thee far hence [afar off, a long way from Jerusalem] unto the Gentiles" (Acts 22:21).

In addition to Paul's statement in Galatians 1:17–18, another reason for believing this was Paul's first visit to Jerusalem after his conversion is the fact that he was told to go to the Gentiles. He learned at the beginning of his ministry that his calling was to the heathen (Gentiles) and not primarily to the Jews. Note carefully Paul's statement in Galatians 1:15–16, "It pleased God to separate me from my mother's womb and [to call] me by his grace to reveal his Son in me that I might preach him among the heathen." To confirm this so-called Gentile calling, Paul stated in Galatians 2:7 that "the Gospel of the uncircumcision [Gospel to the Gentiles] was committed unto me, and the Gospel of the circumcision [Gospel to the Jews] was committed to Peter." There were not two Gospels with different messages for Jews and Gentiles. Although Peter broke the Gentile barrier by going to Cornelius (Acts 10), he was chosen especially to preach the Gospel to the Jews— being known as the "Apostle of circumcision [to the Jews]" (Galatians 2:8). Paul was chosen especially to preach the Gospel to the Gentiles—being known as the "Apostle of the Gentiles," or to the "uncircumcised" (Romans 11:13; Galatians 2:7). Having been called of God, he was now a debtor to all men; he was always ready to preach, and was never ashamed to preach the Gospel (Romans 1:14–16).

On the Day of Pentecost the door of salvation was opened to all flesh, in particular to Gentiles who were then being called out of all nations to be a people for God's name, especially since the Jews had rejected Messiah and were blinded in part (John 1:11; Acts 2:14–18; 15:14; Romans 11:11–12, 25). Paul now had a huge task before him—reach people who were totally ignorant of their spiritual needs. If Gentiles came to God before the Cross, they came to the Jews and became proselytes. Since the Cross, believers are commissioned to go to all who are lost, and Paul, like all believers, was to go where they were, even to the uttermost parts of the earth (Matthew 28:19–20; Acts 1:8).

Thus, Paul's actual commission involved much. He was an ordained preacher, and ordained apostle, and an ordained teacher (1 Timothy 2:7) to preach Christ (Romans 11:13; Galatians 1:15–16; 2:8–9).

In addition to his being ordained, Paul was to be a pattern (1 Timothy 1:16; Acts 13:47). Paul could say "follow [imitate] me" and "be such as I" (1 Corinthians 4:16; Acts 26:29). In being a pattern, Paul was to suffer for Christ's sake (Acts 9:16). Therefore, when he was seized by the Jews in the temple in Jerusalem, he had a clear understanding of his commission and addressed them, saying: (1) The Lord commanded me at my conversion that He would tell me what He had appointed me to do for Him (see Acts 22:10). (2) The Lord told me that He would let me know what His will was for my life, that I should be a witness unto all men (see Acts 22:14–15). (3) The Lord informed me that I was to be a minister and a witness unto the Gentiles (see Acts 26:16–20).

When the church at Antioch commissioned Barnabas and Paul to launch their first missionary endeavor, it was the Holy Spirit who separated them "for the work whereunto I have called them" (Acts 13:1–3). On that trip to Antioch of Pisidia, Paul used an Old Testament passage to remind the Jews it had been prophesied that in keeping with God's covenant or overall purpose of redemption, His servants would be a "light of the Gentiles." Paul was helping to fulfill this calling (cf. Isaiah 42:6–7 with Acts 13:47).

As a chosen vessel Paul was to be a witness to all men (Galatians 1:15–16; Acts 9:15; 22:15; Romans 1:14–16). During his ministry, he was to go to the Gentiles, to go before royalty including kings and governors, and to go to the children of Israel, but he was primarily the Apostle to Gentiles (Romans 11:13; Galatians 2:8–9).

Paul's Apostleship

Paul was, from time to time, questioned about his apostleship. He was not one of the original twelve (Matthew 10:2–4); hence the Judaizers often questioned if he had the right to claim apostleship and preach Christ. Scripture gives us our answer as to the authenticity of his being one. He mentioned at least thirteen times that he was an apostle.

1. He was called to be an apostle (Romans 1:1).

2. He was an apostle of the Gentiles (Romans 11:13).

3. He was an ordained apostle, speaking the truth in Christ, and lying not (1 Timothy 2:7).

4. In 1 Corinthians 9:1, Paul asks, "Am I not an apostle? Have I not seen Jesus our Lord?" Paul's language here prohibits us from thinking that his seeing the Lord was a mere vision. He experienced a personal appearance by Christ, which placed it on the same level as Christ's appearances after His resurrection to His eleven apostles. Christ had risen in a glorified body. After His ascension He was seated on His throne as the Mediator between God and humanity (Hebrews 1:3; 1 Timothy 2:5). To show Himself to Paul, Jesus appeared in the glory of His humility and the light of this glory outshone the sun and blinded him (Acts 9:3–9). His seeing the risen Christ, coupled with his calling as a chosen vessel to preach to all men, qualified Paul to be an apostle.

5. The results of his ministry to those at Corinth had become his seal of apostleship (1 Corinthians 9:2–6).

6. He lays claim to being an apostle—born out of due time, the least of the apostles (1 Corinthians 15:8–10).

7. Paul, on four occasions, said that he was "an apostle

of Jesus Christ by the will of God" (2 Corinthians 1:1; Ephesian 1:1; Colossians 1:1; 2 Timothy 1:1).

8. He was not inferior to the chiefest apostle (2 Corinthians 11:5).

9. Paul was an apostle, not of men, neither by man, but by Jesus Christ and God the Father (Galatians 1:1).

10. Paul was an apostle of Jesus Christ by the commandment of God our Savior and the Lord Jesus Christ (1 Timothy 1:1).

In addition to the ten statements above, Paul's apostleship was confirmed by how he exercised his authority.

11. He preached the Gospel he had received by direct revelation from Christ (Galatians 1:10–23; 1 Corinthians 2:4; 9:16). This preaching of Jesus Christ and Him crucified (I Corinthians 15:3–4) resulted in countless thousands being saved.

12. He exercised his authority as an apostle by preaching the Word, establishing churches and edifying believers on all his missionary journeys (Acts 14:21–22; 15:36; 20:31; 2 Corinthians 10:8; 12:19–21; 1 Thessalonians 3:10). His calling was to preach, to be a witness of things he had seen and heard. He did this by way of his personal testimony and sermons expounding the Scriptures. "That which I received I delivered unto you" (Acts 22:14–15; 1 Corinthians 2:2; 11:23). He said "my speech and my preaching was not with enticing words of man's wisdom, but in demonstration of the Spirit and of power" (1 Corinthians 2:4).

13. He exercised his authority as an apostle by performing signs and miracles. The Lord confirmed Paul's apostleship and preaching of the Word with signs and miracles (Acts 14:3). These were the same signs and miracles given to the other apostles (Acts 4:29–30). Paul reminded the Corinthians that he had worked the signs and miracles and mighty deeds of an apostle (2 Corinthians 12:12).

TEST YOURSELF ON CHAPTER THREE

1. What was Paul's message? List some verses that show that the "gospel of the grace of God" is not only New Testament truth but also Old Testament.

2. Why did Paul go to Arabia? How long was he there?

3. How long did he stay in Damascus after his return from Arabia?

4. Why did Paul leave Damascus?

5. What was his method of escape?

6. Where did he go after leaving Damascus?

7. How did the saints in Jerusalem welcome him?

8. Who befriended Paul on his arrival in Jerusalem?

9. Describe what kind of man Paul was.

10. Who made a special appearance to Paul in the temple?

11. What was the purpose of this vision?

12. Why was Paul told to get out of Jerusalem?

13. To whom was he to go to and preach?

14. What was Paul's commission?

15. What was the order of his commission?

16. Give reasons why we know Paul was an apostle, and how did he exercise his authority as one?

Chapter Four

PAUL'S THORN
IN THE FLESH

Paul's so-called thorn in the flesh has been a controversial subject among Christians for generations. Many have taken the position that the thorn's identity will never be revealed until we get to glory and ask Paul himself. Since the thorn was given to him by the Lord, and it did become a hindrance to his ministry, it is worth examining the Scriptures to see if we can pinpoint what it actually was.

PAUL'S RETURN TO TARSUS Having noted in Acts 22:17–21 that Paul had received his commission and the first warning to leave Jerusalem, he left the city (see map 1, p. 442) and was taken to Caesarea (Acts 9:30). He testified that from Caesarea he went back to his home in Tarsus of Cilicia by way of Syria (Galatians 1:18–21). How long he stayed in Tarsus is unknown; it is possible that he stayed six years or more. The next mention we have of him is in Acts 11:25–26.

Due to the scattering of believers under the persecution of Paul before his conversion (Acts 9:3–4), a church had been established in Antioch (of Syria). This church was desperately in need of a leader, so they sent for Barnabas. Although Barnabas' ministry was highly successful, he felt a need to have Paul with him for a greater in-depth study of Scripture. He set out for Tarsus to find Paul, intending to take him back to Antioch (Acts 11:19–26).

But before Paul went with Barnabas, what happened to him during those years in Tarsus? Luke and Paul both are strangely silent regarding this visit to his home town. It is quite possible that word of Paul's conversion, which had happened several years prior to this visit, had reached the ears of his family and friends in Tarsus. They, no doubt, had heard that their pride and joy had become (to them) a traitor by believing in an imposter called Jesus. Given his background as a Pharisee, this change in Paul was an unpardonable sin. His parents, no doubt, were still in shock and shamed before their friends in the community and in the synagogue. It was bad enough for his family, as things were, with his coming home, but now Paul had a burning desire for his loved ones and friends to be saved, and he proclaimed Christ to all. This was too much, especially for the older Rabbis who had taught him. Opposition from them and his kinsmen was like the opposition he had meted out to believers when he was known as the persecutor of the church (1 Timothy 1:13). His refusal to cease preaching Christ resulted, no doubt, in a public beating by the Pharisees of Tarsus, as Ananias had predicted would happen (Acts 9:15–16).

In spite of the beating, Paul could not be silenced during his stay at home. He had learned enough in his first few years as a Christian to stand up for his beliefs and convictions, and having done all, to continue in the faith. Thus far, his ministry had been primarily to the Jews. Tarsus, a Greco-Roman colony, with the philosophy of both the Romans and Greeks would give him a good opportunity to get some basic training in witnessing to Gentiles of that culture. He probably spent much time in prayer, waiting for God to open a door to begin his Gentile calling while he earned his keep by working at his trade as a tent maker.

Acts 15:23 tells us there were some churches in Cilicia. It does not tell whether Paul was instrumental in helping to establish any of those churches in Cilicia while he tarried in Tarsus, or whether he established all of them while on his first missionary journey. It could be that some of the Jews from Asia (Minor) who were in Jerusalem on the Day of Pentecost were saved and went back home to establish churches (Acts 2:9). Whatever the case, it is probable that Paul was active in the church.

PAUL'S HEAVENLY EXPERIENCE It is also very probable that, during his stay in Tarsus, Paul experienced something extraordinary—an experience that he would later refer to in 2 Corinthians 12:1–10 written about A.D. 56 or 57—being caught up to the third heaven above fourteen years ago. *Above* means "just prior to" or the "exact period of time." By taking the date that Paul wrote this epistle (A.D. 56 or 57), and subtracting fourteen years from it, we arrive at A.D. 42 or 43. Soon after his conversion he was in Arabia, possibly A.D. 36—too early for this third-heaven event. Some have suggested that this memorable occasion took place when he was stoned at Lystra and left for dead (Acts 14:6–19). This stoning took place on his first missionary journey, about A.D. 46 or 47. If the A.D. 42 or 43 date is the correct one for this "heavenly" incident, his Arabian visit had occurred about six or seven years before and his stoning at Lystra about four or five years later. The A.D. 42 or 43 date is the closest one to the time of his being "caught up into the third heaven," and Tarsus was where it happened.

Several things occurred while Paul was "up" there (according to his own account). First he received visions and revelations and heard unspeakable words that were not lawful for him to utter (2 Corinthians 12:1–4). Some say he received the answer to the mystery of the church; some say he received an explanation of the "mystery of godliness" (1 Timothy 3:16); yet others say that he received the answer of the mystery of the ages to come or of God's will or of God's wisdom or of faith or of our bodies being changed, and so forth. Second, he was given a "thorn in the flesh," believed primarily to keep him humble (2 Corinthians 12:7). Third, God gave Paul the assurance that His grace would be sufficient no matter what his trials and circumstances might be.

For fourteen years, the experience of Paul's having been caught up to the third heaven had been kept a secret. And no wonder. It was an unusual event, to say the least. After all, the third heaven is the abode of God—the first heaven is the atmospheric heaven; the second heaven is the solar system. Job tells us that "God is in the height of heaven" (22:12). Lucifer tried to ascend above the stars and sit with God on His throne in heaven (Isaiah 14:13–14). Paul's experience of having been caught up to God's dwelling place in heaven probably would have caused average Christians to capitalize on it, to boast about their relationships with the Lord, and to equate themselves with being God's special representatives on earth.

Not so long ago a leading holiness preacher vowed that he had had a vision of a nine-hundred-foot-tall Christ! Christians know that Christ is big, but they didn't know He is nine hundred feet tall. The preacher, who had received the so-called vision, capitalized on this vision to get people to contribute to his ministry. Paul, however, informs us that, lest he be exalted above measure, God took drastic steps to see that this did not happen to him, that he would not use this wonderful experience to his advantage. What was God's drastic step? Paul himself gives the answer in 2 Corinthians 12:7, "Lest I be exalted above measure through the abundance of the revelations, there was given to me a thorn in the flesh, the messenger of Satan to buffet me, lest I should be exalted above measure."

PAUL'S PRIDE   God, who knows the end from the beginning, certainly knew Paul better than Paul knew himself. Prior to his conversion, Paul boasted about being a Jew, a Pharisee of the Pharisees, more zealous than all others in his desire to stamp out Christianity, and stricter than all of them in their Jewish traditions (Galatians 1:13–14).

There is no doubt that Paul was a proud, boastful Jew. Even after he was saved, he gave every indication that he loved the Jews more than he did the Gentiles. Even though he was called the Apostle of the Gentiles (Romans 11:13), we have no record of his ever having expressed the compassion and concern for them that he did for Jews, "I have great heaviness and continual sorrow in my heart, for I could wish that I myself were accursed from Christ for my brethren, my kinsmen according to the flesh. My heart's desire and prayer to God for Israel is that they might be saved" (Romans 9:2–3; 10:1). Paul was always trying to go back to Jerusalem and preach to his people in spite of Christ's command that he get out of Jerusalem and go far hence to the Gentiles because the Jews would not hear his testimony. True, Paul was concerned for all the lost, but within the providence of God he had the distinction of being the apostle to the uncircumcised (Gentiles) while Peter was the apostle to the circumcised (Jews), as we read in Galatians 2:7–8). Yet it seemed as though Paul would rather be in Peter's shoes—the apostle to the circumcised. The apostle John (4:22) made the statement that "salvation is of the Jews," but just because salvation came to the Jews in Old Testament times and others were saved by becoming proselytes, in no way means that the Jews are elevated above Gentiles. Even Paul himself said, "Are we [Jews] better than they [Gentiles]? No, in no wise: for we have before proved both Jews and Gentiles, that they are all under sin; . . . for all have sinned and come short of the glory of God" (Romans 3:9, 23).

In defense of Paul, we should say that his heading straight for a synagogue the moment he arrived in a town does not necessarily mean he put the Jews first or above the Gentiles. This was merely a custom; a synagogue was where the Law (Word of God) was read and taught, and when a service was held on the Sabbath the Jews had their service first, then when they were finished, the Rabbi would go to the outer court and preach to any Gentile, would-be proselytes. It was by using this method that Paul often found an audience with Gentiles (note Acts 13:44–49).

However, as we consider the overall picture of Paul's concern for his own people, it was his burning desire to go back to Jerusalem to preach to them and possibly win some to his Savior that culminated in his being imprisoned and sent to Rome. It had always been his desire to go to Rome and preach the Gospel, to impart some gift to the believers there, and to fellowship with them, but though he did get there, it was as a prisoner rather than in the freedom and liberty that he had enjoyed on his first three missionary journeys. Who knows what the course of Christianity would have been had Paul, a proud Jew, not gone back to Jerusalem, but rather had removed himself far hence from that city as commanded, putting full emphasis on his Gentile calling. Only God knows.

PAUL'S THORN   In spite of some who call Paul's thorn his "besetting sin," God kept filling him with His blessings and special revelations. In our study of Paul, we find that in addition to his having been caught up to the third heaven, Christ appeared four times to him: (1) at his conversion (Acts 9:4–6); (2) during his first visit to Jerusalem after his conversion (Acts 22:18–19); (3) while in Corinth (Acts 18:19–20); and (4) after his arrest in Jerusalem (Acts 23:11). In addition to these personal appearances by Christ, an angel spoke to him (Acts 27:23). God had a special place for Paul, but He needed a Paul who would be humble when necessary. Possibly Paul himself realized this when he said twice in the same verse, "Lest I be exalted above measure" (2 Corinthians 12:7). Paul's being special never went to his head because it looks as though, even before his first missionary journey, while in Tarsus meditating and resting and being prepared by the Lord for his ministry, he gave Paul a thorn in the flesh lest he become so obnoxious and egotistical that he would drive people away from the Lord, rather than win them to Christ. What was this thorn that God gave to him?

Physical Suffering

Some scholars say that it was his physical sufferings that Paul recalled in 2 Corinthians 11:23–33, plus any other physical suffering that may have been inflicted on him after he wrote this second epistle to the Corinthians. Ananias had said that God would show Paul what "great things he would suffer" (Acts 9:16). But was physical suffering his thorn? As far as we know, Paul did not begin to suffer real physical harm until his first missionary journey. He had met opposition from the Jews in Damascus but managed to escape before any harm was inflicted (Acts 9:22–25). During his first visit to Jerusalem after his conversion some Grecians sought to kill him, but there is no mention of violence or harm being inflicted on him (Acts 9:29; 22:17–18). He suffered no harm in Antioch (Acts 11:25–26) nor while going through Judaea to help the poor (Acts 11:27–30). And he commended those in Galatia for not having injured him (Galatians 4:12).

Thus, it would appear that all the sufferings listed in 2 Corinthians 11:23–33 took place between the time he started on his first missionary journey, about A.D. 45, and the time he wrote the second letter to the Corinthians about A.D. 58, a span of thirteen years. In mentioning these physical sufferings, he is talking about past sufferings, not future ones. Notice his list.

1. He was in labors more abundant, working overtime as it were, so that he would not be chargeable to anyone, plus his "outworking" all other apostles and disciples 2 Corinthians 11:23a; 15:10; 1 Thessalonians 2:9; 2 Thessalonians 3:8).

2. He was in stripes and beaten with rods, like at Philippi (Acts 16:23).

3. He was in prisons more frequently, once in Philippi (Acts 16:23).

4. He was in deaths often, like fighting with wild beasts (1 Corinthians 15:32; 2 Timothy 4:17).

5. He was scourged five times by the Jews (195 lashes).

6. He was stoned at Lystra (Acts 14:19).

7. He was in three shipwrecks; on one occasion in the deep (overboard) for a night and a day.

8. He was in journeyings often, like his missionary journeys over a period of several years in Asia Minor, Macedonia, Greece (Europe), Syria, and Judaea.

9. He was in perils of waters, or overflowing rivers during rainy seasons and floods due to melting snow in mountain regions, notably Galatia; robbers, especially in the mountain passes of Galatia; his own countrymen, the Jews (Acts 9:29; 21:30–31); the heathen (Gentiles), who opposed a message that dethroned their gods, such as at Ephesus (Acts 19:18–20, 23–41); the cities, where sin runs rampant; the wilderness (or desert), where it is terrifically hot in the daytime and extremely cold at night; and false brethren.

10. He was in weariness and pain.

11. He was in watchings often—sleepless nights spent being fearful of his life.

12. He was in hunger and thirst; fastings also, probably many forced on him.

13. He was in cold and nakedness.

14. He was in much mental stress (which leads to ulcers!)

It is incredible the way Paul was treated just because he was a Christian. He was often attacked verbally as well as being ill-treated. He told the Corinthians:

> I am one whom no one respects, am always buffeted or maltreated, going from place to place with no fixed home, laboring to the point of exhaustion so that I will be chargeable to no one, having insulting abuse heaped upon me, persecuted, slandered in public, becoming the offscouring, or as the filth discarded by humanity like dirt scraped off all things to this very moment. (1 Corinthians 4:10b–13; *Wuest's Expanded Translation*)

He was a "fool" for Christ's sake (1 Corinthians 4:10), but to the world he was nothing more than garbage.

It is amazing that Paul survived such physical suffering and abuse. And to think that some scholars have portrayed Paul as a weakling! Paul did admit that he was weak (2 Corinthians 11:29), but who wouldn't be after going through all the physical suffering he had? When one considers everything that Paul went through; yet came out alive, one is amazed at the way Paul rallied from oppression and tyranny and continued "night and day," as it were, to labor more abundantly for his wonderful Savior. No one could have endured labor, suffering, stoning, scourging, and other excruciating torment without having an extraordinary disposition and make-up. Paul may have been short in stature but he had a strong constitution; he bodily dragged people out of their houses and beat them in the synagogues (Acts 8:3; 9:13; 22:19). Paul testified that he was

> hard pressed from every side, but never hemmed in. At times, bewildered, not knowing which way to turn, but not utterly destitute, always looking up for help. At times, persecuted, but never left in the lurch nor abandoned nor let down. Sometimes knocked down but never knocked out. All this that I might bear in my body the dying of the Lord Jesus in order that His life might be revealed clearly and openly in mine. Death is operative in me so that you might see how life might work in you. (2 Corinthians 4:8–12, *Wuest's Expanded Translation*)

In all of this we must not rule out the strength of the Lord that assisted him, that was always made perfect in his weakness. No wonder that Paul gloried in his infirmities, in reproaches, in persecutions, in distress for Christ's sake, for, he said, "when I am weak, then I am strong" (2 Corinthians 12:9–10).

Eye Problem

Other scholars believe that Paul had some physical problem that needed to be healed; a disease that he himself could not heal with his apostolic gift of healing; a malady for which he besought God three times to heal him and was denied each time. The Bible nowhere hints that he had a physical condition labeled *thorn in the flesh*. However, some are of the opinion that he had malaria, having contracted it near Perga on his first missionary journey (Galatians 4:13). There are others who say he was an epileptic. The popular teaching regarding Paul's thorn is that the thorn itself was an eye problem, possibly ophthalmia. This was a common disease in the Near East, involving inflammation of the eyes that made them red, sore, runny, and weak. Those of this school of thought base their arguments on three statements that Paul himself made.

First he records the Galatians saying that they "would have plucked out their own eyes and given them to him" (Galatians 4:15). Paul's world was a rough place, and though he probably suffered physically, we do not know that he suffered any physical torture while in Paphos. He did have a confrontation with Satan while there, no doubt when he blinded Elymas (Acts 13:6–11), but while in Galatia, Paul says nothing about persecution in Perga of Pamphilia (Acts 13:13). However, it was in Perga that John Mark left Paul and Barnabas, possibly due to the ruggedness and persecution of such a ministry. Robbers were at every turn on the road and no one was safe. At any rate, when Paul later wrote to the Galatians he commended them for not injuring him, implying that they had injured others before he arrived in their country. Even though the Galatians never lifted a finger against him, Paul must have been in some kind of pain when he preached to them. Possibly some scars or fresh flesh wounds were visible, because he made mention that he had preached the Gospel to them "through infirmity of the flesh" (Galatians 4:12–13). Nowhere in Galatians, however, does Paul allude to or hint that this thorn or infirmity was eye trouble.

As for the Galatians being willing to "pluck out their eyes" for him, this could well have been an expression similar to what we might use today, saying, "I would be willing to give my right arm for So and So."[1] The Galatians loved Paul while he was with them, not injuring him as others had done. They had received him as an "angel of God, even as Jesus Christ" (Galatians 4:14). They were willing to make any sacrifice for him, therefore, we conclude the expression plucking out their own eyes could mean a number of things relating to warmth and love and sacrifice, not necessarily denoting Paul had bad eyesight.

Second, the incident Paul had in Jerusalem after his arrest in relation to his not recognizing the high priest has led some to conclude that his eyes gave him a problem (Acts 23:1–5). The high priest was Ananias. Paul was well acquainted with Caiaphas, who was the high priest when he was a persecutor of the church and the one from whom he received letters to antagonize believers in Damascus. A new high priest was in Jerusalem now, and we have no record of Paul's having ever met him before this get-together, so it is quite possible he was unknown to Paul. We notice also that when Ananias commanded that Paul be smitten on the mouth, the command was given to those close to Paul. Ananias was not near Paul, and in a closely packed crowd of seventy people plus the Roman soldiers who were present, and with everyone talking and shouting at the same time, it would have been difficult for Paul to have seen the high priest, regardless of whether he had good or bad eyesight. Paul heard the command, but when he said he did not know it was the high priest who had given the command to smite him, this does not necessarily mean that his eyesight was so dim that he could not see who spoke it. In his not knowing the high priest, we can see why he did not recognize the voice. Since Paul was small of stature, and all in the room were standing, it is understandable that he could not see over the heads of some to see the high priest. It appears that his eyesight had nothing to do with this incident.

A third incident that scholars attribute to an eye problem had to do with Paul's handwriting. In writing to the Galatians Paul said, "Ye see how large a letter I have written unto you with mine own hand" (Galatians 6:11). *Large* has to do with size—large, apparently beautifully styled letters. *Letter* in the Greek is *gramma*, denoting individual letters (not a script style). C. I. Scofield attributes Paul's using large letters to his poor eyesight. However, writing in large letters could have been characteristic of Paul. Some people write small, some medium, some large. Since Paul was well educated, knew several languages, and was acquainted with how the Romans spelled their words with large capital letters, he could have developed this as his own style; he could have used this method because the southern part of Galatia was more Roman than Greek. We must take into account that this was Paul's first letter to any group of believers, the first and only letter he wrote to the Galatians. He could have been setting a precedent so that in the future if any of his letters were questioned, people would know his epistles by his unique style of writing.

If Paul really had an eye problem that buffeted him, it is strange that he never mentioned it. He mentioned everything else he had suffered when he wrote to the Corinthians. Even when he said in 2 Corinthians 11:28, "beside all those things that come to me daily, and the care of the churches," he did not add in the list that preceded this statement that he was plagued with an "eye-thorn." Could it be that he did not have an eye malady? Most people in the Near East who had ophthalmia were born with it (as continues to be the case). God would have had to have smitten Paul with it as his thorn after his so-called heavenly ascension. If Paul was bothered with nearsightedness or farsightedness, it evidently was of little consequence since he failed to include it in the other sufferings he mentions in 2 Corinthians 11:23–33.

The three previously mentioned reasons for Paul's having poor eyesight are evidently enough to convince some people that he did indeed have that malady. There are, however, at least six incidents in the life of the apostle Paul that support the theory that his eyesight was not poor—six events that so many have overlooked.

First, when Paul and Barnabas were in Paphos on the island of Cyprus, a sorcerer who was a false prophet withstood Paul as he started to preach the Word of God to Sergius Paulus, a deputy of the country. Paul, being filled with the Holy Spirit, "set his eyes" on the sorcerer, rebuking him, and blinding him (Acts 13:9). The word *set* does not mean that Paul had to look through weak eyes to single out this man and then focus on him. It means that with good eyesight he "fastened" his eyes on him; he "fixed his gaze" on him; he "gazed intently" on him. In our day, we would say that he looked a hole through him.

Second, at Lystra, Paul healed a lame man (Acts 14:6–10). This man sat listening to Paul's preaching, and as he preached, Paul took particular notice of this man and perceived that he had faith to be healed. Ask any pastor—it takes a discerning, scrutinizing look to notice if someone has faith to believe. When he perceived this, verse 9 tells us that Paul "steadfastly beheld him." Here again he "intently gazed" on him, "fixing his gaze" on this one in need, which implies that he had good enough eyesight to single this man out without any trouble.

Third, some have argued that Paul's eyesight was so poor he needed an escort to conduct him from Berea to Athens and that upon arrival in Athens he sent for Silas and Timothy to come from Berea and help him get around (Acts 17:14–15). Actually, when the Bereans "conducted" Paul to Athens, they were with him to keep him company, advisedly showing him the route from Berea to Dium, where they found a vessel sailing the Aegean Sea to Athens. They were not his "seeing-eye dogs" to help him "find his way" to his destination.

Paul's eyesight had nothing to do with the reason that Timothy and Silas went to Athens. Rather, Paul was concerned about the progress of the believers in the church at Thessalonica, hence his desire for these two helpers to meet him and give him a report. They never did arrive in Athens and instead met him in Corinth

(Acts 18:1–5). Scripture makes no mention of an escort for Paul from Athens to Corinth—even later mentioning his going to Jerusalem and Antioch alone (Acts 18:1, 19–22). Why would Paul need help to get around Athens but not during his visit to Corinth?

Fourth, after arriving in Athens, Paul "saw the city wholly given to idolatry" (Acts 17:16). The word *saw* comes from several Greek words: *theoreo*, which means "to be a discerning spectator"; *theaomia*, which means "to took closely, to scrutinize"; and *optanomia* and *optomia*, which mean "to gaze wide-eyed, to take aim, an earnest, continual inspection, watching from a distance." One must have pretty good eyesight to see as Paul did when "he saw the city [of Athens] wholly given to idolatry," wouldn't you think?

Fifth, as Stoic and Epicurean philosophers were taking Paul up to Mars' Hill, they passed an area where there were objects of worship. Paul "beheld" an altar with the inscription: "TO THE UNKNOWN GOD" (see illustration 13). Walking along and reading at the same time takes good eyesight. *Beheld* means to "look again attentively." One cannot look again attentively with poor eyesight. Paul's vision was sufficient to give him some great sermon material to preach the Gospel to these philosophers (Acts 17:22–34).

Finally, the matter of Paul's arrest in Jerusalem and his failure to recognize the high priest, must be pursued just a little further. At the outset of this meeting with the Council, Luke tells us that Paul "earnestly beheld the council" (Acts 23:1). It has been pointed out that Paul could not see over the shoulders and heads of some of the seventy-plus people. Verse 1 is saying the same thing of Paul that was said of him at Paphos and Lystra—he "looked a hole through them," he "fixed his gaze," on them, he "gazed intently" on all he could see.

Some who hold that Paul's thorn in the flesh was an eye malady employ the argument that his so-called eye problems started when he approached Damascus and "suddenly there shined round about him a light from heaven and he fell to the earth." This is when he met Jesus and was converted. When he "arose from the earth, and when his eyes were opened, he saw no man, and those with Paul led him and brought him into Damascus, and he was three days without sight" (Acts 9:3–4, 8–9). This, proponents of an eye problem surmise, was probably the beginning of his physical-ailment thorn. Although his sight was restored after three days, he was left with weak eyesight. One or two things should be noted in connection with this opinion.

Luke tells us in Acts 9:10–16 that God told both Judas and Ananias that Paul's sight was to be restored. Yes, the "eye problem" teachers are correct: he did have an eye problem but just for three days! Ananias, at God's instruction,

> went his way and entered into the house [of Judas]; and putting his hands on him said, Brother Saul, the Lord, even Jesus, that appeared unto thee in the way as thou camest, hath sent me that thou mayest receive thy sight, and be filled with the Holy

13—An altar to an "UNKNOWN GOD." *Courtesy of Felbermeyer, Rome.*

Ghost. And immediately there fell from his eyes as it had been scales: and he received his sight forthwith. (Acts 9:17–18)

No one doubts that Paul's vision returned. The words *received* and *sight* come from the same Greek word, *anablepo*. This is the word that was used to record Jesus' healing the blind, "the blind receive their sight" (Matthew 11:5); when Jesus "touched their eyes, and immediately their eyes received sight" (Matthew 20:34); and when blind Bartimaeus "immediately received his sight" (Mark 10:46–52). The same is said of the blind man in Jericho (Luke 18:41–43) and the man born blind (John 9:7, 11), both of whom were made to see. I know of no Bible believer who would say that any whom Jesus healed were half-healed, saw dimly through weak eyes, or were partially healed and continued to have red and possibly runny eyes. They were either healed completely or they were not healed at all. Jesus did not perform incomplete miracles; only complete ones. According to the Greek text, Paul received such a miracle when his sight was restored through Ananias. Christ Himself could have healed Paul by His own power without human means, but Paul needed to see at the beginning of his Christian life that God's work on earth is done primarily through man. Paul would later see this throughout his own ministry.

After Paul's sight was restored, no mention is made of his being led about the streets of Damascus to preach in the synagogues. Scripture seems to imply that he got around nicely on his own. We assume, rightly I believe, that he went to Arabia alone. This is a dry, desert region, and only a fool would venture alone into a desert made blazing hot by the sun if his eyes were weak, sore, and runny; and he had difficulty getting around. Paul may have been a fool for Christ's sake but he was not as foolish as the so-called ophthalmia brethren would have us believe. When the "scales" fell from Paul's eyes, the result was distinct, 20/20 vision.

It is also rather ridiculous to assume that Paul's blindness at conversion resulted in an eye problem that became his thorn of physical illness (or malady). If Paul were saved A.D. 35 or 36, he did not receive his thorn in the flesh until about six or seven years later. When he wrote his second epistle to the Corinthians, it was in A.D. 56 or 57. The thorn had been given fourteen years before, or, as we said, six or seven years after he was saved. Thus, it is folly to say that his blindness on the way to Damascus was, or precipitated, his thorn. One good brother said Paul's blindness, due to the light from heaven, started his "eye problem" and for six or seven years it was dormant—then the thorn broke through into a disease that was never healed (similar to one's having cancer and not knowing of it until pain strikes). It is a good thing that God made straw, or this fellow wouldn't have anything to grab at (please pardon my grammar).

The grounds on which the ophthalmia group base their claim is mighty weak. They place his thorn in the category of a physical disease—something that was an illness that needed to be healed. Much has been said about Paul's gift to heal others, but he could not heal himself. We cannot put anything past God; He can use the weak to confound the mighty. However, doesn't it seem rather strange that God would afflict a man with such a disease, knowing he was to be the one man who would represent Him before kings, governors, Jews, Gentiles, philosophers, and all mankind in general? Most real Christians, no doubt, would show pity and concern and readily accept such a person full of the joy of the Lord, but such an appearance would turn many people off. It seems, rather, that Paul had this "remarkable power of fascination and cowing a person or enemy with the keenness of his glance,"[2] and that his eyesight was not as poor as so many of us have been taught. It is very doubtful that Paul's thorn in the flesh was poor eyesight—something that needed to be healed.

THE BIBLICAL ANSWER TO THE THORN If Paul's thorn in the flesh was not his physical sufferings or ophthalmia (an eye disease), what was it? I had been taught that the thorn was ophthalmia or possibly Paul's sufferings, which he mentioned to the Corinthians. As one sheep follows another (which so many Christians are prone to do), I accepted this teaching because of my faith and trust in my teachers. I found that most commentators were in agreement about the eye-problem. Finally, putting into practice what the Bereans did and what I had so often preached, I went to the Bible to see what God had to say. It is strange that with all the theories propounded I should find the answer in plain English right from the lips of Paul himself!

In reading 2 Corinthians 12:7, I came to the conclusion and agreed with Paul that his thorn was "a messenger of Satan to buffet him." What other conclusion could one reach? *Messenger* is *angelos* in Greek and is used here to refer to an evil spirit that indwells an unsaved person (Matthew 12:43–45). Oftentimes

Satan uses *angelos* as his ministers or preachers (2 Corinthians 11:13–15). Indwelling humans, their purpose is to hinder God's program or the advancement of the preaching of the Gospel, as in Paul's case. Paul frequently used expressions, like *thorn in the flesh*, to explain or illustrate a point in his messages or writings. He picked up the expressions from Scripture. A look at Scripture, for example, reveals that people, when used by Satan, became to Israel as "pricks in [their] eyes, and thorns in [their] sides, snares and traps, scourges in [their] sides" (Numbers 33:55; Joshua 23:13). Israel's history confirms this truth. The surrounding nations that Israel failed to drive out of the Promised Land became their enemies and so persecuted them that they became "thorns in their flesh [or sides]." This is what happened to Paul throughout his ministry. Satan constantly used people, primarily the Jews, to buffet Paul everywhere he went, many times causing physical sufferings, and at the same time forcing him to abandon his preaching in a given city. Many times his life was threatened. In circumstances that did not involve opposition from people, the "prince of the power of the air" buffeted the seas, causing storm and shipwreck. Although not indwelt by an evil spirit, Paul himself became a thorn in the flesh to the Jews by showing them from their own Scriptures that God's righteousness was obtainable only in and through the Lord Jesus Christ.

When Saul of Tarsus determined to rid the world of Christianity, it is safe to say that either Satan himself, or a messenger of Satan, used him to buffet Christians as they sought to propagate their faith in Jesus Christ. It pleased the Jews for Christians to be killed (Acts 12:1–3), and Paul himself delighted to breathe out slaughterings as he went on a rampage against believers (1 Timothy 1:13). Who else but Satan would motivate people to do such? *Fox's Book of Martyrs* gives a long, long list of saints who down through the centuries forfeited their lives when enemies of the Cross, indwelt by Satan, chopped off their heads, burned them at the stake, crucified them upside down, sawed them in half, scourged them till they died in a convulsive heap with their sinews and organs exposed, threw them to wild beasts, and ripped open the wombs of pregnant women with swords so that their unborn babies would also die.

But Paul was not the only one who had a personal encounter with Satan. Peter, as you recall, was influenced by Satan when he opposed Christ's going to Jerusalem. Peter rebuked Jesus when He mentioned the purpose of His coming—that He would suffer many things, be killed, and raised the third day. When Peter took Jesus to task for such a statement, Jesus said to Peter, "Get thee behind me, Satan," knowing full well that Satan was trying to buffet (hinder) Him by influencing Peter (Matthew 16:21–23). The patriarch Job is another who had a personal encounter with Satan. Satan was permitted to take everything Job had except his life (Job 1). Paul experienced something similar. Satan tried to stop Paul, but Paul pressed on and like Job was able to say, "Though he slay me, yet will I trust in him, and when he hath tried me I shall come forth as gold" (Job 13:15; 23:10).

God permitted Satan's messenger to be Paul's "drill sergeant" not only to keep him humble and on his knees lest he be exalted above measure but also to hinder his preaching. Paul now got a taste of his own medicine, the same type he dished out when he set about to persecute and slaughter saints. Just before he listed his trials and sufferings to the Corinthians, he mentioned the subtlety of Satan and his so-called ministers of righteousness (2 Corinthians 11:13–15). No matter where Paul went, Satan was there in his messenger to meet him, greet him, buffet, and oppose him. A good example is of Satan's hindering Paul when he wanted to go back to Thessalonica to encourage believers—"We would have come to you . . . but Satan hindered us" (1 Thessalonians 2:18). Was it not also Satan who sought to keep Christ from starting out on a ministry that would ultimately end in his death and resurrection for lost sinners (Matthew 4:1–10)? Satan will, if he can, stop any Christian "dead in his tracks."

It is quite true that such opposition by the messenger of Satan resulted in much physical, bodily harm (stoning, scourging, and so forth), but Paul's thorn in the flesh was not eye trouble or physical suffering. It was Satan's messenger to buffet him with physical attacks or curtailed events. Satan simply did not want Paul to exalt Christ in his own life, nor did he want him to win others to Christ. Now that Paul was about to set out on his calling or ministry as the Apostle of the Gentiles, Satan's messenger was ready to use any method—storm, poisonous snake bite, stoning, harsh imprisonment, the mysticism of pagans, unbelieving Jews, and so forth, to be a thorn in Paul's flesh. Satan's goal was to keep him from reaching the lost and establishing churches (1 Thessalonians 2:14–18).

The word *thorn* (*skolops*) originally denoted anything pointed, like briars or a stake. Paul used the word to indicate the effect of Divinely permitted Satanic antagonism, whether physical, painful, or humiliating. *Buffeting* is used in the present tense, denoting recurrent action or a constant repeated attack. *Thorn, messenger of Satan,* and *buffet* have nothing to do with a continuing eye problem. The messenger could attack to humiliate Paul, to endanger his life, to cause painful suffering, or to sideline him in his travels for the Lord.

Many of us have been taught one thing so long that it is difficult to accept another point of view. We too often read the Bible in light of what we have been taught. That is fine when it comes to the fundamental, cardinal truths of our Christian faith, such as the deity of Christ, the Virgin Birth, the Atonement, the Second Coming, the Trinity, and so forth. But in so many subjects, we simply accept what has been preached by good men without taking the time to be a Berean believer. For example, how many times have you heard a minister say, "The Bible says the Rapture is going to take place in a moment, in the twinkling of an eye?" The Rapture may, but the Bible does not say that. It does tell us that "we shall all be changed, in a moment, in the twinkling of an eye [implying a body change]"; for at the Rapture, when we see Him, we become like Him; our corruptible (bodies) must put on incorruption (a glorified body, 1 Corinthians 15:51–57; 1 John 3:2). I was taught that after Paul was saved he spent three years in Arabia. The Bible is silent about his length of stay there. It does say, "then after three years [after his stay in Damascus], . . . [he] went up to Jerusalem" (Galatians 1:17–18). It does not say he spent three years in Arabia. How many times have you yourself said, "The angels in heaven rejoice over one sinner on earth that repenteth"? The Bible does not say that. It does say, "There is joy *in the presence of angels* of God over one sinner that repenteth." This would lead us to believe that the host of the redeemed in heaven do the rejoicing, especially since angels know nothing about blood-washed sinners (1 Peter 1:10–12). How many Christians refer to wine being served at Communion because their pastor or some Bible teacher uses the term. The Bible does not use *wine* in connection with the Lord's Supper; it refers to the drink as "the fruit of the vine" or "the cup" (Matthew 26:26–29; Luke 22:14–20; 1 Corinthians 11:23–26). For us to say that Paul's thorn was an eye problem is to read something into Scripture that is not there. To say that his thorn was a messenger of Satan to actively and periodically buffet him and oppose the fulfilling of his calling is to read something into Scripture that is there.

No real student of the Word of God would for one moment want to contradict Scripture, but a popular, longstanding interpretation is not always correct once we leave good commentaries and look at "thus saith the Lord." When I first presented the view of Paul's thorn being a messenger of Satan to buffet him, one person said: "I know what the Scripture says, but . . . " It is not easy to unlearn what one has been taught, especially in the realm of speculation or supposition. A modernist will continue his unbelief because facts interfere with what he believes and teaches. It isn't easy, even for a believer, to change his or her view on something that cannot be proved; to change his or her view when something different is presented from what was previously believed and taught.

A change is hard to make; pride is a hard thing to swallow, especially if we have to let others know we believe something different. To be sure, there will always be differences of opinion, but whatever our opinion, it must not go contrary to what God says. Taking everything into consideration, however, there is enough Scripture to support the view that Paul did have good eyesight, and that the thorn was something that attacked him often, something different than an eye problem. In no way can a thorn in the flesh, a messenger of Satan, be a disease or a physical ailment, even an eye problem.

It can be argued that we all have opposition from Satan. He goes about as a "roaring lion, seeking whom he may devour" (1 Peter 5:8–9). If we do not have opposition from him, there would be no need to resist him to the point that he flees from us (James 4:7); no need to put on the whole armor of God (Ephesians 6:11–18); we could never be more than conquerors through Christ who loves us (Romans 8:37). But who among us, as well as the other apostles and New Testament saints, was given a thorn in the flesh as a result of having been caught up to third heaven? Who among us was caught up like Paul and heard unspeakable words and was given visions and revelations? Who among us was given a thorn in the flesh, a messenger of Satan to buffet, lest we be exalted above measure? To my limited knowledge of Scripture, only one—Paul.

However, Satan has devices (thought-out ways to defeat us) and wiles (error to deceive us), and with his miraculous power, signs, and lying wonders, his only desire is to keep us from following Christ in total commitment—from being and living in the center of God's will. For this reason he will use any method to keep us from submitting our all to the Lord. Though Satan has been defeated and his emissaries spoiled, his days are numbered. He is like a rat in a corner fighting for his life, fighting against God, His children, and His cause. Since Christ lives in the believer, and Satan's primary attack is against Him, he strikes at Christ through the believer. This means we are caught in the cross fire if we are seeking God's will. When we come to the point of being willing to be a disciple of Christ as outlined in 1 Corinthians 6:19–20, Romans 12:1–2, Matthew 16:24–25, and Mark 8:34, we will (1) realize we have been bought with a price and no longer belong to ourselves, we will present our bodies as a living sacrifice, turn from the things of this world determined that we are going to do God's will; (2) come to Christ, "If a man will come after Me"; (3) denounce (deny) self and selfish pursuits: "Let him deny himself," including everything and everybody; (4) voluntarily take up our cross and follow Jesus. A cross is what one must bear and/or endure for serving God wholeheartedly.

When we take up our cross and follow Jesus, we face the tyranny of the world, the flesh, and the devil because Satan knows we are in the center of God's will. As we take up our cross, his opposition is so great that he will hurl anything at us to ruin our Christian testimony. Why should a Christian expect any better treatment from the world than they gave the One who bore His Cross for us? The world hated Him for His obedience; it will hate us for ours. As we bear our cross, which is a voluntary act on our part, Satan will do his best to cause (1) our friends to forsake us; (2) our enemies to be those of our own household; (3) us to be ashamed of Christ and not witness to others about Him; (4) imaginations to create anxiety, fear, discouragement, depression, worry, and doubt; (5) difficulties, sufferings, persecution, and opposition to get us down; (6) peer pressure and human philosophy to lead us astray; (7) temptation and lust to beset us. Satan will do anything to defeat us and cause us to bring reproach to our Savior. Bearing our cross victoriously is meeting any circumstance or obstacle thrown at us as we bear in our bodies the marks of the dying of the Lord Jesus (2 Corinthians 4:8–12). It is the necessary consequence of one's "abiding in Christ," the "reckoning of ourselves to be dead indeed unto sin but alive unto God" (John 15:4; Romans 6:6, 11). Sometimes it might mean denying ourselves to the point where we are called on to forfeit our own lives.

The believer, who takes up his cross daily, experiences all sorts of opposition from Satan, but this opposition is vastly different from Paul's thorn in the flesh. Taking up our cross is self-denial; death to self; renunciation of the world, the flesh and the devil; being victorious over the flesh and its passions—it is dying to self daily to reveal our spiritual identification with Christ (Romans 6:4–6, 17–18; Galatians 2:20; Colossians 3:1–3).

Paul would *never* have asked the Lord to remove his cross. He knew that he would not be Christ's disciple if it were removed—if he did not bear it. He asked, however, that his thorn be removed. To him, his thorn was not a matter of sickness or some physical ailment. As much as he had already suffered physically, it is doubtful that he would have been more concerned with an eye condition or some physical pain than he would be with something the messenger of Satan did to impede his progress in preaching the Gospel. He was not asking the Lord to be healed of some physical condition like sore eyes; he wanted relief from the beating, buffeting attacks of Satan's messenger. He besought the Lord on three occasions to remove this thorn. It affected his physical being and hindered his journeys to spread the Good News of salvation in Christ Jesus. We do not know how far apart these requests were to have the thorn removed, but the Lord knew Paul better than Paul knew himself, and He knew that if He answered his prayer as he desired, it would do more harm than good.

Paul yielded to his burden, knowing that God had made his back for burdens and that He had also made the burdens for his back. He accepted this thorn knowing that God would "work all things together for good" (Romans 8:28). He believed God's promise that His grace would be sufficient in every trial and situation. We cannot say that Paul was altogether thankful for this thorn, but he was thankful in it—thankful in everything (1 Thessalonians 5:18). He knew that Satan's messenger would be the devil's drill sergeant, but he also knew that Christ was the Captain in his life and of the Lord's host (Joshua 5:13–15). He knew that a Captain outranked a sergeant!

In accepting this thorn Paul testified that no matter what befell him, he would glory, not in all the privileges he had as a servant of Christ, not in what would have exalted him above measure before the eyes of others, but in his "buffeting infirmities." He was assured that, through it all, God's daily grace would be sufficient (2 Corinthians 12:7–10). Paul truly learned that his thorn served a two-fold purpose: (1) to keep him humble lest he be exalted above measure; and (2) to keep him on his knees so that he would be empowered by God no matter where he traveled and met opposition from the Jews and the Gentiles who so vehemently withstood him. The messenger of Satan would buffet, but Paul finally recognized that no matter what success he might have as a servant of Christ, his thorn was to constantly remind him that any accomplishments were all of God, that no flesh would glory in His presence. Whatever glorying Paul did, he learned to glory in the Lord—thorn and all (1 Corinthians 1:29, 32; Galatians 6:4).

TEST YOURSELF ON CHAPTER FOUR

1. After Paul received his first warning to leave Jerusalem, where did he spend the next few years?

2. Who was the successful leader of the church of Antioch in Syria?

3. What unusual event possibly happened to Paul during this period?

4. What three things in particular happened when this event took place?

5. How many heavens are there?

6. Where is the third heaven?

7. What was given to Paul and why?

8. Was Paul a proud Jew? Explain.

9. Was Paul's thorn his physical sufferings or an eye problem? Support your opinion.

10. Give three reasons why some scholars believe that his thorn was an eye disorder.

11. The author lists six reasons why he does not believe Paul's eyesight was his thorn. List them.

12. List the arguments given to refute the statement that Paul's sight was so poor he needed an escort.

13. Does Paul or the Bible ever mention his having an eye malady?

14. List the two points given to support the argument that Paul's thorn was not the result of his having been blinded at his conversion.

15. How is the word *thorn* used in the Bible, and what does it mean in Paul's case?

16. How did this thorn affect Paul?

17. What does the word *buffet* mean?

18. Make a list of the things you think or have been taught that the Bible says but doesn't.

19. Does the Bible mention any other than Paul who had a similar experience of being caught up to third heaven and given such a thorn?

20. In what four ways can a Christian invoke the devil's opposition?

21. How does this opposition against the believer differ from Paul's thorn?

22. Do you believe Paul's thorn was something from which he needed physical healing, such as an eye condition, or something that would go to his head and hinder his traveling, preaching ministry?

23. How many times did Paul ask God to remove this thorn?

24. What did God promise instead?

25. What was Paul's attitude as a result of God's provision?

Chapter Five

PAUL'S FIRST MISSIONARY JOURNEY

W hen Paul made his first visit to Jerusalem after his conversion, he received his commission to go to the Gentiles. Before leaving, he boldly preached in the name of the Lord Jesus. He met with fierce opposition from some Greeks who sought to stop him, but with the help of the brethren, he escaped to Tarsus via Caesarea (Acts 9:26–30). This was his first visit to his home, family, and friends to tell them of his new-found joy in the Messiah of the Old Testament.

Having already considered that Paul was caught up into third heaven while in Tarsus, we noted that it was at this time that he received his thorn in the flesh (2 Corinthians 12:1–10). Assuming that he was saved about A.D. 35 or 36, he spent a little over four years in Damascus, Arabia, and Jerusalem before going to Tarsus. Later he spent a year in Antioch and possibly six months taking an offering to the elders in Jerusalem for the poor brethren throughout Judaea (Acts 11:27–30). Upon returning to Antioch, Paul, with Barnabas and Mark, set out on his first missionary journey about A.D. 46 or 47 (Acts 12:25; 13:1–3). From A.D. 35 or 36 to 46 or 47 we can account for six, maybe seven years, which would make his stay in Tarsus approximately four, maybe five, years. During his stay at Tarsus the churches had rest, were edified, and multiplied (Acts 9:30–31). It was during this time that the Church of Antioch was founded (Acts 11:19–24).

Chapter Five

THE ANTIOCH CHURCH   When Paul pursued Christians, many saints were scattered abroad, some traveling as far as Phoenicia, Cyprus, and Antioch. Some of the founders of the Antioch church were from Cyprus and Cyrene. But why? Why were believers from Cyprus and Cyrene in Antioch? Acts 2:10 tells us that on the Day of Pentecost, Cyrenians from Libya (northern Africa) were present. More than likely some were saved and, due to persecution in Jerusalem, headed north and settled in Antioch rather than returning to their fatherland. We are told in Acts 26:11 that Paul persecuted believers in "strange cities," which implies cities beyond the bounds of Judaea, Samaria, and Galilee. For all we know the cities could have been in Phoenicia and Cyprus, resulting in some Cyprians fleeing to Antioch. Regardless, some from Cyprus and Cyrene were in Antioch active in the things of the Lord. Acts 13:1 mentions some of the leaders of this church. There were Simeon who was called (surnamed) Niger, Lucius of Cyrene, and Manean. Simeon's Latin name was *Niger,* meaning "black," implying an African origin. Simon is a Greek form of Simeon, and one wonders if this might be the same "Simon the Cyrenian" who helped Christ bear His cross (Mark 15:21). Simon, or Simeon, was the father of Rufus and Alexander. Rufus was later mentioned by Paul in Romans 16:13. It is quite possible that Simeon (Simon), Rufus, and Alexander became believers in Christ as a result of helping Christ in His hour of need, seeing and confessing as the Roman soldier had, "Truly this man was the Son of God" (Mark 15:39). The Antioch church was blessed with many active believers.

As previously noted in chapter 3, Barnabas had an excellent reputation among the many believers in Jerusalem. When the Antioch church was established, there was a great need for someone well versed in the Scriptures to be their overseer. The saints in Antioch sent for Barnabas, and when he came and saw the grace of God in their midst, he rejoiced. He exhorted them all that with purpose of heart they should cleave unto the Lord (Acts 11:23–24). In spite of his capabilities, he sensed that Paul would be able to add to his ministry, giving a deeper insight in the Word, so he departed from Antioch to seek him in Tarsus. Barnabas also knew that Paul was especially appointed to preach the Gospel to the Gentiles. Paul appears to have been a thorough master of the Greek language, and consequently was the better qualified of the two to explain the Gospel to the Greek philosophers and to defend it against their frivolous objections. Barnabas found Paul and returned with him to Antioch (see map 1, p. 442). Together for a "whole year they assembled themselves with the church and taught much people" (Acts 11:26).

The results were so great, and believers lived so much like their wonderful Savior, Jesus Christ, that they were called "Christians" first in Antioch (Acts 11:26). They were called *Christianos*, meaning "partisans of the Messiah," but this name seems to have been more of a mockery, a "hissing." They were so Christlike that the unbelieving citizens of Antioch would jeer them as "you Christ followers." They were like those in Jerusalem in that the whole area "took knowledge of them that they had been with Jesus," or like others of whom it has been said: They turned the world upside down (Acts 4:13; 17:6). Followers of Christ were known by many names, but *Christian* was the best known. Sad to say, *Christian* does not have this same meaning today.

PAUL'S SECOND VISIT TO JERUSALEM A year after Paul and Barnabas had ministered in Antioch with great success, several prophets from Jerusalem paid them a visit (see map 1, p. 442).

Famine in Judaea

One of them, named Agabus, warned of an impending famine that would occur during the reign of Claudius Caesar (Acts 11:25–28). While there can be absolutely no doubt as to the historicity of such a famine as predicted by Agabus, it is interesting to note that ancient documents substantiate this biblical account. Already there were famines in the Roman Empire. Suetonius, a first-century Roman historian, in his *Life of Claudius*, made mention of a series of famines and poor harvests during Claudius' reign. The period from about A.D. 41 to 54 was a time of great distress and scarcity over the whole (then known) world. Another first-century historian, Tacitus, reported a famine so severe (possibly the one in Judaea) that it was considered to be a Divine judgment. Eusebius made note of a great famine in Greece and the two above-mentioned Roman historians cited two famines in Rome itself. The famine that Agabus prophesied came to Judaea during the fourth year of Claudius' reign. According to Josephus it was about A.D. 47, possibly a short time after Paul and Barnabas had taken the offering to the elders in Jerusalem, and by this time they had already started on their missionary journey.

NAMES FOR FOLLOWERS OF CHRIST

Christians	Because they were followers of Christ (Acts 11:26)
Believers	Because of their faith in Christ (Acts 5:14; 1 Timothy 4:12)
Children	Because of the Spirit's witness (Romans 8:16; 1 John 2:28)
Children of the kingdom	Because they had been born of the incorruptible Seed, the Word of God (Matthew 13:38; 1 Peter 1:23).
Sons	Because God is Father and they were led by the Spirit (Romans 8:15–16)
Disciples	Because they were taught by Christ and followed Him (Luke 14:26–27)
Friends	Because they obeyed Him (John 15:14)
Sheep	Because He is our Shepherd (John 10:14)
Saints	Because they had been chosen by Him to live a life holy and without blame (Ephesians 1:1–4)
Witnesses	Because they testified of Christ (Psalm 107:2; Acts 1:8)
Servants	Because He is our Master (1 Corinthians 7:22)
Brethren	Because Christ is our Elder Brother (Hebrews 2:11)

NAMES FOR FOLLOWERS OF CHRIST

Ambassadors	Because they represented Christ on earth (2 Corinthians 5:20)
Pilgrims and strangers	Because this world was not their home (Philippians 3:20–21; Hebrews 11:13)
Royal Priests (or a kingdom of priests)	Because they prayed one for another (1 Peter 2:9; James 5:16b; 1 Samuel 23:12)
Ransomed and redeemed of the Lord	Because they had been bought with a price—Christ's precious blood (Isaiah 35:10; 51:11; 1 Corinthians 6:19–20; 1 Peter 1:18–19)
Temples	Because they were indwelt by God the Father (2 Corinthians 6:16–18), Christ the Son (Colossians 1:27), and the Holy Spirit (1 Corinthians 3:16–17)
Pillars	Because as God's Temple, they had a firm and permanent position in spiritual and eternal things (1 Corinthians 6:19–20; Revelation 3:12)
Vessels of honor	Because they had the power of God within them (2 Corinthians 4:7; 2 Timothy 2:21)
Heirs of God; Joint-Heirs	Because of their familial relationship (Galatians 4:7; Romans 8:17); of the kingdom (James 2:5) and of promise (Hebrews 6:17)

Judaea was hit the hardest by the famine. Josephus wrote of Judaea, "The famine was so severe in Judaea that the price of food was enormous and great numbers perished."[1] It was at this time that Queen Helena, a proselyte to Judaism, and her son, King Izates of Adeabene, came to Jerusalem to worship. Moved with compassion for the misery that she saw, she had corn brought in from Alexandria, Egypt, and figs shipped from Cyprus for distribution among the poor. Her son gave large sums of money to help.

God was ever mindful of His own people, probably the poorest and certainly the most disregarded and despised, in Judaea. He had no intention of letting His people die of starvation, especially when the church was still in its infancy and believers were sorely needed everywhere. When the saints of Antioch heard the prophecy of Agabus, they were touched and took up a collection. Having been made partakers of the grace of God and His benefits, they felt it their Christian duty to minister to those in need, although these Judaean Christians were unknown to them. They realized the bond, the oneness that existed between believers, no matter who and where they were, and they determined to send relief according to their means. Barnabas and Paul were chosen to take the offering to the elders in Jerusalem (Acts 11:27–30), which would enable these Judaean believers to afford the inflated price of food.

Suffering of Believers

This was Paul's second visit to Jerusalem after his conversion. It was during his first visit to this city that Christ told him that his testimony would not be received by the Jews there (Acts 21:17–18). On this second visit, he and Barnabas arrived only to witness a worse calamity than that of a famine. One apostle, James, had just been executed at the command of Herod, and Peter was imprisoned awaiting execution (Acts 12:1–4). Paul's heart must have broken as he learned of the pain of persecuted brethren, especially when he was so familiar with having inflicted much pain on believers in the past. We do not know if he visited Peter in prison, but we may assume that after Peter was released and went to the home of Mary, John Mark's mother, that Barnabas, who was related, may have persuaded Paul to visit Mary and Mark (Acts 12:11–12; Colossians 4:10). That Paul and Barnabas met Mark and invited him to go with them to Antioch is plain.

BARNABAS AND PAUL ORDAINED   Mark did join Paul and Barnabas and they returned to Antioch (Acts 12:25). After their arrival, they had great spiritual blessings and fellowship as they ministered to the believers. Paul's time of setting out to fulfill his calling as the Apostle to the Gentiles was fast approaching. Over a span of ten or eleven years in Damascus, Arabia, Jerusalem, Tarsus, and Antioch, Paul had gained experience that would benefit him on his missionary journeys.

The church in Jerusalem has often been called the "mother" church. It was the first church in the New Testament era, and witnessing started "first in Jerusalem" (Acts 1:8). From this church, Stephen preached (Acts 7). Philip had gone from Jerusalem as a missionary to Samaria, Gaza, Azotus, and from city to city up the coast to Caesarea (Acts 8:5–40). Due to the persecution in Jerusalem and the founding of the church at Antioch, the Antioch church soon took over as the missionary headquarters for the churches in general. It was at this church that Paul's foreign missionary endeavor began.

"As they ministered to the Lord, and fasted, the Holy Ghost said, Separate me Barnabas and Saul [Paul] for the work whereunto I have called them. And when they had fasted and prayed, and laid their hands on them, they sent them away. So they, being sent forth by the Holy Ghost, departed unto Seleucia [a Syrian seaport] and from thence they sailed to [the island of] Cyprus" (Acts 13:2–4).

Being sent out by the Holy Spirit Himself (see map 2, p. 444), they were (1) under His influence, (2) under His authority, and (3) under His continual direction. Without the first, they were not qualified to go; without the second, they had no authority to preach, teach, and establish churches; and without the third, they would not know where to go. It was not the praying, fasting, and the laying on of hands that qualified Paul and Barnabas for this work, however. God had already called them, and He who called them qualified them (Acts 13:2).

According to Jewish tradition, ordination was performed by three elders, and the laying on of hands was strictly forbidden. The church at Antioch used three men, Simeon, Lucius, and Manean, but departing from the Jewish custom they put their hands on the heads of Barnabas and Paul, thus designating them to be the ones they, under the direction of the Holy Spirit, sent to preach the Gospel to heathens. Thus we have introduced the custom of the "laying on of hands" in ordination. Having been ordained (commissioned) to this tremendous task, they took John Mark with them as their minister or servant (Acts 13:5).

PAUL'S FIRST Paul, with Barnabas and Mark, went
MISSIONARY JOURNEY through Cyprus (see map 2, p. 444), and into the southern sector of Galatia in Asia Minor (Acts 13–14). The probable date was A.D. 46/47–49/50. The time involved was approximately three years. The traveling distance was about 1,450 miles by land and sea.

What techniques did Paul and Barnabas use when they entered a city to introduce Christ to its citizens? How did they go about it? There would have to be preparation, plans, strategy, and a mind-set to do the impossible among people who were pagans and steeped in superstitious religious beliefs. Paul had truth; the others had error. How might they confront them? How might they open a conversation with total strangers? It is apparent from the visits Paul made to cities on two continents that he, as a stranger, simply walked into town to seek lodging. Having to support himself, he possibly visited the area where tents were made, seeking employment. Knowing Paul as we do, he could not refrain from witnessing to innkeeper and laborers alike. On the Sabbath he headed straight for the synagogue and joined other worshipers in prayer and the reading of Scripture. As was the custom, upon the completion of the service, the leader of the synagogue would ask if anyone present had a worthy comment to make. Paul would go to the "Seat of Moses" (see illustration 14), and because of his educated Jewish background, the authority of his speech would capture their attention. This gave him the opportunity to preach Christ as he had in Antioch (Acts 13:14–43). Such a sermon likely created opposition as well as interest but a seed would have been sown, and sometime during the week Paul and Barnabas and the sermon would be the topic of conversation among the whole city. On the next Sabbath all the Jews, proselytes, and curiosity seekers would attend the synagogue and from there on the Holy Spirit, through Paul's preaching of the Word, was adding to the Lord such as should be saved. Jealous Jews hated to see Gentiles being converted, and oftentimes they would either stir up a mob to oppose Paul's message, or they themselves would plot against his life. Sometimes they would seek the authorities of a city to take appropriate measures to have Paul imprisoned or expelled from their midst.

14—The chief seat: "Seat of Moses" (Matthew 23:2). *Courtesy of Felbermeyer, Rome.*

Regardless of the circumstances, Paul just kept going from one city to another, motivated by his love for Christ and his desire to preach Christ and Him crucified to the unsaved and to see many saved.

So many people have said how wonderful it would have been to have heard John the Baptist, Peter, Paul, or some of the apostles preach. Suppose the apostle Paul were to come to your church to preach. Would you be disappointed in him if he encouraged your pastor to think he, Paul, was the "right" evangelist to "pull in the crowds?" For example, suppose

> he encouraged the church board to put a splashy ad in the local newspaper about their having an international speaker;

> he constantly begged for a generous honorarium;

> he preached a watered-down message that left you comfortable in your sins, instead of labeling sin for what it really is;

he used sensational sermon topics to attract the public and questionable techniques to get people to the altar;

he was just interested in getting people to indicate their profession of faith by signing a card, being baptized, and joining the church;

he did not give an invitation for any present who knew not Christ to respond so that he might have an opportunity to take the Scriptures and show them that they are sinners and need to be saved?

If Paul came to your city and church today, his method of preaching and message would be the same, whether pastors, boards, churches, denominations, religious councils, or people in general liked it or not. "Woe is me," he said, "if I preach not the Gospel" (1 Corinthians 9:16).

CYPRUS: FIRST MIRACLE AND NEW LEADER Departing from Antioch with Mark (see map 2, p. 444), Paul and Barnabas set out on foot to Seleucia on the west coast of Syria, traveling a distance of about sixteen miles (Acts 13:4). Nothing is said about what they did in Seleucia while waiting to board a ship for Cyprus, but rest assured they were "instant in season and out of season" in giving a word of testimony to the old "salt" of the village. Seleucia was founded about 300 B.C. to provide a seaport for Antioch and was a naval base for Rome during New Testament times. Paul must have had a field day conversing with the many Roman citizens of the Imperial navy.

From Seleucia they set sail for the island of Cyprus, landing at the city of Salamis, a distance of about 125 miles (Acts 13:4b–5). Barnabas was a native of Cyprus and this fact may have helped open doors for them. Verse 5 seems to imply that they had great opportunities to preach in the synagogues. Due to its good harbor, Salamis was a heavily populated and busy seaport during both the Grecian and Roman eras. Evidently there was a heavy Jewish population (probably merchants) in Salamis because the word *synagogues* is used. Paul and Barnabas followed the same pattern of going to the synagogues throughout the island until they came to Paphos, a distance of eighty-eight miles (Acts 13:6a).

There was an old and a new Paphos (see map 2, p. 444). The old Paphos dated to the pre-Hellenic times. According to mythology, it was the birthplace of the Grecian goddess Aphrodite, who was born off-shore in the foam of the sea. She was the goddess of love and reproduction. A huge, beautiful temple had been built and pagans from all over Cyprus, as well as from many mainland countries in Asia Minor, came to this cultic shrine to worship her. The Romans called Aphrodite *Venus* and rites performed in worship to her were still very much in evidence when Paul and Barnabas arrived in the new city of Paphos. Worship directed to Venus was sensual and immoral, and the city itself was a cesspool of Grecian iniquity. The new Paphos was the seat of the Roman government but little had been done to wipe out pagan lewdness. Paul and Barnabas began immediately to testify of God's saving grace (Acts 13:6–12).

Sergius Paulus was deputy (the proconsul, or procurator; the governor) of Paphos. Sergius had been appointed to his position and represented the emperor, having gone out from Rome with all the pomp of a military commander, and not expecting to return to Rome until the emperor recalled him. This Roman dignitary, on learning what Paul and Barnabas were doing in his city, desired to hear the Word of the Lord from these two in person. In the audience was a sorcerer, a Jewish false prophet who tried to withstand Paul, seeking to distract Sergius and turn him against the faith (here we find Paul's thorn in the flesh, Satan's messenger, trying to buffet Paul through this sorcerer). As a result, for the *first* time as an apostle, Paul displayed the miracle-working power that God had given him, blinding and disgracing Elymas, the sorcerer. The greater result was that this miracle led pagan Sergius to believe and be saved.

We may rightly assume that a church was established in Paphos. An archaeologist excavating the site of new Paphos uncovered a massive marble block carved with this inscription:

> Appollonius to his father and to his mother consecrated the enclosure and this monument, having filled the offices of clerk and high priest, and having been in charge of the record office. Erected on the 25th of the month of Demarchusius. He also revised the Senate by means of assessors in the time of proconsul [Sergius] PAULUS.[2]

It is interesting, is it not, that this archaeological discovery identifies *this* Paulus? Another inscription of a later date mentions Paulus' son. It is also significant that one whose name was *Paul* would be Paul's first *named* convert on his first missionary journey.

It appears that from the moment of Elymas' blindness and Sergius Paulus' conversion that Paul was now in command, the new leader of the missionary team. Prior to their being in Paphos, Barnabas was always mentioned before Paul and seemingly was recognized as the leader. From these two incidents onward, however, Paul is mentioned *first* with the exception of two times, once at Lystra (Acts 14:14) and the other during the Jerusalem Council (Acts 15:12).

As the missionary team continued on their journey, it was now "Paul and Barnabas," "Paul and his company," "Paul stood up," showing that he was now in charge of the mission. He was the Apostle to the Gentiles. We also note that while in Paphos the name *Saul* is dropped, and the name *Paul* is used from here on out (Acts 13:9). Much has already been said about Paul's names (see chapter 1), but we need to elaborate more on this change that is recorded in verse 9.

The name *Paul* rose to the surface at the moment when he visibly took control of his office as the Apostle to the Gentiles. This Roman name came to the forefront just as Sergius Paulus, the Roman procurator, was converted. The name *Paulus* was also predominant, due to its having been a part of Sergius' name. In Sergius Paulus' case, *Sergius* was not as important as *Paulus*, as noted on the previously mentioned monument. The place where Saul's name was changed to Paul was at Paphos, the favorite sanctuary of a shameful idolatry. At this very spot, which was notorious throughout the world for that which the Gospel forbids and destroys, Paul comes to his own. God made Paul the leader of this missionary tour, enabled him to use his apostolic gift of miracles, and sent him forth as Paul, the Apostle to the Gentiles. We must be reminded that he had this Roman name, as well as his Hebrew name, Saul, in earlier days, long before he became a Christian. It must be observed also that the apostle always speaks of himself under the latter designation in every one of his epistles, without exception. Peter makes mention of him as "our beloved brother Paul" (2 Peter 3:15).

PERGA: Paul, along with Barnabas and Mark,
MARK'S DEPARTURE left Paphos and set sail for Attalia in Asia Minor (see map 2, p. 444). They then went overland to Perga of Pamphilia, a distance of about 175 miles (Acts 13:13). During Greek times a flourishing temple of Diana (Artemis) was located in Perga. In fact ruins of its huge amphitheater are still visible

today. Nothing is said in Scripture about their ministry there, but when Paul came back through Perga he encouraged the believers and appointed elders in churches he had established (Acts 14:21–25). We imply from these verses that a church had been established in Perga during their first visit.

It was at Perga that John Mark deserted the team and returned to Jerusalem (Acts 13:13). The question is why? Scripture does not tell us, but there could have been any number of reasons.

Perhaps Mark was homesick and wanted to get back to his pious mother, Mary, or to fellowship with the saints in the church at home, or to see his dear friend, Peter, to whom he was supposed to be much attached.

Perhaps he was frightened at the prospect of encountering robbers in Galatia—robbers who preyed on those who traveled through narrow mountain passes.

Perhaps he was afraid of hazardous travel. Melting snow from the mountains of Tarsus coursed through narrow passes, creating mighty rushing, overflowing streams, and washing away bridges. Paul later spoke of being in "perils of waters" (or rivers, 2 Corinthians 11:26). Possibly Mark was afraid of drowning.

Perhaps Mark was jealous of Paul since he had become number one in the group, displacing Barnabas as leader. (Barnabas was either Mark's cousin or uncle, a relative on his mother's side, Colossians 4:10). Perhaps Paul's new position over Barnabas offended him because he felt more comfortable under the leadership of Barnabas than he did taking orders from Paul. Despite the hardships that lay before them, Paul and Barnabas forged ahead, knowing that they would confront many dangers, and knowing also that there were countless souls ahead for whom Christ died. The Holy Spirit at the outset of this journey had given assurance that He would lead them, so they continued overland from Perga to Antioch in Pisidia, a distance of 100 miles (Acts 13:14).

ANTIOCH OF PISIDIA: PAUL'S SERMON There are two cities named Antioch in the book of Acts: (1) the city from which Barnabas and Saul started their first missionary journey, located in northern Syria; and (2) the city in which Paul is now ready to preach—Antioch of Pisidia, in Galatia of Asia Minor.

Antioch of Syria was captured by the Romans in 65 B.C. and was made the capital of the Roman province of Syria. The

Chapter Five

Antioch of Syria was captured by the Romans in 65 B.C. and was made the capital of the Roman province of Syria. The Seleucid kings, successors of Alexander the Great, and early Roman emperors had so enlarged and beautified this city that it became known as the Beautiful and Golden City. It had a population of half a million in the first century A.D. A large percentage of its inhabitants were Jews, who were given many religious freedoms, such as building their own synagogues, observing feast days, and so forth. According to Zondervan's *Pictorial Bible Dictionary*, Antioch of Syria gave rise to a school of thought distinguished by its literal interpretation of the Scripture. Antioch was such an important city to Christianity that between A.D. 252 and 380 ten church councils were held there.[3] It is no wonder when we consider the great missionary church and its leaders that Antioch became an important part of Christendom (Acts 11:19–26; 13:1–2).

In 25 B.C. Pisidia became a part of the Roman sector of Galatia. Later, Antioch became its capital and southern Galatia was made a Roman colony. Jews here also enjoyed a measure of religious freedom as they did in Antioch of Syria. Antioch of Pisidia is in Asia Minor. We do not know what day Paul and Barnabas arrived in Antioch of Pisidia, but many wonderful things happened while they were there.

As was their custom, Paul and Barnabas headed for the synagogue on the Sabbath. When given an opportunity to speak (Acts 13:16–45), Paul stood up and preached a sermon similar to the one Stephen preached before the Sanhedrin (Acts 7). Note the analysis of his sermon as given by Adam Clarke.[4]

1. His prologue was to those who feared God (Acts 13:16).

2. During his narrative of God's goodness to Israel Paul spoke of Israel's deliverance from Egypt, of their support in the wilderness, of God's giving them the Land of Canaan, and of the judges and kings that God had given for their governors (vv. 17–22).

3. His proposition was that Jesus was the Christ, the Savior of the world (v. 23).

4. Paul proved his proposition's truth by illustrations from Christ's stock and family (v. 23); from the testimony of His forerunner, John the Baptist (v. 24); from

the resurrection of Christ (v. 30), which was corroborated by the testimony of many Galileans and of David and the prophets (vv. 31–40).

5. Paul anticipates objections relative to Christ's unjust condemnation and to His death and resurrection (vv. 27–29).

6. His epilogue excites his audience to receive the Gospel on two considerations: (1) the benefits that they who embrace the Gospel receive (vv. 28–39), and (2) the danger to which they who should despise and reject it are exposed (vv. 40–41).

Jews and Gentiles alike took to heart this message. They followed Paul and Barnabas, and persuaded them to preach again the next Sabbath (Acts 13:42–43). Curiosity must have run rampant throughout the city that week because on the next Sabbath, almost the whole city gathered to hear Paul preach the Word of God. Though Jews in general could not question the truths he spoke, many revealed their envy over the multitudes (especially Gentiles) that followed these two men of God. Their envy prompted them to speak against Paul, contradicting and blaspheming him (Acts 13:44–45). As with Elymas who withstood Paul in Paphos and now with opposition from the Jews in Antioch, Paul is seeing firsthand how the messenger of Satan, his thorn in the flesh, is becoming active.

As a result of this sermon and Paul's having been rejected by the Jews, he turned to the Gentiles and was warmly received by them as they embraced the Good News (Acts 13:46–49). A great truth is presented in this portion of Scripture. As Paul turned to the Gentiles he said, "For so hath the Lord commanded us saying, I have set thee to be a *light* of the Gentiles, that thou shouldest be for salvation unto the ends of the earth" (v. 47). This truth of being a light to the unsaved applies to every believer. As Christ's representatives on earth, we are the light of the world and we are to "let our light so shine before men that they may see our good works and glorify our Father who is in heaven" (Matthew 5:14–16). As lights we become salvation, so to speak, to the lost. We, however, cannot save anyone. "No man by any means can redeem his brother nor give to God a ransom for him" (Psalm 49:7). We are salvation in the sense that we have the remedy for their sin-sick souls—we know how they can be set free from sin. We don't save them, but we make known the Way whereby they might be. Verses 48 and 49 tell us that when they heard that Paul and Barnabas were salvation unto them—the remedy they needed for spiritual deliverance—"they were glad and glorified the Word of the Lord, and as many as were ordained to eternal life believed. And the Word of the Lord was published throughout all the region" (v. 49). Verse 52 tells us that the disciples were filled with joy and with the Holy Spirit. I am sure, had not Mark deserted them, that his heart would have burst with joy at these results. We so often miss many blessings when the Lord tells us to keep going, but we take our eyes off the work at hand and, like Mark, walk by sight.

It seems that whenever there is victory, the devil works the hardest to defeat or discourage believers. In this case, after many Gentiles were converted "the Jews stirred up the devout and honorable women and the chief men of the city, and raised persecution against Paul and Barnabas, and expelled them out of their coasts" (Acts 13:50).

As a result of their treatment in Antioch of Pisidia, Paul and Barnabas "shook the dust off their feet against them" (Acts 13:51). This was a very unusual and significant rite. By it, they said in effect: "You are worse than the heathen. Even your very land is accursed for your opposition to God and we dare not permit even its dust to cling to the soles of our feet, and we shake it off in departing from your land, according to our Lord's command (see Matthew 10:14). We do this as a testimony against you, seeing that we offered you salvation but you rejected it and persecuted us."[5] The Jews, when traveling in heathen countries, took care when they came to the borders of their own to shake the dust off their feet, lest any of the unhallowed ground defile the sacred land of Israel. Shaking the dust off one's feet was also a graphic display of a complete break of fellowship and the renunciation of any future responsibility.

It was in Antioch of Syria that Paul was most welcomed in a teaching ministry of the Word of God (Acts 11:25–26), and there he also was most despised and hated by those to whom he sought to make Christ known (Acts 13:14, 45, 50; 14:19).

ICONIUM:
CONVERSIONS AND MIRACLES
Having shaken the dust of Antioch from their feet, Paul and Barnabas headed for Iconium (see map 2, p. 444), due

east of Antioch, a distance of eighty-eight miles (Acts 13:51; 14:1–5). As Paul and Barnabas made their way to this area, they saw the beauty of the city as it lay on the edge of one of the greatest plains in Galatia with snow-capped mountains in the distance. Galatia was on a trade route from the East to Rome and was the capital of Lycaonia. Several languages were spoken in this section of Galatia; Phrygian in and around Antioch, and Lycaonian, especially among those in Lystra (Acts 14:11). Iconium, however, did not become a Roman colony until about A.D. 132, under the emperor Hadrian.

Whatever language Paul used, he was able to reason from Scripture in the synagogue and a great multitude of both Jews and Greeks believed. In spite of the unbelieving Jewish opposition, Paul and Barnabas continued in Iconium, speaking boldly in the Lord, giving testimony unto the Word of His grace, and performing signs and wonders. This was Paul's *second* occasion for performing miracles. The opposition on the part of the unbelieving Jews grew. Part of the city's population sided with the Jews and the other part sided with Paul and Barnabas. When Paul saw that the Jews had turned the rulers against them to use them despitefully and stone them, they fled to Lystra and Derbe, cities in Lycaonia, and from there to regions round about.

LYSTRA: A HEALING AND STONING Lystra, a beautiful city, was a twenty-mile journey from Iconium (Acts 14:6–9). This city was steeped in heathenism and mythology. Theirs was not the superstition of an educated mind such as that of Sergius Paulus, nor the refined and cultivated mythology of the Athenians, but the mythology and superstition of a rude and unsophisticated people. They believed two important Greek gods had once visited the earth—Zeus, the father of gods and man, and Hermes, the messenger and herald of the gods and Zeus' son. The Romans named them Jupiter and Mercury (or Mercurius) respectively. Lystra was under the tutelage of Jupiter, and tutelary divinities, thought invisible, were imagined to live in and protect a city. The temple of Jupiter was a conspicuous object in front of the city gate, constantly reminding the Lystrians that someday, as Zeus/Jupiter and Hermes/Mercury had appeared on earth before, they might someday return to Lystra.

When Paul and Barnabas visited the city, they immediately preached the Gospel (Acts 14:7). It is reasonable to assume that there were no Jews living in Lystra because Luke implies that Paul spoke to the Lystrians in the language of the Lycaonians. As Paul was preaching the Word, a certain man, unable to walk, being a cripple from his mother's womb, listened intently. Paul perceived that he had faith to be healed, and the power of God, through Paul, enabled the man to leap and walk (Acts 14:7–10). This is the *third* recorded time that Paul exercised his apostolic gift of healing.

As a result of this miracle the people of Lystra thought Paul and Barnabas were the gods Jupiter and Mercurius. Mercurius was the god of speech and eloquence, Jupiter's special messenger. Barnabas, probably because of his venerable appearance or supposed likeness to their god, was named Jupiter by the Lystrians (see illustration 15). Paul, because of his speech, was called Mercurius (see illustration 16). The priest of Jupiter brought oxen and garlands to the gates and prepared to make sacrifice before the people (Acts 14:11–13).

Paul may have had a little difficulty understanding the Lycaonian language, but when he began to discern what the priest had said and was doing, he realized that the people thought that their gods had returned to earth. Paul and Barnabas ran among the people asking what they were doing. Paul reminded them that he and Barnabas were just humans the same as they, and that they had come to preach the true and living God; that He gives rain from heaven and food for gladness. With difficulty, the

15—Barnabas likened to Jupiter (or Zeus). *Courtesy of author.*

16—Paul likened to Mercurius (or Hermes). *Courtesy of author.*

crowds were restrained from offering sacrifices to Paul and Barnabas (Acts 14:14–18).

In the midst of all this excitement, a group of Jews came from Antioch and Iconium to Lystra to persuade the Lystrians to denounce Paul and Barnabas for their preaching Christ. Evidently there had been no Jews in Lystra who had believed, nor any Lystrians, except the lame man. As a result of being agitated by these Jews, the Lystrians turned against Paul and stoned him, dragging him outside the city, supposing him dead (Acts 14:19). This was yet another act of buffeting by the messenger of Satan.

Just as the Jewish religious leaders were instrumental in provoking Christ's crucifixion, and Paul, as a Pharisee, was an instigator of Stephen's stoning, so Jews were to blame for stirring up the Lystrians (see map 2, p. 444) to stone Paul (Acts 14:19). We can well imagine what went through Paul's mind when he found out he was going to be stoned as well as when each stone struck his body. He could only think of his having given approval for Stephen's death and how Stephen must have felt as each stone found pummeled his body (Acts 7:58–8:1). No doubt Paul said to himself: "Whatsoever a man soweth, that shall he also reap" (Galatians 6:7). We do find in Stephen's home going a beautiful picture. For him it was "absent from the body, present with the Lord" (2 Corinthians 5:8). For the Lord it was "precious in His sight" to welcome him (Psalm 116:15). Christ even stood up Himself to receive Him (Acts 7:56–60)! What a precious truth with which to encourage every believer when a loved one in Christ is taken or when they themselves fall asleep in Jesus. For the unsaved it is a different picture. Just as Jesus welcomes His own, so Satan, the great counterfeiter, has a royal welcome for all who die in their sins and go to a Christless eternity. "Hell from beneath is moved for to meet thee at thy coming" (Isaiah 14:9).

When Paul was stoned, the Lystrians dragged him out of the city, supposing he was dead. As the disciples stood about him, God raised him up the same day—a miracle to behold—and Paul went back into the city unaided (Acts 14:19a). God in His Providence took Stephen home to be with Himself, but He left Paul to continue his ministry in winning souls and establishing churches.

DERBE   The day after his stoning, Paul and Barnabas left Lystra and went to Derbe, a distance of thirty-four miles (Acts 14:20). Very little is known of this city. Its name was derived from the Lycaonian word for Jupiter and it had the name of Claudius as a prefix to honor Caesar. Paul, true to form, preached the Gospel, which resulted in many being saved. Paul and Barnabas stayed awhile and discipled the believers (Acts 14:20–21). No mention is made of any of the Jews there believing or of any Jewish opposition, so it might be assumed no Jews lived in Derbe.

PAUL AND BARNABAS RETRACE THEIR STEPS Derbe evidently was the end of the line in Galatia for this missionary journey (see map 2, p. 444). Being led to retrace their steps back to Perga, they visited all the churches they had established. Their purpose was to confirm and encourage the believers they had led to the Lord, to exhort them to continue in the faith, and to counsel them that they, in spite of much tribulation, would enter the kingdom of God. They also ordained elders in those churches (Acts 14:21–25). Ironically, they went back to Antioch where they had shaken the dust off their feet. Although the Jews there had expelled Paul and Barnabas from their city and had persuaded the Lystrians to stone Paul, he could not, in good conscience, bypass fellow believers who had come to know Christ under his preaching. They, too, needed his encouragement and love. God's love constrained him to do unto others as he would have them do unto him.

JOURNEY'S END: BACK TO ANTIOCH OF SYRIA After paying a visit to all the churches, Paul and Barnabas arrived back at Perga and held services there, preaching the Word (see map 2, p. 444). They left Perga and went to Attilia to catch a ship back to Seleucia and from there overland to the home church in Antioch of Syria, a distance of 330 miles. What a welcome it must have been to return to their home base where they had been recommended and commissioned for the work that they fulfilled (Acts 14:25b–26). Having completed their first missionary journey, Paul and Barnabas reported to the church, telling believers what great things the Lord had done by opening a way that allowed the Gentiles to be saved (Acts 14:26–27).

RESULTS OF THE FIRST MISSIONARY JOURNEY The following list is what they probably reported to those who had sent them:

1. Sergius Paulus, a Roman dignitary, was saved (Acts 13:7–12).

2. Paul exercised his position as an apostle and performed his first miracle by blinding Elymas (13:6, 8–11). As a sign of his apostleship, he performed other miracles on this journey (14:3, 8–10).

3. Paul's name was changed from Saul to Paul (13:9).

4. Paul superseded Barnabas as leader, thus confirming his calling as the Apostle to the Gentiles.

5. An effective sermon was preached in Antioch of Pisidia (13:14–41).

6. Gentiles were anxious to hear the Gospel and many believed, accepting the Gospel with joy (13:42, 46–48).

7. Believers were encouraged to continue with the Lord (13:43).

8. Most of the inhabitants of the city were stirred to hear the Gospel (13:44).

9. Paul's message was opposed by the Jews (13:45).

10. The Word was spread throughout the region of Galatia (13:49).

11. Persecution followed (13:45–50). It appears that a pattern was established in Antioch of Pisidia. Throughout Paul's journeys there was always a rejection of his preaching by many Jews and the acceptance of it on the part of the Gentiles. On this journey Paul had often felt the effects of his thorn in the flesh.

12. In spite of Mark's desertion (13:13), there had been many victories accompanied with joy and the empowering of the Holy Spirit (13:25).

13. Perhaps many questioned Paul about his stoning. He no doubt testified of this incident and of God's miracle in raising him up the same day. Critics down through the centuries have held to the idea that the apostles were only promoting a hoax and that they themselves were impostors or fakes. Up to this point Paul had experienced horrible, terrifying, physical persecution, even a near-death encounter. As far as history records,

all the apostles, with the exception of John, forfeited their lives in defense of, and love for, their Savior and the propagation of His finished work on Calvary. Paul himself was beheaded and tradition tells us that Barnabas suffered martyrdom on Cyprus as a result of Nero's persecution of all Christians in his empire. The Colosseum in Rome stands as a silent monument to the countless Christians who died rather than deny their faith in Jesus Christ. It is not only doubtful but asinine to suppose that all these believers would have experienced such deaths just to promote a hoax. These people were for real. Some Jewish believers at first doubted Paul's conversion (Acts 9:26). They no doubt reasoned that his conversion was a hoax, that his ultimate reason for embracing Christianity was to win the confidence of believers and then strike a greater measure of terror than he had before he had started his Damascus errand. One could hardly be an imposter and at the same time put his life in such danger at every turn of the road, especially since the Lystrians nearly stoned him to death. This, along with his list of sufferings (2 Corinthians 11:23–32), should settle once and for all that Paul's conversion and calling as outlined by Ananias were genuine (Acts 9:15–16).

14. Paul and Barnabas retraced their steps to places where they were able to establish churches to edify believers and to appoint elders, showing their care for the newfound assemblies and the brethren (Acts 14:21–25; 2 Corinthians 11:28).

15. They summarized their report by saying that God had opened a wide door of faith to the Gentiles (Acts 14:27).

Luke does not mention it, but there must have been much rejoicing, many Amens and Hallelujahs echoing throughout their meeting place as this report was given. Afterward, they abide in Antioch a long time with the disciples, having wonderful fellowship in the things of the Lord (Acts 14:28).

TEST YOURSELF ON CHAPTER FIVE

1. What was Paul's reason for going back to his hometown, Tarsus?

2. Approximately how long had he been saved before returning home?

3. What happened to the churches while Paul was in Tarsus?

4. What important church was founded while Paul was in Tarsus?

5. How long did he stay in Tarsus?

6. Where did he go and what did he do when he left Tarsus?

7. Who were some of the saints in the church in Antioch?

8. Who was the pastor who brought Paul to this church?

9. What were believers first called in Antioch? How many different names of Christians can you list?

10. Who was the prophet who came up from Jerusalem and what did he prophesy? Describe the event.

11. Why did Paul and Barnabas go to Jerusalem?

12. Describe the ordination service of Barnabas and Paul.

13. Who went with Paul on his first missionary journey?

14. What was the approximate date of this journey?

15. About how long had Paul been saved before he started on this trip?

16. Describe how Paul approached a city.

17. How do you think Paul would be received in a church today?

18. Where did the missionary team first go to minister? What city?

19. After going through the island, in what city did they arrive?

20. What Grecian mythological goddess was born off-shore? Describe her religion.

21. Who was the deputy of this city?

22. Who was the sorcerer who opposed Paul?

23. What was Paul's first miracle? Why did he perform it?

24. What was the result of this miracle and Paul's message?

25. What evidence do we have that Paul's first recorded convert was actually the deputy of Paphos?

26. What brought about Paul's becoming the leader of this missionary team?

27. Why do you think his name was changed from Saul to Paul?

28. Where did the missionary team go next?

29. List the reasons (or excuses) why John Mark deserted Paul and Barnabas.

30. Describe the two Antiochs and give their locations.

31. Outline Paul's sermon at Antioch of Pisidia.

32. How did the Jews react to this sermon?

33. What did Paul and Barnabas become to the Gentiles?

34. What does the phrase, "They shook the dust off their feet against them" mean?

35. How would you contrast Paul's preaching in the two Antiochs?

36. Describe the events that transpired at Iconium.

37. What was Paul's second miracle?

38. How did the Lystrians receive Paul and Barnabas? What did they call these two servants of God and why?

39. How was Paul able to reason with them?

40. As briefly as possible after reading Appendix 7, explain why Israel was blinded and what were the results of its

disobedience, against itself, Christianity, and the servants of Christ.

41. What happened to Paul at Lystra? Describe the event.

42. List some important results of this first missionary journey.

43. Approximately how many miles did Paul and Barnabas travel on this journey?

Chapter Six

EVENTS BEFORE PAUL'S SECOND MISSIONARY JOURNEY

U pon finishing his first missionary journey, Paul settled in Antioch for a long time (Acts 14:28). How long, we do not know. Nor do we know what Paul did. Possibly much time was spent reflecting on experiences he and Barnabas had had on their travels. In having gotten a taste of his own medicine in the matter of persecution, he must have prayed much, beseeching the Lord to give him wisdom as to how best to approach Jews with the Gospel in the future. Possibly he meditated a great deal on the revelations he had received when he was in the third heaven. During his stay in Antioch, he could have made one of his three requests asking God to remove his thorn in the flesh. He certainly spent time in prayer for his own kinsmen. Possibly he asked the Lord for direction on his next journey. Any number of things could have occupied his mind and time during the first part of his stay in Antioch, while he earned money by making tents.

CRISIS OVER SALVATION As Paul, along with his Antioch brethren, were having wonderful fellowship together in the things of the Lord, certain men (Judaizers) came down from Judaea and began to teach, "Except ye be circumcised after the manner of Moses, ye cannot be saved" (Acts 15:1). This disturbed Paul and Barnabas very much, especially since they had been witnesses to the salvation of so many uncircumcised Gentiles. As a result, there was much discord in the assembly (Acts 15:1–4). This could be the situation Paul referred to later about the false brethren who sneaked in the back door to "spy out our liberty which we have in Christ Jesus, that they might bring us again into bondage" (Galatians 2:4). If salvation were dependent on being circumcised, salvation would be by grace through faith, *plus*, not salvation by grace through faith, *period*. To follow the Jewish teaching would be to step back from freedom to bondage, from maturity to infancy, from a son to a servant, from manhood to childhood. These false brethren, who were teaching that faith plus circumcision equals salvation, supposed that the Christian doctrine was to make perfect the Mosaic religion but not supersede it. As a result, they insisted on the necessity of circumcision because by that, a man was made debtor to the *whole* law, to observe *all* its rites and ceremonies.

The added necessity of circumcision on the part of the Judaizers (Acts 15:1–5) posed a threat to the ministry of Christianity as a whole, both to Jews and Gentiles alike. Not only were false brethren working in Antioch, but churches in Galatia were being drawn away from the simplicity of the Gospel by the subtlety of these Judaizing teachers. These false teachers were wreaking havoc on the Galatian believers. Paul, in writing to them, said, "I marvel that ye are so soon removed from Him who called you unto another gospel" (Galatians 1:6). To make circumcision necessary to salvation is to "frustrate [to make of no value] the grace of God; for if righteousness come by the law, then Christ died in vain" (Galatians 2:21).

So disturbing was this circumcision-for-salvation crisis in Antioch that the elders decided to send Paul and Barnabas, along with certain other disciples, to Jerusalem to confer with the apostles and elders there about this serious question. Having been furnished with the essentials for their trip and possibly a letter giving details of the problem, these men set out for the mother church in Jerusalem. Passing through Phoenicia and Samaria, they told about the conversion of Gentiles to the Christian faith, causing great joy among all the brethren. When they arrived in Jerusalem, they were received by the church, and they told the apostles and elders all the things that God had been doing with them (vv. 2–4). This was Paul's third visit to Jerusalem since his conversion. It appears that where the Gospel had been preached, Judaizers, both unbelievers (false brethren) and believers, were determined to force their belief of the law of circumcision on the grace presentation of the Gospel. Even in Jerusalem there were certain of the sect of the Pharisees who believed but were arbitrarily resolved to see to it that Gentile believers had to be circumcised and that they had to keep the rituals of Moses' law (v. 5) if their salvation was to be complete.

In Old Testament times a Gentile could become a Jew by believing in God and by embracing the Jews' religion, thus becoming a proselyte. There were three initiatory steps that had to be taken in order to embrace Judaism: (1) all males of the family had to be circumcised, (2) there were ceremonial baptisms by immersion or washings for both women and men, and (3) an offering had to be given as long as the temple stood. All of this implied keeping the whole law of Moses. Countless Gentiles had become proselytes down through the centuries, and on the Day of Pentecost, there were numberless proselytes together with Jews from many nations in attendance (Acts 2:10). The mark of salvation for the believing Judaizers was circumcision, which meant in addition to one's embracing grace, one must keep the law also. However, with Christ's coming to redeem those under the curse of the law and to give Himself a ransom for humanity's sins (both Jews and Gentiles), the ordinances of the law were nailed to the Cross, the middle wall of partition between these two was broken down, and now anyone could be saved solely on faith apart from the works of the law (Galatians 4:4–5; Colossians 2:14; Ephesians 2:11–18; Romans 3:28). Tragically, we have a similar problem today among some groups who say that in order for God's salvation to be complete in their hearts they must, in addition to a belief in and an acceptance of Christ as their Savior, become baptized by immersion and then join the local church. Other groups claim that by sprinkling an infant they will bring them into a covenant relation with God, which is confirmed later by a profession of faith. It is amazing how many people today are relying on their baptism and church membership for their soul's salvation and entrance into heaven!

THE COUNCIL AT JERUSALEM   With the background just described of the Jew's belief of salvation being complete by submitting to circumcision and keeping the law, and the Christian's belief of salvation by grace alone, we find the stage set for a thorough investigation and discussion of this subject (Acts 15:6–35). With the Jewish view coming to the forefront and the representatives of the church at Antioch converging on the Jerusalem church at the same time, the apostles and elders called a council to settle the controversy once and for all (v. 6). One could say the theme of this council was salvation by grace through faith in Jesus Christ versus salvation by circumcision according to the Law of Moses. There was much discussion as we observe verses 4 through 11.

1. It would appear from Acts 15:5 that there was heavy debate on the subject with the so-called circumcision Jews trying their best to get their point across. The first part of verse 7 tells us there was much disputing (questioning and debating).

2. After both sides had their say, Peter stood up to testify (vv. 7–11). Peter was well known as a Jew who was for the Jews. He was the apostle of the circumcision (or Jews: Galatians 2:7–8). Peter was so strong a Jew that when God tried to reveal to him that there was no difference between Gentile and Jew, that both were lost sinners, he gave vent to his old self. In the dream (illustration) that God used in the matter of eating meat of both clean and unclean animals (Acts 10:9–20), God had to speak to Peter three times before he realized that he should go and preach to Cornelius, a Gentile. Peter finally went, and Cornelius and his family were gloriously saved. At this Jerusalem Council, Peter told of God's making the choice that the Gentiles, by his mouth (witnessing), should hear the Gospel and be saved. Those in Cornelius' household who believed received the Holy Spirit just like Peter and other Jewish believers had on the Day of Pentecost, showing that God did not distinguish between Jew and Gentile. Peter's plea was that God should not be tempted by putting a yoke (circumcision) upon any believer, Jew or Gentile, that both could be saved by grace through faith in the Lord Jesus Christ. When Peter finished, even the adamant pro-circumcision Jews quieted down.

3. The next two witnesses were Paul and Barnabas, who

not only testified of the miracles and wonders of God, but how many Gentiles had been brought under the sound of the Gospel and had committed their lives to Christ (Acts 15:12). Peter had stated facts. Paul and Barnabas also stated facts but confirmed God's actions by Paul's apostolic gift of miracles and healing. The evidence of Gentiles having been saved by grace through faith minus circumcision was so overwhelming that all in the Council, including the pro-circumcision Jews, held their peace.

4. The moderator of the council was the apostle James (not Peter, the one Roman Catholics call the first pope). As James gave his summation, he brought out that Simeon (a variation of Simon, who is Peter), had declared how that God at first did visit the Gentiles to take out of them a people for His name (Acts 15:13–14). To back up this statement, to prove that it was a fulfillment of Old Testament prophecy, and to settle the issue that Gentiles come under God's grace via faith alone, James quoted Amos 9:11–12. With the authority vested in him as the moderator, James issued a verdict concerning saved Gentiles. His verdict took into consideration that the background of Gentiles was generally idolatrous—vastly different from religious Jews.

James decreed (Acts 15:19–29) that letters should be written to Gentile believers that they (1) abstain from the pollution or contamination of idols, including eating meat that had been offered to them; (2) abstain from fornication, especially prostitution, which was so common among the priestesses in the idolatrous temples; (3) abstain from eating things strangled, which to the Gentiles was a delicacy; and (4) abstain from blood. God had decreed that blood be used only in a sacrifice for sin, for atonement. For spiritual as well as physical reasons He had forbidden anyone to eat blood (Leviticus 3:17; 7:27). James, in realizing the importance and purpose of blood in God's dealings with man, forbade the eating of it from the strangled animals. Some think *blood* here refers to blood from something slain. Since life meant absolutely nothing to pagans, many of their rituals included the offering of human beings in sacrifices (such as in Baal worship). This *blood* could also refer to an established commandment:

"Thou shalt not kill" (Exodus 20:13); the life of the flesh is in the blood (Genesis 9:4). God's commands are explicit: do not eat the life of the flesh, which is blood, and do not take a life. James saw no need to give converted Jews any regulations because they already had ample instructions on these and other points in the Law of Moses (Acts 15:21).

After James rendered his decision concerning the regulations for Gentiles, he declared that a letter spelling out the details should be sent to them. The apostles, elders, and the whole church agreed with his verdict. Letters were drafted in accordance with James' decision and Gentiles in the area of Antioch, Syria, Cilicia, and Galatia in Asia Minor where Judaizers had caused trouble were encouraged to remember that there was no such command to be circumcised and to keep the law in order to be saved (Acts 15:23–29).

PAUL RETURNS TO ANTIOCH To encourage the converted Gentiles, the apostles, elders, and brethren told them that Paul and Barnabas, men who had put their lives on the line for the name of Christ, would be sent, along with Judas and Silas, to confirm these letters verbally (Acts 15:25–27). The men left for Antioch. When they arrived they called the church together, and when they had revealed the contents, they all rejoiced (vv. 30–31). Judas returned to Jerusalem but Silas remained in Antioch. Paul and Barnabas continued there, teaching and preaching the Word of God (vv. 32–35). Here again, we do not know exactly how long Paul stayed in Antioch, but two, possibly three, things happened there before he started on his second missionary journey: Peter blundered in Antioch, Paul wrote to the churches in Galatia, and Paul and Barnabas dissolved their partnership.

Peter Blunders in Antioch

Peter visited Antioch sometime after the Jerusalem Council and its decision concerning Gentiles. Luke is silent about this visit but Paul made mention of it in his letter to the Galatians (2:7–14). Paul refers to Peter as Cephas in verse 9, but reverts back to Peter in verse 2. Both mean the same thing: rock. It appears that Peter was all out for Gentile equality. After his dealings with Cornelius (Acts 10) and the decision of the Jerusalem Council (Acts 15), he knew that God had eliminated the wall that had so long separated Jew and Gentile (Ephesians 2:11–22). Peter had acted on this conviction by his fellowshiping and eating with them. In the Antioch church he witnessed what Paul called a oneness in Christ. There was neither Jew nor Greek, male nor female, master nor slave, circumcision nor uncircumcision, Barbarian nor Scythian, bond nor free, black nor white—all were baptized by the Holy Spirit into the one body of Christ by faith, all one in Christ Jesus (1 Corinthians 12:13; Galatians 3:28; Colossians 2:11). However, when certain Jews, who were partial to James, visited Antioch at this time, Peter started to act as though the Law of Moses was still in force and withdrew himself from the converted Gentiles, giving evidence that he might still be of the opinion that the distinction between Jews and Gentiles should continue. Peter immediately became a stumbling block, and other Jews followed him. Even Barnabas was carried away with them and participated in their hypocrisy. Some of the "old" Peter came to the surface.

> Just as in an earlier part of his life he had first asserted his readiness to follow his Master to death, and then denied Him through fear of a maid-servant, so now, after publicly protesting against the notion of making any difference between the Jew and the Gentile, and against laying on the neck of the latter a yoke which the former had never been able to bear (Acts 15:9–10), we find him contradicting his own principles, and *'through fear of those who were of the circumcision'* he gave sanction by his example to the introduction of a *caste* into the Church of Christ.[1]

Sometimes it is hard for us (Gentiles) to understand Jewish thinking. It was difficult for the average Jew to renounce what he had been taught from his youth up, and Peter was no exception. God had chosen the Jewish people from all other nations and had entrusted them with His sacred oracles, making them caretakers of salvation until the fullness of time when Christ should come to be the end of the law (Galatians 3:19). Anyone outside the Jewish fold had to come to the Jews for hope. Solomon made mention of this in the dedication of the temple when he said that the stranger (Gentile heathen) would come out of a far country for God's name's sake and pray toward His house (temple, 1 Kings 8:41–42). Having chosen His people to make it possible for "salvation to be of the Jews" (John 4:22), those who were afar off and who chose to follow this path became proselytes. To be a Jew (or proselyte) wasn't easy; it was very hard. In making Jews the custodians of this salvation, they were separated from all other peoples; they were different in every aspect of life—food, dress, customs, worship, and so forth. The legality of such restrictions was called the Law, leaving no room for choices. It actually made their religion a heavy yoke of sheer discipline. Regardless of how binding all the regulations were, being a Jew made them feel that as God's chosen people they were better and far superior to all others. Instead of lamenting, they not only accepted the Law as a mark of their identification with God, but added multitudes of regulations and customs to what God had already ordained them to do. Since their mark of identification was circumcision, the Christian Jews at Antioch had said, "Except ye be circumcised after the manner of Moses, ye cannot be saved" (Acts 15:1). All Gentiles, according to them, who received Christ as Messiah had to undergo this rite and accept Jewish Law as well as tradition. Peter had become a Christian but it was ingrained within him to remain a Jew and to follow this procedure. His real problem was that he acted under the influence of a contemptible and sinful motive—the fear of men, just as he had the night before the crucifixion (cf. Galatians 2:12 with Matthew 26:64–75). His behavior was giving a strong sanction to the heresy that was threatening the very existence of the church, namely, that the observance of Jewish ceremonies was essential to salvation.

This was more than Paul could take (Galatians 2:1–16). Call it anger, righteous indignation, infuriation, carnal nature, or whatever, Paul had to let off steam. Peter had really done an injustice to the cause of Christ and something had to be done immediately to nip this teaching in the bud. Picture these two men: Paul, a small, beaten, and scarred man, and Peter, a big, brawny ex-fisherman. Yet Paul stood tall and "withstood Peter to his face" for Peter's cowardly act and rebuked him before all (Galatians 2:11, 14). Paul's rebuke to Peter contained a full statement of the Gospel as opposed to the law:

> You are a Jew, yet you live like a Gentile and not like a Jew. How is it then, that you force Gentiles to follow Jewish customs? We who are Jews by birth, and not Gentile sinners, know that a man is not justified by observing the law, but by faith in Jesus Christ. So we, too, have trusted in Christ, and by so doing we have been justified by the faith of Christ. We are justified not by keeping the law, because by keeping it no one will ever be justified. It becomes evident that we are hypocritical sinners, if on the one

hand we seek to be justified by faith in Christ, and on the other hand we observe the necessary rites and ceremonies of the law, thinking this would save us. This would make Christ a promoter of sin. In no way is this possible! If I rebuild that part of the law which I destroyed by my preaching the Gospel, I only prove that I have been a lawbreaker. I am dead to all expectation that the law could help me obtain my own righteousness and be saved. Since Christ is the end of the law to all who believe in Him, I have died to the law that I might live for God. With Christ I hang upon the cross [or am crucified with Him], and yet I am alive; yet not I, but it is Christ Who lives in me. True, I am living, here and now, this mortal life, but the real life is His and it is His faith that executes it. He is the One who loves me and gave Himself for me. Therefore, I do not spurn, set aside or make void this grace of God, for if anyone can be justified through the law, Christ's death was without a cause; it was meaningless. He died for nothing if this be so.[2] (See Galatians 2:14–21.)

When Paul finished, I imagine Peter was blushing and felt about an inch tall! Although it is not mentioned following Paul's rebuke, Peter was a man who could take it when he was wrong, as seen in his denial of Christ. After denying Christ three times, he was so under conviction of his sin that when the Lord looked at him, he wept bitterly (Matthew 26:69–75). No doubt this same conviction occurred after Paul's stern admonition and evidently there was no future animosity on his part toward Paul. In his second epistle, Peter, in touching on the "long-suffering of our Lord," affectionately mentions Paul as "our beloved brother" (2 Peter 3:15–16). Not only by this heartfelt statement about Paul but also by stating that redemption is only through the "precious blood of Christ" did Peter show that he knew salvation was by grace through faith in the finished work of Christ and not by the law (1 Peter 1:18–19).

Coupled with the incident with Peter in Antioch, Paul, no doubt, must have received word of the devastating results of the pro-circumcision Judaizers in the churches of Galatia. With the discussion and decision of the council in Jerusalem and Peter's actions fresh in mind, what better time for Paul to write his epistle to the Galatians than while he was in Antioch.

Paul's Epistle to the Churches in Galatia

No sooner had churches been established in Galatia than

certain so-called Christian Jews disrupted the Holy Spirit's ministry among these believers by telling them that in order to be fully saved, they had to be circumcised; that this rite was essential to salvation. When Paul got word of this, he wrote to them immediately (ca. A.D. 49/50), saying, "I marvel that ye are so soon removed from him who called you by the grace of Christ unto another gospel" (Galatians 1:6). These Judaizers also complained that Paul's Gospel was not the true Gospel and that he was not an authentic apostle. These Galatians were fickle, foolish people as we noted in Acts 13 and 14. One day they wanted to make Paul and Barnabas gods; the next day they stoned Paul (Acts 14:11–12, 19–20). They were easy prey for Judaizers and when Paul realized what was going on, he wrote to them. In it he vindicates his character as an apostle, establishes the true doctrine of justification by faith in opposition to works of the law, proves that the Gospel he preached was scriptural, and gives a correct description of false teachers and their damnable error, making this epistle the "Magna Carta" or "Declaration of Independence" from the Law of Moses (John 1:17).

Paul's only Bible was the Old Testament, so familiar at one time to the Jews. They had substituted the traditions of their fathers for much of it (Matthew 15:3–6), but Paul sought to get them back to the Book. He frequently used portions to show that Christ was the Messiah as he defended His finished work at Calvary and salvation's being by grace through faith alone. In 1 Corinthians 15:3–4 he stated that all he knew to preach about Christ was what he derived from the Old Testament Scriptures, (see chapter 3). Paul would have been what we call today a Bible-totin', Bible-preachin' preacher. He realized that the Gentiles had no Bible or Scriptures. The Rabbi taught the Gentile proselytes on the Sabbath; this was their only time to hear the Word of God. The only way Christian Gentiles could get the Scriptures was from Christian Jews, and it is very doubtful that these Jews were willing to let a Gentile desecrate the Holy Scriptures by handling and reading it for themselves. The Judaizers were determined to keep believers in the dark and to add insult to injury, they added error to what Paul had preached. Paul, knowing that the Word of God is sharp and powerful, and knowing that Gentiles had no Bible they could call their own, used Scripture frequently to help them see the grace of God in Christ Jesus. Note Paul's use of the Old Testament in his presentation of the Gospel to them:

1. Abraham believed God (cf. Galatians 3:6 with Genesis 15:6);

2. In Abraham . . . all nations were blessed (cf. Galatians 3:8 with Genesis 12:1–3);

3. They were cursed for breaking the Law (cf. Galatians 3:10 with Deuteronomy 27:26);

4. The just shall live by faith (cf. Galatians 3:11 with Habakkuk 2:4);

5. They live in the Law if kept (cf. Galatians 3:12 with Leviticus 18:5);

6. Christ was cursed on a tree (cf. Galatians 3:13 with Deuteronomy 21:23);

7. God made promises to Abraham (cf. Galatians 3:16 with Genesis 13:15; 17:7; 25:5–6);

8. There were two sons of Abraham (cf. Galatians 4:22–23 with Genesis 16:15; 21:2–3): Ishmael, of the flesh; Isaac, of promise (or of the Spirit);

9. The barren who bearest not should rejoice (cf. Galatians 4:26–28 with Isaiah 54:1);

10. The son of the flesh was cast out (cf. Galatians 4:30 with Genesis 21:10);

11. They were to love their neighbor (cf. Galatians 5:14 with Leviticus 19:18);

12. Christ was the Promised Seed (cf. Galatians 4:4–5 with Genesis 3:15).

This epistle has served to free millions of Christians down through the ages from various forms of legalism that endangers spiritual freedom. Galatians was Martin Luther's favorite epistle and provided him with much inspiration and ammunition in his conflict with Romanism. Paul portrayed Christ in Galatians as our Liberator (Galatians 1:4; 5:1).

There is a difference of opinion as to when Paul wrote this Galatian letter. Geographically Galatia was one province, but there were two sectors—northern and southern. The northern was more Grecian, the southern, more Roman. It is apparent that Paul, on his first missionary journey, visited southern Galatia (see map 2, p. 444). Paul did not penetrate the "region of [all] of Galatia" and "all the country of Galatia" until his second and third missionary journeys (Acts 16:6; Acts 18:23). Some scholars have suggested that Paul wrote this letter to the churches of Galatia from Thessalonica on his second missionary journey about A.D. 54. However, soon after the completion of his first missionary journey, Judaizers infiltrated churches with their doctrine that circumcision was essential to salvation. This necessitated the Jerusalem Council's settling the issue that circumcision was not necessary. Word reached Paul that the Galatian churches had fallen prey to this false doctrine. The fact that Paul wrote to them stating that he was amazed that they were "so soon removed . . . from the gospel," would indicate that he wrote the letter soon after the Jerusalem Council when the discussion and decision were still fresh in his mind. Peter had visited Antioch and was rebuked by Paul for not following through with the decision, and it is quite possible that this letter was written prior to the beginning of Paul's second missionary journey when he and Barnabas settled in Antioch for an indefinite period of time (Galatians 1:6; 2:11–14; cf. Acts 15:35). Galatians was probably written about A.D. 49. If so, this epistle was Paul's first.

Paul and Barnabas Dissolve Their Partnership

Ever since Saul became Paul (Acts 13:9), Paul had taken the lead over Barnabas. He had become the motivating power behind their missionary endeavor. He had taken over the reins in Antioch, especially in regard to the episode of Peter and the Jewish believers. Evidently the stationary but rewarding and laborious life in Antioch was wearing on his nerves. He knew that his real calling was far off among the Gentiles and he was itching to be on the move once again (Acts 22:21). He expressed this desire to Barnabas, saying, "Let us go again and visit our brethren in every city where we have preached the Word of the Lord, and see how they do" (Acts 15:36). He knew that one missionary campaign was not enough—it was but the beginning. He was aware that a good soldier of Jesus Christ must endure hardness to please Him who had called him (2 Timothy 2:3–4). Conybeare says of Paul,

> As a careful physician, he remembered that they, whose recovery from sin had been begun, might be in danger of relapse; or, to use another metaphor, and to adopt the poetical language of the Old Testament, he said, 'Come, let us get up early to the

vineyards; let us see if the vines flourish.' The words actually recorded as used by Paul on this occasion are these: 'Come, let us turn back and visit our brethren in every city, where we have announced the Word of the Lord, and let us see how they fare.' We notice here, for the first time, that earnest longing to behold their faces, which appears in the letters which he wrote afterwards, as one of the most remarkable and one of the most attractive, features of his character.[3]

Paul was the speaker, not Barnabas, but Barnabas was as ready to go as Paul. This plan, however, was soon marred by an outbreak of human weakness. After Paul had expressed this desire to begin another missionary journey (Acts 15:36–40), Barnabas determined that Mark should go with them (v. 37). Evidently Mark had been taken to Antioch by his good friend, Peter, when he made his visit there. In spite of the fact that Mark had walked out on them before (Acts 13:13), Barnabas wanted to give him another opportunity to get a taste of missionary life, feeling that he had learned his lesson. Sometimes a young Christian will make a wrong move, and an alert, mature Christian can go a long way in helping him or her get back on the right track. Possibly this was what Barnabas had in mind for Mark. He was Mark's relative (Colossians 4:10), and possibly he knew some of the family traits that Paul did not know.

Paul expressed his feelings about Mark and wanted him left at home. He thought that Mark was too immature, too fainthearted; that he would be excess baggage, so he refused to take him. As a result, Paul and Barnabas got into a heated argument; Barnabas wanting to take Mark, Paul not wanting him to go (v. 38). The argument may have been more personal than that which had recently occurred between Paul and Peter. Paul's natural disposition seemed to be one of impetuousness and one of impatience, easily kindled to indignation and possibly overbearing. Barnabas had shown his weakness when he fell in line under the influence of Peter and the Judaizers. Barnabas could also have been holding a grudge against Paul. When Paul rebuked Peter, Barnabas as well as the other Jews were indirectly rebuked also. And to add insult to injury, Barnabas had once been spoken of as the chief of those at Antioch, while Paul was spoken of last (cf. Acts 11:19–25 with 13:2). Barnabas could have developed an inferiority complex and felt that this was his moment to speak up and be heard.

As we sit on the outside looking in, we can justify both as they argued their points. This is one of those quarrels in which we can agree with each and at the same time see that the purest Christian zeal, when combined with human weakness and partiality, may lead to a misunderstanding. How could Paul consent to take with him one who might prove again to be an embarrassment and a hindrance? The task of spreading the Gospel in a hostile world needed a resolute will and an undaunted courage. This type of ministry was too sacred to be put in jeopardy by any experiments. Mark had been tried once and found wanting. No man, Paul might have thought, *having put his hand to the plow and looking back is fit for the kingdom of God* (Luke 9:62).

Barnabas, however, would not be without strong arguments to defend his claims. It was hard to expect him to resign his interest in one who had cost him much anxiety and many prayers. His dearest wish was to see his young kinsman approve himself as a missionary of Christ. Mark had been won back to a willing obedience to serve the Lord, he had journeyed from his home in Jerusalem, and he was now ready to face all the difficulties and dangers of spreading the Gospel. To repel him now, in the moment of his repentance, was surely "to break a bruised reed" and to "quench smoking flax" (Matthew 12:20). Since we are human, it is not difficult to understand the stubbornness and unyieldedness on the part of both—each clinging to his opinion as though the other were entirely wrong.

Paul's arguments won out. He had been a staunch Pharisee and this made him a strong disciplinarian. For Mark to prove himself, Paul no doubt expected him to keep pace with Barnabas and himself and to tough it out no matter what the circumstances. Mark had failed once; that was enough for Paul. One mistake was one too many, and for Mark, there could be no reconciling with Paul. Matthew Henry said of this incident between Paul and Barnabas: "A timid companion in the hour of danger is one of the greatest evils," and then he quoted Proverbs 25:19, "Confidence in an unfaithful man in time of trouble is like a broken tooth and a foot out of joint."[4]

Paul and Barnabas Take New Partners

We learn from this episode in Antioch between these two spiritual giants that a good work may be blessed of God in spite of violent incidents, such as we see in this passage. God's blessing had been and was on these two, but since neither would bow to the other, "they departed asunder one from the other" (Acts 15:39). It would be wrong to suppose that Paul and Barnabas parted as enemies in anger and hatred. After all, Paul felt a personal obligation to Barnabas for accepting him after his conversion and introducing him to the apostles in Jerusalem (Acts 9:27), and no doubt the feelings of Barnabas would have been deeply hurt if he thought his friendship with Paul had been slighted and was over. It is evident that these two made a deliberate and agreeable settlement in the matter of where each was to go and preach. Paul's desire was to retrace some of the steps of their first missionary journey and go beyond to western Asia Minor. He chose this route with Silas. Barnabas took Mark with him and they headed for Cyprus, his native land (Acts 15:39). Here they had made some of their first converts, notably Sergius Paulus, in Paphos. Here, too, was where Mark had begun his career as a minister with Paul and Barnabas. In spite of Paul's feelings during his argument with Barnabas, the time came when he acknowledged, with affectionate tenderness, not only that Mark had again become his fellow laborer but also that he was profitable to the ministry and one of the causes of his comfort (Colossians 4:10; 2 Timothy 4:11; Philemon 24). In Colossians 4:10 Paul at least mentioned Barnabas, although he didn't have to. In writing to those in Corinth he spoke kindly in exemplifying Barnabas as a faithful steward who worked hard to support himself in their ministry (1 Corinthians 9:6).

Barnabas and Mark no doubt departed first. Evidently the feeling of the church was on the side of Paul when he chose Silas as his partner because these two, in their departure, were recommended by the brethren (Acts 15:40). This is not said of Barnabas and Mark, though the church no doubt prayed, asking God's blessings on them.

As Paul and Silas left, they headed out on Paul's second missionary journey through Syria and Cilicia, confirming the churches (v. 41), and then traveled to western Asia Minor and the European continent.

TEST YOURSELF ON CHAPTER SIX

1. Where did Paul and Barnabas settle after their first missionary journey?

2. Who were the Judaizers and what was their purpose?

3. Describe the purpose and result of the council in Jerusalem.

4. What was Peter's blunder in Antioch? Describe it.

5. How did Paul handle it?

6. What was the purpose of Paul's epistle to the churches in Galatia? Give some of the details of this letter.

7. Describe why Paul and Barnabas dissolved their partnership.

8. Who did Paul select as his new partner?

9. Who did Barnabas select as his new partner and where did they go?

Chapter Seven

PAUL'S SECOND MISSIONARY JOURNEY

T here is much criticism by mainline denominational leaders regarding the matter of church splits, especially those of fundamentalist groups. A split on the part of believers is nothing new. When grace and truth came by Jesus Christ there was a split from the old covenant to establish the new covenant. Some Jews look at the church as a split from the synagogue; a split from worshiping God on the Sabbath to worshiping Him on the first day of the week (Sunday).

Sad to say, many in Christendom became lax and "while good men slept the enemy came in and sowed tares among the wheat" (Matthew 13:25). The books of Jude, 2 Peter, and chapters 2 and 3 of Revelation all speak of the encroachment of error in the church and the need to repent and earnestly contend for the faith (Jude 3). It has been one fight after another to keep truth in the forefront.

When Martin Luther nailed his ninety-five theses to the door of the Roman Catholic church in Wittenberg, Germany, in 1517, the Reformation was born and there was a great split in Roman Catholicism. In fact, there had been a split in the Catholic church long before when some priests condoned marriage and refused to recognize the Pope's voice as *excathedra*. From this came the Orthodox Churches of the East. Denominational churches would not be in existence today if it had not been for the Reformation. These churches got off to a good start but little by little, modernism has crept in. Since institutions do not repent, and the best recourse is for true believers to band together, even if it means a split. Although no one wants split churches, they have played an important role in keeping truth on the right track.

Paul and Barnabas split, not because of any doctrinal differences or a difference in interpretation of Scripture, but because of a personality clash and different opinions concerning John Mark. This split resulted in Barnabas' taking Mark with him to Cyprus, and Paul's taking Silas as his new missionary partner. We saw in the last chapter that somewhere along the line they must have made up, because when Paul commended Mark to the Colossians, he also mentioned Barnabas. It is apparent that any ill feelings against each other had vanished (see 1 Corinthians 9:6; Colossians 4:10). From this split was formed two missionary groups.

Paul and Silas traveled throughout (see map 3, p. 446) Asia Minor, Macedonia, and Greece or what was considered the European continent (Acts 15:40–18:22). The probable date was A.D. 51–54. The time involved was approximately three and one-half years, and the traveling distance was about 2,925 miles by land and by sea.

Paul and Silas left Antioch with the blessing of the church (Acts 15:41). Here again we notice Paul's concern for and care of the churches he and Barnabas had previously established and his desire to visit and comfort them. No doubt he was anxious to check on them and help straighten out any who might still be leaning toward the Judaizers' teachings (any who might have faltered when the Jews pressured them to be circumcised for their salvation to be complete), and to find out what impact, if any, his epistle to the Galatians had made (Acts 15:41; 2 Corinthians 11:28). He also wanted to show them copies of the letters he had in his possession that were decreed for Gentile believers by the Jerusalem Council (cf. Acts 16:4 with 15:19–23).

PHYRGIA AND GALATIA: ENCOURAGING CHURCHES As these two left Antioch, they journeyed overland through Syria, turning westward to Cilicia, probably stopping in Paul's home town, Tarsus. They continued on through Regnum territory to Derbe, the last stop on his first missionary journey in southern Galatia, a distance of 260 miles (Acts 15:41–16:1).

From Derbe they went to Lystra, a distance of thirty-four miles (Acts 16:1). It was at Lystra that Paul had been stoned (Acts 14:8,

19), and he had shaken the dust off his feet at Lystra, implying that he was through with the city, but he remembered the disciples who were standing over him when God raised him up after the Lystrians had stoned him and left him for dead (Acts 14:19–20). The tie that binds our hearts in Christian love would not permit Paul to bypass believers there.

Timothy Joins Paul and Silas

One of those who had stood over Paul when he was left for dead but was raised by God was, no doubt, Timothy. He had been raised by a Jewish mother and grandmother and had been taught the Scriptures, which eventually made him wise unto salvation (2 Timothy 1:5; 3:15). It is reasonable to assume that Timothy was saved when Paul was first in Lystra, although Luke does not mention it. The assumption is based on the fact that Paul calls Timothy "my son in the faith" (1 Timothy 1:2). With knowledge of Scripture and seeing Paul all but die for his faith in Christ, there couldn't have been a better time for God's Word and his mother's prayers to catch up with Timothy as the Holy Spirit convicted of sin. Now after a absence of a year or two, Paul found him held in highest esteem by the brethren of Lystra and Iconium (Acts 16:1–2). When Paul later wrote to Timothy, he reminded him of the personal and intimate knowledge of the sufferings he had endured in Antioch (of Pisidia), at Iconium, and at Lystra, but that the Lord had delivered him out of them all (2 Timothy 3:10–11). Yes, Timothy had seen Paul stoned, left for dead, and then delivered by the Lord. What an impression this must have made on this young convert. What a challenge it must have been for him to commit his life wholly to the Lord. Evidence of his surrender to Christ was witnessed by Paul when he saw that Timothy had an excellent Christian testimony among the Lystrians and Iconium brethren.

It was easy for Paul to single Timothy out above all other disciples at Lystra. Paul saw that natural qualities of an engaging character were combined with Christian faith in this young disciple and his heart was drawn to him in a peculiar tenderness as a result. "Him would Paul have to go forth with him" as a copartner (Acts 16:3). One might ask why Paul would take Timothy, untried, on so difficult a mission. How could he receive Timothy in this inner circle when he had rejected Mark? Evidently it was because of the testimony of Timothy's character and his approval by his brothers in Christ.

Timothy Circumcised; Titus Not

When Timothy became a member of Paul's party he was circumcised because of the Jews in those quarters, for they all knew that his father was a Greek (Acts 16:3). We notice in verse 1 that his mother, Eunice, was a Jewess, thus making Timothy half Greek and half Jew. The most natural inference here is that Timothy's father was living and most probably was not a proselyte to Judaism. It certainly appears, however, that he had no objection to his Jewess wife's bringing Timothy up as a Jew. The fact that Timothy's father was Greek, a heathen to the Jews, made them suspicious of Timothy.

Why was Timothy forced to be circumcised, especially in view of the recent council at Jerusalem that had concluded that circumcision was not essential to salvation (Acts 15:1–35)? Paul worked with Titus, a full-blooded Greek, even taking him to the Jerusalem Council to show that one could be saved without having been circumcised (Galatians 2:1–3), yet at no time did Paul compel him to be circumcised. How did Titus manage to escape this ritual and Timothy was forced, as it were, to submit? Adam Clarke suggests that the Jews, knowing that Timothy was half Greek,

> would never have heard him preach nor would have had any discourse with him had he not been circumcised. Besides, Paul himself would have had no access to the Jews in any place had they discovered that he was associated with one who was not a Jew or part Jew and had not succumbed to this Jewish rite.[1]

Paul's fixed line of procedure was to go from city to city and preach the Gospel first to the Jew in the synagogue and then turn to the Gentiles. This method is seen in Acts 13:14, and 13:42–49 and afforded an opening to make Christ known even though he knew he would meet opposition from many of the Jews. He had no intention of abandoning this system and we know he continued it throughout his entire ministry (see Acts 28:16–28). For Paul to travel among the synagogues with a co-laborer such as Timothy and attempt to convince the Jews that Jesus was the Messiah when his associate and assistant in the work was an uncircumcised half-breed Jewish-Grecian heathen, would evidently have been to obstruct his progress and embarrass his work. For those who say that Paul was inconsistent and blameable for having Timothy circumcised, the question is asked: How could he have done otherwise if he acted with his usual farsighted caution, deliberation, and knowledge of Jewish ways? He did not compromise the Gospel. To imagine that the Jews would overlook the absence of circumcision in Timothy's case is to suppose they had already become enlightened Christians. Difficulties would have increased a hundredfold if Paul had jumped right in and told Jews in their synagogues that circumcision had been abolished. True, it had been, but this was no way to approach a Jew. Paul's meeting with Jews on the Sabbath and during the week would have been hindered and made almost impossible by the presence of a half-heathen companion, for no matter how much relaxing had been done in the matter of circumcision in Antioch of Syria and in Jerusalem, it was still an abomination for the circumcised to eat (fellowship) with the uncircumcised in the rest of the world.

There was no objection on Timothy's part to Paul's request. Timothy's circumcision was not a question of Paul's fearing the Jews as Peter had done in Antioch. Rather, Timothy realized its importance under the circumstances. His mother and grandmother had brought him up in a Jewish atmosphere, enabling him to become thoroughly acquainted with Jewish Scripture. Because his father was Greek and Timothy had not been circumcised, he knew the Jews in those quarters considered him an alien from the commonwealth of Israel. Timothy also knew that it was not right for a Jewess to marry a non-Jewish man. Many of the dispersion Jews had intermarried, but this practice was frowned on by so-called thoroughbred Jews. Timothy, a child of a mixed marriage, was also frowned on, and he knew that he was not being circumcised in order to be saved; he already was saved, and that by grace through faith, plus nothing, minus nothing. Circumcision would in no way prejudice his spiritual state. Possibly Paul also had in mind that to have the kind of hearing that he needed with the Jews, Timothy needed to be readily accepted, having become all things to all men that he might win some to Christ (1 Corinthians 9:19–23).

We must not condemn Paul for having Timothy circumcised. If we say that such action threw a damper on the freedom of the Gospel, that possibly fewer threats would have come their way from the Jews, we say that actions oftentimes become right or wrong according to our knowledge of the situation and what we think the consequences might be. We think Paul was the better judge of the consequences likely to follow from Timothy's submission to this part of the law.

Timothy was circumcised; Titus was not. Titus was a Greek, a son of Greek parents, a Greek by birth. He had been saved by grace through faith apart from the law, apart from any knowledge of Judaism. His salvation was all of grace minus circumcision (Galatians 2:1–3). His ministry was more to Gentile churches that had already been established and circumcision was no problem in the matter of salvation among those believers. There was simply no need for Titus to subject himself to Jewish legalism. His uncircumcision had no effect on the progress of the Gospel whatsoever. It is interesting that Titus is not mentioned in the book of Acts at all. Besides the epistle to the Galatians and the personal epistle that Paul wrote to him, he is only mentioned a few times in 2 Corinthians 9 and only once in 2 Timothy (4:10).

Galatian Churches Established in the Faith

Having taken on Timothy, Paul and Silas departed Lystra to the areas where churches had been established to deliver copies of the letters or decrees that were ordained by the Jerusalem Council, going through Phrygia and Galatia, a distance of about two-hundred miles. There is no record telling us when and by whom the epistle to the Galatian churches was delivered. If Paul wrote it while still in Antioch (as evidence suggests he did since it was his first letter), delivery could have already been made to some of the churches. Having letters from Jerusalem to back up what Paul had elaborated on in that epistle must have been most encouraging to those believers. Maybe some questioned the absence of Barnabas, but Silas, who had been in Jerusalem and was familiar with the decree of the apostles, elders, and the church, was Paul's second witness to back up the truth that circumcision was not essential to salvation. As a result, the churches were greatly established in the faith and many people were saved daily and were added to the church (Acts 16:4–6).

Being established in the faith meant a lot to Paul. It meant many homes had been "Gospel empowered"; homes where truth had come in the demonstration of the power of God; homes where truth had penetrated the hearts of people; homes where relations between former heathen husband and wife were Christ-centered; homes where parents and children, master and slave, had been purified and sanctified by Christian love. This must have thrilled Paul. The changes can be paraphrased and set to the tune of a well-known Gospel song: Since Jesus came into our town, the devil's been wearing a frown; many lives have been changed, many homes rearranged, since Jesus came into our town. Although Christ had moved into many hearts and homes, the symbols of idolatry remained in public places—statues, temples, altars, and various objects of worship were conspicuous in Greek (Gentile) cities. However, Christians in these cities had turned "to God from idols to serve the true and living God" (1 Thessalonians 1:9) Their homes, which had once been decorated with emblems of vain mythology, were now bright with lives that manifested faith, hope, and charity (love). This, no doubt, challenged Paul to keep on keeping on, to press on when every household would prevail against principalities and powers, when every knee would bow at the name of Jesus Christ and every tongue would confess that he is Lord, to the glory of God the Father (see Philippians 2:10–11).

The dumb idols to which these people had formerly been "carried away even as they were led," were now "cast to the moles and to the bats" (cf. 1 Corinthians 12:2 with Isaiah 2:20). Paul was delighted as were those at Athens who had burned their false religious material as a testimony of their acceptance of Jesus Christ (Acts 19:17–20). The remarks about dumb idols can be linked to some archaeological discoveries in Cilicia (Galatian territory). An excavated mound yielded a large collection of objects such as used lamps and idols. Being in a pile with no evidence that they were a potter's rejects, it appeared that they had been thrown there on some occasion—probably conversion to Christianity. One was a statue of Pan; one was the boy Mercury; another goddess mother Cebele; along with Jupiter; Apollo with rays; Ceres, the Roman goddess of harvest crowned with corn; a deified lion devouring a bull; and so forth. The date of this find reveals that these artifacts were from the first century during the period of time Paul was in Asia Minor.

Paul's Preaching Request Denied

Acts 16:6 indicates that after Paul went through the southern region of Galatia (Phyrgia), he also went into the northern region of Galatia. It was from in this area that he wanted to go into Asia and preach the Word of God. In the Roman Empire, especially under the rule of Augustus and Nero, Asia was usually thought of as Asia Minor (presently Turkey), but not exactly limited to just this area. Paul's desire was to penetrate further eastward into Regnum and to Cappadocia. (Peter makes mention of believers in Cappadocia, 1 Peter 1:1.) This eventually could have led to further penetration of eastern territory, possibly of Paul's going into the central regions of the continent of Asia itself. For reasons known only to God, he was forbidden by the Holy Spirit to head in that direction.

MYSIA Paul and his team were not discour-
INSTEAD OF BITHYNIA aged because they could not get their way. Instead, they continued westward about two-hundred miles to a small district called Mysia, in the northwestern corner of Asia Minor (Acts 16:7). Mysia was bounded on the west by the Aegean Sea; on the north by the Hellespont and the Propontis, the waterways that separate Asia Minor from Europe; on the east by Bithynia; and on the south by Pergamos (or Pergamum). Troas was its chief seaport. (Mysia fell to the Romans in 133 B.C.) Paul evidently did little, if any, work in Mysia. Wherever he first arrived in the area of Mysia, he wanted to head northeast into Bithynia (Acts 16:7). Cities in Mysia were small and Paul liked larger cities because usually there were plenty of Jews and synagogues to visit for preaching and witnessing.

Bithynia's history goes back as far as the sixth century B.C., and there were many commercial cities on its shores. Jews populated such cities and Paul wanted to reach them. He also desired to meet Christians there to confirm them in the faith and to show them the letter from the Jerusalem Council. Peter gives verification that believers were in that area (1 Peter 1:1), and he indicates that they knew the cardinal truths of the Christian faith. Peter's letter encourages them to prepare for victory over persecution and suffering. Paul however assayed to go into Bithynia. *Assayed* implies the thought that as they wanted and tried to go in that direction, they were testing the Holy Spirit to make sure they were doing the will of God. If they were in God's will, they would not be hindered. If not, they would rely on the Spirit to stop them and direct them somewhere else. The time, however, was not ripe for them to go in the direction of Bithynia, so the Holy Spirit once again prohibited their going northeastward. Had they gone in that direction as Paul desired, the missionary team might have either stayed too long or continued eastward through Pontus into Asia (Acts 16:7), and the Holy Spirit had already forbidden their going into Asia proper (Acts 16:6).

The Bithynian believers must have been on fire for the Lord, because it was not long before the Gospel had spread from the cities through villages and into rural districts. Evidently, many

Romans (Gentiles) were becoming converts to Christ, which resulted in a decline of emperor worship, and the pagan temples were almost deserted. To check and cure the influence of Christianity in the region of Bithynia, Pliny, the governor, sought to destroy Christianity. The following is a letter he wrote to the emperor Trajan around A.D. 111 or 112.

> The method I have observed toward those who have been accused as Christians before me is this: I interrogated them whether they were believers in this Christus. If they confessed it, I repeated the question twice again, adding the threat of execution. If they were still steadfast in their belief, I ordered them executed. Those who denied they were or had ever been Christians, who repeated after me the invocation to the gods, and offered adoration with wine and frankincense to your image which I had ordered to be brought for this purpose, together with those of the gods, and who finally cursed Christus—these I thought proper to discharge. Those who are really Christian could not be forced into performing these acts.

> Persons of all ranks and ages and of both sexes are and will be involved in the prosecution. For this contagious superstition is not confined to Bithynia and the cities only, but has spread through the villages and rural districts. Having checked and cured it, the temples are now being frequented, and the sacred festivals, after a long intermission, are being revived. There is also a general demand for sacrificial animals, which for some time past have met with but few purchasers.

The first epistle that Peter had written to the Bithynians (1 Peter) had been handed down from one generation to another, and many who were living under the despotic reign of Pliny found comfort in its truths as they suffered the type of persecution mentioned in Pliny's letter to Trajan.

TROAS AND THE MACEDONIAN CALL Since Paul could not go northeastward into Bithynia, he and his companions continued westward (see map 3, p. 446) through Mysia about one hundred miles and arrived in Troas (Acts 16:8). Horace Greeley was not the first person to say, "Go west, young man, go west." The Holy Spirit long before kept telling Paul: Go west, My servant, go west. Troas had been conquered by Alexander the Great from the Persians. It became known as "Alexandria

Troas." After being conquered by the Romans, they often referred to it as just "Alexandria." It was an important seaport city on the Aegean Sea and was also on the trade route between Macedonia and Asia Minor in the days of Augustus (and Paul). Paul's visit to Troas this time was short-lived, but on his return trip from Corinth to Antioch in Syria, he stopped in Troas to take advantage of the open door to preach the Gospel (2 Corinthians 2:12).

Paul's and Silas' journey from Antioch in Syria, and the fact that they were forbidden by the Holy Spirit to go into Asia seems to point to one place—Troas. (Timothy's later arrival confirmed that Troas was where God wanted them.) It was here, soon after his arrival, and at night, that Paul had a vision (Acts 16:8–15). In it a man from Macedonia was praying (or crying) and said unto Paul, "Come over into Macedonia and help us." After seeing this vision, they boarded a ship and headed for Macedonia. This time there was no doubt that the Lord had called them to continue westward to preach the Gospel. How wonderful the providence of God! Ships in the Aegean Sea sailed according to wind conditions, and God had a wind all ready for Paul's journey to Macedonia. They needed a south wind to sail them northward, and as they sailed, I imagine Paul was reminded of the Psalms: "He brought the wind out of His treasures, and by His power He brought the south wind" (135:7; 78:26). They made a straight course toward the island of Samothracia. There is no mention of their taking a port call so they probably bypassed it and landed in Neapolis, sixty-five miles further, the next day (vv. 9–11). What a blessing, too, that God provided a safe voyage. Many storms arise in this region of the Aegean Sea. Paul made mention that he had experienced storm and shipwreck and had been in the sea a day and a night (2 Corinthians 11:25), but God had engineered circumstances on this voyage for His team to have smooth sailing and arrive safely at their destination. It was as if Christ had gone before them whispering, "Peace, be still" (Mark 4:39).

THE GOSPEL INVADES EUROPE It was at Neapolis (see map 3, p. 446) that Paul, for the first time, set foot on the European continent to preach the Gospel, though there is no mention that he actually spent any time at Neapolis. Acts 20:2–3, and verse 6 might indicate that later in returning to Macedonia he visited this city. Verse 6 says that he sailed from Philippi. To sail from Philippi one sailed from Philippi's seaport town, Neapolis, located just a few miles south of Philippi. Luke did not make a mistake by implying that Philippi was on the shore.

We should not overlook the fact that someone else had joined the missionary party with Paul, Silas, and Timothy. It was Luke. We notice that in chapter 16 that Luke, author of Acts and a physician (Colossians 4:4), uses the pronouns *we* and *us*. Pergamos, located less than one hundred miles south of Troas, was a medical center and possibly Luke, somewhere in the province of Mysia, had heard Paul preach. When and under what circumstances he was saved we are not told. By the time he met Paul, his maturity as a Christian was sufficient for Paul to accept him as a partner. What a blessing for Paul, so battered and bruised, to have a medical doctor nearby.

It has been of great importance to Christendom, especially to nations of the West, that Paul answered the Macedonian call and landed in Neapolis. Europe now became his field. Had he gone to Asia Minor as he had desired, the Gospel, no doubt, would have spread eastward and into the full Asiatic continent, eventually reaching all of Turkey, then into Iraq (ancient Assyria; Mesopotamia), Iran (ancient Persia), and on into India, China, and so forth. If Paul had not obeyed the Holy Spirit, the West, no doubt, would be in heathen darkness and missionaries from the East would be coming to us with the Good News of salvation. Instead, the Gospel went into Macedonia, into Greece, Italy, Spain, on up through Europe into Britain, and finally it reached the shores of America. We cannot adequately answer why God permitted this to happen the way it did. We only know that a Sovereign God worked within His providence. We should not only be grateful, but realize all the more how great our missionary responsibility is to those who might have heard the Gospel first if Paul had gone where he wanted to go. Now we know at least two reasons why the Holy Spirit would not allow Paul to go through Cappadocia and Bithynia. The West was waiting for him and God wanted us, in His time, to take the Gospel to the East. God did not forsake His own in those regions because many Jews from there were saved on the Day of Pentecost (Acts 2:9). God later used Peter to write them a letter of encouragement in the midst of all their trials (1 Peter).

PHILIPPI   Disembarking at Neapolis was Paul's first step onto European soil to answer the Macedonian call (Acts 16:11–40). Philippi was about twelve miles north of the port of

Neapolis, and to get there Paul had to travel over the Egnatian Way, the main east-west road to and from Rome.

King Philip, the father of Alexander the Great, had captured this city in 356 B.C. After a fierce battle in 42 B.C. between the forces of Brutus and Cassius and those of Antony and Octavian (who later became Caesar Augustus), Philippi became a Roman colony (a colonial and military outpost).

One characteristic of a *colonia* was that it was a miniature of the city of Rome. It was a free city wherein free citizens governed themselves within the Roman Empire. There was a distinction among its inhabitants between those who were citizens and those who were not citizens. When the Greeks spoke of inhabitants in the world, they divided them into two groups, Greeks and barbarians. Some barbarians were good, some were bad. Paul described them in a bad way in Titus 1:10–12. Anyone not born a Greek was a barbarian. This is why Paul used this distinction in his writings so that all would be included (Romans 1:14; 1 Corinthians 14:11; Colossians 3:11; see also Acts 28:2, 4).

When the Romans spoke of the peoples of their empire, they also divided them into two groups: (1) those who were citizens of Rome and those who were citizens in the empire; and (2) those who had no link with Rome and were called strangers. When Peter wrote his first epistle he wrote to those called strangers or aliens who had no link with Rome (1 Peter 1:1). Romans who lived outside Italy but who were true born Italians were known as "citizens of the dispersion." Those who were strangers, but who had for various reasons received the gift of citizenship, were political proselytes. Such were Paul and Silas in their relationship to the Roman Empire and among their fellow Romans in the *colonia* of Philippi. Both classes of citizens were in full possession of the same privileges, the most important of which were exemption from scourging and freedom from arrest (except in extreme cases such as treason). In all cases each had the right to appeal to the emperor. We will see more of these privileges when we study Paul's arrest in Jerusalem. Paul and Silas, as Roman citizens, had every right to feel at home in Philippi.

Lydia, the First European Convert

Being a military post, Philippi was not a commercial center. As a result, there were not enough Jews residing in the city to have a synagogue. Upon arrival, Paul, on the Sabbath, went out of the city to the riverside for a time of prayer. What Paul was actually looking for was a *proseucha*, a place of prayer where the few Jews in a given place would gather for worship. This was a substitute for the synagogue. The *proseucha* (gathering place), typically was either by a river or by the sea. This is why the Jews during the Babylonian captivity were by the rivers of Babylon (Psalm 137:1). This was the type of place where Timothy's mother and grandmother gathered at Lystra. Paul knew he would find an audience, and sure enough there were some women who had probably arrived a little early. Paul took advantage of this situation and immediately began to witness. Among the women was one named Lydia (Acts 16:14–15), a seller of purple who worshiped God, probably like Cornelius had prior to his conversion (Acts 10:1–2), or like Paul in earlier days as he feared God and went about to establish his own righteousness. Lydia was no doubt a proselyte. Paul had been forbidden by the Spirit to go to other places, but now he is driven by the Spirit, as it were, to this riverbank outside Philippi. He realized that God had prepared Lydia's heart for this moment because she quickly responded to his message and gave her heart to Christ. She became the first recorded European convert. We can only speculate what would have happened to Lydia if Paul had gone where he had wanted to go. Following the biblical pattern of an outward confession of an inward work of grace, she was baptized at the place of the *proseucha*, along with her believing household. She then invited the missionaries to her home for some good old "southern" Macedonia hospitality and good Christian fellowship (Acts 16:13–15). It is mere supposition but Lydia, being from Thyatira, could have won some relatives there to the Lord resulting in the establishment of a church in that city. John later wrote to the church at Thyatira (Revelation 2:18–29). As we think of Lydia, a woman from Asia Minor, we look back at Paul's desire to go throughout the whole of Asia Minor to preach and all the time God had a native from Asia Minor in Macedonia that He wanted saved. God's ways are not our ways, neither are His thoughts our thoughts (Isaiah 55:8–9).

The Gospel vs. Mythology and Evil Spirits

Sometime after Lydia's conversion, as well as the conversion of others (Acts 16:15, 40), Paul and Silas went to pray, and were met by a girl who was possessed with a spirit of divination—a fortune-teller who was a slave to her masters, and who brought them much revenue with this so-called gift (Acts 16:16–19). Evil spirits had preeminence in heathenism because of the mytho-logical system of Grecian idolatry. In the Greeks' imagination, the whole visible and invisible world was peopled with spiritual powers and/or evil spirits, as was this young girl in Philippi. According to Greek mythology, anyone who had a spirit of divination had the spirit of Python, or a spirit of the god Apollos. Python was a huge serpent famous for predicting future events. Apollo slew this serpent, and its spirit, Pythias, became celebrated as the teller of future events. Those who could predict or pre-tended to predict the future, were influenced by the spirit of Apollos/Pythias. This girl had "a spirit of divination," a "divining demon." Although possessed by the devil, the Spirit of God overruled her demon and for many days she followed Paul saying, "These men are the servants of the most high God, which show unto us the way of salvation" (Acts 16:17). We know that demons believe and tremble (James 2:19), but it is doubtful they revealed this truth to her. Finally, Paul sensed that God was at work in her heart. He also realized that the whole city was becoming familiar with her saying, and lest they credit God's salvation via the Gospel to the unholy means of divination, Paul, being grieved and displeased, turned to the spirit and said: "I command thee in the name of Jesus Christ to come out of her. And he came out the same hour" (Acts 16:18). This was Paul's *fourth* recorded miracle. He had followed Christ's command: in My name shall they cast out demons (cf. Matthew 10:34 with Luke 10:17). This young girl was restored to her right mind, she lost her demonic powers, and her masters lost their source of income. We wish that Luke would have continued his narrative about her and told us whether or not she became a Christian.

With the girl no longer in possession of this spirit of fortune-telling, her masters went bankrupt (Acts 16:19–22). Becoming infuriated, they caught Paul and Silas and took them to the public meeting place (see illustration 17). Summoning the rulers of Philippi, they called Paul and Silas before the officials and charged them with troubling the city. No mention is made of their former slave or their loss of income. Possibly they had used this girl in the shadow of the law without a license to practice divination. Maybe they had bribed the officials to use her, or had cheated in the matter of paying taxes. Instead of stating their real cause for performing a citizen's arrest of Paul and Silas, they leveled charges of "foreign customs" that were contrary to theirs. Without saying so in so many words, they were admitting that

17—Forum at Philippi where Paul and Silas were beaten. *Courtesy of author.*

these two missionaries were preaching Christ and that the ways and customs of a Christian were contrary to the ways and customs of pagan Rome. They succeeded in arousing the multitudes of the city against Paul and Silas and the magistrates, and bowing to the whims of the people without giving Paul and Silas a fair trial, the people tore off Paul's and Silas' clothes and beat them (vv. 22–23). We are at a loss as to why Paul did not immediately make it known regarding his Roman citizenship. The whole trial was based on their being slaves. Yet Paul opened not his mouth. It wasn't until after his ignominious treatment and the Philippian jailer was saved that he made it known that he was a Roman citizen (v. 37).

Paul and Silas Beaten and Imprisoned

At the command of the magistrates, they were then cast into the prison (Acts 16:23–29), and their feet were put in stocks (see illustration 18). The jailer was charged with keeping them secure (Acts 16:23–24). It is difficult for us to know the severity of a Roman beating. To beat someone was the delight of the soldier whose duty it was. He showed absolutely no mercy as he inflicted his heavy blows, delighting as the blood oozed from the flesh-

18—Stocks in Roman prison.
Courtesy of author.

torn back of his victim. The usual number of stripes was forty save one, making it thirty-nine. Whether Paul and Silas received thirty-nine each we do not know. Luke only says many, but Paul does make mention of his having been in "stripes above measure" (2 Corinthians 11:23).

The jailer fulfilled the verdict of the magistrates with inhuman cruelty, not placing them with other prisoners as was the Philippian custom, but "thrust them into the inner prison, and made their feet fast in the stocks" (Acts 16:24). What excruciating pain this must have been. Already bleeding from the lash (or rod), their limbs, lacerated as they were, were forced into a painful and constrained posture, causing great torture. The inner prison itself was nothing more than a rat-infested hole, typically dark, damp, and cold, where chains rusted on the limbs of the prisoners. Not only were their legs squeezed into and twisted by the stocks, but their arms and even necks were stretched, making breathing difficult. The jailer had them put into the inner prison to die and rot. Here again we question why Paul did not appeal to his Roman citizenship. He had every right to since the "law of Rome" was Philippi's strength as a free city. Had he done so, the arrest, beating, and imprisonment would have been avoided. However, God had a jailer He wanted saved and Paul's thorn, the messenger of Satan to buffet him, ultimately resulted in the salvation of the jailer and his family.

A Midnight Singspiration in Prison

Paul had learned as a Christian that whatsoever state he was in, he would be content. Years later he wrote to the Philippians to remind them of this Christian characteristic (Philippians 4:11). Being content in the state of imprisonment and pain, he, with Silas, prayed and began to sing at midnight (Acts 16:25). Here again, as with his stoning at Lystra and quick recovery (Acts 14:19–20), God must have performed some kind of miracle to relieve pain just a matter of hours after their beating. Maybe they sang their version of "Amazing Grace," or "Down at the Cross," or "At the Cross." What Paul and Silas were actually doing, I am sure, were "in psalms and hymns and spiritual songs, singing and making melody in their hearts [and vocally] to the Lord" (Ephesians 5:19; Colossians 3:16). They, along with the apostles, were counting it worthy to suffer shame and physical pain for their Lord (Acts 5:41). They knew that the Lord, our maker, giveth songs in the night (Job 35:10). The songs they heard in the night and probably sang were several Psalms, such as:

For he [God] hath looked down from the height of his sanctuary; from heaven did the LORD behold the earth; to hear the groaning of the prisoner; to loose those that are appointed to death (Psalm 102:19–20).

Let the sighing of the prisoner come before thee; according to the greatness of thy power preserve thou those that are appointed unto death (Psalm 79:11).

Which [God] executeth judgment for the oppressed; which giveth food to the hungry. The LORD looseth the prisoners. (Psalm 146:7)

Possibly their last song, just prior to the earthquake, was Psalm 107:10, 13–16.

Such as sit in darkness and in the shadow of death, being bound in affliction and iron; Then they cried unto the LORD in their trouble, and he saved them out of their distress. He brought them out of darkness and the shadow of death, and brake their bands in sunder [apart]. Oh that men would praise the LORD for his goodness, and for his wonderful works to the children of men! For he hath broken the gates of brass, and cut the bars of iron in sunder.

What cursings and complaints they might have gotten from other prisoners didn't faze them at all—they were too engrossed in the blessings of the Lord and at the same time too far removed from them to be in any danger. Maybe their singing put the jailer to sleep! It was customary for the jailer's house to be adjacent to the prison. As Paul and Silas sang, "Amen," at the close of their song service, there was a great earthquake (Acts 16:26). The jailer was so hardened he slept right through the singspiration, but being awakened out of his sleep by the shaking of his house, he came outside and saw the prison doors open and the prisoners standing around unshackled. Supposing they were going to flee, and aware of the inevitable death that awaited him by his superiors had any escaped, he resolved that suicide was better than disgrace and he "drew out his sword" (Acts 16:26–27). (Suicide was common in Philippi's history. It was here that Cassius, unable to face defeat, covered his face in his tent and compelled his orderly to strike the blow; here Brutus said farewell to his friends, exclaiming "certainly we must fly, not with the feet, but with the hands."[2] Many, according to Roman history, whose names were never recorded, ended it all by suicide. Cassius' messenger, Titinius, "held it to be a 'Roman's part' to follow the stern example [of Cassius]."[3]) Had it not been for Paul's loud voice, saying, "Do thyself no harm for we are all here," the jailer would have followed this tradition. Everyone was excited, but Paul and Silas were self-controlled, as was Paul to be later in a storm at sea (Acts 27:20–25). Paul calmly turned the occasion to a spiritual end. This quieted the jailer, who called for a light and came trembling into the inner prison and fell down before Paul and Silas (Acts 16:29).

The Philippian Jailer Saved

Somewhere along the line the message of the Cross had gotten to the heart of this jailer. Maybe he had heard repeatedly from the lips of the damsel that these two men were "servants of the most high God who show us the way of salvation." Paul had to have been preaching Christ for this girl to say this, so the jailer, somewhere along the line, must have heard that Christ died for the lost, that He came to seek and to save the lost. Up to the time of the earthquake he had turned a deaf ear to his spiritual need. He now knew that he was lost, and that he desperately needed help. Frightened by the earthquake, the thought of where he would spend eternity had he ended his own life, and seeing there was no hope in the paganism of Rome, he now realized that God had engineered all these circumstances in order for him to find out what was needed to be saved. He called for a torch and went into the inner prison to Paul and Silas and fell down, trembling, before them.

No doubt he was embarrassed not only because he knew that Paul and Silas knew of his hard-heartedness but also for the awful way he had treated them. One thing was on his mind now, and it was his own soul's salvation. He cried unto them saying, "Sirs, what must I do to be saved?" The answer Paul gives implies that the jailer's use of the word saved meant spiritual deliverance, not any deliverance to save his skin from the government. It would have been stupid to ask Paul and Silas for that kind of deliverance, knowing full well these men were only prisoners. When Paul answered, he literally said: Believe, not in us, but in the Lord Jesus Christ, and you shall be saved; and not only you, but the like faith shall bring salvation to all your house (see Acts 16:30–31).

Since the jailer's house was next to the prison, these verses infer that in the excitement of the earthquake the jailer's family had crowded around the jailer, Paul, and Silas. Upon moving to the jailer's house (Acts 16:32), no time was lost in Paul's making known to them the way of salvation. The meaning of faith in Jesus was explained in the darkness of the midnight hour and the light of the Gospel enlightened their hearts and faces. Paul had preached Christ, and God commanded the light to shine out of darkness to give their hearts the light of the knowledge of the glory of God in the face of Jesus Christ (2 Corinthians 4:5–6). Contrary to the teachings of what is known as covenant theology, the sprinkling of an infant does not in any way give that baby future access to salvation, to be confirmed at the age of accountability. Salvation is personal, an act on the part of the individual for himself. Each must come to the place of decision such as did the jailer. "None of them can by any means redeem his brother, nor give to God a ransom for him" (Psalm 49:7). Some have supposed that Acts 16:31 teaches household salvation, that a man's house will be saved when the head of the house believes. Notice the Greek text again. To the jailer Paul said: Believe, not on us, but in the Lord Jesus Christ, and *you* [the jailer) shall be saved; and not only you, *but the like faith* shall bring salvation to all your house. "The like faith" is an individual faith, only for those in the household who have faith to believe to the saving of the soul.

Early New Testament saints had something that is woefully lacking in our dog-eat-dog society, especially among believers. Very few among us are hospitable. Few missionaries are welcome in homes. Neighborliness is almost a thing of the past, and few seem to have a desire to be involved with other believers. Many are content to attend only the morning worship service in their church and then to hibernate until the next Sunday. Not so with these early Christians. In Jerusalem they had all things in common (Acts 2:44–46). Lydia immediately opened her home after her conversion (Acts 16:15). Now the jailer, upon conversion, immediately took care of Paul's and Silas' bleeding wounds. Then

Paul saw to it that the jailer and all believers in the house were taken to a place where they could be baptized. Here again he followed the biblical pattern: evangelize and baptize.

After performing so-called believer's baptism, they returned to the house where they had an early breakfast and enjoyed fellowship together. Paul no doubt put into practice the third step of the Great Commission and taught these new converts some needful steps to follow in their new-found faith (vv. 32–34). In the course of that night great changes had taken place: (1) The prison keeper's heart was changed; (2) his family was changed; (3) his relation to the world and the world to come was changed; and (4) he had been transformed from an ignorant slave of a heathen magistracy to the spiritual head of a Christian family!

A change had also taken place in the minds of the magistrates themselves. Maybe it was the earthquake that caused this sudden change. Possibly they realized that they had acted hastily and unfairly without giving Paul and Silas an opportunity to defend themselves; maybe they wished they had heard more accurate facts in the case. Being pagans, maybe they thought there was something to the girl's proclamation that these men were of the most high God and in their superstitious beliefs thought Paul's God had caused the earthquake. One thing was for certain, Christianity was established in Philippi through Lydia's and the jailer's conversions. The foundation had been laid for a great church, and the magistrates realized that their hands were tied concerning Paul and Silas. They now had to get rid of these so-called religionists. They sent officers to the jailer's house to inform the jailer to "let these men go" (Acts 16:35). This expression could be translated, "Let these 'way of salvation' followers go." But Paul said unto them,

> they have beaten us openly uncondemned, being Romans, and have cast us into prison; and now do they thrust us out privily? nay verily; but let them come themselves and fetch us out. And the sergeants told these words unto the magistrates: and they feared, when they heard that they were Romans. And they came and besought them, and brought them out and desired them to depart out of the city (Acts 16:37–39).

There is no record of an apology from these magistrates. Paul's name, in a sense, had been vindicated as a Roman citizen in that he was set free. This meeting between Paul and Silas and the magistrates must have taken place in the prison, because when the case was closed, they went out of the prison and entered Lydia's house. Here they met with the brethren, had fellowship together, and departed to continue their missionary journey (Acts 16:40).

PAUL'S EPISTLE No mention is made of Luke's staying **TO THE PHILIPPIANS** in Philippi after Paul and Silas depart. What a blessing that this physician was there to help in the matter of dressing wounds as the jailer washed their stripes. But, by the use of the pronoun *they* in Acts 17:1, it is inferred that only Paul, Silas, and Timothy left Philippi. (One thing about Luke's writing of Acts is that he never mentions his own labors nor even praises himself. Paul referred to him as "the beloved physician" and "my fellow laborer" [Colossians 4:14; Philemon 24]. Luke reappears again on Paul's third missionary journey when he made his second visit to Macedonia [Acts 20:1–5]. Here Luke uses the pronoun *us*, which included himself.) The prospects of a church in Philippi looked good and there was the need for a mature Christian to stay behind and help the believers there become rooted and grounded in the faith. The testimony of the Philippian church, established in A.D. 52, gave evidence of a growing, stable assembly.

Twelve years later, Paul, in prison in Rome, wrote his letter to the Philippian saints (ca. A.D. 64). Not only was Lydia the first European convert, the church at Philippi was the first to be established on that continent. Lydia, the Philippian jailer, and other converts were mostly Romans and Greeks, hence the absence of Jewish names in this letter. There was little need for Paul to use the Old Testament in witnessing to these Gentiles; however, there is one indirect reference to the Old Testament Scriptures, "every knee shall bow" (cf. Philippians 2:10 with Isaiah 45:23).

In the twelve years since its inception, this church had experienced phenomenal growth. Taking their cue from Lydia, it was also hospitable. These believers had helped Paul financially (4:16), and when they heard of his imprisonment in Rome, they sent Epaphroditus with another gift. This letter was more than a thank-you note to these people, and it is the most personal one he wrote to any of the churches he had established. Paul sent Epaphroditus, who had become gravely ill while in Rome (Philippians 2:27), back to Philippi with his epistle to them.

The overriding theme of Philippians is joy and rejoicing.

These words are used at least seventeen times. No one is without problems, but Paul desired that all believers be content, whatever their lot might be or in whatsoever state they were (4:11). It had been evident to Paul that down through the years these people had been overcomers and the joy of the Lord had been their portion. However, as with every church, because its members are human, there were some problems. Human beings, though saved, are not capable of perfection; they are not omniscient, nor are they infallible. Epaphroditus had filled him in on some disturbing situations.

> First, they wondered why Paul was in prison. Paul answered this question (1:12–24).
>
> Second, there were some selfish, ambitious members; rivalries; and pride in abundance (chapter 2:3–4).
>
> Third, Judaizers, false brethren, were trying to make inroads with their damnable circumcision-for-salvation doctrine. Paul told the Philippians that such a law was a thing of the past and that all he had been as a Jew was now counted as dung that he might win Christ (3:1–10).
>
> Fourth, some converts were prone to believe that since they were set free in Christ they were free from the moral law, which gave them license to satisfy their own desires. Paul answered this problem in 3:11–19.
>
> Fifth, there were some petty differences among members, resulting in friction and the grieving of the Holy Spirit (4:2).

Paul not only mentioned *joy* and *rejoicing* many times but also mentioned *mind* and *think* thirty-one times. He wanted those at Philippi to have the right attitude in every situation and circumstance. He wanted them to realize that whatever problems they had, they were based on 10 percent circumstance and 90 percent attitude. Paul reminded these members that he himself had not attained perfection (3:12), and though he didn't quote Proverbs 23:7, the principle was there concerning the mind: As one thinks in his heart, so is he. Paul knew from experience that the key to living a victorious Christian life was attitude. How else could he have had such a good attitude at midnight in the middle of excruciating pain unless he had learned therewith to be content in whatsoever state he was in (see 4:11–13). Paul had learned the principle that life is 10 percent what happens to us and 90 percent how we respond to those circumstances.

Philippians provides a constructive outline in the matter of Christian living:

OUTLINE OF CHRISTIAN LIVING FROM PHILIPPIANS	
Chapter 1	Circumstances will ultimately rob us of joy in our lives. Paul's answer to this situation is to think on Jesus Christ, and God will give us *confidence*.
Chapter 2	Selfishness will ultimately rob us of joy in our lives. Paul's answer to this problem is to think of others more than we think of ourselves, and God will give us *purpose*.
Chapter 3	Looking to people will ultimately rob us of joy in our lives. Paul's answer to this issue is to think of heaven where our home really is, where our fellowship awaits us, and where everything will be straightened out, and God will give us a clear *perspective*.
Chapter 4	Worry will ultimately rob us of joy in our lives. Paul's answer to this depressing circumstances is to pray and think on those things that are pure, and God will give us *peace*.

The secret of experiencing the right attitude and basking in the joy of God's salvation is that we can do it (4:13); we have the mind of Christ to give us the right attitude (cf. 2:5–8 with 1 Corinthians 2:16); and whatever we need in order to live above our circumstances, God will supply (4:19).

Paul's great challenge to the Philippians was his own testimony: "For to me to live is Christ" (1:21). To live for Christ means many things, some of which are

1. letting one's manner of living be becoming to the Gospel (1:27),

2. suffering for Christ (1:29),

3. letting Christ's mind rule in all humility (2:5–8),

4. doing all things without murmuring and strife (2:14),

5. holding on to the Word of God (2:16),

6. constantly pressing on (3:13–14),

7. rejoicing always (4:4),

8. praying (4:5–7),

9. thinking on the positive, mixed with faith (4:8),

10. practicing daily what has been learned—doing what you know is God's will through Christ's strength (4:9, 13),

11. relying on God to supply your every need (4:19),

12. realizing that regardless of the circumstance, God's grace is always sufficient (4:23).

Paul presents Christ to the Philippians as the Sacrifice for our sins (2:5–8), as Lord (2:11), as the Supreme Prize in life's struggles (3:8), as our Strength (4:13), and as the Supplier of our every need (4:19).

THESSALONICA Having established a promising church in Philippi, the missionary team spent their last hours in the city with Lydia, her household, and many of the new converts. Later, Paul, Silas, and Timothy departed (Acts 16:40). We have already noted that Luke at this point did not accompany them but stayed in Philippi for an indefinite period of time (note the use of the pronoun *they*, not *we* in Acts 17:1). The team journeyed westward over the Egnatian Way to Amphipolis, a distance of thirty-three miles and on to Apollonia, a further distance of thirty miles (Acts 17:1–10). No mention is made of any ministry in either of these cities. Later Paul covered the territory in Macedonia where these cities are located—in the region of Illyricum, stating that "from Jerusalem, and round about Illyricum, I have fully preached the Gospel of Christ" (Romans 15:19). Quite possibly he returned to either or both of these cities.

Leaving Apollonia, Paul and company continued westward to the city of Thessalonica, a distance of thirty-seven miles (Acts 17:1). Long before Alexander the Great started his conquest of the world, Thessalonica was named Therma. Persia's territory extended this far west when Xerxes ruled, but when the Macedonian power began to overshadow the Persians, and Alexander the Great finally defeated them, he named this city after his sister, Thessalonica. The Romans captured the city in 168 B.C., and it became a free city under Augustus, who permitted the Thessalonians to appoint their own city officials (magistrates) called *politarchs*. Many liberal scholars have questioned Luke's use of the term *politarch* since secular history made no mention of the term, but archaeological records have shown it was a common word where cities had liberty to appoint their own governing body. The message that the Macedonians (Philippi, Thessalonica, and so forth) should be free was proclaimed by one Paulus Eamilius after the battle of Pydna. Isn't it ironic that another Paulus (Paul) visited Macedonia and was in the area to proclaim a better freedom—that of the soul set free!

Thessalonica (see map 3, p. 446), like Philippi, was on the Egnatian Way, which contributed to its importance in the Roman Empire. It was an important seaport, located on the northwest corner of the Aegean Sea, near Mt. Olympus, the legendary home of the Greek Parthenon. Paul arrived here about A.D. 52 and stayed at the home of Jason (Acts 17:7). From Romans 16:21 we learn that one of Paul's relatives was named Jason, and if Jason of Thessalonica is the one mentioned in Romans, we have an explanation of why Paul lodged with this particular person. This metropolis boasted a citizenship of perhaps 200,000, plus a sizeable population of slaves. It also had a sizeable Jewish population. As was Paul's custom, he headed straight for the synagogue and preached to the Jews that Jesus was the Christ. For three Sabbaths he reasoned with them out of the Scriptures, which resulted in some Jews', many Greeks' (the Greeks were God-fearing men who were probably proselytes delivered from idolatry), and leading women (probably wives of these Greeks) believing. Running true to course, there were many Jews who did not believe (Acts 17:2–5). Jealousy is one of Satan's best tools, and as more Gentiles believed and were thrust into the limelight, Jews, who saw their influence declining, began to buffet Paul as they had in Antioch of Pisidia and Lystra (Acts 13:14, 44–50; 14:6–19).

After spending three Sabbaths with the Jews, Paul, in turning to the idolatrous Gentiles, probably remained longer in Thessalonica, though most scholars say he was in the city only three Sabbaths. This could, however, have entailed almost five weeks, taking a Sunday before the first Sabbath and going through the Friday after the third Sabbath. Or, conversely, it could have been just a little over two weeks if he arrived the Friday before the first Sabbath and left the Sunday after the third Sabbath. Note some circumstantial evidence that might point to a much longer stay.

First, his letter to them is more to former Greek idolaters. Because most of these converts came out of idolatry, it is understandable that with no biblical background they would need an extended, lengthy ministry, especially in view of all that Paul taught them (see next paragraph). Paganism was ingrained in these citizens. With the Greek Parthenon nearby, any or all Grecian gods had preeminence. Paul mentioned that when they came to a saving knowledge of Christ they "turned to God from [their] idols to serve the true and living God" (1 Thessalonians 1:9). They turned to God from idols not from idols to God. To express it the latter way, would imply that they looked at an idol, then to God, back to an idol, then to God, thinking: *Should I turn from my favorite idol to a living God?* They did not spend time comparing their gods (idols) to God. This could have been a long drawn-out process with the devil there as the god of this age to blind their minds "lest the light of the glorious Gospel of Christ, who is the image of God, should shine unto them" (2 Corinthians 4:4). In the case of these idolaters, when God "commanded the light to shine out of darkness, . . . [it] shined in their hearts, to give them the light of the knowledge of the glory of God in the face of Jesus Christ" (2 Corinthians 4:6). When God did this, their minds were blinded to their gods and they immediately turned to God from their idols. They might not have comprehended everything that Paul taught, but much of it got through to them and they became rooted in God's overall plan for lost mankind.

However long Paul stayed, they learned about election (1:4), the ministry of the Holy Spirit (1:5–6; 4:7; 5:19), assurance (1:5), the Trinity (1:1, 5), conversion (1:9), the second coming of Christ (1:10), the believer's walk (2:12; 4:1; 5:22), sanctification (4:4;

5:23), the Resurrection (4:14–17), the Day of the Lord (5:1–3), prayer (5:17), and man's tripartite nature (5:23).

Second, during Paul's stay in Thessalonica he received two separate offerings from the church at Philippi (Philippians 4:15–16). It is true that the saints at Philippi could have sent two separate offerings within three weeks (more or less), but that was not likely, considering the distance.

Third, while in this city Paul worked "night and day" to support himself (1 Thessalonians 2:9; 2 Thessalonians 3:7–9). What orders he had in tent making would require much time to fill if he worked this hard. It would take many hours away from going about preaching, teaching, and evangelizing. Having to work could easily have prolonged his stay in this city.

Jewish Opposition at Thessalonica

Evidently the Gentiles were most kind to Paul and Silas. Not so the Jews (Acts 17:5–9). After much success with these idolaters, jealous Jews organized a mob to persecute the servants of the Lord. Their opposition arose mainly because Paul was declaring the kingship of Jesus (v. 7). Like the Pharisees who accused Jesus before Pilate of being a king in opposition to Caesar, so these Thessalonian Jews accused Paul of opposition to Rome. The Jews saw that Paul's influence was undermining their businesses, so the logical thing to do was to silence them and chase them out of town. Because Thessalonica was a free city, anyone had the right to take a complaint to the city rulers. Following the example of the Jews at Antioch of Pisidia in going to Lystra to encourage the stoning of Paul, these Jews, moved with envy against Paul and Silas, "took unto them [the rulers] certain lewd fellows of the baser sort [vile loafers] . . . and set all the city on an uproar, and assaulted the house of Jason, and sought to bring them out to the people" (Acts 17:5). These base, vile loafers were common in the agoras or forums of Greco-Roman cities. They invariably, if paid, assembled themselves together and would gather around the platform to heckle the speaker, or if the money was good enough they were ready at a moment's notice to start a riot. Cicero gave them the apt designation of *subrostrani*, meaning "those-under-rostrum." When the Jews found out Paul and Silas were not in Jason's house, they, at the enjoyment of the *subrostrani*, dragged Jason before the magistrate with trumped-up charges that Jason was harboring men who were teaching that Jesus was a new king (vv. 6–8).

Not only were the Jews determined to rid the city of Paul and Silas, but in all probability Jason was also on their hit list because (1) he had befriended Paul and Silas, and (2) the name *Jason* is a derivative of "Joshua." Being a Hellenistic Jew he had conformed enough to Grecian culture to have eliminated his Jewish name. The Jews however tolerated no such change. Since Paul and Silas were not there at that time, the Jews accused Jason of protecting his guests, whom they labeled as traitors to Rome. Venting their rage against him and his fellow brethren, they took them before the politarchs. These Thessalonian magistrates were much more alert and cautious than those at Philippi. They realized that these will-do-anything-for-a-buck *subrostrani* must be quelled, so they accepted bail from Jason and the brethren and then let them go (Acts 17:9). The hostility and opposition on the part of the Jews was so great that Paul and his team were forced to flee the city by night (v. 10). Once again, Paul's thorn was evident.

An archaeological discovery has come to the rescue of Luke's account of Jason's being taken before the rulers of Thessalonica (Acts 17:6, 8). Luke uses the Greek word *politarchs* for rulers. Thessalonica, being a free city with a peoples' assembly, was headed by six or seven *politarchs*. This term for the rulers has been seriously questioned by critics of Luke's writings since it does not appear elsewhere in Greek literature. Many inscriptions however have been discovered that have vindicated Luke. The most famous was one inscribed on the arch of the Vardar Gate (see illustration 19b), which stood in Thessalonica over the Egnatian Way. The gate was taken down but the inscription, carved on a six-foot-thick marble block, is now in the British Museum in London. On this particular monument there are the names of seven *politarchs*. It is perhaps worth observing that three of the names are identical with three of Paul's friends in this region: Sopater of Berea, and Secundus of Thessalonica (both mentioned in Acts 20:4) as well as Gaius, the Macedonian (Acts 19:29). We can only speculate as to whether these were the same men that Paul mentioned and whether or not these officials were saved under Paul's ministry.

PAUL'S FIRST EPISTLE TO THE THESSALONIANS After Paul's missionary endeavor was completed in Berea, he left Silas and Timothy with these believers and went to Athens (Acts 17:14–15). In Athens he sent for his companions to return to him from Macedonia (Berea). Luke makes no mention that they

Paul's Second Missionary Journey

19a—Reconstructed Gate of Vardar at Thessalonica. *Courtesy of author.*

ΠΟΛΕΙΤΑΡΧΟΥΝΤΩΝ <u>ΣΩΣΙΠΑΤΡΟΥ</u>[1] ΤΟΥ ΚΛΕΟ
ΠΑΤΡΑΣ ΚΑΙ ΛΟΥΚΙΟΥ ΠΟΝΤΙΟΥ <u>ΣΕΚΟΥΝΔΟΥ</u>[2]
ΠΟΥΒΛΙΟΥ ΦΛΑΟΥΙΟΥ ΣΑΒΕΙΝΟΥ ΔΗΜΗΤΡΙΟΥ
ΤΟΥ ΦΑΥΣΤΟΥ ΔΗΜΗΤΡΙΟΥ ΤΟΥ ΝΙΚΟΠΟΛΕΩΣ
ΖΩΙΛΟΥ ΤΟΥ ΠΑΡΜΕΝΙΩΝΟΣ ΤΟΥ ΚΑΙ ΜΕΝΙΣΚΟΥ
<u>ΓΑΙΟΥ</u>[3] ΑΓΙΛΛΗΙΟΥ ΠΟΤΕΙΤΟΥ. . . . .

1. Sopater   2. Secundus   3. Gaius

19b—Facsimile of inscription on Gate of Vardar. *Courtesy of author.*

PAUL'S FIRST EPISTLE TO THE THESSALONIANS   175 arrived in Athens, but they probably did as we will see later (see p. 179 ff.). Paul evidently sent Timothy back to Thessalonica and later met Paul in Corinth with his report of the state of the Thessalonian church. Paul learned that some saints were questioning his character, some were concerned about loved ones who had passed away, and many needed encouragement due to persecution. The fact that Paul had commended them for turning to God from their idols indicates that the bulk of the members were Greeks (Gentiles) who had worshiped Athenian gods and goddesses, and, with such a background, Paul understood why so many questions had arisen in their minds. This precipitated his writing to them from Corinth about A.D. 53. He wrote to defend his character (2:3–9), to encourage them to be faithful to the Lord in spite of opposition (2:13–16), to help babes in Christ (3:1–4:2), to urge them to live a holy life (4:3–8), to comfort those whose loved ones had fallen asleep in Jesus (4:13–18), and to show them how to have an acceptable walk before others (ch. 5).

His preaching the Word to these people really demonstrated that the "Gospel is the power of God unto salvation to everyone who believes" (Romans 1:16). These idolaters (1) received the Word of God (1 Thessalonians 1:6; 2:13), (2) were saved from wrath (1 Thessalonians 1:10), (3) turned to God from their idols (1 Thessalonians 1:9), (4) presented their bodies as a living sacrifice (2 Corinthians 8:1, 5), (5) followed the Lord (1 Thessalonians 1:6), (6) served the true and living God (1 Thessalonians 1:9), (7) suffered persecution for godly living (1 Thessalonians 1:6; 3:3, 6–7), (8) were joyful in the Spirit (1 Thessalonians 1:6), (9) had works of faith and love (1 Thessalonians 3:6–7), (10) were examples to others (1 Thessalonians 1:7–8), (11) supported missionaries and prayed for them (2 Corinthians 8:3–4), and (12) looked for Christ's return via the Rapture (1 Thessalonians 4:13–18).

Because of such growth in grace and knowledge of their Lord and Savior Jesus Christ, and because Paul mentioned few faults, the Thessalonians became a model church.

1. As a *model church* they had a work of faith (chapter 1).

2. As *model servants* they had a labor of love (chapter 2).

3. Living a *model life* they were unblamable in holiness (chapter 3).

4. Having a *model faith* they had a hope of Christ's return (chapter 4).

5. Having a *model action* they were walking in the light (chapter 5).

Due to their unfamiliarity with the Old Testament Scriptures there are no Old Testament references cited in either epistle. Paul portrayed Christ to them as the believer's Hope (1:3) and the coming Savior (4:13–17), who delivers from wrath to come (1:10; 5:4–11), who will reward (2:19–20), who will perfect (3:13), and who will resurrect His own (4:13–17).

Archaeological discoveries reveal that the pagans of Thessalonica believed that "after death no reviving; in the grave no meeting again."[4] It is hard sometimes for Christians to forget some old things they were taught and believed as sinners, and Satan is anxious to capitalize on that. Possibly after their conversion, some believers in this church wondered just what happened to a loved one who died after being saved. "Will I ever see them again?" they wondered. "If there is life beyond the grave, will I be able to recognize my loved ones?" Paul's answer must have sent them into spiritual orbit:

I would not have you to be ignorant, brethren, concerning them which are asleep [like your unsaved friends are with their pagan beliefs and like you used to be before you were saved], that ye sorrow not, even as others which have no hope. For if we believe that Jesus died and rose again, even so them also which sleep in Jesus will God bring with him. For this we say unto you by the Word of the Lord, that we who are alive and remain unto the coming of the Lord shall not prevent them which are asleep. For the Lord himself shall descend from heaven with a shout, with the voice of an archangel, and with the trump of God: and the dead in Christ shall rise first: then we which are alive and remain shall be caught up together with them in the clouds, to meet the Lord in the air: and so shall we ever be with the Lord (1 Thessalonians 4:13–17).

And then to put the icing on the cake, Paul said to them: "Wherefore comfort one another with these words" (4:18). What a comfort that after death there will be a reviving (resurrection) and after the grave there will be a meeting in the air with, and a recognition of our saved loved ones.

PAUL'S SECOND LETTER TO THE THESSALONIANS After the saints in Thessalonica received Paul's first letter, word got back to him that some had fallen prey to false teachings concerning the Day of the Lord, thinking that this day had already begun. They had interpreted the first epistle to mean that they would be exempt from such judgments. They thought that the end of the world was at hand and as a result, some believers were compromising their Christian stand and walk by fraternizing with unruly or carnal brothers (2 Thessalonians 3:6). Paul had previously encouraged them to have a walk pleasing to God and to continue pursuing holy living (1 Thessalonians 4:1, 4, 7). Not only were they now walking unworthy of their calling, but some had even stopped working (2 Thessalonians 3:11). They probably reasoned: *Why work if the Lord is coming back today?* In Paul's first letter, he had encouraged them to live by love and in peace with one another (5:13). Now they were busybodies and gossipers, living in idle strife.

This second epistle (ca. A.D. 54) was written to show what events must take place before the Day of the Lord and the wrath to come, and to show that laboring for the Gospel's sake, rather than living in idle resignation, is the only way to be consistent in the things of the Lord. Paul portrays Christ in this epistle as the Soon Coming One to be glorified in His saints (1:10).

AT BEREA AMONG THE SCRIPTURE SEARCHERS Paul's pattern in his travels was to stay in a particular location until he was compelled to depart. Such was the case in Thessalonica. Due to the opposition on the part of the Jews because of his and Silas' success in preaching the Gospel, the believers sent them away by night to Berea (Acts 17:10–14), southwest of Thessalonica, a distance of about sixty miles (see map 3, p. 446). The city was sufficiently populated by Jews, and according to his custom, Paul went to the synagogue. Here he found a different breed of Jews than he had encountered elsewhere. Just as there had been a faithful remnant in Isaiah's day (Isaiah 1:9), there was a remnant of Jews who relied on the Scriptures rather than the traditions of their fathers at Berea. There was a maxim among the Jews that stated, "None was of a noble spirit who did not employ himself in the study of the Law." The Bereans practiced this. Their minds were not narrowed by prejudice as were those of Thessalonica and Antioch of Pisidia, and they were more willing to receive the truth. When Paul preached the Gospel to them, they "were more noble than those in Thessalonica, in that they received the word with all readiness of mind, and searched the scriptures daily, whether those things [that Paul was preaching] were so" (Acts 17:11). These Bereans not only listened to Paul's arguments but instead of taking the preacher's word for it, they examined the Scriptures themselves to see if Paul's arguments were true. They had to be sure that the Scriptures, as preached by Paul, corresponded to what they had heard concerning its fulfillment in the person, work, and suffering of Christ. To their credit they made this scrutiny their daily occupation. Truth sought in this spirit cannot long remain undiscovered. The promise that they who seek shall find was fulfilled, and as a result of Paul's visit, many were converted. The blessing of abundant salvation was not limited to the Jewish colony. The same Lord who responds to all who call on Him also called Gentiles, both men and women of the highest rank (v. 12).

The blessings of Berea were short-lived. The length of Paul's stay in this city is not known. The fact that the Bereans "searched the scriptures daily" implies that Paul tarried a sufficient number of days for them to be convinced that he was telling the truth. Then the old thorn in the flesh appeared and the violent Jews of Thessalonica came to Berea to buffet him. It never took Jewish bigots long to come upon Paul like hunters in search of their prey. They could not arrest the spread of the Gospel but they "stirred up the people" against God's man, using the same method that they had at Thessalonica by employing the *subrostrani* to influence the city rulers so that they would inflict some method of torture or persecution on Paul. "Immediately the brethren sent away Paul to go as it were to the sea: but Silas and Timothy abode there still. And they that conducted Paul brought him unto Athens" (Acts 17:14–15). Once before, because of threats, Paul had been escorted from Jerusalem to Caesarea (Acts 9:30–31). At Berea we find a repeat performance—this time from Berea to Athens. Silas and Timothy were left behind to help the saints overcome discouragement in their trials and to support them in persecutions.

ATHENS The journey by land and sea from Berea to Athens (Acts 17:15–34) was 325 miles (see map 3, p. 446). Having left Berea, Paul and a company of believers likely hiked to Dium where they found a vessel going to Athens. Sailing into Piraeus, the harbor entrance to the city of Athens, Paul was

20—Athens as Paul saw it. *Courtesy of author.*

confronted with gross idolatry—the devotion of the Athenians to pagan religious ceremonies and the dialogues of unbelieving philosophers (see illustration 20). Having left Timothy and Silas in Berea, Paul sent word for them to come to Athens to be with him (v. 15). Luke makes no mention that these two co-laborers arrived in Athens, but it is quite possible that they did. If so, Paul immediately sent them to Thessalonica in Macedonia to check on the newborn saints. The reason for the supposition that they visited Athens is that the last time Luke mentioned them they were in Berea (Acts 17:13–14), yet Paul said in his letter to the Thessalonians that he sent Timothy (and no doubt Silas with him) to "establish you and to comfort you concerning your faith" (1 Thessalonians 3:16). Later, we note that Timothy and Silas returned from Macedonia where Thessalonica is located and met Paul in Corinth (Acts 18:5).

As Paul entered the city of Athens, his spirit was stirred (tormented) when he saw that this metropolis was given to idolatry (v. 16). Named after its patron goddess Athena, Athens greatness occurred in the period of Pericles (459–431 B.C.) when many temples and public buildings were erected. It was under Pericles' leadership that Grecian art and literature flourished.

21—Numerous Athenian gods and idols. *Courtesy of author.*

Although under Roman rule, Grecian culture was still in vogue when Paul visited there. The city itself boasted a population of over a quarter-of-a-million people, controlled by religion and philosophy.

Religion of Greeks

The Greeks were polytheistic, having gods for any occasion (see illustration 21). Even as one views the ruins of Athens today, one takes note of Luke's statement—it is a city full of idols. According to the records of antiquity, there was no other place where as many idols were to be seen. One ancient Greek historian wrote: "Our region is so full of deities that you may more frequently meet with a god than a man."[5] The Greek religion was a deification of human attributes and the powers of nature. It had gods too numerous to mention, some of which were Jupiter, Apollo, Theseus, Hercules, Venus, Artemis (or Diana), and Bacchus. Many of their great heroes were deified—Solon the lawgiver, Conon the admiral, Demosthenes the orator, Augustus, Agrippa, and so forth. Every god found a niche in the agora. Every public place and building was a sanctuary; even streets were named for gods.

To give a true picture of the Athenian religion we must go beyond the beauty and art of their temples and statues into their ignorance and the deeper darkness of corruption and sin. Their shameless religion was encouraged by public works of art (nudes in many cases), by popular belief concerning the character of the gods, and by established worship ceremonies. One Greek philosopher said that "No other effect could possibly be produced but that all shame on account of sin must be taken away from men, if they believe in such gods."[6] Plato seriously censured the Athenians when he spoke of the depravity of the Grecian gods. In their religion they admired the beauty and the good but hopelessly followed the bad. From the standpoint of lewdness and vulgarity, no religion stooped lower than that of the Athenians (unless it was the worship of Baal as described in the Old Testament). It is no wonder that Paul remarked that they were very religious (too superstitious), and that the whole city was given to idol worship (Acts 17:16, 22). Their whole religious system blinded them to the reality of life and to the consciousness of their own sin and eradicated any desire for a cure or remedy. Unbeknownst to them, Paul was in town to preach the Gospel.

Philosophy of Greeks

Socrates was the first to call humanity to the contemplation of itself and became the founder of philosophy. He also led the Greek mind to investigate moral truth. Plato and Aristotle were also pioneers in the search for truth. Paul, with knowledge of Greek philosophy, plus a knowledge of the truth, had come to Athens for one purpose and one purpose only—to give the Athenians the truth, salvation as found only in Christ Jesus.

There were numerous philosophical schools among the Greeks, but Luke mentioned only two groups of philosophers—the Stoics and the Epicureans—as dialoguing with Paul (Acts 17:18). These two systems, out of all the philosophies, had the most influence in the matter of moral investigation.

The Stoics regarded images and temples as ornaments of art. They accepted polytheism as the norm in religious life, yet they recognized a god who did not create but merely organized. Their philosophy was akin to today's so-called doctrine of secular humanism. To them, the wise lived according to reason, and living thusly, were perfect and self-sufficient. Humanity reigned supreme as god and was justified in boasting of itself as god, even being equal to the chief god, Zeus (Jupiter). Nothing was more repugnant to a Stoic than the news that they needed a Savior, who had atoned for their sins, and who was ready to help in time of need. Christianity was the school of humility; Stoicism was the education of pride. Stoicism's first two leaders died by suicide, and they denied the resurrection of the body and did not believe in the immortality of the soul. They did not believe that the Gospel provided a message of hope and an escape from the disgrace of death. Stoicism in its full development was utterly opposed to Christianity. It offered no hope.

The Epicureans were atheistic. Their philosophic system was one of materialism. In their view, the world was formed by an accidental concourse of atoms; it was not created or even modified by the Divinity. If there were any gods at all, these divinities were merely phantoms, impressions on the popular mind or dreams that had no objective reality. The universe was a great accident, and explained itself without any reference to a higher power. Since there was no belief in a Creator there was no moral government. All notions of retribution and of judgment to come were forbidden by their creed. They also did not believe in resurrection; the soul was nothing without a body. Both body and soul dissolved together and dissipated into the elements and when this occurred life ended. Their idea was to live and let live, believing that good consisted in the gratitude of the appetite of the senses. They set out to deliberately do what the animals instinctively do—gratify self. The Stoics sought to resist the evil that surrounded them; the Epicureans endeavored to console themselves in this world with a tranquil, self-gratifying, and pleasurable life.

Upon arrival in this city, Paul immediately plunged into a daily witnessing ministry with the Jews in the synagogue (Acts 17:17); with the devout people, probably God-fearing Greeks who had become proselytes (v. 17b); with anyone in the market place (see illustration 22), regardless of their walk of life (v. 17c); and with the philosophers (vv. 18–19). The market was the agora where people assembled to buy, sell, converse, hear public announcements, and so forth. Paul visited the marketplace daily because he knew that this was where the crowds would be. Word soon reached the ears of the Epicureans and the Stoics about Paul's effective preaching concerning so called "strange gods: because he preached unto them Jesus, and the resurrection" (v. 18).

22—Ancient marketplace in Athens. *Courtesy of author.*

Sermon to Greeks on Mars' Hill

The Epicureans and Stoics often spent all day in dialogue, discussing life and delving into the mysteries of the mind. They were ever seeking to hear or learn some new thing. Paul's message about Jesus, a strange god to them, and His resurrection was a "new thing" or philosophy to them, hence they desired to hear him elaborate on this new doctrine. These philosophers took Paul to the Areopagus, the highest place on Mars' Hill (Acts 17:18–21). Mars' Hill (see illustration 23) is nothing more than a rock knoll near the Acropolis where the Parthenon and other temples and buildings were located. The Acropolis was in full view from Mars' Hill. There were any number of places where these philosophers could have taken Paul—to an amphitheater, the agora, a grove, and so forth. Why Mars' Hill, and not some place where they could sit comfortably?

According to archaeological discoveries, Mars' Hill received its name from the god Mars, who, in Greek mythology, was first tried at this spot by other gods. To the Greeks, Mars' Hill was where the court of judicature had sat from time immemorial to pass sentence on the greatest criminals and to debate and decide the most solemn questions connected with religion. The judges (gods) sat in the open air on seats hewn out of the rock; Athena, the goddess of wisdom, presided.

Their judicial system however, was corrupt; these gods made a mockery of justice. A notable example is the case of a god named Orestes who was charged with the murder of his mother. As the trial progressed with all the Athenian gods and goddesses in attendance, they played politics, offering enormous bribes and making plea-bargains. Finally, Orestes had pulled enough strings to get the majority of the gods on his side and he was found innocent. Dishonesty was the order of the day.

The Stoics and Epicureans had all this knowledge concerning Mars' Hill's being the "Court House" of the gods as well as the unethical trials that the gods had conducted. Paul also had this knowledge. Although the Stoics and Epicureans had little, if any respect for these Athenian gods, they accepted Mars' Hill as the place to discuss matters and make decisions, since Paul's so-called new thing involved religion. One might say that by taking Paul to Mars' Hill, these philosophers were putting Paul on trial. After arriving and seating themselves (on hard rock), they motioned for Paul to speak. What a magnificent case he made for his belief

23—Mars' Hill (foreground) and Acropolis (background). *Courtesy of American School of Classical Studies in Athens, A. Frantz.*

ATHENS   185

24—Paul before Athenian philosophers. *Courtesy of author.*

in the God who made heaven and earth (see illustration 24). His main points were as follows (see Acts 17:18–34 for the context of the Mars' Hill sermon):

First, he called attention to their superstition because whenever mythology and gods (religion) have become a part of one's philosophy, the result is superstition. Because the Greeks did not know the exact number of gods, their superstitious beliefs necessitated an altar to be erected to an unknown god for fear that they might have overlooked a god and offended it. Numerous altars of this nature had been erected throughout the countryside. Paul immediately capitalized on their reasoning and said, "whom therefore ye ignorantly worship, him declare I unto you" (see Acts 17:22–23). He redeemed the time, so to speak, by saying in effect: Once God was unknown to me but I had a head-on collision with Him in the Person of His Son, and now I know who the true God is. Luke probably doesn't record everything Paul said, but we can assume Paul had a field day on this point. It only takes about a minute and forty seconds to read this sermon (Acts 17:22–31), and this is far too short a time for any preacher to preach. We believe Luke only hit the high points.

Second, Paul mentioned that all Grecian temples, the dwelling places for their gods, were not the abode of the God who made heaven and earth (Acts 17:24). How easy it was for Paul to simply turn and point to a temple (possibly the Parthenon [see illustration 25], since it was the largest on the Acropolis) and say that the "God that made [created] the world and all things therein, seeing that he is the Lord of heaven and earth, dwelleth not in temples made with hands" (v. 24). Possibly the Holy Spirit reminded Paul of his having heard Stephen make this statement while he consented to his stoning (Acts 7:48–50). Paul knew that the Greeks in general believed that there was a god who made the world and all things. He knew that the philosophers of this school tolerated a belief that this god could not be confined within temples made by men because this god was the lord or governor of heaven and earth. To be shut up in a temple would make this god less than the place in which it was confined.

Third, Paul brought out in Acts 17:25–28 that humanity, the offspring of God, has a personal relationship with Him, not an impersonal relationship such as in a worship of gold or silver or stone (v. 29). Wherever Paul's eye turned, he saw a succession of statues in every variety and form. Paul's argument here is simply this: If we are the offspring of God, then He cannot be like these images of metal and stone. The parent must resemble his offspring. Since humanity is living and intelligent, then He from whom humanity came must be living and intelligent, for like produces like. Paul was simply showing these philosophers that the object of worship should be more excellent than the worshiper, and humanity, the worshiper, is more excellent than an image made of gold, silver, or stone. In using this argument, Paul reminded the Stoics and Epicureans that some of their own poets had said, "we are also his offspring" (v. 28).

The Importance of Creation

In summarizing the philosophy of both the Stoics and the

25—Parthenon: A building made with hands. *Courtesy of author.*

Epicureans, we see that they recognized the necessity of a religious life but that both were basically atheistic. They tolerated the temples and idols of many gods. They denied the true God, the God of creation. Their belief system tolerated no absolutes; thus there were no rights or wrongs, no truth, no universal laws given by a master designer (even though they were not acquainted with the laws that govern our universe). However, humans have always lived in a law-abiding universe, and there are certain laws that cannot be attributed to other humanity or chance. If the God of creation is Lawgiver, He has the right to make and impose laws. Such a Creator will make laws for the good of His creatures. If such laws are ignored, and the Lawgiver, or Creator, is denied, then one's philosophy will be that man is his own god, controlling his own destiny, and living according to the "lust of the flesh, and the lust of the eyes, and the pride of life" (1 John 2:16)—living according to the world, the flesh, and the devil.

As any Bible believer knows, there are two kinds of people in the world. There are those who believe in God as Creator and those who believe in evolution or humanism. The latter will sneer at the creationist, not only for his or her belief in direct creation, but in his or her proclamation of the Gospel and other biblical truths. When creation was taught in our churches, there was a sense of the presence of God our maker. Creation was not denied in our public schools when the Bible was read, the Ten Commandments were posted, and prayer was offered. Then there was a measure of respect for law and order; for moral laws. But as Darwin's theory of evolution, Marx's philosophy of society (communism), and Freud's psychoanalysis got a foothold in our educational system, the Bible took a back seat. Its laws and morals were questioned, and society went berserk morally, or rather immorally. Human nature, being what it is (Jeremiah 17:9), threw law and order overboard and replaced it with the evolutionists' doctrine of humanism with self taking complete control of the mind. The Bible says "As a man thinketh in his heart [mind], so is he" (Proverbs 22:7). Jesus said, "Out of the heart [mind] proceed evil thoughts, murders, adulteries, fornications, thefts, false witness [lying], blasphemies: These are the things which defile a man" (Matthew 15:19–20).

The outward acts of people's hearts today are evidence of what people will do when Creator-God, and his law and order, are dethroned. Illegal drugs, murder, permissive sex, homosexuality, abortion on demand, divorce, and many other sins, have become the norm in our society. When one does not acknowledge God the Creator, he turns to the creature, and a permissive lifestyle is the result, making humanity no more than so-called advanced animals that live according to animalistic instincts. Humanity becomes a product of chance. There are no laws. There are no absolutes. There is no right or wrong. Humanity is its own god, thinking it can determine its own destiny.

Whether we realize it or not, Darwin's theory of evolution, which eliminates a Creator and absolutes, is no more than ancient pagan, religious and philosophical beliefs. Such beliefs confronted Paul in Athens and throughout the Greco-Roman world. Wherever Paul traveled, he faced two philosophies: Jewish and Greek. Before Jews and Greek proselytes he was determined to know no one save Jesus Christ and Him crucified, using the Old Testament Scriptures of the Jews (Moses and the Prophets), to show that Jesus was Messiah, the Son of God (Acts 9:20; 1 Corinthians 2:2). When the Jews refused to believe, Christ then became a "stumbling block to them" (1 Corinthians 1:23a). Paul would then turn to Greeks who were familiar, to a degree, with the Jews' Scripture (Acts 14:42–49).

With Greeks, however, such as with the pagans in Athens who were totally ignorant of the Word of God, his approach was entirely different. His first concern was to get them to realize that they were not in the world by chance; that all humans were the offspring of the Creator (Acts 17:24–29). Before he could preach the Cross, which was "foolishness" to them (1 Corinthians 1:23b), he had to show that their belief in a form of evolution had made them ignorant of their need for a true God; a God who created them; a God who had authority over them. This was a truth that they sorely needed to know and believe. Therefore, Paul approached first on the basis of creation by the God who made the world and all things therein, the Lord (authority) of heaven and earth (Acts 17:24). These Athenian Greeks did not believe in such a God. They were just as ignorant of Him as multitudes are in our day. One meets with scorn, contempt, and ridicule when witnessing to a humanist today. Truth, absolutes, right and wrong, and law and order are foreign to their thinking. They, like the fool, say in their hearts, "There is *no* God" (Psalm 14:1a). The Cross is as foolish to them as it was to the pagan Greeks in Paul's day. In Acts 14, where the people of Lystra thought that Paul and Barnabas were gods, we note that Paul's first approach to these pagan Gentiles was to present the true God of creation,

"We also are men of like passions with you, and preach unto you that ye should turn from these vanities unto the living God, which made [created] heaven, and earth, and the sea, and all things that are therein" (v. 15). He then proceeded to talk about people who were "walking in their own ways." Although Luke does not elaborate further, knowing Paul, we know that he could not have left without telling them about Christ (vv. 14–18).

In our study of Paul's famous Mars' Hill sermon to the philosophers, in particular, and to Athenians and strangers, in general, we find that his approach to them, totally ignorant as they were of the Jewish Scriptures, was to first familiarize them with the true God of creation (Acts 17:24–30). He also made the point that since we all are God's offspring, having been created by Him, we all have a responsibility to repent, because He has appointed a day of judgment for those who are His offspring (vv. 29–31). Since some believed, notably a chief philosopher, we can be assured that Paul concluded his message with a Gospel presentation.

In our day and age when we face the same problem as did Paul with those pagan Greeks, we too can use the same method to reach those steeped in the unbelief of evolution and humanism. Something must be done to turn the tide. Although the gates of hell shall not destroy the church, that which gave the world absolutes, a knowledge of right and wrong, law and order, authority, and so forth, is being eroded and replaced by error. As long as the philosophy in America is such that people regard the preaching of the Cross foolishness, it is high time we wake up to some biblical methods and try to stem the tide of humanism. It will work with some if we try, just as it did for Paul.

Every philosopher on Mars' Hill must have felt the power of Paul's reasoning, for there is no record that they argued against it. They were shown that ignorance of the living God is no excuse because He has revealed Himself in the person of His Son, Jesus Christ and has appointed a day in which He will judge all men. In view of Mars' Hill's being the place of decision or judgment, it was a fitting place for Paul to conclude his sermon with an appeal to make a decision to repent and believe the Gospel, and then face the Judge who would judge in righteousness and justice (Acts 17:31). These philosophers knew well of the corrupt judgment of unrighteous gods at many of the trials at Mars' Hill. Paul was trying to get them to see that all men must stand alone before the God of heaven and earth, and when they do there will be no bribery, no politicking, no plea bargaining. In God's court house there will be a righteous judgment based on what God's offspring has done with His Son.

Paul's sermon (reasoning) convinced some that there is a living, intelligent God; that there is a resurrection; that repentance and belief must take place (cf. Acts 17:30 with Hebrews 9:27). Paul's argument doomed the Athenian gods. Mythology said the gods were the judges; they made decisions even though most of them were not made in the name of justice. In reality, the Athenian gods were on trial and it was Paul's God who judged them. How ironic it was that Paul's defense of the Gospel in Athens took place on Mars' Hill, the site of the mythological court of the Athenian gods.

What was the result of Paul's sermon to the Epicureans and Stoics? "When they heard of the resurrection of the dead [Jesus], some mocked: and others said, We will hear thee again of this matter" (Acts 17:32). The moment Paul mentioned Christ's resurrection the philosophers interrupted him, some rudely. They mocked; literally they jeered, laughed him to scorn, ridiculed him, and "lipped" (all talked at once). The doctrine of the resurrection was to them ridiculous, just as the notion of equal religious rights with the Gentiles was offensive and intolerable to the Jews. Others of those who were present on Mars' Hill were more courteous, telling Paul that they would hear him again on the matter. As the old saying goes, "You win some, you lose some." God does not force anyone to believe. Opportunity is given to exercise faith, but a person can say no. Each sermon is adapted to win and rebuke. A true sermon will make one mad, sad, or glad. God's Word always accomplishes its purpose (Isaiah 55:6–11). The majority of these philosophers were not impressed with Paul's sermon. The same sun that melts ice will harden clay—the Word of God either softens or hardens. "Howbeit, certain men clave unto him [Paul], and believed: among the which was Dionysius the Areopagite, and a woman named Damaris, and others with them" (Acts 17:34). In spite of the sneering and overwhelming unbelief, some did believe. Before Paul was taken to this hill, he had been preaching Jesus and the resurrection, and though his discourse was interrupted, this was the last impression he left on the minds of these philosophers. The impression was not so much to merely excite or gratify their intellectual curiosity but to startle them and make them search their consciences.

Speaking of those who were saved and named by Paul, we know nothing of Damaris. Considering the obscurity of Greek women, the mention of her name in connection with these well-known philosophers is remarkable. Dionysius, however, was a mighty, noble individual believing on Christ. There can be no doubt that Dionysius the Areopagite was one of the judges of this great court. No person was a judge of the Areopagus who had not borne the office of *archon*, or chief governor of the city, and none bore the office of judge in this court who was not of the highest reputation among the people for his intelligence and exemplary conduct. Paul said that not many wise, mighty, or noble men are called (1 Corinthians 1:26). Queen Victoria of England, who was a Christian, thanked the Lord for the letter "M" in *many*, otherwise the verse would read "not any . . . are called." One of the reasons God saved Dionysius was to show that the simplicity of the Gospel is His method of saving those who will believe (1 Corinthians 1:24–29). In this wise man's case, he was not confounded but enlightened.

It should be pointed out that in most cases when philosophers gathered on Mars' Hill to discuss and judge matters, many of the more ignorant of the population went along to listen. Paul's audience was not limited to just the philosophers. It is likely that many of these so-called ignorant people also believed because Paul said, "and others with them" (Acts 17:34). Those on Mars' Hill who left in unbelief, were without excuse. The Seed, the Word of God, had been planted in their hearts.

In spite of the fact that there were some who did not believe and receive Paul's message, his speech on the Areopagus is an enduring monument of the first victory of Christianity over paganism per se. Other individuals who were pagans had been won to Christ, but this was Paul's first encounter with those of the headquarters of philosophy and pagan religion, and some of them saw and accepted truth as found in Jesus Christ. Although Paul met with a measure of success in this confrontation, there is no record that he established a church in Athens or that he ever wrote a letter to these people.

On Paul's third missionary journey he did go back to Greece, but there is no mention that he ever saw the Athenian believers again, though we may assume that he did (see Acts 20:2–3). He had been a faithful steward in fulfilling his calling, but it is evident that the Gospel made little progress in this city of pagan religion.

CORINTH Paul was all alone in Athens; his co-workers were elsewhere and, being human, we can be assured he desired help from fellow believers. Loneliness and little success contribute to discouragement, but Paul forged ahead and set his sights on Corinth (Acts 18:1–18). We do not know if he made the seventy-two-mile westward trip by land or by sea (v. 1).

Corinth was a flourishing city under the Greeks but had been destroyed by the Romans in 146 B.C. Julius Caesar rebuilt it as a Roman colony in 46 B.C., and it grew to become the capital of the province of Achaia. It had become a wealthy city by Paul's day with a population of approximately seven hundred thousand. It was located on the narrow isthmus between the Aegean and Adriatic Seas (see map 3, p. 446). In Paul's day, smaller ships were dragged on logs across the isthmus to avoid dangerous sailing around the southern tip of Greece. The idea of cutting a canal through the narrow neck of the isthmus had been thought of in classical times of the Greek empire and was seriously investigated by several Roman emperors, Nero in particular. After centuries of consideration, a canal was finally cut about four miles through solid rock in the nineteenth century, shortening the voyage around Greece by about two hundred miles.

Corinth was given to much luxury and immorality. To live like a Corinthian was to live recklessly in sin and debauchery. Living like a Corinthian meant to get drunk, stay drunk, and practice fornication. This city was more corrupt, more vulgar, and more sensual than Athens. The Grecians would often build temples to their deities on the highest hill or mountain near their city, and on the high mountain overlooking Corinth was a temple to Aphrodite, the goddess of lust and love (see illustration 26). A thousand prostitute priestesses were ready at a moment's notice to serve any men who desired to buy their services. The city was filled with taverns and the drunkards they produced. There was also a large temple to Apollo, the god of youth, manly beauty, music, and song. Marble statues of nude males were placed throughout his temple.

Soon after Paul's arrival in this city, he met Aquila and Priscilla and took up lodging with them (Acts 18:2–3). Aquila and his wife had formerly lived in Rome, but because Jews were continually revolting, Claudius Caesar (see illustration 27) expelled them. We are not told how Paul met this couple. Oftentimes strangers who engage in the same trade gravitate toward one another. Since all were tent makers, it is easy to understand how they met (v. 3).

26—Aphrodite's Mountain and Gallio's Bema in foreground. *Courtesy of author.*

We do not know if this couple had been converted to Christianity when they first met Paul, but having been drawn together because of their trade and their religion, it is quite possible that they became Christians some time during the year and a half that Paul lodged with them (v. 11). In their close association with Paul they no doubt knew well how Old Testament prophecy relating to Christ and His resurrection had been fulfilled. Later, they were able to help Apollos see the "full" Gospel (complete New Testament truth about Christ) just as Paul had helped them (Acts 18:24–28).

27—Emperor Claudius, A.D. 41–54. *Courtesy of the American Numismatic Society, New York City.*

Following his usual custom when entering a new city, Paul immediately went to the synagogue on the Sabbath and "persuaded" both Jews and Greeks (Acts 18:4). In the meantime Silas and Timothy arrived in

Corinth from Macedonia to rejoin Paul (cf. v. 5a with 1 Thessalonians 3:1–2). Whatever they reported to him must have encouraged him to testify boldly to the Jews (v. 5b). However, the Jews rebelled and Paul discharged his responsibility to preach to them and turned to the Gentiles (v. 6) even though in Romans 1:14 Paul stated that he was debtor to all men. It is the obligation of all believers to witness to those without Christ. We cannot be like the one of whom the Psalmist said: "I looked on my right hand, and beheld, but there was no man that would know me: refuge failed me; no man cared for my soul" (142:4). Ezekiel brought out the truth that we must warn unbelievers; we cannot make them believe, but we *must* declare the Good News of salvation to them. If we do not, their blood is on our hands; if we do, then their blood is on their hands (Ezekiel 3:17–19). In Corinth Paul was forced to tell these synagogue Jews that since he had made known to them the truth of their Scriptures concerning Christ they were responsible for their refusal to believe—their blood was on their own head (hands), thus clearing Paul of his indebtedness to them.

Paul stalked out of the synagogue and entered a house adjacent to the synagogue that was owned by a God-fearing man named Justus (Acts 18:7). Although he had read the riot act, so to speak, to the Jews (v. 6), he must have sensed the Spirit's working among some of them. This could be the reason he stayed in the vicinity of the synagogue—to take advantage of the situation if any Jews wanted to discuss further the Scriptures concerning Messiah. Paul's decision paid off, and Crispus, the chief ruler of the synagogue, believed in the Lord with all his house (v. 8a). The chief ruler of the synagogue had authority. It was his responsibility to preside in all the assemblies, interpret the law, decide concerning things lawful and unlawful, punish the unmanageable, excommunicate the rebellious, solemnize marriages, and grant divorces. His conversion must have shocked and infuriated the Jews, especially when he publicly accepted Christian baptism. Luke tells us that many Corinthians believed and were also baptized (v. 8b).

Baptism was not a problem in New Testament days. It was commonly understood that when one believed on Christ, following the Lord in baptism was not only an act of obedience but also a renunciation of one's former religion and a vow to the Lord that one's life would exemplify Christ as he or she walked in newness of life. After all, this is what Christ had taught in the

Great Commission (Matthew 28:19–20). There was no question as to how it was done. Whenever water is mentioned in connection with baptism, the baptizer and the one being baptized always went *down* into the water and came *up out of* the water. The act was always performed where there was *much* water (Mark 1:9–10; John 3:23; Acts 8:35–39).

Paul and Baptism

The big argument among many Christians today is that it is not necessary to be baptized since it is not necessary for salvation. This is true, but baptism is necessary for obedience to Christ and is the answer of a good conscience (1 Peter 3:21). The first thing done on the Day of Pentecost after three thousand souls were saved was that these people were baptized. The Scripture seems to be so plain in the matter that baptism follows salvation, yet the "nonbaptism" and the "baptism is not important" groups will take some verses out of context to support their views. Stephanas and his family were Paul's first converts in Corinth (1 Corinthians 16:15), though many others believed, including Crispus and Gaius. Paul baptized only Crispus, Gaius, Stephanas and his household. We do not know how many were in Stephanas' household, which included not only his believing family but his believing servants as well (1 Corinthians 1:14, 16). Paul could have baptized as many as ten or twelve. After Paul said who he had baptized, he went on to say that "Christ sent me not to baptize, but to preach the Gospel . . ." (v. 17). On the basis of these verses, the "nonimportant, no-baptism" adherents use the following verses to rule out baptism as a part of church order today (they still, however, observe the Lord's Supper).

First, they say baptism is not important because Paul said that, while in Corinth, he had only baptized a few (1 Corinthians 1:14, 16). As previously mentioned, the figure could actually have been as many as ten or twelve.

Second, they say that no mention of baptism is made while Paul and Barnabas were on their first missionary journey, hence the practice of baptism is not relevant. Just because baptism is not mentioned every time someone (or many) believed does not mean that baptism did not take place. Luke, as we have noticed throughout our study of Paul's life, did not mention many things. We are justified in saying that Paul did such and such on the basis of what he did elsewhere. Paul did not preach one thing and practice another. We believe Paul stuck to Christ's Great–Commission pattern everywhere he went, and he, or his helpers, baptized believers in obedience to the Lord whether Scripture mentions it or not.

Third, they say that baptism is not important because Paul himself said, "Christ sent me not to baptize, but to preach the Gospel" (1 Corinthians 1:17). Once we understand the situation in the Corinthian church, we will see why Paul made such a statement, and once we see the clear meaning of his statement, there will be, no doubt, the admission that baptism is as important an ordinance as Communion, that it is a *must* in one's Christian experience.

The church at Corinth was carnal. These believers, at the time Paul wrote this epistle to them, were babes in Christ of their own choosing. They had not grown in grace as they should have. There were contentions (quarrels and strife) among them, as well as personality conflicts. There were at least four factions: the followers of Paul, the followers of Apollos, the followers of Cephas, and the holier-than-thou followers of Christ. They all bragged about who baptized whom. Paul said to them, "Is Christ divided? Was Paul [or Apollos or Cephas] crucified for you? Or were you baptized in the name of Paul [or Apollos or Cephas]?" (1 Corinthians 1:13). Paul sought to help the Corinthians see that who baptized whom was not important; reminding them that he had only baptized a few. Had he baptized more, the division, no doubt, would have been greater. Paul was not in any way minimizing baptism; he was trying to get these church members to see that it was not important who did the baptizing, but that it was important to be baptized as a confession of faith in Jesus Christ. Just because Paul did not remember everyone he had baptized (v. 16b), is beside the point. He certainly did not want everyone he baptized going around bragging that he had done so. When Paul said that Christ had not sent him to baptize, but to preach the Gospel, the Greek text, is saying: Christ sent me not to be known as a baptizer [possibly like John the Baptizer], but to be known as a preaching minister of the Gospel. The implication is that baptism is not essential to salvation; preaching the Gospel is: "How shall they believe in him of whom they have not heard? and how shall they hear without a preacher? And how shall they preach [the Gospel], except they be sent?" (see Romans 10:13–17).

It must be understood that if Paul had not been sent to baptize, he baptized some without a commission, but since he had been sent, he was sent also to baptize, or see to it that new converts were baptized. He discharged his duty aright. We must remember that the main function of the apostles in preaching was to pray and study the Word of God, and let others do other tasks (Acts 6:4). While Paul baptized some, he saw to it that his helpers, in this case Timothy and Silas, baptized the other many Corinthians who believed (Acts 18:8a).

After the euphoria of seeing the salvation and baptism of many Corinthians, Paul apparently was very discouraged by the Jews' opposition. The word *opposed* in verse 6 means that the Jews "systematically" opposed him, putting themselves in warlike order against him. Paul's thorn had been activated again, this time in Corinth.

These Jews, having made a covenant with unbelief, began to blaspheme when pressed to believe in Christ as Messiah. They blasphemed not so much against Paul as against God (as the children of Israel did against Moses, Exodus 16:2, 8). Paul was not only discouraged but probably also feared for his life and could have been seriously considering leaving Corinth. In the midst of Satan's buffeting, suddenly Christ made his *third* appearance to Paul (Acts 18:9–11). In 1 Corinthians 2:3 we find recorded that Paul said, "I was with you in weakness and in fear, and in much trembling." Christ's comfort and assurance convinced Paul that no matter what happened, with Christ's presence he could not be stopped. He knew that one plus God make a majority; that if God be for him, who could be against him? (see Romans 8:31). God, who knows the end from the beginning, knew that there were many Corinthians who were sick of their sin and were ripe for salvation. God's telling Paul there were many in the city who would believe encouraged him to speak boldly. He did not hold back in proclaiming the Gospel. This vision so encouraged Paul that he remained in this great city for a year and a half (vv. 9–11).

Paul before Gallio

During the eighteen months Paul was in Corinth (Acts 18:12–17), opposition from the Jews intensified. Charges of insurrection were made against Paul before Gallio, the deputy of the province of Achaia where Corinth was located. (An inscription has been found at Delphi that mentions the emperor Claudius and Gallio, proconsul, or Deputy of Achaia [see illustration 28]. Gallio's seat of government was in Corinth in A.D. 51–53. This record gives evidence of Paul's visit to Corinth during

Gallio's tenure.) Judaism was a licensed religion under the Romans, and Paul, according to these Corinthian Jews, was persuading men to worship God contrary to their law (religion, Acts 18:13). The Jews took Paul to Gallio's courthouse—*bema* (judgment seat) to make these charges. In spite of the fact that the Jews' religion was licensed, they had no power, under Roman law, to punish Paul. If they had, they, no doubt, would have murdered Paul. Luke simply says that the Jews charged Paul with persuading people to worship God contrary to the law. If we read between the lines, we see that since the Jews had Roman permission (or license) to worship their God in their own way and that the Roman worship was also licensed or established by law, they probably intended to accuse Paul of acting contrary to both laws. They intended to accuse him of not being a Jew because he did not admit that circumcision was necessary in his unlicensed religion, of not being a Gentile because he preached against the worship of gods, of being an unlicensed religionist setting up a worship of his own in opposition to theirs and Rome's, and of persuading many people to follow him.

As Paul was about to defend himself, Gallio, who saw through

28—Gallio's inscription. *Courtesy of Ecolé Francaise D'Athens.*

the hypocrisy of the Jews and the selfish desire on their part for him to side with them, let it be known in no uncertain terms that their accusation had nothing to do with Roman law pertaining to matters of wrong, wicked lewdness, destructive mischief, lawlessness, or a crime against society or the state. He let them know his opinion was based on *their* religious law and threw the case out of court. The Jews were so hated by these Greeks in Corinth that when court was adjourned the Greeks beat Sosthenes, the chief ruler of the synagogue, who had replaced Crispus when he was saved and the perpetrator of the allegations against Paul. Sosthenes no doubt brought these charges in reprisal because Paul had led the former ruler, Crispus, to the Lord. When Paul later wrote to the Corinthians, he mentioned a fellow helper named Sosthenes (1 Corinthians 1:1). If this is the same Sosthenes who was beaten by the Greeks after Paul's trial before Gallio's *bema*, it could be that God engineered the beating to bring him to his knees and confess his need of Christ.

The Haircut Vow

Before leaving the province of Achaia, Paul, Priscilla, and Aquila visited Cenchrea, a few miles southeast of Corinth. During this brief visit, and probably while waiting for a ship to sail for Ephesus, mention is made of Paul's keeping a vow (Acts 18:18).

According to Deuteronomy 23:21–23, if a person made a vow, it was considered sacred and binding, and it was sinful to break it. If no vow were made, there was, of course, no guilt involved. The vow mentioned in Acts 18:18 evidently was part of a "Nazarite vow" because it involved a haircut. Looking at Numbers 6:1–23, we notice that mention is made of a Nazarite vow. A Nazarite was known for his consecration, and during his days of separation (or vow) he drank no wine nor strong drink, no razor was applied to his head, and he touched no dead body. The vow was to continue for a certain season, at least long enough to grow a full head of hair. Then at a proper time, the hair was shorn and burned in the fire beneath the sacrifice of the peace offering (Numbers 6:17–21).

The question is raised when reading Acts 18:18: Whose hair was cut? Just about everyone has been taught that it was Paul's. As we examine the verse, we notice the order of names that are given before mention is made of the vow and the haircut. Paul's name is first, Priscilla's is second, and Aquila's is last. It would appear from the grammatical structure of the verse that the last person named, Aquila, was the one who had the haircut. This is the only time that Luke mentions Priscilla before Aquila. In Acts 18:2 and 26, Aquila precedes Priscilla. No mention is made in the Scripture or in Jewish historical writings that Pharisees were Nazarites; Paul would be eliminated. Aquila was a Jew. He was a master of Scripture and the "way of the Lord" (Acts 18:24–26). Before conversion, any number of Jewish laws and traditions could have been a part of his life. Spending eighteen months with Paul in Corinth could have shown Aquila that he needed to sever all connections with any Old Testament vows, and having his head shorn in Cenchrea would have been a wonderful testimony as to his convictions that he was "free from the law."

If however, the correct interpretation of this verse means that Paul himself had made a vow and that his head was shorn, it is really nothing that would have violated his Christian testimony. A vow of consecration is often made by Christians today, especially in revival and evangelistic meetings. If the act of consecration is real, change is seen in the life of the believer, not in some outward sign like the Nazarite haircut. If Paul did make a Nazarite vow that culminated in a haircut, it was because he was "becoming all things to all men, without compromising his faith, that he might win some to Christ." He could also have done it as a way to open a door to speak to Jews. In this case, we are at liberty to take our pick between Paul and Aquila. (We will note later [see chapter 9] Paul's involvement in a Jewish vow in connection with his arrest in Jerusalem [Acts 21:12–26].) After the vow was performed in Cenchrea, Paul, Aquila, and Priscilla sailed to Ephesus. Paul met with the Jews briefly and set sail for Antioch, leaving his friends behind (Acts 18:18–22).

Apollos, Aquila, and Priscilla

After Paul left Ephesus, Apollos arrived. We are not as familiar with Apollos as we are with the others that Paul mentioned. Apollos was, no doubt, a traveling Jewish merchant from Alexandria, Egypt (Acts 18:24–28). He was an eloquent man, able to communicate in classical Greek as well as Hellenistic and the vernacular (*koine*) Greek. He was well versed in the Old Testament Scriptures, which suggests that he was not only a master of the text, but had the ability to present it in an understandable way. The fact that Apollos had a knowledge of "John's baptism" and had been "instructed in the way," implies that much of the message of Christianity had reached Alexandria by A.D. 50.

Although his knowledge was limited, Apollos was familiar with John's being the forerunner of Christ, of his baptism in reference to a confession of sins, of his message of the One coming after him who was mightier than he, and of the fact that John's message was that all would believe in this mighty One, namely Jesus Christ (Mark 1:1–8; John 1:29; Acts 19:4). Apollos was an "active soul-winning Christian," as we would say. He, like Paul, upon arrival in a city, would head straight for the synagogue and boldly and accurately begin to declare his knowledge of the Scriptures concerning Christ. Aquila and Priscilla listened carefully to his message. They were, no doubt, awestruck with his eloquence but detected that he wasn't going far enough—something was missing because he knew "only the baptism of John" (Acts 18:25b).

Aquila and Priscilla faced a dilemma. With the characteristics that Apollo possessed, should they tell him that he was not preaching the full Gospel? Did they have the nerve to tell a learned man that he was preaching only half the truth? It was evident to Aquila and Priscilla that Apollos knew nothing of the finished work of Calvary or of what happened on the Day of Pentecost. Aquila and Priscilla followed the leading of the Holy Spirit, called Apollos aside, and "instructed him in the way of God more perfectly [to its fullest]" (Acts 18:26). They explained to him that God had fulfilled John's prophecy of Christ's coming to be the Lamb of God to take away the sin of the world, that Christ had already accomplished that work at Calvary by His death for our sins, and that He had been raised from the grave for our justification (John 1:29; Romans 4:25). Although Apollos was a great and mighty man, he was humble enough to listen to other saints. He was approachable, teachable, and responsive to instruction from an average church member. Apollos desired to learn the truth, to grow in grace and the knowledge of His Savior; hence he was willing to listen to two meek servants of the Lord who knew something he did not. Upon being brought up to date concerning Christ's fulfillment of Old Testament prophecies concerning His coming as Messiah, Apollos was able to "mightily convince the Jews, . . . publicly, showing by the Scriptures that Jesus was Christ" (Acts 18:28).

When Apollos finished his business in Ephesus, he left for Corinth. So impressed were Aquila and Priscilla and the brethren with Apollos that they gave him a letter of recommendation to the church at Corinth—to the disciples of the church, rather than to the synagogue (Acts 18:27). Upon arrival in Corinth, many members were overwhelmed with his eloquence and gifts, and soon they attached themselves to him as his disciples. These Apollonian disciples were most likely the ones who criticized Paul for his "contemptible speech" (2 Corinthians 10:10), which prompted others to defend Paul, the one who had led them to Christ and who was the founder of their church. Also in Corinth were those who knew Cephas, or the apostle Peter. Paul had made mention of other apostles, including Cephas, who took their wives with them as they traveled about preaching the Gospel (1 Corinthians 9:5). We have no record that Peter ever visited Corinth but believers there knew enough about him for some to claim him as their leader. The disciples of Peter probably said that they were "of him" because he had worked and walked personally with Christ. Yet another faction in Corinth who believed that "Christian liberty" gave them license to do "all lawful things." They said they were followers of Christ. Paul had to remind each contentious group that each was wrong; their motives were not compatible with their oneness in Christ. To those who said they were of Christ and exercised a new freedom, Paul reminded them that, although many things were lawful, all things were not necessary because they did not edify (1 Corinthians 10:21–31). To others he called attention to the fact that no matter who expounded the Scriptures to them, Christ was not divided and that only God could give an increase (1 Corinthians 1:11–13; 3:1–8).

PAUL'S FIRST EPISTLE TO THE CORINTHIANS   Paul founded the church at Corinth on his second missionary journey about A.D. 50 or 51 (Acts 18:1–18). Evidently the first letter he wrote to them was lost (1 Corinthians 5:9). The epistle that we call 1 Corinthians, was written from Ephesus, probably at the end of his first visit there, A.D. 55 or 56. Due to their background, the "saints" at Corinth (1:2) found it difficult to become dedicated Christians, and for this reason they were classified as "babes in Christ" (3:2). Paul had received disturbing reports about their moral laxity from Timothy; hence this letter to them, rebuking them for their schisms (1:11–17; 3:1–8); their regard for man's wisdom and Greek philosophy (1:18–31; 3:18–23); their permitting incest to go unchecked (5:1–8); their lack of seriousness regarding separation from the world, the flesh, and the devil (3:9–17; 6:9–20. See also 2 Corinthians 6:14–18); their going to court against each other before heathen magistrates (6:1–8); their views on marriage and divorce and the breakdown of homes (ch. 7); their continuing to follow idolatrous practices (8:1–13); their not trusting his apostleship and their lack of support in supplying the need of God's servants (9:1–18); their getting drunk at the Lord's Table (11:2–33); their lack of love for and their need to love one another (ch. 13); their misuse of spiritual gifts (ch. 14); their misunderstanding of the importance of the resurrection of Christ (15:12–20); and their lack of consideration for the poor (16:1–2).

Although Paul turns from these rebukes to encouragement in 1 Corinthians 16:13–16, these admonitions were necessary for these weak Christians who seemed to care little about their deviating from the great truths preached to them by Paul during his stay with them. Sad to say, however, these problems continued in the church. As late as A.D. 95, Clement of Rome wrote to the Corinthians and cited Paul's epistle regarding their situation, especially the factions among them.

On several occasions, Paul used Old Testament Scripture to fortify truths that the Corinthians needed to know, such as in the chart on the next page. Paul portrayed Christ to the Corinthians as

the "Lord of Glory" (2:8),

the "Only Foundation" (3:11),

the "Sacrificial Lamb" (5:7),

the "Object of our Faith" (15:12–20),

the "Conqueror of Death" (15:24–26), and

the "Epitome of Love" (13:4–8a).

First John 4:8b tells us that "God is love." John also tells us that God and Christ are one (John 17:21). Since God and Christ are one, and God is love, then both God and Christ are "Love." Substituting the word "Charity" or "Love" for Christ, we note in 1 Corinthians 13:4–8b that Christ suffers long (v. 4a); is kind (v. 4b); envies not (v. 4c); vaunts not Himself, is not boastful, is not puffed up or conceited (v. 4d); does not misbehave (v. 5a); seeks not His own, is not selfish (v. 5b); is not easily provoked,opened not His mouth (cf. v. 5c with Mark 16:60–62); thinks no evil (v. 5d); rejoices not in iniquity (v. 6a); rejoices in truth (v.6b); bears all things (cf. v. 7a with Matthew 11:28–30);

PAUL'S USE OF OLD TESTAMENT IN 1 CORINTHIANS

Subject	1 Corinthians	Old Testament
Man's wisdom being brought to naught	1:19	Isaiah 29:14
Glorying in the Lord	1:31	Jeremiah 9:24
Truth revealed by the Spirit	2:9–10	Isaiah 64:4
Possessing the mind of Christ	2:16	Isaiah 40:13
Foolishness and the wisdom of the world	3:19	Job 5:13
God's omniscience	3:20	Psalm 94:11
The mystical union in marriage	6:16	Genesis 2:24
God's supplying all needs	9:9	Deuteronomy 15:4 (cf. Matthew 6:33)
Profiting by Israel's wilderness experience	10:7, 11	Exodus 32:6
God, the Possessor of all things	10:26	Psalm 24:1
The gift of prophecy	14:21	Isaiah 28:11–12
The first Adam	14:45	Genesis 2:7
Death swallowed up in victory	15:54	Job 14:14; 19:25–27
Christ's reign till His enemies are subdued	15:25	Psalm 110:1
All things under His feet	15:27	Psalm 8:6
Reveling, for tomorrow we die	15:32	Isaiah 22:13
O death, where is thy sting?	15:55	Hosea 13:14

believes (knows) all things (cf. v. 7b with John 1:1–2; 2:24 –25); hopes all things (v. 7c); endures all things (cf. v. 7d with Hebrews 12:2); and never fails (cf. 8a with His complying with His Father's will in Luke 2:48; Hebrews 10:5–12).

In seeking to have the Corinthians understand the meaning of love, Paul not only used the so-called love chapter (chapter 13) to show that God and Christ are love but also to show what love does that they might realize that the believer and Christ are "one" (John 17:20–23). Being one in Him (as He is, so are we, 1 John 4:17b), we too are love, and the above outline must be applied to the believer as well. Had the Corinthians applied this love to themselves, there would have been no need for all the rebukes found in this epistle.

PAUL'S SECOND EPISTLE TO THE CORINTHIANS Paul was in Ephesus when he wrote his first epistle to the Corinthians. He expected Timothy to visit Corinth and return with a report on conditions of the church (1 Corinthians 16:10–11). The report Timothy apparently brought back to him told of the opposition that had developed against Paul. Luke does not record Paul's making a third trip to Corinth but it can be inferred from 2 Corinthians 12:14 and 13:1–2 that he did. Because he retraced his steps to many places he preached, Paul was in Macedonia when he wrote this letter about A.D. 58. His heart was broken when he learned of developments in the church. Little had been done to correct wrongs and forsake sins (2:4). With a heavy heart he wrote this sorrowful letter to (1) discipline the leader of opposition (2:1–11; 7:8); (2) vindicate his apostleship, answering charges made against him (1:1a; 11:5); (3) remind them of the subtlety of Satan and his ministers appearing in their midst as angels of light and ministers of righteousness (11:13–15); (4) remind them of his sufferings in the defense of the Gospel (11:23–33); (5) remind them to be considerate of others in giving to their support, to follow the example set by those in Thessalonica (8:1–15; Paul appears to be saying here that when you are defeated and living in sin, look to the Lord and to someone in whom the strength and grace of God are working, then give yourselves to the Lord and open your pocketbooks to help others); (6) express his joy for their salvation even though there needed to be many changes in their lives (8:16–18).

A final note of interest about this epistle is Paul's desire that those at Corinth realize that someday they would have to face

God and give account to Him for what they had or hadn't done as believers. During his first missionary journey there, Paul appeared before Gallio's judgment seat to face charges brought against him by the Jews (Acts 18:12–17). To drive home the truth that these Corinthians (and all believers) are answerable to God for everything they do, "especially their loose living," he reminded them that one day they would stand before the *bema*, and give account for their behavior (5:10). In today's vernacular, Paul would likely have said: Not everyone will have to appear before an earthly judge like I did before Gallio, but *every* believer, including the Corinthian saints, will have to appear before the judgment seat of Christ that he may receive the things done in his body, according to *everything* he ever did since he was saved, whether good or bad.

Although most Corinthian believers were Gentiles, Paul did refer to some Old Testament passages in this epistle:

PAUL'S USE OF OLD TESTAMENT IN 2 CORINTHIANS		
Subject	**2 Corinthians**	**Old Testament**
A veil over Moses' face	3:13	Exodus 34:33
Spirit of faith	4:13	Psalm 116:10
Now is the day of salvation	6:2	Isaiah 49:8
God's indwelling the believer	6:16	Leviticus 26:11–12
Separation from the unclean thing	6:17	Isaiah 52:11
God a Father	6:18	Jeremiah 31:1, 9
God's abundantly supplying our need	8:15	Exodus 16:18
God's care for the poor	9:9	Psalm 112:9
Glorying in the Lord	10:17	Jeremiah 9:24
Truth established by two witnesses	13:1	Deuteronomy 17:6

Paul portrays Christ in this epistle as

our sufficiency (3:5),

the image of God (4:4),

the righteousness of God (5:21), and

the strength in our weakness (12:9a).

EPHESUS: Upon completion of his missionary visit in
A BRIEF VISIT   Corinth, Paul set sail with Aquila and Priscilla
for Syria (Antioch, Acts 18:18). After crossing the Aegean Sea he
landed on the western shore of Asia Minor at Ephesus (Acts
18:21), a distance of 265 miles. Paul's stay in Ephesus was very
short, just one Sabbath, as he visited the synagogue to reason
with the Jews. He made a great impression on these Jews, and
they desired that he stay with them longer, but Paul was in a
hurry to get to Jerusalem to keep a feast (possibly either Pentecost
or Passover). He promised these Jews that, Lord willing, he would
return. Leaving Aquila and Priscilla he set sail from Ephesus to
Caesarea, a distance of 650 miles (vv. 18–21). We have already
discussed the encounter of Apollos with Aquila and Priscilla in
the outline of the first epistle to the Corinthians (see p. 201 ff.).

JERUSALEM: Paul landed at Caesarea and went up to the
A FOURTH VISIT   church. Here Luke is referring to his going
to Jerusalem, although he does not say in so many words (Acts
18:22). Geographically, Jerusalem is southeast of Caesarea and is
about 2,500 feet above sea level. Since Jerusalem is the capital
city of all Jewry and the location of the temple, this city is always
referred to as being *up*. The expression *went up* is used seventeen
times in the New Testament in reference to Jerusalem (e.g.,
Matthew 20:17–18; Luke 2:42; John 5:1; Galatians 1:17–18). The
expression about Paul, and his having gone up, is the same. Often
the expression *went down* from Jerusalem is used, even if one were
headed north or northeast or northwest (Mark 3:7–8, 22; Acts
15:7). This is Paul's *fourth* visit to Jerusalem after his conversion,
but Luke does not give us any details as to what Paul did in
Jerusalem on this visit, except that he saluted or paid his respects
to the church and then journeyed to Antioch in Syria. From
Caesarea to Jerusalem it was 70 miles and from Jerusalem to
Antioch it was 325 miles (see map 3, p. 446). In leaving Jerusalem
for Antioch, Paul went north, but he went down from Jerusalem.

Upon arrival in Antioch, he completed his second missionary journey (Acts 18:22–23). The length of his stay in Antioch this time is unknown. He had spent about three years on this second missionary trip and had traveled approximately 2,925 miles on land and on sea.

RESULTS OF THE SECOND MISSIONARY JOURNEY

1. He fortified the churches that he and Barnabas had established on their first missionary journey throughout Galatia, delivering letters of the Jerusalem Council's decision that circumcision was not essential for salvation (Acts 15:22–27).

2. Paul received the Macedonian call and led the first European to the Lord (Acts 16:10–15).

3. The church at Philippi was founded (Acts 16:14–40).

4. The church at Thessalonica was established (Acts 17:1–9).

5. At Berea, he found a different breed of Jews; those who searched the Scriptures daily to check out the fulfillment of messianic prophecies (Acts 17:10–14).

6. Paul gave a sermon on Mars' Hill (Acts 17:22–34).

7. Only a few were saved in Athens and no church was established there (Acts 17:15–34).

8. The church at Corinth was established (Acts 18:1–18).

9. Aquila, Priscilla, and Apollos entered the Lord's service (Acts 18:2, 24–28).

10. As usual, Paul's thorn in the flesh was very active on this second journey, especially in Thessalonica and Berea. He also met some drastic Gentile opposition and persecution in Philippi, but it resulted in the salvation of the Philippian jailer and his family (Acts 16:22–34).

TEST YOURSELF ON CHAPTER SEVEN

1. What was the approximate date of Paul's second missionary journey?

2. Who was Paul's new missionary partner?

3. Why did Paul go through Galatia again?

4. What was a possible reason for Paul's return to Lystra?

5. Who joined Paul and Silas at Lystra?

6. What was his background?

7. Why did Paul accept him as his partner?

8. Why was Timothy circumcised but Titus was not?

9. Describe the idols of Galatia.

10. After Paul had delivered the letters of the Jerusalem Council, where did he want to go?

11. What happened in Troas?

12. Where did Paul go after leaving Troas?

13. What is a *colonia*? Describe Philippi.

14. Describe the name that the Greeks gave to those who were not Greeks.

15. Describe the name that the Romans gave to those who were not Roman citizens.

16. What is a *proseucha*?

17. Who was the first European convert?

18. In retrospect, why do you believe that God did not permit Paul to go into Asia and Bithynia?

19. Describe what type of girl Paul dealt with in Philippi.

20. What was Paul's fourth miracle?

21. Why were Paul and Silas imprisoned?

22. Describe their prison.

23. What testimony did Paul and Silas give in prison?

24. What disrupted their testimony and what happened to the jail?

25. What course of action did the jailer plan to take?

26. What was the result of Paul's imprisonment?

27. What was Paul's answer to the jailer?

28. How many were saved as a result of Paul's imprisonment?

29. How can a person be saved?

30. How did the jailer show his appreciation to Paul and Silas?

31. What did Paul perform as a result of their salvation?

32. What Scriptural proof do we have that believers were baptized after they were saved?

33. List the changes that took place in the jailer and his family.

34. What was the reaction of the magistrates to Paul's release from prison?

35. Give a brief outline summary of Paul's letter to the Philippians.

36. Where did Paul and Silas go and what did they do before leaving Philippi?

37. Describe Thessalonica.

38. How long did Paul reason with the Jews in Thessalonica?

39. In your opinion, how long do you believe Paul stayed in Thessalonica?

40. To whom did Paul witness after leaving the Jews? Describe these people.

41. List the truths Paul preached to these people.

42. What did Paul receive from the Philippians while in Thessalonica?

43. How did Paul support himself in Thessalonica?

44. What type of opposition did Paul meet in Thessalonica and by whom?

45. Define *subrostrani*.

46. What role did Jason play in Paul's visit to Thessalonica?

47. Name some *politarchs* who were saved under Paul's ministry.

48. What type of Christians were these Thessalonians?

49. What type of church was the one at Thessalonica? Describe it.

50. Give the archaeological background of 1 Thessalonians 4:13–18.

51. What was the purpose of Paul's second epistle to the Thessalonians?

52. What set the Bereans apart from other Jews?

53. Why did Paul have to leave Berea?

54. What upset Paul when he arrived in Athens?

55. Describe the religion of the Athenians.

56. Describe the philosophy of the Athenians.

57. Describe the philosophy of the Stoics.

58. Describe the philosophy of the Epicureans.

59. What was the significance of Mars' Hill? Give details.

60. Give an outline of Paul's sermon on Mars' Hill.

61. What did Paul observe and use as an illustration in his sermon?

62. Why is it necessary to believe in direct creation by God?

63. What beliefs and results follow when creation by God is denied?

64. What were the results of Paul's sermon on Mars' Hill?

65. Name the important philosopher who was saved. What was his position?

66. Where did Paul go after leaving Athens? Describe the city and the philosophy of its inhabitants.

67. Describe the reaction of the Jews in this city to Paul's ministry.

68. Where did Paul then go to preach and teach the Gospel?

69. What were some of the results of this ministry?

70. Outline Paul's attitude toward baptism.

71. What type of Christians were the Corinthians?

72. Why was Paul brought before Gallio's judgment seat? What is the Greek name for Gallio's courthouse? List the accusations against Paul.

73. What was Gallio's reaction and decision to the charges by the Jews?

74. What did the Greeks do to the chief ruler of the Jews who instigated the charges against Paul?

75. Describe the haircut vow.

76. In your opinion, who made the vow?

77. What was the purpose of the vow?

78. Who were Aquila and Priscilla?

79. Who was Apollos? How did Aquila and Priscilla help him?

80. What influence did Apollo have on the church at Corinth?

81. How was the church at Corinth divided?

82. Why did Paul reprimand the Corinthian church? List his charges.

83. Outline 1 Corinthians 13:4–8a in relation to love and your life.

84. List the reasons why Paul wrote his second letter to the Corinthians.

85. Where did Paul go in Asia Minor when he left Corinth?

86. What was the result of his visit there?

87. Where did he visit after he left this city?

88. Where did Paul settle after he completed his second missionary journey?

89. How many years did he spend on this missionary journey?

90. List several important results of this journey.

91. How many miles did he travel on two continents on this trip?

Chapter Eight

PAUL'S THIRD MISSIONARY JOURNEY

aul concluded his second missionary journey by visiting
the brethren in Jerusalem and settling in Antioch of Syria
for an indefinite period of time (Acts 18:22–23a). Luke
abruptly makes mention that after this intermission in Antioch,
"he [Paul] departed" Antioch to begin his third missionary journey. Paul had a four-fold purpose in making this third trip. He
wanted to keep his promise to the brethren in returning to
Ephesus (Acts 18:19–21); to preach in an Occidental/Oriental
city; to encourage believers along the way in churches he had
established on his other journeys (Acts 18:23; 19:1a); and to
receive a collection (offering) from these believers to take to the
poor believers in Jerusalem. The steady pursuance of this collection in the whole course of this journey can be traced from the
following verses: Galatians 2:10; 1 Corinthians 16:1–4; 1 Corinthians 8:3–4, 20; Romans 15:25–26; and Acts 24:17.

As Paul started on this journey, it is apparent that Silas was
no longer his partner, but that Timothy continued to be. Silas is
no longer mentioned in connection with Paul, although Paul
does refer to him in three of his letters as "Sylvanus" (2 Corinthians 1:19; 1 & 2 Thessalonians 1:1). The last time he is mentioned is by Peter—"Sylvanus, our faithful brother." Sylvanus
(Silas) was Peter's "dictation" secretary (1 Peter 5:12).

That Timothy was with Paul throughout this whole journey
is abundantly clear as mention is made of him in both Acts and

the epistles (Acts 19:22; 20:4; 1 Corinthians 4:17; 16:10; 2 Corinthians 1:1; Romans 16:21). In fact, he is mentioned at least twenty-four times by Luke and Paul. It is quite possible that Titus also accompanied Paul on this third journey. If he did not set out with Paul and Timothy from Antioch, he later joined Paul and was sent out on three occasions by Paul to go to Corinth (2 Corinthians 2:12–13; 7:5–7,10–15; 8:6,16–24). We will later mention others who joined Paul on this journey.

The probable date of Paul's third missionary journey (see map 4, p. 448) is A.D. 54–58, and it takes Paul from Antioch in Syria, throughout Asia Minor, to Ephesus, into Macedonia and Greece (see map 4, p. 448), then from Troas to Tyre, and from Tyre to Caesarea and on to Jerusalem (Acts 18:22b–21:17). In his journey from Antioch, he went through all Galatia (both the northern and southern sectors) and Phrygia, strengthening the disciples from his first and second missionary trips (Acts 18:22c–23). The phrase "he went . . . in order" (18:23) includes all the places he had previously visited in these regions. He continued onward to the upper coast of Asia Minor (probably to Troas), and then south to Ephesus (Acts 19:l). The distance from Antioch to Ephesus alone was approximately 1,000 miles. The total number of miles of this third journey was 3,900 miles (which included his second round-trip visit to Corinth).

EPHESUS Ephesus was located 35 or 40 miles north of Miletus. With the decline of Miletus, Ephesus rose to greater prominence and, in Paul's day, it was the greatest city in Asia Minor (see illustration 29). Although it was Greek in origin, it was also half Oriental and served as a gateway to Rome from the East and as a gateway from the West to the Orient (Asia). It was a port city on the river Cayster, which flowed into the Aegean Sea, and was continually visited by ships from all parts of the Mediterranean, particularly from the Oriental cities of Asia Minor. Great roads united it with the markets of the interior; hence Ephesus was the common meeting place for many nationalities. It was the capital of the western sector of Asia Minor, as well as being the metropolis of the whole province of Asia Minor. Ephesus boasted a famous stadium, or sports arena, about 687 feet in length. It was probably here that Paul, because of his staunch stand for Christianity, fought with wild beasts (1 Corinthians 15:32). The city had a vast amphitheater, seating over twenty-five thousand (see illustration 30). This was the place

29—Ruins of Ephesus. *Courtesy of author.*

where the mob, in response to Demetrius, shouted, "Great is Diana of the Ephesians," for over two hours (Acts 19:34).

Ephesus was a very immoral city as well as a very religious one. Brothels were numerous, and footprints were carved in the marble streets giving directions to these dens of iniquity. Prostitute priestesses gave their earnings for the upkeep of their patron goddess, Diana, the multibreasted goddess of sex, lust, and fertility. Her temple in Ephesus was imposingly beautiful, a sight to behold (see illustration 31). It was considered to be so holy that citizens of foreign countries brought gifts and deposited huge sums of gold and silver for safekeeping. From the monetary standpoint, the temple of Diana was to her subjects what Fort Knox's gold deposit is to America. This colossal temple was 425 feet in length and 220 feet in breadth. There were 127 columns, each 60 feet high, and each of them a gift from a king. Thirty-six were enriched with ornament and color. The staircase was formed with the wood of one single vine from the island of Cyprus. It is said that the sun, in its course, saw nothing more magnificent than Diana's temple.

It is probable that there were no two religious buildings in the world in which were concentrated a greater amount of admira-

30—The vast amphitheater at Ephesus where the unruly crowd cried to Diana. *Courtesy of author.*

tion and enthusiasm than the temple of Diana and the temple of Solomon (later Herod's temple). The cult of Diana surpassed all religions in immorality and superstition. The temple was one of the Seven Wonders of the Ancient World. Pillaged by the Goths in A.D. 111 and burned by a madman in A.D. 365, all that exists today are a few pillars and statues in museums in Ephesus, Naples, and in the Archaeological Museum in Istanbul, Turkey. The "Marble" street led to the site of Diana's temple (see illustration 32).

Diana is the Roman name for the Greek goddess Artemis, the patron goddess of the Phoenician navigators long before Ephesus became important. She supposedly fell from heaven (Acts 19:35) and became the nursing mother of gods, man, and animals, and was the patron goddess of sexual instinct. So sacred was Diana that when Alexander the Great offered the spoils of his eastern campaign if he might inscribe his name on the building, his request was denied. Any number of coins were minted in her honor, bearing her image on the obverse, and the cult image of this lewd, vulgar religion on the reverse.

The worship of Diana was more Oriental than Greek. Images

31—Temple of Diana (artist's conception). *Courtesy of the American Bible Society, New York.*

found of her remind us of idols of the Far East (see illustration 33). Multibreasted statues depict a religion in which the life of all its beings is supported by the many breasts of nature. The lower part of the pictured statue depicts small-sized animals of Greek fables—bees, lambs, heads of lions, crabs, deer, and bulls. The image of Diana, which stood for life, was the object of the utmost veneration, and numberless smaller images were patterned after it.

The ceremonies of the actual worship of Diana at Ephesus were conducted by her priests and a "swarm" of "virgin" priestesses. At least they had been virgins at the time they offered themselves as "sacred" slaves to Diana, but they ended up selling their bodies in the numerous brothels to help support the upkeep of the temple.

This, then, is the Ephesus that Paul came to visit. What an opportunity to make Christ known at the crossroads of the Occidental and Oriental cultures of that day, as well as in the seat of world-wide paganism (Acts 19:27).

Upon his arrival in Ephesus (see map 4, p. 448), Paul immediately met with certain disciples, about twelve, who knew only

32—"MARBLE STREET" leading to Diana's temple. *Courtesy of author.*

33—Statue of Diana. *Courtesy of Naples Museum, Italy.* Coins minted in her honor. *Courtesy of American Numismatic Society.*

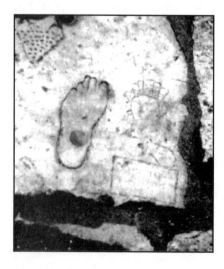

34—Footprint pointing to brothel. *Courtesy of author.*

the baptism of John the Baptist (Acts 19:1–20:1). They themselves had been baptized "unto John's baptism of repentance, believing on Christ who was to follow John" (19:1–4).

Questioning the Disciples of John the Baptist

There are at least two thoughts concerning these men and why they knew only John's baptism. First is the theory that on a visit to Jerusalem in the days of John, they had heard him preach and had believed the Old Testament Scripture concerning his being the forerunner of Messiah (Christ). Upon hearing that message, they repented and were baptized. Second is the theory that they had heard Apollos preach in Ephesus before he learned the full truth of Christ's coming, His work of redemption at Calvary, and the coming of the Holy Spirit at Pentecost (Acts 18:24–28). No doubt Apollos did not have any personal contact with these disciples after he was shown the way of God more perfectly. Nevertheless, whether they had heard John in person or Apollos, verse 4 implies that they were believers in Christ. Having believed John's message of repentance, baptism, and belief in Christ, and having shown it by their repentance and baptism, their faith was counted unto them for righteousness (Romans 4:4; Hebrews 11:4).

Paul recognized their faith in the truth they knew and had experienced. He immediately asked these disciples two ques-tions: (1) Have you received the Holy Spirit since you believed? and (2) Unto what were you baptized when you repented and believed? Pentecost had heralded the indwelling presence of the Holy Spirit to all believers; Christ had set the pattern for baptism to be in the name of the Father, the Son, and the Holy Spirit (Matthew 28:19–20). These men were totally ignorant of what had transpired since John's preaching. They knew that John had said Messiah, who was to come, would baptize with the Holy Spirit (Matthew 3:11), but knew nothing of the Spirit's gifts. When they heard Paul's message, filling them in on fulfilled truth as Aquila and Priscilla had enlightened Apollos, these Ephesian disciples readily accepted "the way of God more perfectly" and were baptized in the name of the Lord Jesus (Acts 19:4–5), whose name embraces the Father and the Holy Spirit. As Paul laid his hands on them, they were "endued with power from on high" (Luke 24:49b) as the Spirit came upon them, and they spoke with tongues (believed to be different languages) and prophesied (Acts 19:6).

Preaching the Kingdom of God

Upon leaving the Ephesian elders, Paul "went into the synagogue and spoke boldly, . . . disputing and persuading the things concerning the kingdom of God" (Acts 19:8). This is just another way of saying that Paul preached the Gospel to the Jews—presenting Christ as their Messiah, trusting God to convert them.

We do not know all that Paul learned by revelation when he was caught up to third heaven and/or when he went to Arabia, but it is logical to assume that because of his knowledge of the kingdom of God, he made known to them

1. that Christ was God's Lamb slain from before the foundation of the world; that this was in the mind of God in eternity past for lost sinners; and that it was the will of God for Christ to be delivered by the determinate counsel and foreknowledge of God unto death, burial, and resurrection (see Revelation 13:8; Hebrews 10:7–10; Acts 2:22–24; Romans 5:6, 8).

2. that Isaiah spoke of a coming righteousness and salvation that was to be forever and shall not be abolished (46:13; 51:5–6; 56:1); also that none other than the One of Isaiah 53 could bring such salvation and righteousness.

3. that it was prophesied of John the Baptist that he would be the forerunner of the One who would give knowledge of salvation onto His people by the remission of their sins (Luke 1:76–77).

4. *that Christ was to be named Jesus* because he would save His people from their sins (Matthew 1:21).

5. that the angel announced to the shepherds that "unto you is born this day in the city of David a Savior who is Christ the Lord" (Luke 2:8).

6. that those who really knew the Old Testament Scriptures did not rely on the traditions of the elders. Simeon and Anna are good examples of this truth. Both were cognizant of the fact that Jesus was born to be God's redemption (salvation) for all people, Jew and Gentile alike (Luke 2:25–38). When Simeon first saw the baby, Jesus, he remarked, "now mine eyes

have seen the salvation of the Lord," indicating that salvation is in a Person, not a ritual, church, baptism, or creed.

7. that Isaiah had prophesied that Messiah would have the Spirit of the Lord upon Him to preach good tidings . . . to bind up the broken . . . to proclaim liberty to the captives, to open the prison to them that are bound, and to proclaim the acceptable year of the Lord (see Isaiah 61:1–2).

8. that Messiah had come to be about His Father's business, which was to be God's sacrifice for sin (cf. Luke 2:49 with Hebrews 10:5–10).

9. that Christ had been presented by John as the "Lamb of God"—the "Passover sacrifice," who takes away the sins of the world (John 1:29; 1 Corinthians 5:7b).

10. that Christ repeatedly revealed Himself as Messiah by His works of mercy and healing as the "Son of God" (John 12:32–37).

11. that Christ came not to be ministered unto, but to minister and give His life a ransom for many (Matthew 20:20).

12. that Christ thought it not robbery to be equal with God, but made Himself of no reputation, and took upon Himself the form of a servant, was made in the likeness of men, was fashioned as a man, was obedient (to the will of God) unto death, even the death of the Cross (see Philippians 2:6–8).

13. that Christ came to seek and to save the lost (Luke 9:56; 19:10).

14. that Christ was the seed of the woman who came in the fullness of God's time "to redeem those under the curse of the law" (Galatians 4:4–5).

15. that the faithful saying, worthy of all acceptation, is that Christ Jesus came into the world to save sinners (1 Timothy 1:15).

16. that Christ's finished work on the Cross would break down the middle wall of partition between Jew and

Gentile, making each nigh to God through Christ's blood, and that Christ as the Way would open a new and living way for all believers to have direct access to God (see John 14:6; Ephesians 2:13–16; Hebrews 10:19–20).

17. that as Moses lifted up the serpent in the wilderness, Christ had to be lifted up so that whosoever believes in Him might not perish (John 3:14–21).

18. that Christ had a destiny, a destiny to defeat Satan at Calvary (Genesis 3:15), that He was manifested to destroy (undo) the works of the devil by tasting death for every man, thus conquering the one who had the power of death (Hebrews 2:14; 1 John 3:8). Paul also knew that Christ, in His death struggle with Satan, had bruised the head of the serpent, which resulted in His total victory over Satan, His judging the prince of this world, His blotting out the handwriting of ordinances that were against us by nailing them to the Cross, His spoiling principalities and powers, and by His coming forth from the grave with the keys of hell and of death. This same Christ was the Messiah of the Old Testament, the King of Kings and the Lord of Lords (see John 2:31; Colossians 2:14–15; 1 Timothy 6:15; Revelation 1:18).

Paul's whole message in presenting the kingdom of God is summed up in his words in 1 Corinthians 15:3–4, "how that Christ died for our sins according to the Scriptures; and that he was buried, and that he rose again the third day according to the scriptures." The apostle always reasoned with his hearers out of Scripture that Jesus was Christ, the very Son of God (Acts 9:20), the One of whom Peter spoke as having been delivered by the determinate counsel and foreknowledge of God to be crucified and slain (Acts 2:23–24). This was Paul's basis for preaching that "the kingdom of God is not meat and drink; but righteousness [God's], and peace [with God], and joy [as one is controlled by the Holy Spirit] in the Holy Ghost" (Romans 14:17).

What a pity many of the Jews who heard Paul's message on the kingdom of God were hardened and believed not, and spoke evil of "that way" (Acts 19:8–9a). Being Jews, who were going about to establish their own righteousness, they felt no need to repent and resented Paul's admonition that they had to believe in Christ in order to be right with God. Paul sensed he had hit a dead end with them. He probably felt like he was casting pearls before swine, so he departed from them and took with him those who had believed and were being discipled.

Not too far from the synagogue was the school of one Tyrannus, who was probably a teacher of Grecian philosophy or ethics. His classes are thought to have been held in the mornings, which made it possible for traveling teachers, such as Paul, to have access to the classrooms the rest of the day. Not much is known about this man, but whether Jew, proselyte, or pagan, he had no objection to Paul's preaching Christ in his school, even though there were Jews who publicly opposed Paul. Many transients from all parts of Asia would come and listen to Paul who taught both Jews and Greeks the necessity of repentance toward God and faith in the Lord Jesus Christ (Acts 19:10; 20:21). Paul's teaching continued for two years, not only in the school, but publicly from house to house (Acts 20:20). Such teaching and preaching resulted in the Word of the Lord Jesus being spread throughout the region of Asia Minor (Acts 19:10).

Performing Miracles

While in Ephesus, Paul exercised his apostolic gift of healing and casting out evil spirits once again (Acts 19:11–12, "And God wrought special miracles by the hands of Paul; so that from his body were brought unto the sick handkerchiefs or aprons, and the diseases departed from them, and the evil spirits went out of them."

We must remember that Ephesus was renowned throughout the world for the worship of Diana and the practice of magic, and though it was a Greek city, like Athens and Corinth, it was half Oriental. The image of Diana, the guardian goddess, resembled an Indian idol rather than the beautiful forms seen in the acropolis of Athens. The enemy that Paul had to oppose in Ephesus was not a glorified philosophy, as he had tackled in Greece, but an Asiatic superstition associated with the practice of magic. To worship Diana was to practice magic. One ancient Greek writer, Eustathius, said that mysterious symbols, called the "Ephesians Letters," were engraved on her crown, her girdle, and her feet. When pronounced, they were regarded as a charm and were used by those who were under the power of evil spirits. When written, they were carried about as amulets. Curious stories were told about their influence. Croesus is said to have repeated the mystic symbols on his funeral pyre. An Ephesian wrestler is said to have always been victorious until he lost the scroll (or book) that had acted like a charm of magical protection. The study of these symbols was an elaborate science, and books, both numerous and expensive, were in great demand.

This background knowledge of the superstitious worship of Diana throws some light on the peculiar character of the miracles wrought by Paul at Ephesus. We are not to suppose that the apostles were always able to work miracles at will. It appears that supernatural power was given to them according to the circumstances that required it, and the character of the miracles was not always the same. Some were accommodated to the peculiar forms of sin, superstition, or ignorance they were required to oppose. The miracles that Paul performed in this city should be equated with Peter's miracles in Jerusalem when "many signs and wonders [were] wrought among the people; . . . insomuch that they brought forth the sick in the streets, . . . that at least the shadow of Peter passing by might overshadow some of them" (Acts 5:12–16).

We know that in the case of Christ's miracles (though His were usually performed by speaking a word) that an agency was sometimes used. For example He made "clay of spittle" to anoint the eyes of a blind man who was then told to wash his eyes in the Pool of Siloam (John 9:6–7), and the hem of His garment was made effectual to the healing of a sick woman (Matthew 9:20). Here, at Ephesus, Paul faced magicians like Moses and Aaron faced Pharaoh, and it is distinctly said that Paul's miracles were not ordinary miracles; they were special, different from those that he usually performed. On the particular occasion of Acts 19:11–12, handkerchiefs and aprons were made the means of communicating healing power to those who were at a distance, whether they were possessed with evil spirits or afflicted with ordinary diseases (Acts 19:12). The effects, which were publicly manifested, were a definite refutation of the charms, the amulets, and the mystic Ephesian Letters. Paul's miracles were a signal that what had been performed had been done by God Himself, who "wrought miracles by the hands of Paul" (v. 11), that "the name," not of Paul, but "of the Lord Jesus was magnified" (v. 17). This is the only recorded Scripture of such a means used to perform miracles of this nature. There is no record in church history where this was ever repeated, contrary to reports by some so-called healers today. Healing the sick and casting out evil spirits in Ephesus were Paul's *fourth* and *fifth* times to perform miracles.

The miracles that Paul performed must have affected those who practiced curious arts. Among the magicians in Ephesus were several Jewish exorcists, even though we note the stern severity with which sorcery was forbidden in the Old Testament (Deuteronomy 18:9–12). This passage implies that the Israelites were fascinated by witchcraft, and the Talmud bears witness to this practice during Israel's history. There were Jewish magicians throughout the Roman Empire, and Paul had encountered one sorcerer on the island of Cyprus when he preached to Sergius Paulus (Acts 13:6–12).

At the time Paul was in Ephesus, superstition, deception, and fraud, and their evil manifestations were powerful. It is no wonder that Paul classified witchcraft among the works of the flesh and solemnly warned that those who practiced such could not enter the kingdom of God. It is because of witchcraft that Paul wrote to Timothy that "evil men and seducers [wandering magicians] shall wax worse, deceiving and being deceived" (Galatians 5:20; 2 Timothy 3:13), probably as the result of Timothy's experience among the sorcerers when he was in Ephesus. These exorcists, believing that the name of Jesus acted as a charm, and recognizing the apostle as a Jew like themselves, attempted his method of casting out evil spirits (v. 13). But He to whom the demons were subject, and who had given to His servant "power and authority" over them (Luke 9:1), had shame and terror in store for those who presumed they could take His holy name in vain.

Attempting to Cast Out Evil Spirits

One specific instance is recorded that produced disastrous consequences for those who made the attempt, and led to public shame among the population. Among those who attempted to cast out evil spirits "in the name of Jesus" were seven brothers, sons of Sceva (Acts 19:13–19). Sceva was a chief priest, who had either held the office at one time in Jerusalem, or he was chief of one of the twenty-four courses of priests. The demons, who were subject to Jesus, and by His will subject to those who preached the Gospel and knew Christ personally, scorned those who used Jesus' name without being converted: "Jesus I recognize, and Paul I know, but who are you?" (v. 13). And straightway the man who was possessed leaped on the brothers, overcame them, and

35—Burning books of magic at Ephesus. *Courtesy of author.*

prevailed against them (tore off their clothes) so that they fled out of the house naked and wounded. The name of Jesus, used under the leading of the Holy Spirit, is the only answer to exorcism.

The fearful result of the profane use of that holy name, which was proclaimed by the apostle for the salvation of all men, soon became known throughout Ephesus, and many believed, confessed their sins, and manifested fruit in keeping with repentance. One great evidence was that the Word grew mightily and took effect in many lives (Acts 19:20). For those who became new creatures in Christ, old things passed away. These believers, who had used the mystical and magical arts of Diana, had purchased books and silver idols of Diana from the silversmiths of the city (see illustration 35). After their salvation, they brought their books as well as their magical spells, amulets, charms, idols, and arts and destroyed them by fire in the sight of all (see illustration 36). Their conscience was moved by what had recently occurred, and knowing that their charms and religion were worthless, as babes in Christ they came and made full confession before Paul and publicly acknowledged and forsook their deeds (or practices) of darkness. This mass burning proved to be a financial loss for the silversmiths because the people were not likely to replace what they had burned, calculated at 50,000 pieces of silver (Acts 19:19). We do not know the exact value, but speculating, if the silver was in drachmas, it was worth about $10,000. If in shekels, it was worth about $35,000. It was such a financial loss to the silversmiths that they caused a riot that culminated in the city's amphitheater (Acts 19:24–41).

This scene must have been long remembered in Ephesus. It was a strong argument against the error and evil of the sorcerers, and a striking affirmation of the triumph of Jesus Christ over the powers of evil and darkness. The workers of corruption were put

36—Ruins of the silversmiths' shops. *Courtesy of author.*

to scorn, like the priests of Baal by Elijah on mount Carmel (1 Kings 18:1–39). It is no wonder the Scripture grew mightily and had great force among the Ephesians, taking root in many and flourishing in their lives. They were like the demoniac who had been healed by Jesus—they told and showed what great things God had done for them (cf. Mark 5:19 with Luke 8:39).

CORINTH: A SECOND VISIT Paul first visited Corinth on his second missionary journey (Acts 18:1). Leaving Achaia, the province in which Corinth is located, he made a brief visit to Ephesus and then set sail for Caesarea, and from thence to Jerusalem and Antioch of Syria (Acts 18:18–22). Now on his third missionary journey (see map 4, p. 448), and after his three-year stay in Ephesus, he departed for Macedonia, where he wrote his second epistle to the Corinthians (Acts 19:1–20:1a). After leaving Macedonia he went to Greece and spent three months. He visited Athens and Corinth. It was at this time that he wrote his epistle to the Romans. This visit to Corinth was Paul's third, because when he wrote his second letter to them from Macedonia, he said on two occasions, "Behold, the third time I am ready to come to you," and "This is the third time I am coming to you" (2 Corinthians 12:14; 13:1).

When, however, did he visit the second time? Luke's record

makes no mention of a second visit, but if there was a first and a third, there must had been a second. But where do we place the second? Paul mentions "a painful visit again" in 2 Corinthians 2:1. Was his second visit the painful visit? Possibly a little arithmetic will help determine when he could have easily made the second visit. The time he spent in Ephesus was three years (Acts 20:31). After taking a brief time to deal first with the Ephesian elders (Acts 19:1–7), he spent three months reasoning with the Jews in their synagogue concerning the kingdom of God (Acts 19:8). Rejected by the Jews, Paul spent two years teaching and preaching in the school of Tyrannus (Acts 19:9–10). The last few days of Paul's stay in Ephesus revolved around the silversmiths' starting a riot that ended in the amphitheater, and Paul's exodus from Ephesus to go to Macedonia and Greece (Acts 19:23; 20:2). There is about an eight-month-plus period of time between Acts 19:11 and 22 (after Paul's two-year ministry in Tyrannus' school and then his leaving Ephesus). During this period he performed some miracles and sent Timothy and Erastus to Macedonia.

Having written his first epistle to the Corinthians while in Ephesus, his heart was still heavy because of their carnality. With the possibility that he had received reports of abounding sin among the babes in Christ there, Paul made a hurried visit to see them during this eight-month period of time. Trade between these two cities across the Aegean Sea was booming and there was no problem in catching a ship to go back and forth without delay. This would have been about a four hundred-mile round trip. As mentioned, it was a painful visit, but one that he felt had to be made. He needed to deal with them in person again. Although he had denounced them in his first letter for their abuse of Christian liberty, conditions were such that possibly Paul felt that this polluted church should not continue to use the name Christian. Yet, Paul knew the believers were also saints, and his love for them constrained him to try and help by making this unscheduled visit. Because of Luke's silence in this matter, we can only say that there was a second visit, probably while Paul was nearby in Ephesus.

Assuming that Paul had visited Corinth and returned before or after he had performed many special miracles in Ephesus (Acts 19:11–19), his heart yearned to learn how the believers were in Macedonia—Philippi, Thessalonica, Berea, and Achaia in Greece. He expressed a desire to go into Macedonia later; also giving an indication that he would like to visit Rome to meet Roman believers and impart some gift to them (cf. Acts 19:21 with Romans 1:11). He finally did get to Rome, but not under the circumstances he desired (see chapter 12).

Before expressing his desire to go to Rome, he expressed a desire to go to Jerusalem again (see chapter 9). Evidently it was Paul's Jewish heritage and love for his lost Jewish kinsmen that caused him to repeatedly yearn to go back to Jerusalem in spite of Christ's warning to get out of that city and go to the Gentiles (cf. Romans 9:1–3; 10:1–3 with Acts 22:17–21).

Paul sent Timothy and Erastus to Macedonia and Corinth to get firsthand information about the churches in those areas (Acts 19:21–22). This is Paul's first mention of Erastus as one of his helpers. We do not know exactly when he joined Paul and Timothy, but it is reasonable to assume that he became a follower in Ephesus. Erastus had previously been a "chamberlain," a high political figure in Ephesus or Corinth (possibly a city treasurer).

EPHESUS At the beginning of this chapter, I gave a description of the images of Diana. One of the idolatrous customs of the ancient world was the use of portable images and shrines, which were little models of the more elaborate objects of devotion, and the temple of Diana was no exception. These images were carried in processions, on journeys, and on military expeditions. In most instances they were set up as household gods. Many heathen historians have alluded to the shrines of the Ephesian Diana, which are mentioned in Acts 19:24.

The material of which these images were made were wood, sometimes overlaid with gold or silver, or solid gold and solid silver. The latter material was that which was used by Demetrius' workmen and his competitors. From the expressions used by Luke, it is evident that an extensive and lucrative trade grew up in Ephesus from the manufacture and sale of these silver shrines. Few of those who visited this fair city and the temple of Diana would willingly return home without a memorial of Diana and possibly a model of her temple. Since so many citizens were coming to know Christ as their Savior, they were not purchasing these idols and shrines. Not only were sales of these items falling off, but new believers in Ephesus were burning their books of magic and causing havoc in the business of the silversmiths who made the idols (see illustration 36).

When Paul wrote his first letter to the Corinthians he said that he would remain in Ephesus until Pentecost, which would extend Paul's visit into the spring and the "month of Diana" (May). The month of Diana precipitated the greatest religious gathering in the area. This meant that the city would be crowded with people from the whole of Asia Minor and possibly from many European areas such as Macedonia and Greece. Doubtless the silversmiths were expecting to make a killing in sales. They found out, however, that sales of these objects of superstition were declining and that Paul's preaching was the cause of their financial loss, which resulted in "no small stir [or tumult] about that way" (v. 23).

A certain Demetrius, who was a master silversmith (maker of these shrines and temples), inflamed fellow artisans in a speech that blamed Paul for their misfortune. He accused the apostle of turning away many people by his saying "that they be no gods, which are made with hands" (Acts 19:26), that the great goddess Diana should be despised, and that her magnificence should be dethroned, thus robbing her of her divine majesty. It is true that as Paul preached many were turned away from worshiping this goddess, but the rest of the accusations were false (v. 37). Demetrius appealed first to the interest of his hearers and then to their fanaticism (vv. 25–27), whipping them into a frenzy by telling them that the great temple of Diana was in danger of being lost. As a result, not only were the silversmiths infuriated, but as the cry, "Great is Diana of the Ephesians" rang out, the whole city was aroused. As this "infection" spread, a general rush was made to the amphitheater, the most obvious place of assembly. They dragged along two of Paul's companions, Gaius and Aristarchus, because they were not able to locate Paul. Because of Paul's desire to come to the rescue of his friends, and possibly to speak for himself before the mob, he made an effort to go to the stadium but was persuaded to stay away by some "friends" from Asia. These so-called friends were known as Asiarchs and were either political figures or religious leaders (priests, but not Christians). They became friends only because they knew that Paul would be killed if he ventured near the mob. Once the mob was inside the theater, there was much confusion as to why they were really there.

The Jews, knowing that many pagans equated the Jewish religion with Christianity because Paul was a Jew and often met with Jews, sent Alexander to try to quiet the people so that the Jews of Ephesus would not be blamed for the gathering nor the effect of the Gospel. When the crowd recognized Alexander as a

Jew, they all with one voice for about the space of two hours cried out, "Great is Diana of the Ephesians" (Acts 19:33–34).

The frenzy of an angry multitude will dissipate after a time, and they became disposed to listen to words of counsel and reproof. At the moment that they quieted, the town clerk stepped in. He reminded them of four things. First, he reminded them that everyone knew that the Ephesians were worshipers of Diana and that no one had attempted to contest it (vv. 35–36). In effect he said, "The contradiction of a few insignificant strangers in town [Paul and company] cannot affect what the whole world knows." Second, he reminded them that the persons accused were not guilty of any public offence, nor of any breach of city laws (v. 37). Third, he reminded them that an unruly gathering was not a legal method of prosecuting the strangers. Finally, he reminded them that they themselves, by this tumultuous meeting, had exposed themselves to the displeasure of Rome—there was no reason for the uproar and for however great were their liberties, they were in danger of being called into question for it (v. 40). Having rapidly brought his argument to a climax, he dismissed the assembly (v. 41). The stone seats gradually emptied, the uproar ceased, and the rioters separated to their various occupations, amusements, and homes.

PAUL'S EPISTLE TO THE EPHESIANS Paul wrote this letter during his first imprisonment in Rome about A.D. 63 or 64 (Ephesians 3:1). He had been in Ephesus briefly on his second missionary journey when he left Aquila and Priscilla there. This couple was either responsible for Christianity's originating in this city, or were largely responsible for paving the way for Paul's return on his third journey when he spent three years with the Ephesians (Acts 18:18–19:1). Now, led of the Holy Spirit while in prison, he pens this letter, commonly titled "The Letter [or Epistle] of Paul to the Ephesians." This is not much of a personal note to the believers at Ephesus. The letter itself is more doctrinal, having to do with the position of all believers (chapters 1–3), and how they are to practice their position (chapters 4–6). Conspicuously absent is any mention of friends or fellow workers and any problems or controversies such as we find in some of his other writings. Many Greek manuscripts omit the phrase "at Ephesus" in 1:1, which strongly supports the possibility that this letter was a general epistle for many churches throughout Asia Minor where Paul had preached (similar to his general letter to the churches of Galatia). It was likely sent first to the Ephesian believers, being delivered to them by Tychicus (Ephesians 6:21). When Paul wrote his circular letter to the Colossians, he asked that his letter "that is coming out of Laodicea" be read by them (Colossians 4:16). Some have suggested that this refers to the circular Ephesian letter. One thing is for certain, Ephesians was written to believers in Christ.

The theme of this epistle is God's eternal purpose to establish and complete His body, the church of the living God. According to this inspired letter, believers are rich beyond measure.

Outline of the Book of Ephesians

I. The Believer's Position (1:3–3:21)
  A. The Believer "In" Christ
     This phrase, or its synonym, "in Christ," is used about thirty-four times by Paul in this book; more than in any of his other writings. Note how Paul characterizes the Christian. The believer is:
     1. *in* Christ (1:1)
     2. in heavenly places *in* Christ (1:3)
     3. chosen *in* Him (1:4)
     4. adopted *by* (or *through*) Christ (1:5)
     5. accepted *in* the Beloved (1:6)
     6. *in* whom we have redemption *through* His blood (1:7)
     7. *in* Him from whom we have received an inheritance (1:11)
     8. *in* Him from whom we are sealed by the Holy Spirit (1:13)
     9. made alive *with* Him (2:5)
     10. raised *with* Him and seated together with Him in heavenly places (2:6)
     11. created *in* Christ to bear fruit (2:10)
     12. brought nigh God *in* Christ by His blood (2:13)
     13. reconciled *in* one body by the Cross (2:16)
     14. given access *through* Him by the Spirit to the Father (2:18)
     15. *in* Him and are built together as God's temple (2:20–22)
     16. a partaker of God's promises *in* Christ (3:6)
     17. one who has the unsearchable riches *of* Christ (3:8)
     18. *in* Him with whom we have boldness *by* the faith of Him (3:12)
     19. grounded *in* love *with* Christ *in* our hearts (3:17)
     20. one who has God the Father *in* him or her (4:6)

21. the gift *of* Christ (4:7)

B. The Believer Has Been
   1. blessed with every spiritual blessing (1:3)
   2. chosen to be holy and without blame (1:4)
   3. predestinated unto adoption (1:5)
   4. made recipients of free grace (1:6)
   5. redeemed through His blood (1:7–8)
   6. given God's wisdom and insight (1:8)
   7. given knowledge of His will (1:9–10)
   8. given an inheritance (1:11–12)
   9. sealed with the Holy Spirit (1:13)
   10. given life (2:1, 5)
   11. raised to sit in heavenly places in Christ Jesus (2:6)
   12. saved by His grace through faith apart from works (2:8–9)
   13. made His workmanship, created unto good works (2:10)
   14. made nigh God (2:12–13)
   15. given God's peace (2:14a)
   16. given access to God (2:14b–15, 18)
   17. made fellow citizens with other saints (2:19a)
   18. made God's household (2:19b)
   19. made God's dwelling place (2:22)
   20. made fellow heirs and fellow members of Christ's body (3:6)
   21. given the unfathomable riches of Christ (3:8)
   22. given the revelation of the mystery of the church (3:9–11)
   23. strengthened with the Holy Spirit's power (3:16)
   24. given the presence of the indwelling Christ (3:17a)
   25. rooted and grounded in love (3:17b)
   26. given a full knowledge of God's love (3:18–19)
   27. blessed above and beyond all we could ask or think (3:20–21)

II. The Believer's Practice (4:1–6:20)
   A. The cause of the believer's practice (effect) is his position in Christ. Verse 1 of chapter 4 draws the line between one's position and one's practice—"Walk worthy of the vocation wherewith ye are called," or walk in a manner worthy of our position in Christ. How does one walk in Christ?
      1. with all humility and gentleness, with long suffering (or patience) (4:2a)
      2. by showing forbearance to one another in love (4:2b)

3. by endeavoring to keep the unity of the spirit in the bond of peace (4:3)
4. by doing the work of the ministry (4:12b)
5. by growing in grace; becoming mature (4:13–14 with 2 Peter 3:18)
6. by speaking the truth in love (4:15)
7. by walking contrary to the world (4:17–5:7)
8. by putting off the old man (self) and putting on the new man (Christ) (4:22, 24)
9. by being kind one to another, tender hearted and forgiving (4:32)
10. by walking as children of light (5:8)
11. by proving what is acceptable unto the Lord (5:10)
12. by reproving those who walk in darkness (5:11–12)
13. by walking circumspectly (wisely, carefully, orderly) (5:15)
14. by redeeming the time (5:16)
15. by understanding the will of God (5:17)
16. by being filled with the Holy Spirit (5:18)
17. by singing and rejoicing (5:19)
18. by giving thanks for all things unto God (cf. 5:20 with 1 Thessalonians 5:18)
19. by submitting self to one another in the fear of God (5:21)
20. by exhibiting a happy home; the husband living under the authority of Christ and the wife living under the authority of the husband (5:22–6:4)
21. by servants working for their masters as unto Christ (6:5–9)
22. by putting on the whole armor of God to withstand all the fiery darts and schemes of the devil (6:10–17)
23. by being in an atmosphere of prayer at all times (6:18)
24. by boldly making known the Gospel (cf. 6:19 with Romans 1:16)

Summary of the Believer's Position and Walk

1. He is saved by grace through faith; becoming a new creation in Christ Jesus, created unto good works to be a fruit-bearing child of God (cf. 2:8–10 with John 15:1–8).
2. He is to walk in a manner worthy of his calling with all humility and meekness, proving by his life that Christ did not die in vain (4:1–3). If he were to be arrested for

being a Christian, there should be enough evidence to convict him.

Since the bulk of believers at Ephesus were Gentiles, Paul seldom quoted from the Old Testament. However, he did use a few Old Testaments references:

    a. cf. 4:8 with Judges 5:12; Psalm 68:18: leading captivity captive

    b. cf. 4:25 with Zechariah 8:16: speak truth with thy neighbor

    c. cf. 4:26 with Psalm 4:4: sin not

    d. cf. 5:31 with Genesis 2:24: husband and wife one flesh

    e. cf. 6:1–3 with Exodus 20:12: honoring parents

    f. cf. 6:17 with Isaiah 59:17: helmet of salvation

Paul presented Christ to the Ephesians as "the head of the church and of the believer" (1:22; 5:23).

Suggested Outlines of Chapters[1]

The Book of Fullness

Chapter 1—The Boundless Chapter; "Before the Foundation of the World" (v. 4)

Chapter 2—The Limitless Chapter; "Ages to Come" (v. 7)

Chapter 3—The Measureless Chapter; "Above All that We Ask or Think" (v. 20)

Chapter 4—The Fathomless Chapter; "Fill All Things" (v. 10)

Chapter 5—The Faultless Chapter; "Without Spot or Wrinkle" (v. 27)

Chapter 6—The Dauntless Chapter; "Able to Stand" (v. 13)

The Book of What God Is Doing Now

Chapter 1—He Is Composing a Body

Chapter 2—He Is Constructing a Building

Chapter 3—He Is Conveying a Blessing

Chapter 4—He Is Combining a Brotherhood

Chapter 5—He Is Counseling a Bride

Chapter 6—He Is Commanding a Battalion

Chapter Eight

The Book of Established Truths

They are without "shadow of turning."

Chapter 1—A Blessing That Can Never Be Depleted (v. 3)

Chapter 2—A Building That Can Never Be Demolished (v. 21)

Chapter 3—A Blessing That Can Never Be Disputed (v. 8)

Chapter 4—A Body That Can Never Be Decomposed (vv. 12–16)

Chapter 5—A Bride That Can Never Be Divorced (v. 27)

Chapter 6—A Battalion That Never Can Be Defeated (v. 13)

All of this is ours because we are under a blood that can never be diluted!

The Book of Perfection

Chapter 1—The Perfect Riches

Chapter 2—The Perfect Temple

Chapter 3—The Perfect Mystery

Chapter 4—The Perfect Body

Chapter 5—The Perfect Bride

Chapter 6—The Perfect Armor

The Wonderful Book

Chapter 1—The Most Wonderful Story Ever Told

Chapter 2—The Most Wonderful Building Ever Erected

Chapter 3—The Most Wonderful Body Ever Assembled

Chapter 4—The Most Wonderful Walk Ever Initiated

Chapter 5—The Most Wonderful Bride Ever Wooed and Won

Chapter 6—The Most Wonderful Warfare Ever Fought

The Book of the Church's Function

Chapter 1—The Church Is a Body for Service

Chapter 2—The Church Is a Temple for Worship

Chapter 3—The Church Is a Family for Fellowship

MACEDONIA AND ILLYRICUM After the uproar over Diana had died down in Ephesus, Paul left. God had used the eloquence of a Greek magistrate in the amphitheater to protect His servant (Acts 19:35–41). As in the case of Philippi, the narrative of Paul's sojourn to Ephesus concluded with an affectionate farewell (Acts 16:40; 20:1). The danger was now over and Paul headed for Europe (Acts 20:1–2a; Romans 15:19). Luke does not tell us how he journeyed to Macedonia, whether by land or sea, or by both (see map 4, p. 448). Upon his arrival, he journeyed throughout the region (Acts 20:2). We must assume he visited Philippi, Thessalonica, and Berea, and he wrote his second letter to the Corinthians while in Macedonia. Luke does not mention in Acts that Paul preached the Gospel in Illyricum, which is in the northwestern part of Macedonia. However, Paul made mention of it in Romans 15:19, and it is reasonable to assume that he visited this area on this his third missionary journey because Luke was so meticulous in recording his first Macedonian visit on his second missionary trip, and nothing was said then about a visit to Illyricum.

How far Paul penetrated this area is not known. "Unto Illyricum" could mean just to its borders, or it could mean traveling through to the Adriatic Sea. Under Roman rule it did not encompass the same area that it does today (Albania). In ancient times there was a Greek area of Illyricum, a district in the south, and a Roman area of Illyricum, which ran along the coastline of the Adriatic. The Roman Illyricum was barbarous and was referred to as "one of those ill-fated portions of the earth, which, though placed in immediate contact with civilization, has remained perpetually barbarian."[2] Paul, in writing to Timothy, made mention that Titus had gone into Dalmatia, which was a district in the southern part of Illyricum. To the Greeks, however, barbarian did not necessarily mean a ruthless, uncouth person. Rather, anyone who was not a full-blooded Greek was a barbarian. However, those in Roman Illyricum were of a barbarous nature.

GREECE (CORINTH) Having fulfilled his mission in Macedonia, Paul then went into Greece (see map 4, p. 448). During the course of his stay at Ephesus his heart had continually been in Corinth. We noted the possibility that he made a second visit to Corinth during his three-year stay in Ephesus. He had been in frequent communication with these inconsiderate and rebellious converts. A total of three letters had been written to them, one of which has been lost (1 Corinthians 5:9–12). Besides his own personal visits, he had sent several messengers who had been authorized to speak in his name. In his going now, he also had in mind to collect the money that they were giving to the poor in Jerusalem. Regardless of where he was in Macedonia, there was a good Roman road on which he made his journey southward into Achaia. Opportunities would not be wanting for preaching the Gospel at every stage of this foot journey. When he wrote to the Romans about his having been to Illyricum, he said, "but now, having no more place in these parts [to preach]" (15:19–23), indicating he had fully covered that area of Macedonia and Illyricum. Luke does not mention where Paul visited in Greece, though he must have visited the believers there (Acts 17:34). It had been several years since Paul had been there, and even if a church had been established in Athens, they had long been in a weak state. Paganism was flourishing as much as it had when Paul was there before. (The Christian community by the time of the Antonines was almost entirely disposed, but there seemed to be a revival of Christianity about A.D. 165. By the end of the second century, Christianity was almost extinct in Athens.) In considering three of the main cities Paul reached with the Gospel, Corinth was noted for its immorality, Ephesus for its idolatry, and Athens for its polytheism.

When Paul left Athens and went to Corinth (Acts 20:2b-6),

we learn from Romans 16:23 that he visited the home of Gaius. Two things in particular happened during the apostle's third stay in Corinth. First, he completed the great collection for the poor Christians in Judaea. These Achaian Christians had already prepared their contributions by laying aside a portion for the fund every first day of the week (1 Corinthians 16:2) for more than a

year (2 Corinthians 8:10; 9:2), and it must have been a considerable sum. It had been collected from individual believers and entrusted to certain treasurers elected by the church. These men would carry it to Jerusalem in the company of Paul (1 Corinthians 16:3). The second important occurrence was Paul's writing the epistle to the Romans (Romans 16:1–2). It was probably written while he stayed in the home of Gaius, and mention is made that Phoebe took this letter to the believers in Rome (see illustration 37). Shown is a leaf from the University of Michigan Library, Papyri P46, of Romans 14:4–13, which could well represent what Paul's letter looked like to them. The rolled-up parchment below probably indicates what an Epistle looked like before delivery, such as the one Phoebe took to Rome.) She was a member of the church in Cenchrea, the eastern seaport of Corinth. Scripture also indicates that Paul's three-month stay in Greece was in Corinth. Quite possibly he visited other Christians in and around Corinth (throughout Achaia, Acts 20:2–3a; 2 Corinthians 1:1; 10:16).

37—Above: Papyri P46, Romans 14:4–13. *Courtesy of University of Michigan Library, Ann Arbor, Michigan.* Below: sealed epistle or parchment. *Courtesy of Brooklyn Museum, New York.*

PAUL'S EPISTLE TO THE ROMANS In Paul's day, Rome (which means "strength"), was the recognized mistress and metropolis of the world. It was at the height of its greatness, with a population estimated to be almost three million. It was noted for its untold wealth, beauty, luxury, and fame. Jews, however, were not looked on with favor because Gentiles were in the majority. On one occasion Emperor Claudius had all Jews expelled from the city (Acts 18:2). The ban was later lifted, and many Jews were able to live there in spite of hatred on the part of some Romans. It was to Jews, proselytes, and Gentiles that Paul wrote his letter.

He desired to visit not only Rome but also Spain after taking the offering to Jerusalem (Romans 15:25–26). He also wanted to give the Roman believers proof of affectionate interest that he felt for them, although many of them had not seen his face in the flesh. Many Roman believers were personal acquaintances as we see from the many salutations at the close of the epistle.

From the personal friends he had thus formed and from information he had received about them, Paul had every reason to have a very high opinion of the character of the church in Rome. He made mention that their "faith was spoken of throughout the world" (Romans 1:8). In no other epistle did Paul expound so fully the great doctrines of the Christian faith and the rules for Christianity. He desired not only to remind them of every man's need for the wonders of God's so-great salvation by grace through faith apart from the works of the Law but also to let them know that he was justified in exhorting them because of the special commission that Christ had given him to the Gentiles—the majority of the Roman believers being of Gentile origin. We must take into account, however, that the original nucleus of this church, as well as that of many other great churches throughout the Roman Empire, was formed by Gentile proselytes more than by Jews who had separated themselves from the Jewish synagogue. We must also keep in mind that a Gentile proselyte was a Gentile who had become a "Jew" in belief; a convert to Judaism; one who had submitted to circumcision and was taught the Law of Moses, the Prophets, and the Psalms. This is evident from the familiarity with the Old Testament that Paul assumes of his readers and from the multiple references to Jewish readers in his whole argument of chapters 3, 4, and 9 through 11. Acts 28:17–29 tells us that some Jews in Rome were believers, but the majority were not.

The name of the original founder of the Roman church has not been preserved for us in the Bible, by history, or even by tradition. This is remarkable when we consider how soon this church attained the great faith that was spoken of throughout the world. Had any of the apostles laid the foundation, the fact would have been recorded. As active as Peter was in helping to establish the first church in Jerusalem, it is apparent that somewhere in Scripture, mention would have been made if he had ever gone to Rome or had a part in the establishment of the church there. The tradition that the apostle Peter was the founder of the Roman church is contrary to the evidence. It is significant that Paul never once mentioned his name in this epistle or in 2 Timothy during his second imprisonment. Nor did Luke in Acts after Paul arrived in Rome. We note that on the Day of Pentecost there were strangers, Jews, and proselytes from Rome present (Acts 2:10). Some of these could have been among the almost three thousand saved that day. Going back home, they could have started the assembly of believers, or it could have been started by Christians led to the Lord throughout Asia Minor, Macedonia, and Greece, who had moved to Rome. Whatever the hypothesis, the Roman Christians were Jews and proselytes. This is evident from the fact that a large number were of Gentile blood, and it appears still more plainly from Paul's writing throughout his epistle.

Yet, at the same time, the Judaizing element was not entirely absent. There was opposition to the Gospel by those who argued against it on the ground that one was not justified by faith alone. They thought that because they were Jews they were all right with God; that they were better than others (Romans 3:1–30). Some could not bring themselves to acknowledge that their uncircumcised Gentile brethren were their equals and privileged as they were in the kingdom of God (Romans 3:9, 29; 15:7–11). Moreover, the Gentile converts were inclined to treat the lingering Jewish prejudices with scornful contempt (Romans 14:1–8). It was Paul's aim throughout this letter to instruct all believers to win the Jews to the truth of liberty in Christ and for the Jews and the Gentiles to love and understand one another. Paul sought to remove all stumbling blocks from both groups by setting before them the summary of the doctrines and the practice of Christianity.

This epistle was written about A.D. 57, near the end of Paul's third missionary journey. The **key phrase** in Romans is the "righteousness of God" (1:17). The **key thought** is, "I am not ashamed of the gospel of Christ; for it is the power of God unto salvation to everyone that believeth; to the Jew first and also to the Greek" (1:16). The **key words** are righteousness (66 times);

faith (62 times);

justification (justify) (17 times);

impute (19 times);

in Christ (33 times);

law (78 times);

sin (60 times);

flesh (20 times);

death (42 times).

Outline of the Epistle to the Romans

  I. Introduction (1:1–15)
    A. The Gospel Declared by the Prophets (vv. 1–6)
    B. Greetings to the Roman Believers (vv. 7–13)
    C. Paul's Indebtedness to the Gospel (vv. 14–15)
  II. Righteousness Revealed (1:16–17)
    A. Through the Gospel (v. 16)
    B. From Faith to be Saved (cf. v. 17 with Ephesians 2:8–9)
    C. To Faith to Live (cf. v. 17 with Habakkuk 2:4; Galatians 2:20)
  III. Righteousness Required (1:18–3:20)
    A. Gentiles Guilty (1:18–32)
    B. Jews Guilty (2:1–3:8)
    C. All Mankind Guilty (3:9–20)
  IV. Righteousness Received (3:21–5:21)
    A. Righteousness versus the Law (3:21–30)
    B. Righteousness by Faith Illustrated (4:1–25)
      1. Abraham (4:1–5, 9–25)
      2. David (4:6–8)
    C. Righteousness Results in
      1. Peace with God (5:1)
      2. Access by Faith into His Grace (5:2a)
      3. Hope (5:2b)
      4. Joy in Tribulation (5:3–4)
      5. Love of God in Our Hearts (5:5)
      6. Saved from Wrath (5:6–9)
      7. Reconciled to God (5:10–11)
    D. Righteousness and Judgment Contrasted (5:12–21)
  V. Righteousness Realized (6:1–8:39)

    A. Believer's Death to Self (6:1–14)
    B. Believer's Death to Sin (6:15–23)
    C. Believer's Death to the Law (7:1–6)
    D. Law Cannot Deliver from Sin (7:7–23)
    E. Believer's Deliverance from the Power of Sin (7:24–8:11)
    F. Believer's Position (8:12–39)
      1. Sonship (8:12–17)
      2. Future Glory (8:18–30)
      3. Present Victory (8:31–37)
      4. Final Victory (8:38–39)

VI. Righteousness Rejected (9:1–11:36)
    A. Paul's Compassion for Lost Individual Jews (9:1–5)
    B. God's Sovereignty (9:6–29)
    C. Israel's Rejection by God (9:30–10:21)
      1. Israel Lost; Seeking Salvation by Works (9:30–10:3)
      2. Israel Rejected Christ (10:4–15)
      3. Israel Rejected the Prophets (10:16–21)
    D. Israel's Future (11:1–36)

VII. Righteousness Reproduced (12:1–15:13)
    A. Righteousness Personified in Christian Living (12:1–2)
    B. Righteousness Promoted Toward Fellow Believers, Governments, and Fellowmen (12:3–13:14)
    C. Righteousness Prevailing in Christian Love and Liberty (14:1–15:13)

VIII. Conclusion (15:14–16:27)
    A. Personal Notes (15:14–33)
    B. Personal Greetings (16:1–23)
    C. Benediction (16:24–27)

The Old Testament in Romans

Paul used over sixty references from fourteen Old Testament books because of the Jewish influence among those to whom he was writing in Rome, and also because of the key doctrines mentioned throughout this epistle, especially since he sought to emphasize justification by faith, based on Habakkuk 2:4. It was the truth of this portion of Scripture that precipitated the Reformation by Martin Luther. Note the following Old Testament references:

THE OLD TESTAMENT IN ROMANS

Subject	Romans	Old Testament
The just shall live by faith	1:17	Habakkuk 2:4
God's name blasphemed	2:24	Isaiah 52:5
Justified in speaking	3:4	Psalm 51:4
None righteous	3:10	Psalm 14:1, 3
None understands	3:11	Psalm 14:2
All gone out of the way	3:12	Psalm 14:3
Throat an open sepulchre	3:13	Psalm 5:9; 140:3
Mouth full of cursing	3:14	Psalm 10:7
Feet swift to shed blood	3:15	Isaiah 59:7
Destruction and misery in their ways	3:16–17	Isaiah 59:7–8
No fear of God before their eyes	3:18	Psalm 36:1
Abraham's faith counted for righteousness	4:3	Genesis 15:6
David's iniquities forgiven	4:7–8	Psalm 32:1, 2, 5
Abraham the father of many nations	4:17	Genesis 17:5
Abraham's seed to become many nations	4:18	Genesis 15:5
Thou shalt not covet	7:7	Exodus 20:17
For thy sake they are killed all the day long	8:36	Psalm 44:22
In Isaac shall Thy seed be called	9:7	Genesis 21:12
Sarah shall have a son	9:9	Genesis 18:10
The elder shall serve the younger	9:12	Genesis 25:23
Jacob have I loved	9:13	Malachi 1:2–3
God's mercy upon us	9:15	Exodus 33:19
Pharaoh raised up for God's purpose	9:17	Exodus 9:16
Gentiles called a people	9:25	Hosea 2:23
Jews not called a people	9:26	Hosea 1:10
Only a remnant of Israel saved	9:27–28	Isaiah 10:22–23
God's provision of a seed	9:29	Isaiah 1:9
Christ a stumblingblock	9:33	Isaiah 28:16a
Living by the Law	10:5	Leviticus 18:5
Who shall ascend into heaven	10:6–7	Deuteronomy 12–13
God's Word is nigh	10:8	Deuteronomy 30:14

THE OLD TESTAMENT IN ROMANS

Subject	Romans	Old Testament
Belief in Christ eliminates shame	10:11	Isaiah 28:16b
Call upon the name of the Lord	10:13	Joel 2:32
The beautiful feet of those who preach	10:15	Isaiah 52:7
Believing the Lord's report	10:16	Isaiah 53:1
Hearing the Gospel	10:18	Psalm 19:4
Provoked to jealousy	10:19	Deuteronomy 32:21
God found by those who seek Him	10:20	Isaiah 65:1
God's outstretched hands	10:21	Isaiah 65:2
The prophets killed	11:3	1 Kings 19:10, 14
God's reserved prophets	11:4	1 Kings 19:18
The spirit of slumber	11:8	Isaiah 29:10
Israel's conduct a snare	11:9–10	Psalm 69:22–23
A Deliverer from Zion	11:26–27	Isaiah 40:13
The mind of the Lord	11:34	Isaiah 40:13
Given to the Lord	11:35	Job 41:11
Vengeance is the Lord's	12:19	Deuteronomy 32:35
Feeding our enemies	12:20	Proverbs 25:21–22
Various Commandments	13:9	Exodus 20:13–17; Leviticus 19:18
Every knee shall bow to the Lord	14:11	Isaiah 45:23
Being reproached	15:3	Psalm 69:9
God's mercy among the Gentiles	15:9	Psalm 18:50
Gentiles rejoicing with the Jews	15:10	Deuteronomy 32:43
Gentiles praising the Lord	15:11	Psalm 117:1
Christ, from the root of Jesse	15:12	Isaiah 1, 10
Christ preached to the heathen	15:21	Isaiah 52:15
Companion References Render . . . according to their deeds	2:6	Psalm 62:12
God is no respecter of persons	2:11	Deuteronomy 10:17
Shall clay speak to the potter	9:20	Isaiah 45:9
Potter's power over the clay	9:21	Jeremiah 18:6
Eyes that see not	11:8	Isaiah 29:10

Paul portrays Christ in Romans as "the end of the law for righteousness to everyone who believes" (Romans 10:4). He is the One whose righteousness and substitutionary death provides justification for all who exercise faith in Him. Having borne man's sins and wrath, his righteousness is offered as a gracious gift to lost, sinful mankind. His death and resurrection are the basis for the believer's redemption, reconciliation, justification (salvation), righteousness, sanctification, and glorification (Romans 4:25; 5:8–11; 8:28–29).

TROAS VIA MACEDONIA Paul had had a confrontation with the Jews in Corinth on his first visit, and had sternly rebuked them (Acts 18:5–6). During this three-month stay there, these agitated Jews opposed Paul (as his thorn in the flesh). They "laid in wait for him," probably to seize his person, sell him for a slave, rob him of the offering he was taking to the poor in Jerusalem, or kill him (v. 3). Paul set his sights on returning to Antioch in Syria (before going back to Jerusalem), purposing to go back through Macedonia (Acts 20:3) to once again encourage the believers (see map 4, p. 448). Several of his co-workers accompanied him to Philippi—Sopater of Berea, Aristarchus and Secundus of Thessalonica, Gaius of Derbe, Timothy of Lystra, and Tychicus and Trophimus of Asia (Acts 20:4–5). Paul and Luke tarried in Philippi for the Feast of Unleavened Bread. Afterward, they sailed from Philippi (the seaport of Neapolis) to Troas to meet these co-workers and other brethren and spend a few days with them (Acts 20:6–12).

We previously noted that on Paul's second missionary journey it was doubtful that he had preached in Troas because the Macedonian call necessitated a hurried visit to Philippi (Acts 16:8–12). That trip from Troas to Neapolis took about two days. The trip this time by Paul and Luke took five days, possibly due to rough waters.

Now in Troas again, Paul preached to the disciples on the first day of the week (another indication that Christians worshiped and took communion on Sunday, the day of Christ's resurrection, instead of on the Sabbath). To say that Paul was a long-winded preacher is to put it mildly. Assuming he started preaching after they had eaten supper and observed Communion, which early Christians combined into a "love feast" (1 Corinthians 10:21–22), Paul may have preached as much as four or five hours, or until midnight. During the sermon, Eutychus fell asleep—and no wonder (it is amazing that the whole congregation didn't). Eutychus, having fallen asleep, fell from the third loft and was taken up for dead. Paul, like Elisha with the Shunammite's son (2 Kings 4:33–36), fell on him, embraced him, and announced that the young man was all right. Continuing their love feast, Paul, along with the disciples, talked and fellowshipped till the break of day (Acts 20:11).

MILETUS AND THE EPHESIAN ELDERS In Paul's sermon at Troas, he had said that "on the morrow" he would be ready to depart (Acts 20:13–18). Leaving Troas (see map 4, p. 448), those with him sailed to Assos, but he left by foot. There was a good Roman road from Troas to Assos, a distance of about seventeen miles, which would make his solitary journey both safe and fast, and at the same time enable him to be alone with the Lord for prayer and meditation. He knew that on a crowded ship this would be impossible. Just as Christ had need for such occasions (Mark 1:35), Paul felt he needed strength from and communion with God, especially since he was deeply conscious of his weakness and filled with apprehension about his trip to Jerusalem (see Romans 15:30–31; cf. Acts 20:3 with 20:22–25 and 21:4, 13).

Having been refreshed by the Lord, filled with enthusiasm, and exhibiting the joy of God's salvation, he entered the city of Assos and headed for the shore to board the ship without delay, rejoining his fellow workers. Docking overnight, they set sail the next day for other southward ports (Mitylene, Chios, Samos, and Trogyllium, Acts 20:14–15). The distance from Assos to Miletus was 168 miles. Although Paul desired to go back to Ephesus, they had boarded a ship that would bypass this city. No doubt he figured he would miss arriving in Jerusalem in time for Pentecost if he visited them.

Having arrived in Miletus, Paul was not going to neglect the Ephesian brethren (Acts 20:17–38). He sent a messenger to ask the elders of the church to come and visit him (v. 17). There was so much on his heart that he wanted to say to them. The excitement and joy must have been great among these Christians of Ephesus when they heard that their honored friend, to whom they had listened so often in the school of Tyrannus, wanted to see them. They must have gathered together in all haste to comply with his request and went with eager steps to Miletus. Those people were used to traveling on a journey of some thirty miles. To them, the trip was not long and tedious, nor was time a factor, whether day or night. These elders must have arrived the next day. Had there been any weariness in coming from Ephesus to Miletus, it would soon be forgotten at the sight of their friend and instructor. They gathered together, probably somewhere on the shore, to listen to what Paul had to say. Paul testified to them of his faithfulness in preaching Christ and the opposition he had endured, especially from Jewish unbelievers. He warned them of impending apostasy, as well as opposition they might have from the Jews. And then, as though he had a premonition about his being bound if he did go to Jerusalem, he more or less, in his closing address, gave these believers of Ephesus his "swan song." Of all the messages Paul preached and words spoken to fellow Christians, none was more touching and tender than those addressed to these men. The close of his speech was followed by a solemn act of united supplication. Paul knelt down on the shore with all those who had listened to him, and offered up a prayer to Christ who was establishing His church in the midst of so many difficulties. There followed an outbreak of natural sorrow and weeping. With reverence and love these men fell on Paul's neck, embracing and kissing him again and again, realizing they might never behold his countenance again this side of heaven.

If Paul's address to these Ephesian believers teaches us nothing else, it teaches us that if the church is to forge ahead, *all* its members must be faithful, be watchful, and be growing in the faith.

If the date of Paul's visit to Miletus of A.D. 58 is correct, in less than thirty-seven years none other than the Lord Jesus Christ was taking the church of Ephesus to task for not being evangelical. They were solid, fundamentally speaking, but had no interest in the lost (Revelation 2:1–7). They were admonished to repent and do their first works, else the light of their testimony would be darkened and would be taken from them. It is a tragedy that there is no church, no Christian testimony in or around Ephesus today. They once were a Bible-believing church, but they forgot and left their first love, and with no evangelical outreach in their community as well as a refusal to repent and do what they knew they should do to reach the lost, their light went out. What a challenge for us today to be faithful and to abide in Christ, so that when He comes for His bride, we will not be ashamed before Him at His coming (Luke 18:8; 1 John 2:28).

TYRE   As the Ephesian brethren left, Paul and his company boarded a ship (Acts 21:1–14) and sailed out into the open sea. Luke is very thorough in giving details and says that with a good wind they went due south to Coos on the island of Cos, thence to Rhodes. After a port call at Rhodes, they sailed straight to Patara. Fortunately for Paul, they found a ship sailing over to Phoenicia. No doubt they went aboard without a moment's delay, and it seems evident from Luke's expression that they sailed that very day (Acts 20:15). Since the voyage was to take them across the open sea with no dreaded shoals or rocks, and since the winds were in their favor during this time of year (spring), there could be no reason for not sailing through the night. There is a freshness and cheerfulness in such a voyage with a fair wind at night. The sailors are on watch, the passengers are in good spirits, and the feeling is often expressed in songs or long conversations into the wee hours of the morning. Such cheerfulness must have been felt by Paul and his companions as they thanked God who gives songs in the night and who hearkens unto those who fear Him, speak often to one another, and think upon His name (see Job 35:10; Malachi 3:16).

The distance from Troas (Acts 20:6) to Tyre is about 650 miles (about 340 from Patara to Tyre). From Acts 20:6 we note that Paul stayed in Troas to observe the Feast of Unleavened Bread. He wished to reach Jerusalem by Pentecost. The Feast of Unleavened Bread, eaten during Passover Week, was followed by Pentecost, forty-nine days later. Paul stayed seven days in Philippi for Passover week. It took him five days to sail to Troas, and he spent seven days there (Acts 20:6–7). About five days were taken by the voyage to Miletus, and at least two days were spent in this city. It would take about four days to go from Miletus to Patara, and at least another three days to go from Patara to Tyre. He spent seven days in Tyre (Acts 21:3–4), one day at Ptolemais (Acts 21:7), an unknown number of days in Caesarea (Acts 21:8–10), which would have enabled Paul to arrive in Jerusalem in sufficient time for Pentecost. Luke does not go into detail about events on board this journey from Miletus—only where they sailed and docked.

When Paul came to Tyre in Phoenicia (see map 4, p. 448), Tyre was not in the glorious state described by Old Testament prophets when its merchants were princes and its traffickers the honorable of the earth (see Isaiah 23:4), nor in its desolation of fulfilled prophecy, being a place to spread nets (see Ezekiel 26:5). Alexander the Great had done a good job in destroying the city, but Rome still utilized its harbor and had made it free. Upon docking, the ship unloaded its cargo and Paul and his friends lost no time in seeking out the Tyrian disciples (v. 4). The church was probably small, but one had existed there ever since the dispersion that took place after the death of Stephen (Acts 11:19). Paul had previously visited the brethren on his mission of charity with Barnabas to attend the Jerusalem Council (Acts 15:3).

Paul Warned Not To Go to Jerusalem

Paul found a closeness among the Christians at Tyre. Although he was the man of God, so to speak among them, they too, had great spiritual knowledge mingled with spiritual insight. They endeavored to discourage his going to Jerusalem, saying "to Paul through the [Holy] Spirit, that he should not go to Jerusalem" (Acts 21:4). Luke does not tell us why they were so directed by the Holy Spirit, but possibly being as close as they were to the Holy City, and knowing the unrest there among Jews due to Paul's preaching to the Gentiles, they encouraged him not to go there. Paul evidently looked on the coming danger from a higher point of view. What to others was imminent danger, appeared to Paul only as a passing storm that would disappear with his presence and report (see chapter 9).

The seven days spent with these believers (Acts 21:4) afforded many opportunities to confirm those who were already Christians and to make the Gospel known to others, both Jews and Gentiles. When the time came to sail to Ptolemais, a touching scene unfolded like the one when the apostle's departed from Miletus. A long procession walked through the city gate—Paul, his companions, and all the Tyrian Christians, including their wives and children. On the shore, they knelt and prayed together. We are not to imagine here any Jewish place of worship like the *proseucha* at Philippi, but simply that they stopped on the way to the ship. The last few moments were precious as they fellowshiped together, but the time spent in prayer soon passed. As they tore themselves from each other's embrace, Paul and his group went aboard and the Tyrian believers returned home, no doubt sorrowful and anxious about Paul's safety.

Blest Be the Tie That Binds

There is something about the tie that binds Christians that cannot be explained. There is a togetherness that only Christians understand; they are members one of another.

COMMON TRAITS OF CHRISTIANS

Trait	Passage
Christians are to be kindly affectioned one to another	Romans 12:10a; Ephesians 4:32
Prefer one another in honor	Romans 12:10b
Be of the same mind one toward another	Romans 12:16
Love one another	Romans 13:8; John 13:34–35
Edify one another	Romans 14:19; 1 Thessalonians 5:11
Admonish one another	Romans 15:14
Care one for another	1 Corinthians 12:25
Bear one another's burdens	Galatians 6:2
Lie not one to another	Colossians 3:9
Speak not evil one of another	James 4:11
Grudge not one against another	James 5:9
Forbear one another in love	Ephesians 4:2
Be tenderhearted one to another	Ephesians 4:32b
Forgive one another	Ephesians 4:32c
Submit one to another	Ephesians 5:21
Esteem others better than self	Philippians 2:3
Teach one another	Colossians 3:16
Comfort one another	1 Thessalonians 4:18
Exhort one another	Hebrews 3:13
Consider one another	Hebrews 10:24
Fellowship one with another	Hebrews 10:25a
Confess faults one to another	James 5:16a
Pray one for another	James 5:16b; 1 Samuel 12:23
Have compassion one for another	1 Peter 3:8
Use hospitality one to another	1 Peter 4:9
Minister the same one to another	1 Peter 4:10

PTOLEMAIS Sailing southward from Tyre, Paul's next stop was Ptolemais (see map 4, p. 448), a distance of only fourteen miles (Acts 21:7). Ptolemais was the Roman name for this city. During the days of the judges it was called Accho (1:31). In the Middle Ages the Crusaders renamed it St. Jean d'Acre. It is called Acre today and is located just north of the port city of Haifa in Israel. Luke mentions that the missionary party spent only one day here having fellowship with the believers. It is also apparent that Paul's voyage from Assos ended here. Although they had accomplished the voyage in plenty of time for Paul to meet his determined deadline in Jerusalem, they hastened onward so that they might spend some time with the Christians in Caesarea.

CAESAREA: Paul hiked the distance of about
AGABUS' WARNING thirty-eight miles from Ptolemias to Caesarea (Acts 21:8–14). At Caesarea there was a Christian family with whom they were sure of receiving a welcome—Philip the evangelist and his daughters.

We know of Philip from his great meeting in Samaria and when he made the Gospel known to the Ethiopian eunuch near Gaza (Acts 8:4–17, 26–40). This was just prior to Paul's conversion. Now, after many years, the apostle and the evangelist are brought together under one roof in Caesarea—the place where Philip's labors ended, or where he had his headquarters if he continued on missionary circuits throughout Judaea. The term *evangelist* is applied to those missionaries who, like Philip (Acts 21:8) and Timothy (2 Timothy 4:5), traveled from place to place to bear the glad tidings of Christ to unbelievers. Hence it follows that the apostles were all evangelists, but not all evangelists were apostles.

Philip's family consisted of four daughters who were an example of the fulfillment of Joel's prediction, quoted by Peter on the Day of Pentecost, that said that at the opening of the dispensation of grace, God's Spirit would come on His handmaids as well as His bondsmen, and that the daughters as well as the sons should prophesy about the Spirit (cf. Acts 2:17–18 with Joel 2:28–29).

News of Paul's arrival in Caesarea at Philip's home reached the church in Jerusalem. Since Paul tarried in Caesarea many days (Acts 21:10), the prophet Agabus, who before had prophesied of a famine in Judaea (Acts 11:28), came to visit Paul. Agabus' first prophecy came to pass, resulting in Paul's and Barnabas' taking an offering to Jerusalem to help those in that crisis (see chapter 5). When Agabus had gathered Paul and the disciples together, he told Paul of his clear knowledge of the danger that awaited him in Jerusalem. His revelation was made in a dramatic form that impressed a stronger sense of reality than mere words could have done. We read of other dramatic events such as that of Isaiah when he loosened the sackcloth from his loins and put off his shoes from his feet to declare how the Egyptian captives would be led away into Assyria naked and barefooted (Isaiah 22), or how Jeremiah, using a girdle in its strength and its decay, revealed to Israel her glory and her fall (Jeremiah 13). Agabus, in like manner, used action imagery in communicating his revelation. He took Paul's girdle and then fastened it around his own hands and feet and said, "Thus saith the Holy Ghost, So shall the Jews at Jerusalem bind the man that owneth this girdle, and shall deliver him into the hands of the Gentiles" (Acts 2:11). It would be a mistake to suppose that Agabus bound Paul's hands and feet. Agabus does not say, "the man whom I bind," but the "man who owns this girdle."

The effect of this startling, dramatized prophecy was very great. The saints wept and implored Paul not to go to Jerusalem. Such a prophecy must have had some effect on Paul's mind also. When he had written to the Romans, he had asked them to pray for him, that on his arrival in Jerusalem he might be delivered from the Jews who hated him and be well received by those Christians who questioned his authority (Romans 15:31). At Miletus he had told the Ephesian elders that he was concerned because he did not know what would befall him when he went to Jerusalem (Acts 20:22), and he had just received a stern warning from his friends in Tyre (Acts 21:4). Paul certainly must have been touched by the earnest supplications and the sorrow that was caused by Agabus' prophecy.

Agabus' act placed Paul in an awkward, peculiar position. Yet Paul, no doubt, felt that the Holy Spirit Himself should tell him what to do and what not to do. With his own inward convictions about the trip to Jerusalem, he did not falter for a moment in giving his answer to what others thought was a direct warning from God through His Spirit: "What mean ye to weep and to break mine heart? For I am ready, not to be bound only but also to die at Jerusalem for the name of the Lord Jesus" (Acts 21:13). When Paul would not be persuaded to reconsider his trip to

Jerusalem, the believers ceased trying and said, "The will of the Lord be done" (Acts 21:14).

JERUSALEM: FIFTH AND FINAL VISIT Paul's third missionary journey was coming to an end (Acts 21:14–17). Having made the necessary arrangements with regard to their baggage, Paul and his companions proceeded to Jerusalem (see map 4, p. 448). Some of the Caesarean believers went along with them, not only out of respect and sympathy for Paul, but to secure his comfort by taking him to the house of Mnason, a native of Cyprus and an aged convert to Christianity.

This missionary journey was Paul's last recorded Gospel-preaching tour. I say last because Luke does not mention anything after Paul's imprisonment in Rome. However, I believe that there is evidence to support two imprisonments, and that a fourth missionary journey is quite possible, though it is not specifically recorded (see chapter 13). The third journey was full of incidents and Luke relates it more minutely than Paul's other journeys. We know about all the places—whether he passed or visited and stayed. In addition we are able to connect each place with historical backgrounds. We can point to places where his vessels anchored for the night, the courses his ship followed, the weather conditions, and the direction of the wind. We have been made fully aware of the apostle's mind and of the burdened feeling he had for many he had led to the Lord (especially the Corinthians).

Paul had never gone to Jerusalem without a heart full of emotion. As a young Jew, Paul dreamed of going to the Holy City and was later privileged to go as an enthusiastic lad from Tarsus, sitting at the feet of Gamaliel and learning of Moses and the prophets. There were the days after his conversion and his leaving Damascus when he went back and faced not only his old cohorts of the Jewish faith but also the believers themselves, who at first doubted his faith in Christ but who finally accepted him after Barnabas befriended him. He went with Barnabas to take an offering for those who would need help during an impending famine. Then there was the time when he, with Barnabas, helped convince the church that Gentiles—the uncircumcised—who by faith had believed in Christ, were as welcomed by God as were Jews who had believed in Christ. Now we find him arriving in Jerusalem calmly and resolutely, though doubtful of his reception among the Christian brethren, and not knowing what would happen on the morrow.

SOME RESULTS OF PAUL'S THIRD MISSIONARY JOURNEY

1. The Ephesian elders were informed of "the way of God more perfectly" and were baptized in the name of the Lord Jesus (Acts 19:1–7).

2. The Word spread throughout Asia Minor (19:8–10).

3. Paul, with many tears and much persecution from the Jews, witnessed from house to house to reach people for Christ (Acts 20:19–20).

4. Paul performed special miracles to show the exorcists the fallacy of Diana's amulets and the Ephesian letters (19:11–12).

5. Sceva's sons were defeated by demons because they dishonored the name of the Lord Jesus (19:13–16).

6. Many Ephesians believed on Christ as a result of Paul's miracles and the defeat of Sceva's sons. They gave evidence that they were new creatures in Christ by burning their books of magic—a great financial loss to them (Acts 19:17–20).

7. Because of Paul's concern for those at Corinth, it is quite possible that he made a second visit to see believers there while he abode in Ephesus for three years.

8. A riot broke out in Ephesus because of the effect of the Gospel against Diana (Acts 19:23–34).

9. At the close of the riot, a city official exonerated Paul (Acts 19:35–41).

10. Paul visited Macedonia and wrote his second epistle to the Corinthians (Acts 20:1; see chapter 7).

11. Paul completely covered the area of Macedonia in preaching the Gospel and went as far west as Illyricum (Romans 15:19–23).

12. The state of Christianity in Athens must have been very discouraging to Paul.

13. While in Corinth for three months, he concluded his efforts to collect an offering for the poor and wrote his epistle to the believers in Rome.

14. Once again God spared Paul's life while in Corinth (Acts 20:3).

15. Paul, in Miletus, encouraged the Ephesian elders to be faithful (Acts 20:17–35).

16. At Tyre, Paul was warned by the Holy Spirit not to go back to Jerusalem, but had a blessed time of fellowship with these believers (Acts 21:2–7).

17. Paul had wonderful fellowship with Philip the evangelist and his daughters in Caesarea (Acts 21:8–9).

18. The Holy Spirit warned Paul by Agabus not to go to Jerusalem (Acts 21:10–12).

19. Paul made a decision to go to Jerusalem in spite of warnings by the Holy Spirit through believers in Tyre and Agabus in Caesarea (Acts 21:3–4, 8, 11–16).

TEST YOURSELF ON CHAPTER EIGHT

1. What was Paul's four-fold purpose in making this particular missionary journey? What was the approximate date of this trip?

2. Who was Paul's partner at the outset of this journey?

3. What role did Silas play after being Paul's co-worker?

4. After going through most of Asia Minor from Antioch, where was Paul's first lengthy stay? How far had he traveled overland from Antioch to this city?

5. What was the character of the city of Ephesus?

6. Why did Paul have to fight with wild beasts?

7. Describe Diana's temple and tell its purpose.

8. Who were the first to whom Paul ministered in Ephesus? What was their problem?

9. What is the real need in the life of the average Christian?

10. What was Paul's theme as he preached to the Jews?

11. What was the result of Paul's teaching and preaching in the school of Tyrannus?

12. What was the significance of Paul's special miracles?

13. What was so unusual about these miracles?

14. Why were the sons of Sceva tormented by an evil spirit?

15. What was the twofold result of Paul's victorious miracles?

16. Why is it likely that Paul paid a second visit to Corinth?

17. Why was there a riot in Ephesus? Who instigated it? How long was the uproar? What was the cry of the people?

18. How was the uproar in the amphitheater in Ephesus

quelled, and what was the argument used to quiet the
people?

19. Where did Paul go after he left Ephesus and what
    epistle did he write?

20. How far west did Paul penetrate in preaching the
    Gospel in Macedonia?

21. What was the character of those in Illyricum?

22. What had been the effect of the Gospel on Athens?

23. How long and where did Paul stay in Corinth?

24. How was his life endangered while there?

25. What two important things happened while Paul was
    in Corinth?

26. Who delivered Paul's epistle to those in Rome?

27. How many Old Testament references did Paul use in
    his letter to the Romans?

28. What unusual event happened during Paul's sermon
    in Troas?

29. Name as many "members one of another" as you can.

30. When and with whom did Paul stay in Caesarea?

31. What kind of warning did Agabus give Paul in Cae-
    sarea?

32. What was Paul's reply to the prophecy of Agabus?

33. What was the response of the believers to Paul's reply?

34. What was the total mileage of Paul's third missionary
    journey?

Chapter Nine

PAUL'S LAST VISIT TO JERUSALEM AND HIS ARREST

Wherever Paul went and regardless of the strength of hostility or persecution that dogged his footsteps, Paul found some believers who loved the glad tidings he preached and loved him as the messenger of the grace of God.

RECEPTION BY THE JERUSALEM BRETHREN "When we were come to Jerusalem, the brethren received us gladly" (Acts 21:17). This is Luke's description of the welcome given the Apostle to the Gentiles upon his arrival in the metropolis of Judaism (see map 5, p. 450). Having left Caesarea with certain disciples, Paul's group lodged with Mnason, an aged believer (Acts 21:16). Paul must have been encouraged by the kind reception of these sympathizing Christians. A more formidable ordeal awaited him, however.

The next day, Paul and the trusted deputies of several churches whose alms he bore visited James and the elders of the Jerusalem assembly. The elders received the travelers with the touching symbol of Christian brotherhood—the "kiss of peace" (see Acts 21:18–19a; 1 Thessalonians 5:26). Although Luke makes no mention of it, the offering for the poor was presented—a proof of love from the churches of the Gentiles to the mother church from which they derived their spiritual beginnings. Then the main business of the assembly got underway with an address by Paul (Acts 21:19b).

This was not the first occasion on which he had been called on to take a stand before this same audience. He had done so in the days of the apostolic council when he declared to the body of believers the Gospel that he had preached to the Gentiles and the great things God had wrought among those "outcasts." The majority of the church had been brought under the truth of his testimony and had ratified his views by their subsequent decree (Acts 15:12–26). Here he is again before these same men, four years after he last left Jerusalem, to give another detailed account of all that God had done among the Gentiles by his preaching. The founding of the church at Ephesus must have comprised the majority of his testimony, but he mentioned also the progress of churches in Phrygia, Galatia, and other parts of Asia Minor, and in Macedonia; his witnessing in Illyricum and in Achaia; and his fellowship with his associates as well as the wonderful fellowship with believers at Tyre and Caesarea.

During his discourse, he could not avoid some subjects that excited painful feelings and roused bitter prejudices in many Judaizing believers in his audience. He knew that James and these elders were still harboring certain Jewish beliefs and condoning many Jewish customs. He could hardly speak of Galatia without mentioning the attempted perversion of his converts there. He could not speak of the state of the church in Corinth without alluding to the emissaries from Palestine who had introduced confusion and strife among the Christians of that city. Yet we know that Paul, with the grace and courage noted both by his writings and speeches, was able to convince his hearers of the might and power of the Gospel in the lives of all who had believed. As a result, the majority of the assembled elders were favorably impressed with his address. Their response was to glorify God. They joined in thanksgiving with one accord as they praised the Lord for these results (Acts 21:17–20a).

PAUL REQUESTED TO APPEASE THE JUDAIZERS Beneath this outward joy, however, there lurked elements of bitter discord that threatened to disturb the whole assembly, especially the apostle (Acts 21:20–25). A Pharisaic faction continually strove to turn Christianity into a sect of Judaism. We have already seen that this faction had recently sent their henchmen into Gentile churches and had endeavored to turn the minds of Paul's converts from truth to error. These men were restless agitators, controlled by a bitter sectarian spirit, and although they were a small minority party, their relentlessness kept the church in a turmoil.

Beside these Judaizing zealots, there was a large number of Christians at Jerusalem, whose Christianity, though sincere, was very weak and imperfect. The many thousands of Jews who had believed had by no means attained the fullness of the Christian faith. They were still in a state of transition from Judaism to Christianity, from law to grace. Many Christian leaders, therefore, thought it best not to shock their prejudices too rudely lest they be tempted to renounce their Christianity altogether.

Although James appeared to be the apostle of the transition church, he seemed afraid to take a definite, positive stand against the hostility of the Judaizing bigots, which appeared to be the attitude of the elders, also. This lack of action regarding the Judaizers might explain the resolution that followed Paul's testimony. To them the strength of the Jewish element in the Jerusalem church was great, and it appeared that they did not want to agitate any further Jewish patriotism. They told Paul that the majority of the Christian church had been taught to hate his name and to believe that he had gone about the world "teaching all the Jews . . . to forsake Moses, saying that they ought not to circumcise their children, neither to walk after their customs" (Acts 21:21). They also told Paul that his arrival would become known; that his fame was too great to allow him to go unnoticed; that his public appearance in the streets of Jerusalem would attract a crowd of curious spectators, most of whom would be violently hostile. It was needful then that he should do something to disarm these Jewish rabble-rousers and refute the injurious slander that was being circulated throughout the city about him (Acts 21:20a–21).

The plan that they recommended, as outlined in Acts 21:23–26, was that he should take charge of four men who were under a Nazarite vow, accompany them to the temple, and pay for the necessary expenses involved in their attending to the fulfillment of their vow; thus purifying himself with them. These four men were evidently Jewish Christians. According to Josephus, Agrippa I had given the same public expression of his sympathy with the Jews on his arrival from Rome to take possession of the throne. On arriving in Jerusalem he offered many sacrifices of thanksgiving and ordered that many of the Nazarites should have their heads shorn.[1] What the king had done for popularity, the elders felt Paul should do for the sake of peace. Paul's friends thought that if he publicly exhibited himself by purifying himself as a "paying" observer of this Mosaic ceremony, he would then refute the accusations of his enemies. They sought to convince Paul that doing so would in no way have a bearing on any Gentiles because it had already been decided that Jewish ceremonial observations of the law were not obligatory for them.

As previously noted in chapter 3 while Paul, Aquila, and Priscilla were in Cenchrea, Aquila had taken a similar vow and had had his head shorn. It was a Nazarite vow, one of consecration—a customary vow among the Jews who had received deliverance from some great peril or for giving thanks. In keeping a vow, a Nazarite publicly testified of his dedication to God. These four men were near the end of their vow—close to the time when they would fulfill it. If Paul would now take these fellows into the temple, purify himself with them, and pay for the sacrifices that needed to be offered, this would let the contentious Judaizers know that Paul walked orderly and kept the law. In this way, all the gossip about his teaching the Jews among the Gentiles to forsake Moses and not to circumcise their children would come to naught—the Jewish church would be reconciled. According to Charles C. Ryrie, "Paul was being asked to pay the expenses involved in the offerings required at the completion of the Nazarite vow these four men had taken. He was being urged to take actions that would indicate that he was, after all, a 'middle-of-the-road' Jewish-Christian."[2] We find in Numbers 6:13–21 what Paul was asked to do in purifying himself with these four men.

> And this is the law of the Nazarite, when the days of his separation are fulfilled: he shall be brought unto the door of the tabernacle [temple] of the congregation. And he shall offer his offering unto the LORD, one he lamb of the first year without blemish for a burnt offering, and one ewe lamb of the first year without blemish for a sin offering, and one ram without blemish for peace offerings. And a basket of unleavened bread, cakes of fine flour mingled with oil, and wafers of unleavened bread anointed with oil, and their meat offering, and their drink offering. And the priest shall bring them before the LORD, and shall offer his sin offering, and his burnt offering. And he shall

offer the ram for a sacrifice of peace offering unto the LORD, with the basket of unleavened bread: the priest shall also offer his meat offering, and his drink offering. And the Nazarite shall shave the head of his separation at the door of the tabernacle of the congregation, and shall take the hair of the head of his separation, and put it in the fire which is under the sacrifice of the peace offerings. And the priest shall take the sodden shoulder of the ram, and one unleavened cake out of the basket, and one unleavened wafer, and shall put them upon the hands of the Nazarite, after the hair of his separation is shaven. Then the priest shall wave them for a wave offering before the LORD: this is holy for the priest, with the wave breast and heave shoulder: and after that the Nazarite may drink wine. This is the law of the Nazarite who hath vowed, and of his offering unto the LORD for his separation, beside that that his hand shall get: according to the vow which he vowed, so he must do after the law of his separation.

Strange as it may seem, Paul willingly complied with the advice of the assembly, and while he removed the prejudice of the strong Judaizing element within the group, he no doubt provoked those who had hoped he would refuse, since they knew the charges against him were false. The meeting was adjourned and the next day Paul took the men to the temple (see illustration 38). They went well inside the area where only Jews could go. These sacred limits were fenced off by low pillars supporting a handrail, with columns set at intervals on which inscriptions in Greek and Latin warned all Gentiles against advancing beyond them on pain of death. This fence is mentioned by Josephus in a striking passage where Titus said to the Jews after a horrible scene of bloodshed within these sacred limits as he was destroying Jerusalem:

Was it not yourselves, you wretches, who raised this fence before your sanctuary? Was it not yourselves that set the pillars therein at intervals, inscribed with Greek characters and our characters, and forbidding anyone to pass the boundaries? And was it not we that allowed you to kill anyone so transgressing, though he were a Roman?[3]

From this it appears that the Jews had full permission from the Romans to kill anyone, even a Roman, if he went beyond the boundaries. It was in this sacred spot of the temple that Paul took

PAUL REQUESTED TO APPEASE THE JUDAIZERS   265

38—Temple model of Paul's day. *Courtesy of author.*

these men, purifying himself with them to signify the accomplishment of the days of purification and offering the necessary sacrifices mentioned by Moses for such a ceremony.

PAUL SEIZED IN THE TEMPLE BY THE JEWS Just before the seven days of purification would have ended with the offerings or sacrifices being made, certain Jews from Asia recognized Paul (Acts 21:27–31). They stirred up the people—worshipers from every land who had come to Jerusalem to celebrate Pentecost. They seized Paul and cried out,

> Men of Israel, help. This is the man that teacheth all men every where against the people [Jews], and the law, and this place: and further brought Greeks also into the temple and hath polluted this holy place (For they had seen before with him in the city of Trophimus an Ephesian, whom they supposed that Paul had brought into the temple). (vv. 28–29)

A vast multitude that had gathered on the spot, as well as others in the temple, was excited to fanatical madness by this announcement that spread throughout the whole area. The pilgrims who flocked to Jerusalem for feasts were the most zealous of their nation—very Hebrew of the Hebrews. We can only imagine the consternation, the horror, and the indignation that gripped their minds when they heard that an apostate from the faith of Israel had been seized in the temple in the very act of profaning that sacred spot at that holy season. With the madness of demons, they rushed Paul, and it was only their reverence for the sacred holy place that kept them from profaning it with his blood. They hurried him out of this sacred enclosure, and as the Levites shut the gates, the mob took their victim to the court of the Gentiles and began beating him with violent blows. Their next course might have been to stone him or hurl him over the temple precipice to the valley below. To Paul's delight, however, they suddenly stopped beating him. It is quite possible that Paul was again reminded that he was reaping what he had sown.

PAUL RESCUED BY All the commotion came to the atten-
A ROMAN CAPTAIN tion of the Roman sentries on guard
nearby (Acts 21:31–40). They sent news immediately to their captain, Claudius Lysias, the commandant of the garrison, that "all Jerusalem was in an uproar" (v. 31). As someone has said, "a spark had fallen on materials the most inflammable, and not a moment was to be lost if a conflagration was to be averted."[4]

Lysias with some of his soldiers rushed immediately to the spot where Paul was surrounded by angry Jews. At the sight of the heavily armed guards, the Jewish mob immediately let go of their victim: "they left beating of Paul" (Acts 21:32). They had for the moment forgotten the proximity of the Roman fortress to their temple and that the eyes of Rome were ever on them. They also knew that they were helpless when soldiers took over. Lysias and his company of men went straight to Paul when they realized he was the recipient of the cruel actions. Paul, suspected to be an Egyptian rebel who had previously caused trouble, was seized and chained to some soldiers. Because the crowd was now silent, the commandant questioned the bystanders, and when some cried one thing and some another, he wisely took Paul back to the barracks under heavy guard. The multitude pressed and crowded the soldiers as they sought to have Lysias turn Paul back over to them, but Paul was actually carried up the staircase and into safety. The multitude continued to demand his life, crying: "Away with him."

Chapter Nine

Paul, no doubt, had heard about the time at this same praetorium when Pilate was ruler of Judaea that the Jews had cried out against Jesus: "Away with him, away with him, crucify him" (John 19:15). It is easy for us to realize how heavy Paul's heart must have been at this moment as he mulled over what the Jews had done to his Savior. How heartbreaking it must have been as he thought of the times he had wished that the Christ of Christianity had never appeared on the scene and how glad he had been that his brethren were responsible for His death. Now, as a believer and a staunch soldier of the Cross, his kinsmen were crying for his blood, just as their fathers had done. He was now in the same role as his Savior.

PAUL'S SPEECH IN HEBREW BEFORE THE JEWS With the words, *Away with him*, ringing in his ears, Paul turned to the commanding officer who was near him, and said respectfully, "May I speak with thee?" (Acts 21:37). Claudius Lysias was shocked when he found himself addressed in Greek and asked whether he was then mistaken in thinking that Paul was the Egyptian ringleader of a recent rebellion. Paul replied calmly that he was not Greek but a Jew, and at the same time he asserted his claim to respectful treatment by saying that he was a native of Tarsus in Cilicia, a citizen of no mean city. Still taking advantage of the officer's surprise, Paul requested that he be allowed to address the Jews.

Paul's request was a bold one and could have been the beginning of Paul's gaining an influence with this Roman officer (Acts 21:39–22:24). Possibly Lysias granted permission because he "owed Paul one." After all he had arrested the apostle and had bound him with chains before learning the cause of the upheaval or that his prisoner was a Roman citizen. When Paul began to speak, he stood on the stairs between the fortress Antonia and the temple. Immediately the whole scene changed as Paul made a motion with his hand and said, "Men, brethren, and fathers, hear ye my defense which I make now unto you" (22:1). The language he used was Hebrew. Had he spoken in Greek the majority would have fully understood his words, but the sound of their "mother tongue" brought silence. No one spoke; no one moved. These Jews riveted their attention on what Paul had to say, even when he talked about Jesus, Ananias of Damascus, and his vision in the temple. There were those in the crowd who could testify on their own evidence the truth of what he said about

Gamaliel, his persecution of Christians, and the stoning of Stephen.

It is also quite possible that Gamaliel was present as Paul delivered this speech (Acts 22:1–21). In a book titled *Horce Paulince*, the author mentions that Gamaliel died about two years after this meeting took place. Gamaliel was known for his level-headedness when vehement Jews confronted him about Peter's and the apostles' preaching "none other name" but Christ (Acts 4:12; 5:17–18). Gamaliel had reminded them that if this doctrine was of men, it would come to nought; but if it was of God, it could not be overthrown (Acts 5:34–39). This revered Hebrew was known as the "aged *Rabban*," a title given to only seven men because of their eminent learning and holy character. The title *Rabban* is the same as *Rabboni* that Mary Magdalene gave to Christ. Gamaliel was not swayed by the narrow bigotry of Jews. He rose above their prejudices. There is a saying in the Talmud that when Gamaliel died, "the glory of the Lord . . . ceased."[5]

If Gamaliel was present in this gathering before Paul, why, then, did he not remind these Jews of what he had said years ago, seeing that this doctrine had not come to nought? We must remember that there was dead silence while Paul was speaking, but at the mere mention of his going to the Gentiles, the rabid, fanatical Jews screamed so loudly they could not even hear their own voices, which prohibited anyone else from being heard. Even if he had shouted, Gamaliel would have never been heard. Paul himself was silenced; the outburst of indignation was too great for "right" to be considered. The Jews' national pride shot down every argument that could influence their reason or their reverence for any of their leaders, such as Gamaliel or the high priest. They could not bear the thought of uncircumcised hea-thens (Gentiles) being made equal with the sons of Abraham. They cried out that a wretch like Paul ought not to pollute the earth with his presence; that it was a shame to preserve his life. In their rage and impatience they tossed off their outer garments, as had been done when the Sanhedrin stoned Stephen. They continued to vent their hatred against this servant of God by throwing dust in the air as a sign of contempt. (Shimei did the same thing to express his contempt for David. It is said he "cursed [David] as he went, cast stones at him, and cast dust" [2 Samuel 16:13]). They also throw dust to express rage and vexation because they could not get their hands on Paul again. He was too far removed from them by the soldiers.

The Jews' demonstration threw Lysias into a state of perplexity. He had not been able to understand Paul's speech in Hebrew and when he saw the results, he had no choice but to suppose that his prisoner was guilty of some enormous crime. He ordered his men to take Paul back up the stairs to the barracks and to "beat" out of him the reason these hot-headed, violent Jews demanded his life (Acts 22:24). The instruments necessary for this scourging would be in readiness inside, and before long Paul's body would be stretched out to receive the lashes from a hardened soldier.

We now find Paul on the verge of adding another suffering and disgrace to his long list of afflictions, which he had enumerated in 2 Corinthians 11:23–25. Five times scourged by the Jews, once beaten with rods at Philippi, and twice on other unknown occasions, he had indeed been "in stripes above measure." Here in the Roman barracks, among rude Roman soldiers who hated Jews as much as the Jews hated them, Paul knew that the man who was to scourge him would have no mercy on him, so he rescued himself with a few words to the centurion who stood by, saying: "Is it lawful for you to scourge [torture] a man that is a Roman, and uncondemned?" (Acts 22:25).

Paul bought some time with his claim of Roman citizenship, and the centurion immediately reported the words to his commanding officer, saying: "Take heed what thou doest, for this man is a Roman" (Acts 22:26). Possibly Lysias, in the heat of all the excitement and frustration of the Jews' reaction to Paul's speech, had forgotten for the moment that Paul had said that he was a citizen of Tarsus. Rome had made Tarsus in Cilicia a free city, and the bulk of its residents were Roman citizens. When Lysias was reminded that Paul was a Roman citizen, he was both astonished and alarmed. He knew full well that no man would dare claim the right of citizenship if it did not belong to him, and he hastened in person to his prisoner to check it out. A hurried discussion took place, and Lysias found that Paul was "free born" (Acts 22:28), while he had purchased his citizenship for "a great sum" (v. 28). Orders were immediately given to remove the flogging instruments, but Paul still had to be kept in custody because Lysias was still ignorant of the nature of his offence, and because keeping Paul a prisoner was the only sure method of saving him from physical harm from the Jews. We must also keep in mind that this Roman officer was really on the defensive; for in his treatment of Paul, he had been guilty of a flagrant violation of the Roman law concerning citizenship. He knew it, and Paul knew it (see Acts 22:25–30).

PAUL BEFORE THE SANHEDRIN The day after Lysias and Paul discussed the matter of their Roman citizenship, the captain came up with a plan to determine the nature of the charges against his "prisoner." He summoned a meeting of the Sanhedrin (see illustration 39) and the high priests and brought Paul down from the fortress and set him before them, doubtless taking precautions to prevent a repeat of sudden violence against his prisoner (Acts 22:30–23:10). Only a narrow space existed between the steps of the fortress and those that led up to the hall Gazith, the meeting place of the Sanhedrin. The hall was off-limits for

39—How the Sanhedrin might have looked. *Courtesy of author.*

all but Jews, and Lysias, realizing Paul was his responsibility, wisely kept him in a proper area, which gave license for Roman soldiers to be there to protect Paul if necessary.

Although Roman soldiers were present, the scene was entirely Jewish. Paul was now in the presence of that council before which many had been judged, including Stephen. That moment could hardly have been forgotten by him, but he looked steadfastly at them, recognizing some of his fellow classmates under Gamaliel, and some of his associates in the persecution of Christians.

Earnestly beholding the council he spoke unto them and said: "Men and brethren, I have lived in good conscience before God until this day" (Acts 23:1). These words so enraged Ananias, the high priest, that he commanded those who stood by to strike Paul on the mouth. This insulted Paul to the point that he blurted out, "God smite thee, thou whited wall" (v. 3). When Paul used the words *whited wall* it was his way of saying, "you hypocrite!" Jesus had likened the Pharisees to hypocritical "whited sepulchres"–whitewashed or clean on the outside but full of dead men's bones and uncleanness on the inside (Matthew 23:27). If we consider Paul's words as an outburst of anger—returning evil for evil—it would be difficult to blame him when we remember his temperament and how he was provoked at times, like when he "had it out" with Barnabas about Mark (Acts 15:38–39), and when he "withstood Peter to his face" (Galatians 2:11–14).

We noted in chapter 1 that Paul, being a member of the Sanhedrin, was personally acquainted with Caiaphas, the high priest. Now Paul is before a high priest who is new to him. It would have been difficult to recognize him as such since being in an area with Roman soldiers, he would not be wearing his high priestly garments. Paul's eyesight was good enough to *earnestly behold* those near him, but being short of stature, his view of those at a distance was obscured; hence he did not know it was the high priest who had shouted at him. Or, maybe he only knew that whoever the high priest was, he was not in that position legally. Josephus informs us that there was great irregularity in the appointments of high priests at that time. Others think that Paul spoke sarcastically—that the priesthood had been abolished with the rending of the veil of the temple when Christ was crucified; thus establishing the sole priesthood of Christ. Some look at Paul's rebuke as a prophetic denunciation since this hypocritical leader of the Sanhedrin was soon murdered by assassins in the Jewish war.[6]

Regardless, Paul, when reminded it was the high priest who had commanded him to be struck, did, with meekness and humility, apologize saying that he had not known it was the high priest, otherwise he would not have spoken so, "For it is written, Thou shalt not speak evil of the ruler of Thy people" (Exodus 22:28). The apostle had seen enough to satisfy him that he would not get a fair trial and a just verdict. Knowing how to "get their goat" and throw them into a state of confusion, he enlisted the sympathies of those who agreed with him in one doctrine that was questioned by some in Judaism but was an essential truth in Christianity. He knew that both Pharisees and Sadducees were among his judges, so he cried out, "Brethren, I am a Pharisee, the son of a Pharisee: of the hope and resurrection of the dead I am called in question" (Acts 23:6). The Sadducees did not believe in the resurrection, and Paul was forgotten for the moment while the Pharisees and Sadducees were engaged in a heated doctrinal debate. Some think that the Pharisees hated the Sadducees more than they hated Christianity. The two groups shouted vehemently at each other. Paul was probably to the side laughing, as was Elijah when he had his contest with the prophets of Baal (1 Kings 18:27).

During the argument, the scribes that were of the Pharisees stood up and pleaded with the whole group that Paul was not evil and that if an angel or a spirit had spoken to him, far be it for them to fight against God. Maybe it was Gamaliel who led these scribes. This speech only lit another flame of bitter anger since the bulk of the Jews wanted to be rid of Paul. The judgment hall became a scene of the most violent contention. In this melee one group pulled Paul one way and another group pulled in the opposite direction. When the Roman officer saw that the Jews were about to literally pull Paul to pieces, and fearing that this Roman citizen whom he was bound to protect would be murdered on the spot, ordered his troops to go and bring Paul back to the soldiers' quarters within the fortress.

WAS PAUL DISOBEDIENT IN GOING TO JERUSALEM? The apostle Paul, in Roman quarters, was for the time being safe from his kinsmen. The morning had been one of violence. Paul passed the rest of the day in isolation from both his Jewish enemies and his Christian friends. He was no longer physically opposed by the presence of his persecutors nor supported by any of his sympathizing brethren. We can imagine that his heart had sunk and that he looked with dread on the vague and unknown future that was before him. Where were James and the elders who had put him up to going into the temple? Maybe they felt guilty for requesting this of Paul. Maybe they felt too ashamed to face Paul and admit that they had given him bad advice. Right or wrong, they certainly could have been an encouragement to him at this moment of despair, but there is no record that any of the Jerusalem brethren ever came to his rescue. On the surface this seems to be a victory for the opposing forces.

When one is alone in solitary confinement as was Paul, "thinking" is about all one can do. The afternoon must have passed slowly, and Paul, no doubt, began to wonder if Agabus had not been right in warning him not to go to Jerusalem (Acts 21:10–12) because he would be bound by the Jews and then delivered to the Gentiles (Romans). This prophecy, like the one about the famine, literally came to pass. There in the barracks Paul sat reflecting on what the Jews had done and seeing himself at the mercy of the Gentiles. Human nature in this type of situation usually asks, "Why me, Lord?" Paul was probably no exception.

In putting the pieces together as to the why of this event, we must go back and review Paul's ministry from his encounter with Christ on the road to Damascus until this moment in prison. On his first visit to Jerusalem, Christ appeared to him in the temple and gave him specific instructions concerning his service.

> And it came to pass, that, when I was come again to Jerusalem, even while I prayed in the temple, I was in a trance; and saw him [Christ] saying unto me, make haste, and get thee up quickly out of Jerusalem, for they [the Jews] will not receive thy testimony concerning Me . . . And He said unto me, Depart: for I will send thee *far hence* unto the Gentiles (Acts 22:17–18, 22).

This was warning *number one* to stay clear of witnessing to the Jews in Jerusalem. This warning alone should have told Paul that he was not the one to be a minister to the Jews in Jerusalem. Warning *number two* not to go to Jerusalem came from the Holy Spirit through the saints at Tyre (Acts 21:3–4). Warning *number three* as to what the Jews would do to him if he went to Jerusalem came from the Holy Spirit through Agabus (Acts 21:8–12). All these warnings seemed to fall on deaf ears.

Although Paul was labeled the "Apostle or minister to the Gentiles, the 'Gospel preacher' to the uncircumcised" (Romans 11:13; 15:16; Galatians 2:7), such a calling would not exclude his witnessing to Jews elsewhere. We have noted that one of his best methods in reaching Gentiles was to go first to the synagogues to win Jews that they in turn might help him reach Gentiles. It appears, however, that Paul, in spite of his saying that he counted his Jewish heritage and all the prestige that goes with being a nationalistic Jew as dung that he might win Christ, could never shake this heritage. He bragged about his being a Pharisee, and was willing to go into the temple and offer sacrifices—including the sin offering. His burning compassion for his lost brethren was uppermost in his mind, and on one occasion he even said he would "wish himself accursed from Christ for my brethren, my kinsmen according to the flesh" (Philippians 3:4–8; Romans 9:1–3). *Accursed* means "anathema." Paul was saying that if it were possible he would be willing to be excommunicated from Christ—literally would be willing to die and go to hell if it meant bringing about the salvation of any of his kinsmen, but he *never*, to our knowledge, made such a statement concerning the Gentiles, though no one can deny his undying devotion to and concern for the many Gentile converts, as we see in his letters to the Corinthians.

In his travels he often made mention of a desire to go back to Jerusalem (Acts 18:21; 19:21; 20:16). After Christ warned him to make haste, leave Jerusalem, and depart far hence to preach to the Gentiles because the Jews there would not hear him, he visited Jerusalem three times. There were no warnings given against his going when he went with Barnabas to take an offering to the poor (Acts 11:27–30; 12:25). There was no warning given when Paul returned for the Jerusalem Council where he testified of God's grace to the Gentiles (Acts 15:1–12). There was no warning against his third visit to Jerusalem when he completed his second missionary journey (see chapter 7, Acts 18:22). There was a warning by the Holy Spirit through believers, however, against his going to Jerusalem this fourth time (Acts 21:3–4; 10–12).

Paul knew that the prophecy of Agabus about the famine had literally come to pass as noted in chapter 5. Yet he ignored the last prophecy of Agabus. Why? Possibly Paul was more of a Jew than he thought he was, and in his thinking he figured he might be the one who could win over the Judaizers in the Jerusalem church as well as win many unbelieving Jews and bring about peace and harmony to the Christian community. His arrival in Jerusalem and his ready willingness to do what James and the elders asked of him shows that he would go to great lengths to win peace. If he could win this church to the full truth of the finished work of Christ, or could avert its open hostility to himself, more would be accomplished for the diffusion of the Judaizing error than had already been accomplished. Paul was ready to adopt every lawful means for such an end. He had just written to the Romans about what ceremonies to observe—what day to worship, what to do or what not to do, what to eat or what not to eat—all so that they would not be a stumbling block to others (Romans 14). He was responsible for Timothy's circumcision, though he knew that circumcision or uncircumcision meant nothing; only faith in Christ counted for salvation. He had been with Aquila in the cutting of his hair in a Nazarite vow. Paul had become a Jew to the Jew that he might gain the Jews as willingly as he had become a Gentile to Gentiles that he might win them. He had previously written this principle in his first letter to the Corinthians (9:19–23). It was for this principle that he gave assent to the request of the elders and took these men into the temple to fulfill their Nazarite vow.

Two questions must be asked at this point. First, did Paul disobey the Lord in going to Jerusalem for this visit? We have already discussed the warnings given to Paul. The force of these warnings by Holy Spirit should have, I believe, caused Paul to think twice about going, and then do what he had been called to do—be on the move for God by going far hence to the Gentiles (Acts 22:17–18, 21). One can witness when bound, but there is greater liberty when one is free to go as the Lord commands. He had been warned twice by the Holy Spirit through the saints in Tyre and by Agabus in Caesarea but in his determination to go, he ignored these warnings. It is interesting to note that the desire to go to Jerusalem was always his and not the Lord's. On two occasions in Asia Minor he wanted to go into Asia to Bithynia to preach, but he obeyed the Holy Spirit's leading and continued westward (Acts 16:6–8). He did not obey the Holy Spirit's direction about going to Jerusalem.

We notice that on three occasions that it was Paul's spirit or Paul's determination that pressed him into going. Acts 19:21 tells us that he purposed or committed himself in the spirit to go to the Holy City. Spirit here begins with a small *s*, which denotes that it was his spirit and not the Holy Spirit. In Acts 20:16, we find that "Paul had determined [resolved or decreed within himself] . . . to be in Jerusalem for Pentecost." In Acts 20:22 he said, "I go bound in the spirit [my own mind] unto Jerusalem. . . ." Here again the word spirit begins with a small *s*, indicating his own desire rather than the Holy Spirit's. When Agabus along with the saints at Tyre warned Paul, it was by the Spirit—capital *S*, indicating the Holy Spirit. *Spirit* with a small *s* in the above mentioned verses is the neuter gender, indicating that Paul made it up in his *own mind* to go. Holy Spirit and Spirit in Acts 21:4 and 11 are in the masculine gender, meaning "the person" of the Holy Spirit. Here we have Paul's spirit or mind versus the Holy Spirit. Would this not imply that he went to

Jerusalem in opposition or in possible disobedience to the Holy Spirit?.

Paul told those at Philippi when he wrote his epistle to them that they should understand that what happened to him (in these bonds) had been for to the furtherance of the Gospel (1:12). It is amazing how God works in spite of us. Peter willfully and woefully disobeyed the Lord when he denied Him three times. Yes, he was sorry for what he had done and wept bitterly, and from this experience of weakness he became preacher on the Day of Pentecost, boldly pointing an accusing finger at those who crucified Christ, and later joining in with those who said they would "obey God rather than man" (Acts 2:14, 22–23; 5:29). Peter's wrong worked together for his good and God's glory. Paul was in a similar situation. God used Paul's wrong to give him a greater challenge in witnessing in prison, on board ship, in shipwreck, among heathens, and even in Caesar's household. He did this by giving Paul his *fourth* vision of Christ, and told him that as he had testified of Him in Jerusalem, he would bear witness of Him also in Rome (Acts 23:11). We should never, however, interpret God's taking a wrongdoing and turning it into something for His glory as a license to continue disobeying: "Shall we continue in sin that grace may abound? God forbid" (Romans 6:1). Both Peter and Paul learned their lessons.

Second, was Paul disobedient in following through on the request of the elders to purify himself and pay for the sacrifices to be offered by the four men who had made the Nazarite vow? When Paul said in effect that "he became all things to all men that he might win some," we note in 1 Corinthians 9:21 that he mentioned that these deeds were done under the law of Christ. Paul would not get drunk to win a drunkard, or commit fornication to win a pagan prostitute to the Lord. One does not get down in a pig pen to rescue a pig stuck in the mud; otherwise both will be in the mire.

Up to this point, we believe that Paul had not compromised his convictions or the truth in seeking to reach both Jew and Gentile. Now, however, in the face of the complete finished work of Christ at Calvary for sin—the Lamb of God offered once and for all as an atonement for sin—we find Paul going into the temple to purify himself and pay for the following sacrifices for the Nazarite vow (cf. Acts 21:20–26 with Numbers 6:13–21): one he lamb for a burnt offering, one ewe lamb for a sin offering, and one ram for a peace offering.

The same man who is about to go through this ceremony, which includes a sin offering, wrote to those at Colossae and said that Christ had nailed such ordinances to the Cross (2:14). Romans, written by the same author, tells us that Christ is the end of the law for righteousness to everyone who believes (10:4). Paul may or may not have written Hebrews, but he knew the truth that Christ was better than the priests and sacrifices of the Old Testament; that all the sacrifices of this dispensation were imperfect, worldly (earthly), carnal ordinances, patterns, and at best, a shadow of good things to come (cf. Hebrews 7:11 with 9:1, 10, 23; 10:1–4).

In light of what Scripture teaches and what Paul himself wrote about Christ and His redemptive work, how can we justify his willingness to participate in this vow and pay for sacrifices? Was this disobedience to truth and the revealed will of God? In his desire for his kinsmen to know the Messiah and be saved, was he momentarily blind to such a great compromise? Few have ever felt such a compelling desire to witness to one certain group, and Paul did not yet realize that these Jews would reject his testimony. His one desire was to tell them that Jesus saves. He thought that if only he could tell them in person, they would listen. But, alas, here he was in a Roman fortress, all alone. Possibly he thought about how he had withstood Peter to his face for being a strict Jew among the Jews in Antioch and ignoring Gentile believers (Galatians 2:11–14). He no doubt was asking himself, *Why did I ever let James and the elders get me into such a mess?*

The apostle Paul was one of the greatest Christians who ever lived. Even though there may be many who think that he could do no wrong, the man was human and at times he was weak. He admitted that there were times when he would do what he should not do and would not do what he should (Romans 7:15–21). He also acknowledged that he was not perfect (Philippians 3:12). In spite of his going into the temple in compliance with the wishes of the church leaders, God engineered circumstances in such a way that Paul did not participate in the sacrifices and offerings. The days of purification had been accomplished. The next thing on the agenda would have been the offering of the animals. God stopped His servant from partaking of an Old Testament ritual of a sin-offering that would have slapped Him in the face in view of the Cross "and when the seven days were *almost* ended, the Jews . . . stirred up all the people and laid hands on Paul" (Acts 21:26–27). However, damage was done to Paul's independence and his being free to go far hence to the Gentiles. Such actions were costly, and he paid dearly, even though God forgave (Numbers 32:23; Proverbs 28:13; Galatians 6:7; 1 John 1:7).

With many thoughts going through his mind as a result of this temple episode he was, no doubt, weeping as bitterly as Peter had. God will chastise His own, but He will never forsake them. Although Peter had denied Christ three times just before He was crucified, immediately after His resurrection an angel of the Lord told the women at the empty tomb that Christ had risen and for them to go tell the good news to His disciples, *and Peter* (Mark 16:7). Peter had sinned greatly but the forgiving Savior had singled him out by name from all the others—he had not been forgotten. As Paul reflected throughout the afternoon on the events that had ensnared him, "the Lord stood by him, and said, Be of good cheer, Paul, for as thou hast testified of me in Jerusalem, so must thou bear witness also at Rome" (Acts 23:11). Isn't it amazing how the Lord always comes through when we seem to be at our lowest! It was at this low period in his life that Paul was miraculously comforted and strengthened by Him who is "the confidence of all the ends of the earth, and of them that are afar off upon the sea; who by his strength setteth fast the mountains; who stilleth the noise of the seas and the tumult of the people" (Psalm 65:5b–7). Paul would get to Rome as a prisoner, with God's seeing to it that he got free transportation and a Roman guard who would permit him to have certain liberties—liberties that no Roman prisoner had ever had. Paul must have slept like a log that night with the good cheer of the Lord being his portion. He knew that his life was in God's good and gracious hand.

THE JEWISH CONSPIRACY TO ASSASSINATE PAUL When it was day, more than forty of the Jews entered into a conspiracy to assassinate Paul (Acts 23:12–15). To give their crime a religious overtone, they bound themselves by a curse that they would eat and drink nothing until the deed was accomplished. Josephus tells us that such an oath (for anyone) was well and piously taken.[7] Pliny, the Roman historian, said that assassinations of apostates (Paul was an apostate to these Jews) was justified. The Talmud shows that those who were implicated in an oath that resulted on another person's death could obtain absolution. Thus fortified by this dreadful oath, these Jews came before the chief priests and members of the Sanhedrin and proposed the following plan, which seems to have been readily accepted.

These members of the Sanhedrin were to present themselves before Claudius Lysias with the request that he allow the prisoner to be brought once more before the Jewish court for further investigation. As the soldiers brought Paul down, the assassins would lie in wait and murder him. They brought their request to Lysias and, to him, it seemed like a good idea because he still didn't know why the Jews were so upset with Paul. He would be glad to have his perplexity removed by the results of a new inquiry. Unbeknown to him, of course, was the danger to which Paul would be exposed and the trouble he would be in if he let a Roman citizen under his care be murdered. Seldom has there been a more horrible example of premeditated crime clothed in religious zeal. Lysias would have granted the Sanhedrin's request if God had not intervened.

The instrument of Paul's safety was one of his own relatives, his nephew (Acts 23:16). We assume that Paul's sister lived near or in Jerusalem, but why he stayed with Mnason instead of her, we do not know (Acts 21:16). In any case, the young man came into the barracks and related what he knew of the conspiracy against his uncle. Evidently Lysias had granted Paul the liberty of receiving visitors, as noticed by the free access of his nephew. Upon learning of this plot, Paul immediately called one of the centurions over and requested that his nephew have permission to tell Lysias what he had just told him. Lysias received him kindly, "took him by the hand, and went with him aside privately" (Acts 23:19). As the story was related with much feeling, the Roman commander, with all promptness and yet with caution, decided what should be done. He dismissed Paul's nephew, cautioning him to tell no man what had transpired between them (Acts 23:22).

ESCORTED FROM JERUSALEM TO CAESAREA As soon as Paul's nephew was dismissed by the commanding officer (Acts 23:22–33), two centurions were immediately summoned and ordered to have in readiness two-hundred soldiers (see illustration 40), seventy men of the cavalry, and two-hundred spear men. They were to depart at nine o'clock that same evening and take Paul in safety to Felix, the governor, in Caesarea (see map 5, p. 450).

The journey was long and it was imperative to accomplish it

as rapidly as possible. Although the four-hundred foot soldiers had to march, the prisoner (Paul), was privileged to have a horse provided for him! We may be surprised that so large a force was sent to secure the safety of one man, but we must remember that this man was a Roman citizen, and the garrison at the fortress consisted of more than a thousand men. The number sent with Paul could easily be spared. Besides, robberies and rebellions were frequent at this time in Judaea, and there was the great possibility that the Jews might find out what Lysias was up to and try to assassinate Paul during this trip. Lysias was right to have sent this large a company of soldiers for Paul's safety. Prior to their leaving, the captain wrote a letter to Felix of Caesarea explaining the purpose of sending Paul to him (Acts 23:26–30). When the

40—Roman soldier in full armor. *Courtesy of Felbermeyer, Rome.*

time for departure arrived, the troops, with Paul in the midst of them, marched out of the city of Jerusalem and headed northwest toward their destination. After a good two-day journey, a distance of about forty miles, they arrived at Antipatris (near Joppa), roughly halfway between Jerusalem and Caesarea. At this point the horsemen continued on to Caesarea with Paul, and the foot soldiers returned to Jerusalem. Being this far from Jerusalem, they considered Paul to be safe.

TEST YOURSELF ON CHAPTER NINE

1. How was Paul welcomed when he arrived in Jerusalem?

2. What was the reaction of the Jerusalem Jews when Paul gave his third-missionary-journey report?

3. What did James and the elders request of Paul? Why?

4. What kind of vow was Paul requested to participate in and what was his reaction?

5. What kind of sacrifices were involved in completing such a vow? Where is this vow recorded in the Old Testament?

6. Where did Paul have to go to fulfill this vow?

7. Describe the location where Paul went. Who did he go with? What was he asked to do in their behalf?

8. In your opinion, do you believe Paul compromised in participating in such a vow, especially because of his willingness to offer blood sacrifices after he had made it clear that Christ was the fulfillment of all sacrifices? If not, why not?

9. What happened to Paul just before he was to have participated in the offering of these sacrifices?

10. Who were Paul's accusers and what were their charges?

11. What course of action did they take against Paul?

12. How was Paul rescued?

13. Who was the Roman commander who rescued Paul?

14. What did this commander suspect Paul to be?

15. What did Paul request of this Roman officer?

16. What language did Paul use in addressing these Jews and how did it affect them?

17. What was the Jews' first reaction to Paul's speech?

18. What one word did Paul use to cause the Jews to turn against him again?

19. How did they react?

20. What was the commander's reaction to this turmoil, and what did he plan to do with Paul?

21. What "magic" word did Paul use to escape scourging?

22. Explain what effect this had on his captor?

23. Why did he keep Paul in custody?

24. Who did Paul appear before again to defend himself?

25. What unusual experience did he have with the high priest? Explain.

26. How did Paul confuse this group?

27. Do you believe Paul was disobedient in going to Jerusalem? Defend your answer.

28. How many warnings was Paul given not to go to Jerusalem? By whom were these warnings given, and why were they given?

29. How burdened was Paul for his unsaved kinsmen?

30. How burdened was Paul for Gentile believers?

31. Answer briefly the two questions revolving around whether Paul disobeyed the Lord in going to Jerusalem, and whether he compromised truth in a willingness to offer Old Testament sacrifices.

32. What animals were to have been offered?

33. What was the Jewish conspiracy against Paul?

34. Who warned Paul of this plan?

35. What did the commanding officer do about it?

36. Where and how did he take Paul?

Chapter Ten

PAUL'S TWO YEARS IN CAESAREA

When the Roman soldiers arrived in Caesarea (see map 5, p. 450) with Paul, they went immediately to the quarters of governor Felix. He was given the letter from Claudius Lysias, the captain of the fortress Antonia in Jerusalem. Paul was also presented to him. Opening the letter, Felix read as follows:

> Claudius Lysias unto the most excellent governor Felix sendeth greetings. This man was taken of the Jews, and should have been killed by them: then came I with an army, and rescued him, having understood that he was a Roman. And when I would have known the cause wherefore they accused him, I brought him forth into their council: Whom I perceived to be accused of questions of their law, but to have nothing laid to his charge worthy of death or of bonds. And when it was told me how that the Jews laid wait for this man, I sent straightway to thee, and gave commandment to his accusers also to say before thee what they had against him. Farewell. (Acts 23:26–30)

According to Roman custom, Felix asked what province Paul was from and upon learning that he was from Cilicia, commanded that he be kept in Herod's judgment hall, or praetorium. He then informed Paul that he would hear and decide his case when his accusers arrived (Acts 23:31–35).

Unbeknown to Paul at this time was the fact that he would

be in Caesarea at least two years before going to Rome. We might well ask what it was like in Herod's praetorium. How confined was Paul as a Roman prisoner? When an accusation was brought against a Roman citizen, the magistrate, who had criminal juris- diction in the case, appointed the time for hearing the case and detained the accused in custody during the interval. He was not bound to fix any time for the trial, and could defer it at his own pleasure or commit the prisoner at his discretion to any of the several kinds of custody stipulated by Roman law.

TYPES OF ROMAN IMPRISONMENTS There were three types of Roman impri- sonments. The first was confinement in the public jail (*custodia publica*), which was the most severe kind. These common jails throughout the empire were dungeons of the worst kind where prisoners were kept in chains or were even bound in positions of torture. This was the type of jail in which Paul and Silas were confined in Philippi.

The second type of imprisonment was free custody (*custodia libera*), which was the mildest kind. Here the accused party was committed to the magistrate or senator, who became responsible for his appearance on the day of trial. This type of detention applied only to those of high rank.

The third type of imprisonment was military custody (*custodia militaris*), which had been introduced at the beginning of the Imperial Roman regime. In this form of custody, a soldier, respon- sible with his own life for the safe keeping of his prisoner, was given charge of the accused. The prisoner's right hand was usually chained to the soldier's left. The soldiers of course relieved one another in this duty. The prisoner was usually kept in the barracks but sometimes was allowed to reside in a private house under guard (as was Paul in Rome).

It was under *custodia militaris* that Paul was now placed by Felix: "And he commanded a centurion to keep Paul, and to let him have liberty, and that he should call his acquaintances to come and minister unto him" (Acts 24:23). Close confinement was necessary, both to keep him safe from the Jews and because he was not yet acquitted. Paul had been under this same of type custody in Jerusalem. This arrest in the apostle's career when his labors were so critical to the church is hard for us to under- stand—especially because it involved two years of the best part of Paul's life. Providential workings seem so mysterious to us.

Sometimes though we must realize that God has an inner work to accomplish in the lives of those who have been chosen as His instruments for His special service. As Paul needed quiet preparation in Arabia before he entered his career, so his imprisonment at Caesarea would give him time to meditate, have less-interrupted prayer, and gain a deeper knowledge of the unsearchable riches of Christ. Certainly the care of all the churches was still weighing heavily on his heart. He needed time for message preparation, and possibly some time was spent in writing of which we know nothing. When he wrote to those at Colossae, he suggested that they read the letter he had sent to the Laodiceans (Colossians 4:16). Maybe he wrote this letter while in Caesarea. It was possibly lost since we have no record of it. Some have suggested that Luke, fellowshiping with Paul in Caesarea, wrote his Gospel account with Paul's help during this time.

FELIX, GOVERNOR OF JUDAEA (CAESAREA) Caesarea of Judaea had been built by Herod the Great and named in honor of Augustus Caesar. It had a splendid artificial harbor and became the military headquarters for Roman forces in that area. Its location gave easy access from the troubled capital of Jewry, which was under Roman rule, to Rome itself. Whoever governed Judaea at Caesarea had to be highly favored by the emperor. Pilate had once governed from this city. Now we find that Felix is governor.

Felix, a freedman, had once been a slave in the household of Antonia, daughter of Mark Antony and Octavia, widow of Drusus (Tiberius' brother), and mother of Emperor Claudius. Felix had found favor with Claudius and was given this high position in Roman government. His title, according to the Roman historian, Tacitus, was "procurator," a financial officer whose duty it was to obtain funds for Rome, which he seemed to have accomplished with all sorts of tyranny. Because he had been made a free man he thought he could rule as he pleased, so he governed with all the authority of a king and the baseness, arrogance, and hatred of a former slave. He revelled in cruelty and lust. He was a greedy, unrighteous governor.

Tacitus said of Felix that before he became governor of Caesarea he had occupied an administrative post in Samaria of Judaea. While there, he won the confidence of Jonathan, the son of the powerful ex-high priest, Annas. While Jonathan was in

Rome voicing certain Jewish grievances against Cumanus, who then was the governor of Caesarea, he also put in a plug for Felix to become the next governor. Because of Felix's favorable position with Claudius, coupled with Jonathan's request, Felix was appointed the next governor of Caesarea.

One of the first things Felix did was to select a group of knife-wielding terrorists who butchered everyone they disliked but Jews in particular. One of their first victims was Jonathan, who had befriended Felix. That act on the part of these agitators elevated the new governor's ratings in Rome.

Felix had three wives, each born of royalty, one of whom was a granddaughter of Antony and Cleopatra. Drusilla, at the age of twenty, became his third wife. She was the youngest daughter of Herod Agrippa I, and evidently she had become a Jewish proselyte. As a girl she had been engaged to the crown prince of Commagene, but since he would not embrace the Jews' religion, they were never married. She was then promised by her younger brother to Azizus, king of Emesa in Syria, who was willing to embrace Judaism. Felix, at this point, came upon the scene and with the help of a Cypriot magician, persuaded her to leave her husband, Azizus, and become his third wife. According to Josephus, there seems to be little doubt that Felix became a Jew in name only, in order to marry her. He is said to have promised her every desire if she married him.[1] They had one child, Agrippa, who died with Drusilla in the eruption of Vesuvius, which happened in A.D. 79.[2]

Because Drusilla was Jewish, Felix learned much of Jewish life and customs. Christianity was well established in Caesarea, and Cornelius and Philip lived there, along with many believers as we noted when Paul was there just prior to his going to Jerusalem (Acts 10; 21:8–12). Not only had Felix learned much about religion and customs but because he resided in Caesarea, where Christianity had been known for many years and had penetrated even among his troops (Cornelius was a centurion, Acts 10:1), he had a "more perfect knowledge of that way" (of Christ, Acts 24:22). The evidence of his giving Paul a measure of freedom shows that he evidently thought some Christians were not so bad after all.

PAUL'S DEFENSE BEFORE FELIX Roman law required that cases such as Paul's be heard speedily (Acts 24:1–23). The apostle's enemies at Jerusalem knew this. They must have learned soon after Paul's departure from Jerusalem where the Roman soldiers had taken him, and it is quite possible that Ananias, the high priest, and certain members of the Sanhedrin headed for Caesarea the next day to level charges against their enemy. Their journey took about five days, which would have placed their arrival in this port city a day or two after Paul's. This information is inferred from Paul's statement that it had been only twelve days since he had entered the temple to worship (Acts 24:11). Among those who came along with the Sanhedrin was a certain orator named Tertullus. Under Roman law the accuser and the accused could either plead in person or have a representative, like a lawyer. Paul pled his case personally. The Sanhedrin chose to employ the professional services of an orator/lawyer—Tertullus, who was Roman. There is little doubt that he was an Italian because he spoke on this occasion in Latin. He laid before Felix the criminal charges against Paul, who was then summoned before the tribunal. Tertullus began by lauding Felix with unmerited praise, and then he leveled three distinct charges against the accused.

First, he charged him with causing factious disturbances among all the Jews throughout the empire—an offense against the Roman government that amounted to *majestas* or treason against the emperor.

Second, he charged him with being a "ringleader of the sect of the Nazarenes," which involved heresy against the Law of Moses.

Third, he charged him with an attempt to profane the temple, an offense not only against the Jewish, but also against the Roman law, which protected the Jews in the exercise of their worship. He concluded by asserting, with serious deviations from the truth, that Lysias, the commander of the garrison in Jerusalem, had forcibly taken the prisoner away when the Jews were about to judge him by their own ecclesiastical law; thus improperly bringing the matter to Felix. The underlying intent of this representation was to persuade Felix to turn Paul back over to the Jewish courts, in which case his assassination would soon be accomplished. The Jews gave a vehement assent to all that Tertullus said, making no secret of their hostility against Paul.

The governor now made a gesture to the prisoner, signifying that he could make his appeal. The Jews were silent, and the apostle, after briefly expressing his satisfaction that he could plead his cause before one so well acquainted with Jewish customs, refuted Tertullus step-by-step. He declared that on his recent visit to Jerusalem no disturbance had been caused in any part of Jerusalem. As to heresy, he had never swerved from his belief in the Law and the Prophets, and that, in conformity with that belief, he held to the doctrine of a resurrection, which was a belief held in common with the Pharisees. He told his hearers that he had sought to live conscientiously before God. Regarding his alleged profaning the temple, he had been found in it deliberately observing one of the very strictest ceremonies. The Jews of Asia, he added, who had been his first accusers, ought to have been present as witnesses now. Those who were present knew full well that no other charge had been brought against him by the Sanhedrin.

Paul's argument left no doubt in Felix's mind that Paul had the same freedom under Roman law to worship God in his way as the Jews did in their way. Paul was inferring in Acts 24:14–16 that since Rome tolerated religious parties called sects—the sect of the Pharisees; the sect of the Sadducees—they should tolerate him because he was of the "sect of the Nazarenes" (Acts 24:5). Paul was declaring that he expected the same toleration for his beliefs that Rome extended to others. He said in effect: "I claim the right to worship my God, the same right you permit other nations to claim under your government, that of worshiping their national gods." Paul's defense was truthful and everything harmonized 100 percent with the statement contained in the dispatch sent by Claudius Lysias. Paul made a strong impression on Felix, but this wicked governor was one of those characters who was easily affected by feelings, and he put off making any decision until Lysias could come and testify. Although he knew the Jews had no case against Paul, he had an ulterior motive in keeping him in custody, as we shall see.

PAUL, FELIX, AND DRUSILLA   We read nothing of Lysias' coming to Caesarea, or of any other judicial proceedings. A few days later Felix came into the audience chamber with his wife, Drusilla, and Paul was summoned before them (Acts 24:24–26). A summons like this was unusual, but by this time Felix knew Paul to be a man of integrity. Evidently Drusilla, being a Jewess, had taken a lively interest in what Felix had told her about Paul and was curious to hear something of this faith that had Christ as its object. What a great opportunity Paul had, even in bonds, to preach the Gospel. His audience consisted of just three people, a hardened Roman soldier, a governor known for his crimes, and an adulterous Jewish princess. In speaking of Christ he spoke of "righteousness and temperance, and of judgment to come" (v. 25). The Holy Spirit brought about great conviction, causing Felix to tremble, but he made no decision. Paul was escorted back to the barracks with these words, "Go thy way for this time; for when I have a convenient season [or time], I will call for thee" (v. 25). We are told explicitly why this governor shut his heart to conviction and even neglected his official duty by keeping an innocent prisoner in cruel suspense: "He hoped that he might receive from Paul a bribe for his release" (Acts 24:26). Josephus tells us that this was common practice among governors of Judaea. Albinus, who succeeded Festus, is said to have released many prisoners, but only those from whom he received a bribe.[3] Felix, knowing how the Christians aided one another in distress, probably thought they would bail Paul out and thus set him free. With the thought of enriching himself, he frequently sent for Paul and had many conversations with him. But his hopes were never realized. Paul, who was ever ready to proclaim the protection of the law, would not seek to break it by any dishonorable act. Neither would his Christian friends, who knew how to pray for an apostle in bonds (such as Peter, Acts 12:5). They would pray and use any persuasive methods available, but would not be a party to a known violation of the law. As a result, Paul remained in Herod's praetorium for two years. Paul did not appeal to Caesar while Felix was in office, possibly because he knew that Felix was mindful of his innocence and was simply postponing his release to a more advantageous time.

As these two years slowly slipped away, the maladministration of Felix became increasingly worse. Disturbances took place in the streets. Troops, who were chiefly recruited in the province to keep order were relaxing the laws and becoming party to the whims of the people. The Jews were making money and trusting in their wealth. The political state of Judaea under this governor grew unruly. In the end, Felix was summoned to Rome and the Jews, who knew he hated them, followed him with their accusations. However, before he left, and as a gesture, no doubt, to appease the Jews, he left Paul bound (Acts 24:27). He violated the law and trifled with the rights of a Roman citizen. His conduct was that of a man who knew truth, was convicted by it, but in rejection struck back at God and His people. As someone put it, he, in seeking to make himself popular, "riveted the chains of an innocent man of God" and left Paul a prisoner.

PAUL, FELIX, AND DRUSILLA

FESTUS REPLACES FELIX   Very little is known of Porcius Festus, who followed Felix (Acts 24:27–25:12). He was appointed by Nero and died while serving as governor of Judaea in Caesarea, about A.D. 62. He was a much better and more efficient ruler than his predecessor. No change seems to have taken place in Paul's outward circumstances when Festus took command of the province. Paul was still confined as before. However, immediately upon Festus' enthronement, the Jews made a fresh attempt to get Paul.

When a Roman governor came to his new province, whether his character was rough and cruel like Felix's, or reasonable and just like Festus', his first step was to acquaint himself with the habits and current feelings of the people over which he was to rule and to visit places he thought would be associated with national interests. Jerusalem was to the Jews what Rome was to a Roman, and we are not surprised that three days after his arrival in Caesarea, Festus went up to Jerusalem.

Upon his arrival, he was met by the high priests and leading men of the Jews, plus many people of rancor. They asked a favor of Festus, having good reason to believe, as a new ruler, that he would not refuse them. They wanted Paul brought to Jerusalem to be tried again before the Sanhedrin. The real reason, however, was to assassinate him somewhere along the road between Caesarea and Jerusalem. We have previously noticed that those antagonizing Jews never gave up. Their philosophy had always been an eye for an eye and a tooth for a tooth. They were not satisfied until they crucified Jesus. Now, they are not giving up on Paul. To them there was nothing left to do but exterminate him once and for all. They bitterly hated this Christian who was now an apostate Pharisee to them.

The answer Festus gave to them was dignified, just, and worthy of his office. He declared that Paul was in his custody, and that he himself would shortly return to Caesarea, adding that it was not the custom of the Romans to give up an uncondemned prisoner as a mere favor. Such had not been the case with Pilate, who, as a favor to the Jews of his day, gave up Barabbas that Christ might be crucified. Festus suggested to these Jerusalem Jews that if they persisted in their demand to have Paul tried again, they should come down to Caesarea and make their charges there (Acts 25:4–5, 16).

Festus remained ten days in Jerusalem and then returned home. Paul's accusers also went down that same day. This is not to imply that these Jews were in the company of Roman royalty; just that they lost no time in following Festus. The day after arriving at the tribunal with his council, Festus ordered Paul to be brought before him. The Jews were given opportunity to speak first, and as they stood around, they laid many and grievous complaints against Paul, which they could not prove. The charges were still classed under the same three heads as before; viz., heresy, sacrilege, and treason. But Festus plainly saw that these offenses were all connected with the religious opinions of the Jews instead of relating, as he at first expected, to some political movement. He was soon convinced that Paul had done nothing worthy of death (Acts 25:18–19, 25). At the same time, possibly to ingratiate himself to the Jewish community in his province, he proposed to Paul that he should go up to Jerusalem and be tried there, in his presence, or at least under his protection.

PAUL'S APPEAL TO CAESAR Paul knew full well the danger that lurked in that proposal. He knew he would either be killed in ambush on the way or put to death in Jerusalem. We cannot help but think of Paul's bold statement when Agabus and the Caesarean Christians warned him not to go to Jerusalem. He replied with a note of pride and with possible arrogance: "What mean ye to weep and to break mine heart? For I am ready not to be bound only, but also to die at Jerusalem for the name of the Lord" (Acts 21:13). Now, before Festus, we see once again the human side of Paul. Maybe he wasn't quite as homesick for heaven as he thought he was! His martyrdom certainly would have challenged James, the elders, and all believers to be more bold in their faith and witnessing, but as with all humans, when death stares us in the face, there is something in us that makes us want to live a little longer. Such was the case of Hezekiah, who begged for an extension on his life and had fifteen years added (2 Kings 20:1–11). Paul was no exception, even though he knew that to be absent from the body meant to be present with the Lord (2 Corinthians 5:8).

Paul refused to go to Jerusalem and said boldly to Festus:

> I stand at Caesar's judgment seat, where I ought to be judged: to the Jews have I done no wrong, as thou very well knowest. For if I be an offender, or have committed any thing worthy of death, I refuse not to die: but if there be none of these things whereof they accuse me, no man may deliver me unto them. I appeal to Caesar. (Acts 25:10–11)

PAUL'S APPEAL TO CAESAR

Paul knew that this appeal would free him from these Jerusalem Jews, though Festus was probably as surprised by this appeal as were the Jews. Paul's appeal terminated the proceedings and left Festus with no choice. Paul had taken advantage of his prerogative to be tried by Roman law, not by Jewish law—a claim already admitted by Festus, who had just proposed a transfer to the jurisdiction of the Sanhedrin with himself present. But, as stated, Paul knew deep down inside that the Jews would never let him get to Jerusalem alive. By availing himself of one of the most important privileges of Roman citizenship, he instantly sent his case to the supreme tribunal of the emperor at Rome by simply saying, "I appeal unto Caesar." What a blow Paul's appeal must have been to the Jews who would have torn him limb from limb if allowed. Paul had outfoxed his own kinsmen, knowing his life would be spared: "Then Festus, when he had conferred with the council, answered, Hast thou appealed unto Caesar? Unto Caesar shalt thou go" (Acts 25:12). Festus now had to make his official report. He was bound to forward to Rome all the facts and documents pertaining to the trial—the dispositions of the witness on both sides, and the record of his own judgment in the case. It was also his duty to keep the accused in safe custody and to send him to Rome for trial at the earliest opportunity. But the governor was still confused. Although an appeal had been allowed, the information elicited at the trial had been so vague that he hardly knew what statement he should send in his dispatch to the emperor. It seemed a foolish thing for him to send a prisoner to Rome and not be able to indicate the charges against him (Acts 25:27). But he must send something—it was the Roman law.

AGRIPPA VISITS FESTUS IN CAESAREA It happened about this time that Herod Agrippa II (see illustration 41), king of Chalcis, with his sister Bernice, made a complimentary visit to the new governor and stayed "some days" at Caesarea (Acts 25:12–26:32). This Agrippa was the son of Agrippa I (Herod in Acts 12). Agrippa I had been very cruel, being responsible for James' murder and Peter's imprisonment (Acts 12:1–4). Agrippa II was only seventeen years old when his father died (Acts 12:20–23), but six years later, at the age of twenty-three, he was made king of Chalcis, a chief city of the island of Euboea in the Aegean Sea. The king had been familiar from his youth with all that related to the laws of the Jews, and was an expert in all customs as well as the many Jewish controversies. He was also familiar with the Old Testament prophets, especially in relation to the mission of Jesus Christ, and in particular to His crucifixion. It was common knowledge, even in Caesarea, that Jesus had been crucified, for His trial and death had not been "done in a corner" (Acts 26:3, 22–27a).

Festus took advantage of Agrippa's presence, knowing he was much better qualified on the points in question. He recounted to Agrippa what had been related to and experienced by him, confessing his ignorance of Jewish theology and mentioning especially Paul's reiteration of one Jesus who had died and was alive again. This cannot be the first time Agrippa had heard of either Jesus' resurrection or of the apostle Paul. After Festus told him about the matter at hand, Agrippa said, "I would also hear this man myself" (Acts 25:22). The tense of this statement might seem to imply he had longed to meet Paul and have a one-to-one talk with him. Festus then set a time for this get-together, and they met the next day.

PAUL'S DEFENSE BEFORE AGRIPPA   At the time appointed, Agrippa and Bernice came with great pomp and cere-

41—King Agrippa. *Courtesy of author.*

42—Paul's appeal before Agrippa and Festus. *Courtesy of author.*

PAUL'S DEFENSE BEFORE AGRIPPA

mony and entered the audience chamber with a contingent of military officers and the chief men of Caesarea (Acts 25:23–26:32). They probably convened "court" in the amphitheater. At Festus' command, Paul was brought before them (see illustration 42). Festus opened the proceedings with a ceremonious speech describing the circumstances under which his prisoner had been brought to his notice and ending with a statement of his confusion concerning what should be written to the emperor since the charges against Paul were of a religious nature and did not pertain to civil law.

When Festus finished, Agrippa turned to Paul and said: "Thou art permitted to speak for thyself. Then Paul stretched forth the hand, and answered for himself" (26:1). We notice the following in his defense in Acts 26: (1) He described his conversion (vv. 1–15). (2) He specified his call or mission (vv. 16–17). (3) He rehearsed his convictions (vv. 18–23). (4) He exhibited the courage of his convictions (vv. 19, 21–27).

We must remember that Paul was in the presence of Roman nobility. Each dignitary, and all Romans for that matter, gave allegiance to Caesar as "God and Savior." This was the purpose of emperor worship throughout the Roman Empire (see illustration 43). A decree had been issued by a Caesar that he in fact was God and Savior and all Roman citizens had to affirm allegiance to him, obtaining a certificate to validate it (see illustration 44). Many early saints, particularly in Rome, forfeited their lives in defense of their faith in Christ because He was their God and Savior. This was the purpose of the "sign of the fish": to announce to Caesar and all Rome that "Jesus Christ, God's Son, Savior," was the One in whom they trusted, not Caesar. The initial letters *J. C. G. S. S.*, of the expression, spell *Ichthus*, which means "fish" in Greek. Wherever and whenever a Christian could carve or paint this symbol, they indelibly engraved their testimony (see illustration 45). Paul knew that Festus and Agrippa worshiped the emperor, but he dared to tell them that Jesus Christ was the *only* Savior, the only One who could open their eyes and turn people from darkness to light and from the power of Satan unto God that they might receive forgiveness of sin and an inheritance among the saints by faith in Christ. He fortified this truth by saying he was not disobedient to his calling and convictions. We can only wonder what was going on in Bernice's mind. She was a very wicked woman—the consort of her brother, Agrippa. She concluded her life in abandonment to vice and a criminal con-

43—Pantheon: seat of emperor worship. *Courtesy of author.*

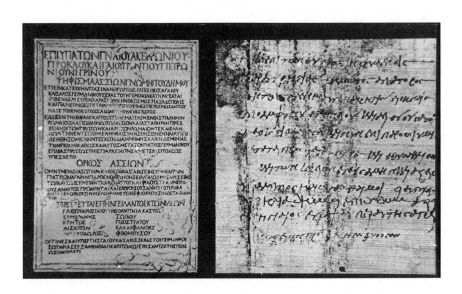

44—Caesar's decree and certificate. *Courtesy of John Rylands Library, Oxford, England.*

PAUL'S DEFENSE BEFORE AGRIPPA   297

45—Sign of the fish: "ICHTHUS."
Courtesy of author.

nection with Titus, who destroyed Jerusalem. She, at least, could never point a finger at God and say she never heard the Gospel.

As Paul continued and began to quote Moses and the Prophets concerning the sufferings, crucifixion, and resurrection of Christ, Festus interrupted with a loud voice, expressing surprise and ridicule. To an out-and-out pagan, the doctrine of the resurrection was foolish, and Festus accused Paul of incessant study that had made him mad. When Paul mentioned Moses and the Prophets, Festus no doubt thought that the writings of these people, whoever they were, had caused Paul, during his two-year imprisonment, to become "stir crazy." He no doubt concluded that he had before him a defendant whose head had been turned by poring over strange mythical tales of days gone by. Paul's reply was courteous and self-possessed, but in dead earnest. Knowing that King Agrippa knew he was telling the truth, he replied:

> I am not mad, most noble Festus, but speak forth the words of truth and soberness. For the king knoweth [or has knowledge] of these things before whom I speak freely [with boldness]; for I am persuaded that none of these things are hidden from him, for none of these things were done in a corner. (Acts 26:25–26)

Then Paul, turning to the one who sat beside the governor made a most solemn appeal to him: "King Agrippa, believest thou the prophets?" (v. 27). Agrippa replied, "Almost thou persuadest me to be a Christian" (v. 28). These words were doubtless spoken ironically and in contempt. The phrase here cannot mean "almost" as we have it in our Authorized Version. It carries with it the connotation, "Do you think that in a few words, or in a short time, you can make me a Christian with little persuasion?" Agrippa and those present with him would never have the Gospel presented to them any better than Paul had on this occasion. Regardless of how Agrippa took this testimony and invitation, Paul took it as though his reply had been spoken in earnest.

Paul's defense had been convincing (see v. 28). Although Agrippa responded the way he did, Paul knew deep down inside that the king at least gave mental assent to what he had said about Moses and the Prophets, and the historical fact that Christ's sufferings had not been done in a corner (see v. 3).

Paul also manifested compassion (see v. 29a). Instead of letting the tone of Agrippa's remark discourage him, Paul, no doubt with tears streaming down his cheeks, said in effect, "O king, would to God that not only you, Bernice, Festus, and all the rest present in this court today were not only almost but were fully convinced that this Christ of whom I speak were your Savior. He could be if you would but believe on Him as I have."

Paul then challenged them with his consecration (see v. 29b), saying, "O how I wish you were such as I, except these bonds" (or these chains). Agrippa and his assembly could not help but realize that this saint of God had an inner peace and freedom which was unknown to them. Paul had won a Roman proconsul on the isle of Cyprus (Acts 13:7, 12), he had won some Greek philosophers of renown (Acts 17:34), he had won a Roman subordinate (jailer) in Philippi (Acts 16:31–33), but at Caesarea it appeared the Word of God had fallen on deaf ears. Before Claudius Lycias, Paul had almost been killed (Acts 21:31–32; 23:26), before Felix he was almost released (Acts 24:24–26), and before Agrippa he almost won a king for the Lord (Acts 26:27–29).

VERDICT: INNOCENT, BUT MUST APPEAR BEFORE CAESAR   Paul had appeared before the Jews, including the Sanhedrin, Lysias, Felix, Festus, and Agrippa. All had heard his defense. Yet, no one could come up with a guilty verdict.

1. The Jewish leaders tried unsuccessfully to say he was guilty of blasphemy and sedition, but none of their arguments stood up in the Roman courts.

2. Captain Lysias, in his letter to Felix, said the Jews had laid nothing to his charge worthy of death.

3. Felix knew he was innocent, but for personal reasons to favor the Jews and for mercenary purposes he kept Paul under house arrest, hoping for a bribe to free him.

4. Festus could find none who could produce evidence to convict Paul, but in an effort to protect his legal rights as a Roman citizen he accused him of being mad

(crazy; a religious fanatic) when he didn't understand his defense before Agrippa.

5. Agrippa, knowledgeable of the Prophets and Moses regarding Christ's death, burial, and resurrection, turned thumbs down on truth, though he acknowledged Paul's innocence.

As Paul concluded his defense before Agrippa with a salvation appeal, Agrippa had no desire to hear more, so he arose from his seat. Along with Festus, Bernice, and those with him, they retired and discussed the case one with one another. They all agreed that Paul was guilty of nothing worthy of death or even imprisonment. Agrippa said positively to Festus, "This man might have been set at liberty if he had not appealed unto Caesar" (Acts 26:30–32). Festus had no desire to delay any further sending his prisoner to Rome. All that remained was to wait for a convenient opportunity to get him on board a ship headed west. With his appeal to Caesar, Paul had forfeited his freedom to be on the go—to go anywhere for the Lord. Possibly this action of appeal haunted his mind until his dying day, but being the man of God that he was, he rose above his circumstances and was determined by the grace of God to "press toward the mark for the prize of the high calling of God in Christ Jesus" (Philippians 3:14).

TEST YOURSELF ON CHAPTER TEN

1. To whom was Paul taken in Caesarea?

2. What was contained in the letter of Lysias to the governor of Caesarea?

3. What questions did the governor ask Paul and where was he kept?

4. What are the types of Roman imprisonments? Describe each.

5. In which type was Paul kept?

6. What kind of man was Felix?

7. Who was Felix's wife?

8. What was her "religion"?

9. How did Felix go about winning her hand in marriage?

10. What did Felix know about Christianity?

11. What were the charges Tertullus and the Jews made against Paul?

12. What argument did Paul use to defend his right to follow the "sect of the Nazarene"?

13. What was Felix's reaction to Paul's defense?

14. What was Felix's reaction to Paul in his private conversation with him and his wife Drusilla?

15. What do you think Felix knew about Christianity?

16. Did Paul have other occasions to meet with Felix?

17. Why would Felix not free Paul even though he knew that he was innocent?

18. Why did Felix lose his position as governor of Caesarea?

19. Who replaced Felix?

20. When Paul made his defense before Festus and the Jerusalem Jews, what was the governor's decision?

21. Why was Paul reluctant to go back to Jerusalem?

22. What appeal did Paul make to avoid this trip?

23. Why did Festus find it difficult to state the charges against Paul in his report to Caesar?

24. Who came to Festus' rescue?

25. Why was the king willing to hear Paul?

26. What did he know about the Jews' customs and religion?

27. What did he know about Paul?

28. Outline Paul's defense before Agrippa as he gave it in Acts.

29. What was Festus' reaction to Paul's defense?

30. What was King Agrippa's reaction to Paul's testimony?

31. What had been the decision of all those before whom Paul had made his defense?

32. What was the decision of his trial before Agrippa and Festus?

Chapter Eleven

PAUL'S VOYAGE
TO ROME

Luke gives us a vivid description of Paul's voyage to Rome in Acts 27:1–28:13 (see map 5, p. 450). Because of his appeal to Caesar, Paul was classified as a prisoner and he had to be sent to Rome under guard. Along with certain other prisoners, he was put in the charge of a centurion named Julius, of the company of Augustus. Luke and Aristarchus accompanied him (later Mark and Demas joined him in Rome, Philemon 24). We do not know if Luke paid his own fare or signed on as the ship's doctor. Neither do we know if Aristarchus signed up on the passenger list to be Paul's companion, Paul's servant, or was a prisoner himself. Luke's description of the voyage is one of a skilled navigator: It is a masterpiece, as we shall see. Not only is his account enlightening as to the seamanship of that day, it is profitable in portraying Paul's personality under adverse circumstances.

Before we set sail with Paul on this voyage, a remark or two should be made concerning the vessels of this period of time (see illustration 46). Luke gives some details about navigation and the winds, but nothing about the ships. We must not entertain the notion that all ancients' commerce was conducted by small craft that sailed only in the daytime or only in the calm summer months. Ships of that day were not equipped with compasses, but sailors were skilled in matters of changeable weather and when neither sun nor stars were visible, they were cautious and

46—A ship of Paul's day. Courtesy of the American Numismatic Society, New York.

47—Harbor of Caesarea where Paul sailed to Rome. *Courtesy of author.*

hesitated to try the open seas (as we note in Acts 27:9–12 and 28:11). The ships were large enough to be steered by double rudders, hence Luke mentions *rudders* (plural) in Acts 27:40.

The ship of Alexandria that they boarded in Myra must have been a rather large vessel with an estimated weight of 75 to 1000 tons and carried cargo of wheat (Acts 27:38). Two hundred and seventy-six people were on board when it went down (Acts 27:37).

The transportation of state prisoners to Rome from various parts of the empire was an event that frequently took place. We are told by Josephus that Felix "for some slight offence, bound and sent to Rome several priests of his acquaintance, honorable and good men, to answer for themselves to Caesar."[1] These prisoners often left Caesarea (see illustration 47) and other eastern ports in merchant ships bound for the west. A ship from Adramyttium on the northwestern coast of Mysia was docked at Caesarea. (Paul had once passed through Mysia on his way to Troas where he had his Macedonian vision (Acts 16:7–9). Festus was aware that this ship was not scheduled to go to Rome, but he felt that the sooner he got rid of Paul the better, since Jewish opposition might crop up again even though Paul had appealed to Caesar. He knew that in some port the trusted guard, Julius, would find another ship sailing for the Italian coast; thus ultimately taking his prisoners to Rome.

SIDON After sailing out of the harbor of Caesarea, the first port call was Sidon (see map 5, p. 450), about seventy miles northward (Acts 27:3). Paul's knack for friendship soon won the heart of Julius, his guard, and he was allowed to go ashore and visit friends. After his imprisonment in Caesarea for over two years, he needed a spiritual shot in the heart, so to speak, from those of like faith. He had previously visited Tyre, and with its proximity to Sidon, many of the saints from Tyre probably came to see him. Luke does not record any conversations that took place in Sidon, but they certainly praised the Lord for their free salvation, many blessings, and Paul who was now a member of their group and not a persecutor.

Sidon had had a long biblical history, and possibly they talked about the fact that after the flood, Ham's descendants settled at the border of the Canaanites' land, which began at Sidon (Genesis 10:19–20). When Jacob was giving his blessings to his sons, he said that "Zebulun shall dwell at the haven of the sea; and he shall be for an haven of ships, and his border shall be to Zidon [Sidon]" (Genesis 49:13). During the occupation of the Promised Land, Joshua and the Israelites chased the enemy to Sidon, but were never able to fully conquer the city (Joshua 11:18; Judges 1:31). It was a city that had been built up by "merchants who pass over the sea" (Isaiah 23:2). Sidon was also mentioned in the earlier years of the founding of Christianity. Many from both Tyre and Sidon came to hear Jesus preach (Luke 6:17–19). Christ also rewarded the Syrophenician woman from this area for her faith (Mark 7:24–30).

CRETE   Paul's visit to Sidon was short-lived; the wind was unfavorable, blowing against them from the west and the time of his departure arrived quickly (Acts 27:4–13). Instead of sailing southward (below) Cyprus, they sailed "under the lee" of this island (see map 5, p. 450), which was northeast and north, sailing over against (or under) Cilicia and Pamphilia (Acts 27:4 NIV). The ship finally docked at Myra, a city in Lycia (see map 5, p. 450) and a busy port city. It was common for ships from Alexandria to sail due north to Myra; thus it was no surprise when Julius found an Egyptian vessel sailing for Italy. All prisoners were transferred to this ship, but due to bad weather they reached Cnidus with difficulty. The wind changed their course, however, and they sailed under the island of Crete, bypassing Salmone, and finally docking at Fair Haven on this island (Acts 27:4–13).

The timing of the voyage was not good. Festus was so anxious to get rid of Paul that he had put him on the first vessel heading west. Luke tells us that "the fast was now already past" (Acts 27:9), which meant the Jewish Day of Atonement was over. At this time (A.D. 59), this day fell in early October, and the dangerous season for sailing had begun three weeks earlier. The ancients could count on fairly dangerous seas from about the middle of September to the middle of November. After that, it was so dangerous that just about all open sea travel ceased for the winter.

Paul suggested that if they were to continue their journey to Italy, there would be much hurt and damage not only to the ship and its cargo but also to their lives; whereas the city of Lasea was nearby, and there would have been accommodations for all for this period of time. His arguments not to continue were addressed to all fellow voyagers. The master would naturally want to avoid danger to the ship; the owner, who was on board, would be thinking about his cargo; the centurion would be thinking about his responsibility in getting all prisoners safely to Rome, and the passengers were thinking of themselves. That Paul, as a prisoner, was allowed to give advice at all implies the esteem Julius and others had for him. No doubt his words held a commanding sway over the entire group, yet we are not surprised that Julius, thinking that Paul was a much better preacher than a navigator, overruled his advice, being more influenced by the words of the owner and master. There can be no doubt that their present anchorage was not suitable for winter, and those in authority thought it best to sail farther west to Phenice, which was sheltered from the winds.

PAUL, THE STORM, AND THE SHIPWRECK Just about the time the decision had been made to leave Fair Haven, a soft wind came into port, and this signal was all Julius and the captain needed to sail (Acts 27:13–44). To them this proved their judgment to be right; thus refuting Paul's argument. No sooner had they cleared the harbor, however, than there arose a tempestuous wind called Euroclydon. It came down from the mountains of Crete and struck the ship with great force, stirring mountainous waves. This was a wind that was extremely dangerous to ships with large sails, such as the one on which Paul was sailing. There was nothing left for the sailors to do but let the wind drive it.

Luke does not mention that Paul was apprehensive, but who wouldn't be in a storm at sea, especially when the sailors had left the ship to the mercy of the storm! The ship now was south of the small island of Clauda, and there was fear of falling in the quicksand. All hands on board were undergirding the ship by passing large ropes or cables under the keel, over the sides and top, and then drawing them tight by means of pulleys or levers. Momentarily, the ship seemed safe, but with the sky overcast, and having no idea where they were at this point, it is doubtful that those on board even knew the time of day. Luke tells us that all hope was gone that any would survive. Surely we are beginning to see what Paul meant by being "in perils in the sea, a day and a night in the deep," although at the time that he wrote to the Corinthians, this experience of going to Rome had not occurred (2 Corinthians 11:25–26).

In the midst of all this uncertainty, Paul must have been thinking of the promise the Lord had made to him after he had appeared before the Sanhedrin in Jerusalem (Acts 23:11). This promise assured Paul that he would bear witness of Christ in Rome. As Paul reflected on this promise, an angel of the Lord appeared to him and gave assurance that regardless of the consequences of the storm, no lives would be lost and he would arrive safely in Rome to appear before Caesar (Acts 27:22–25). It appears that at this point the centurion and captain were willing to listen to this man of God when he told them that they should have listened to him in the first place and not left Crete. As reckless as sailors are in the absence of danger, there can be no doubt that they, at this time, were open to any religious act—even praying out loud—when their lives were at stake.

After fourteen days of being tossed about in Adria (the Aegean Sea), the sailors "smelled" land. The roar of breakers is a peculiar sound and can easily be detected. When it was reported that they must be close to some country, even though it was midnight, orders were given to sound. With each sounding the water was shallower, indicating that the ship would soon fall on rocks and be dashed to pieces. The sailors dropped four anchors, hoping for dawn so they could see just where they were.

From Acts 28:2 we learn that it was raining. Even though the sailors were trying to save the ship, their selfish desire was to save themselves and leave the ship and the passengers to their fate. Paul saw through their little game, and knowing that if they left, none on board would know what to do, he said "except these abide in the ship, ye cannot be saved" (Acts 27:31).

As day approached, Paul encouraged all to eat after a fourteen-day fast (Acts 27:33) and give thanks to God. He assured them that "not a hair shall fall from the head of any of you" (v. 34). This cheered everyone on board, and they all went to work to cast the cargo of grain overboard so that the ship would be lighter. In the meantime, the soldiers cut the cables and ropes around the boat and later that morning, seeing a small stream, they took up the anchors, hoisted up the mainsail to the wind, and made toward the shore. They ran the ship aground, and it was broken by the violent waves. Sensing that the prisoners would now be able to swim ashore and escape, the soldiers advised Julius to kill them. The centurion, who by now trusted Paul implicitly and who desired to save Paul, commanded that those who could swim to shore do so, and the rest could save themselves by clinging to broken pieces of the ship. Not only were all prisoners saved but all the passengers as well.

MALTA   Upon coming on shore, the passengers, prisoners, and crew knew they were on the island of Melita (see map 5, p. 450). The people of Melita/Malta (Acts 28:1–11), though part Greek, were barbarous since they were not Greeks by birth. They were kind hosts to their unexpected guests, seeking to give them a warm welcome in spite of the rain and cold weather. Paul was not a typical preacher who did not want to get his hands dirty, and he helped gather wood for the fire. In the course of picking up sticks, a viper fastened on his hand. The implication of *fastened* is that this poisonous snake had sunk its fangs in his hand. The immediate reaction of the island natives was that Paul was some sort of criminal, a murderer, and that the snake bite was justice being meted out. Paul shook the viper into the fire and suffered no harm. The natives watched, expecting his body to swell or him to suddenly fall dead. In due time, after they had watched in vain and saw that nothing happened, their feelings changed, and they said he was a god. The Lystrians had once proclaimed Paul and Barnabas to be gods, but later stoned Paul (Acts 14:11–12, 19). Luke does not tell us that Paul refuted their claim, but knowing Paul, he did the same here that he had done at Lystra.

Taking advantage of the situation, Paul immediately began to preach Christ. He was able to work many miracles during his stay on Malta. The first that is recorded is the healing of Publius' father. Publius was the governor of the island who had given a hospitable reception to the shipwrecked strangers. This man's father had suffered from fever and a "bloody flux," or dysentery, in an aggravated form. Many others were healed also, and as a result, the islanders honored Paul and the others and supplied whatever they needed for their three-month stay. This was the *sixth* time Paul used his apostolic gift of healing.

ITALY   Having ended a wonderful stay at Malta (see map 5, p. 450), the centurion was able to get his prisoners on board another Alexandrian ship whose sign was Castor and Pollux (Acts 28:11–15), semideities that were reported to be the sons of Jupiter, whose figures were on the prow of the ship. This ship was a more modern one with a navigational device that assured the captain of the ship's location at all times. They sailed to Syracuse, a city on the island of Sicilia (modern Sicily) and were there for three days. Local tradition today regards Paul as the founder of the Sicilian church, so it is probable that Julius permitted Paul to go ashore. He doubtless found Jews and prose-lytes to whom he announced the glad tidings of his resurrected Savior.

The next stop was Rhegium, located on the "toe" of Italy. The patron divinities of the city, by curious coincidence, were the hero-protectors of seafaring men, the great twin brothers, Castor and Pollux, to whom Paul's ship was dedicated. After waiting for a south wind to carry them northward, they set sail the next day for Puteoli (see map 5, p. 450), just south of the modern city of Naples, arriving a day later. It did not take Paul long to find Christians. He met with these disciples and as soon as he was among them they sent a messenger to Rome to inform them of his arrival. The Italian Christians had long been looking for a visit from the famous apostle, though they had not expected to meet him as a prisoner in chains. But Paul's sufferings only brought their hearts closer to him. They besought him to tarry with them for a few days, and Julius complied with their wish. Even when the voyage first began, we noticed that this Roman soldier was courteous and kind toward Paul, and after all the varied incidents that Luke recounted on this trip, it is understandable that he would grant such a favor to the one who had saved his life.

APPII AND   At the end of his seven-day visit in Puteoli,
THREE TAVERNS   believers at Rome had already received the message that Paul was headed there (Acts 28:13–15). Many believers immediately headed south to meet him. They travelled by foot along the Appian Way (see illustration 48), a distance of a little more than one hundred miles. Going through Paul's mind, no doubt, was the words he had written in his letter to the

48—Appii: the Appian Way. *Courtesy of the American Bible Society, New York.*

believers at Rome: "I am ready to preach the gospel to you that are at Rome also" (Romans 1:15).

Now he found himself, an old, gray-headed, broken man; a chained prisoner, just escaped from a shipwreck, exhausted, feeling he could hardly take another step. As he approached the Appii (see map 5, p. 450) forum, unbeknown to him a group of believers from Rome were waiting. Ten miles further north he met a second group at the Three Taverns. Evidently the zeal of some enabled them to outrun the others. Altogether they gave their "ambassador in bonds" a great welcome. Paul's spirit was buoyed and he thanked God for a safe voyage and took courage that he was about to have his dream of visiting Rome fulfilled.

TEST YOURSELF ON CHAPTER ELEVEN

1. Who was Paul's trusted Roman guard?

2. What friends accompanied Paul to Rome?

3. How kind was Paul's guard to him in Tyre?

4. What advice did Paul give the captain of the ship and his guard concerning an impending storm?

5. What was their reaction?

6. Describe what type of storm came upon them below Crete.

7. How severe was the storm?

8. How many days did the passengers fast?

9. Who appeared unto Paul in the storm and what promise was given to him?

10. What assurance did Paul give his guard?

11. After fasting and then eating, what assurance did Paul give the passengers?

12. How many people were aboard?

13. After the ship ran aground and broke into pieces, what did the soldiers want to do to the prisoners and why?

14. After all got ashore, where were they?

15. What near incident happened to Paul?

16. What was the reaction of the natives to this incident?

17. How did they treat Paul and the other passengers?

18. What miracles did Paul perform?

19. After leaving this island, where did they sail?

20. Where did they land in Italy?

21. How long did they stay in this city and what favor did Julius grant Paul?

22. Where did Paul meet some believers on his hike to Rome?

Chapter Twelve

PAUL'S PRISON YEARS IN ROME

And when [he] came to Rome . . . (Acts 28:16), bonds or no bonds, this was a happy occasion for the apostle (see map 5, p. 450). He had left Caesarea in August or September and had arrived in March (A.D. 61). He had traveled well over two-thousand miles according to the course mentioned by Luke; more when we consider their being tossed in the Aegean Sea during the storm. Julius, his Roman captor, delivered him to the captain of the guard. Evidently Julius spoke a good word for his prisoner, and Paul was put under house arrest in his own rented house. He was given liberty to stay virtually alone—with but one soldier to guard him. Nothing is said about Paul's winning Julius to the Lord, but the life and witness of this great apostle had changed him from a hardened Roman soldier to one who had admiration for his special prisoner.

What was Rome like—this metropolis to which Paul had come in high hopes of having fellowship with the believers who had settled in the capital of the Roman Empire (see illustration 49)? Nero was the emperor (see illustration 50), and he tolerated all the inhabitants of this imperial city. Possibly one quarter of the three million population were slaves. Jews had played an important role among the merchants, and the Jewish community no doubt had been fully established in Rome when Pompey, in 63 B.C., brought captives back from his eastern campaign. According to Philo, a Roman historian, the Jews had been privileged to

49—Rome: first century A.D. *Courtesy of author.*

50—Nero's headquarters: the Roman Forum. *Courtesy of author.*

be freemen. Many were wealthy and they had annually sent large sums to Jerusalem for religious purposes. Only when the Jews became excited about a temporal Messiah or when Rome became suspicious about some of their mysterious customs were they cruelly treated or banished, such as the time when Claudius had commanded that all Jews be deported from the city (Acts 18:2). When Paul arrived during the earlier years of Nero's reign, which were distinguished as a mild and lenient period of Roman history, the Jews at Rome were fully tolerated and were free to worship in their synagogues.

The Christians doubtless shared the same protection that was extended to the Jews. They were not yet distinguished as a self-existent community; thus they did not provoke any hostility. It is even possible that the Christians were more tolerated than the Jews simply because they did not have the same expectation of an earthly hero to deliver them, and with no political ends in view, they would not be in the same danger of exciting the suspicion of the government.

The bulk of the Roman believers were Gentiles, but no doubt the earliest ones had been Jews and proselytes who were in Jerusalem on the Day of Pentecost (Acts 2:10; *strangers* would imply proselytes). It is quite possible that when Claudius expelled all Jews that the Christians enjoyed great freedom and growth. When we see the list of names Paul mentions in Romans 16 of those then living in Rome, we must remember that he had met many of them in his travels—Aquila and Priscilla, in whose home the church of Rome met; Epaenetus of Achaia; relatives of Paul now living in Rome; and Rufus of Antioch of Syria to name just a few.

We have no idea what the Roman believers told Paul after meeting him in Appii and Three Taverns and what discussions they had as they continued their journey to Rome. In writing to the Philippians, Paul gave some insight concerning some believers at Rome who had, no doubt, hostile feelings toward him. Many other believers, encouraged by Paul's preaching and convictions, became aggressive in their defense of the Gospel (Philippians 1:13–18). Paul had set a good example by his preaching the Gospel as a debtor to all men and by his being ready at a moment's notice to witness to all who crossed his path—he was not ashamed of His wonderful Savior (Romans 1:14–16). One would think that Luke might have included in Acts Paul's telling these Roman believers how he had prayed for them and done all the things he had promised them in his epistle to them, but he mentions none of these things.

PAUL MEETS WITH THE Three days after arriving in Rome,
CHIEF JEWS AT ROME Paul wasted no time in calling the chief of Jews together (Acts 28:17–29). His purpose was twofold: (1) to explain to them the purpose of his visit to their fair city in bonds, and (2) to preach the Gospel to them. He was concerned that someone representing the Sanhedrin from Jerusalem had preceded him to Rome with accusations that he was an apostate Pharisee or traitor to his country. He no doubt thought it highly probable that the prejudices of these Roman Jews might already be aroused against him. With a desire to set them straight, he addressed his hearers on this point at once, showed them that his enemies were guilty of false accusations, and told them that because of his enemies' desire to kill him he had appealed to Caesar. His only crime had been his firm faith in God's spiritual deliverance of His people through the Messiah as promised by the Prophets. "For the hope of Israel," he concluded, "I am bound with this chain" (Acts 28:17–20).

Their answer to his address was reassuring. They said they had not received any word or written communication from Judaea or Jerusalem concerning him, and that none of the brethren who had arrived from the East had spoken evil of him. They expressed a desire to hear what he had to say about his own religious beliefs, adding that the Christian sect was everywhere spoken against. It appears that this answer was anything but honest because it seems to imply a greater ignorance with regard to Christianity than we can suppose to have prevailed among the Roman Jews. They probably were downplaying the importance of Christianity and its influence in the community. With regard to Paul, and to his delight, they probably did not know why he was in bonds. Although he had been in Caesarea a long time, his appeal had been made a short time before winter, and since there had not been much sea travel during the stormy winter months, it is likely that no one had arrived in Rome to inform these Jews about Paul. All these circumstances gave Paul a favorable opening for the preaching of the Gospel, and he hastened to take advantage of it. A day was set for a meeting in his private lodging (Acts 28:23–29).

The time of the meeting arrived and the Jews came in great numbers. Paul pleaded long and earnestly from morning till evening, bearing testimony concerning the kingdom of God and endeavoring to persuade them with arguments drawn from out of the Law of Moses and out of the Prophets. This must have been an impressive, lengthy session, something like that at Troas (Acts 20:6–9). The result was a division among his hearers—"not peace, but a sword,"—a division that always comes when one encounters truth. After a long and stormy discussion, the unbelieving Jews departed, but not until Paul had warned them that they were bringing on themselves the blindness that was denounced in their own Scripture against obstinate unbelievers, and the salvation that they were rejecting would be withdrawn from them and would be given as an inheritance to the Gentiles. The sentence or condemnation with which he gave emphasis to this warning is originally found in Isaiah 6:9–10:

> Go unto this people and say, Hearing ye shall hear and shall not understand; and seeing ye shall see, and not perceive: For the heart of this people is waxed gross [become calloused], and their ears are dull of hearing, and their eyes they have closed, lest they should see with their eyes and hear with their ears, and understand with their heart, and should be converted, and I should heal them (Acts 28:26–27).

Christ had used this same Scripture in denouncing the Pharisees of His day (John 12:37–43).

Just before the Jews left, no doubt chafing under the Scripture they had just heard, Paul took a parting shot at them with these words: "Be it known therefore unto you, that the salvation of God is sent unto the Gentiles, and they will hear it" (Acts 28:28). Luke does not follow up on any further discussions with these Jews, but we can well imagine that the Apostle to the Gentiles reminded them that God is no respecter of persons, that salvation was to the Jew first and then to the Gentiles, and that the prophet Isaiah, on numerous occasions, had prophesied that Gentiles would come under God's favor. Possibly Paul even reminded them that through Abraham "all the families [nations] of the earth would be blessed" (see Genesis 12:3; Isaiah 11:10; 49:6, 22; 60:5; 61:6; 62:2; Acts 10:34; Romans 1:16; 2:9–11; 3:29–30;).

Luke tells us that the Jews departed from Paul "and had great reasoning [arguing and disputing] among themselves" (Acts 28:29) concerning the sect that was making such inroads on their prejudices. Paul continued in his own rented house for two years. In all probability, thanks to the courtesy of Julius, he was allowed to receive all who came to visit him, and was permitted without any interference to boldly preach the kingdom of God and teach all about Jesus Christ and His redemptive work, especially His resurrection (Acts 28:30–31).

Thus was fulfilled Paul's long-cherished desire "to proclaim the Gospel to them that were in Rome also" (Romans 1:15). Luke closes his narrative on the life of the Apostle to the Gentiles rather abruptly. Our knowledge of the incidents of his time in Rome and of his subsequent history must be gathered almost exclusively from the letters he wrote during his two-year imprisonment. No mention is made of any Jews' coming from Jerusalem to press charges. There is nothing about a trial and nothing about a guilty or not-guilty verdict. Nothing is even mentioned about a release after these two years. The probability of his release and a fourth missionary journey will be discussed in the next chapter.

PAUL'S PRISON EPISTLES Not only did Paul have great preaching opportunities during his tenure in Rome, but he wrote several letters (see illustration 51), which have been designated as "prison epistles." Four have been attributed to him during this two-year term: Ephesians, Philippians, Colossians,

51—Paul writing an epistle in prison. *Courtesy of author.*

and Philemon. Ephesians (see chapter 8) and Philippians (see chapter 7) have already been considered.

Paul's Epistle to the Colossians

Colossae was located in the Lycus Valley, about one hundred miles east of Ephesus, near Laodicea and Hierapolis (Colossians 4:13). It was on an important trade route that ran from the Aegean Sea at Ephesus to the Euphrates river. It later lost its importance due to a change in the road system and Laodicea became the greater city (Revelation 3:7).

The church at Colossae was established on Paul's third missionary journey, not by the apostle himself but in all probability by Epaphras who had come to know Christ as his Savior under Paul's ministry at Ephesus (Colossians 1:7). Some have speculated that he evangelized many cities in the Lycus Valley and helped establish churches in Hierapolis and Laodicea also (4:12–13). Onesimus later became a member of the Colossae church (4:9), as was Philemon, in whose house the church met (Philemon 2).

During Paul's visit to Rome and his two-year imprisonment there, his path crossed that of Epaphras. In his letter to the Colossians, Paul called Epaphras a "servant of Christ" and "my fellow prisoner" (cf. Colossians 4:12 with Philemon 23). We do not know if Epaphras came to visit Paul in Rome, or if he himself had been arrested for his zeal in Gospel preaching and was put into custody with Paul. It could be that because of his willingness to be identified with Paul that he was likened as his fellow prisoner.

As Epaphras conversed with Paul, he mentioned the state of the Colossae church. It had not yet fallen prey to forms of heresy, yet the enemy was threatening to destroy its testimony. Prevalent among the believers was a religious system that involved the error of Greek philosophy (Colossians 2:4, 8–10); Jewish legalisms such as circumcision, dietary regulations, and ritual observances of feasts and offerings (Colossians 2:11–17); Oriental mysticism that included asceticism, worship of angels, and magical or mystical encounters as an approach to spiritual things (Colossians 2:18–23); and a low view of the body (Colossians 2:20–23). All these errors led them to deny the supremacy and universal mediatorial ministry of Christ. As a result, Paul wrote this letter to them "that in all things [in their thinking and in their conduct] He might have the preeminence" (1:18). Colossians is probably the most Christ-centered book in the Bible. Paul wrote to remind these believers that they were complete in Christ and lacked nothing because "in him dwells all the fullness of the Godhead bodily [or that in Him, Deity dwells in bodily form]" (2:9); that because He has "all the treasures of wisdom and knowledge," they had their inheritance in Him (2:3). He wrote to commend and confirm them in the faith of the Gospel that they had believed under the preaching of Epaphras, and to encourage them to "continue in the faith, grounded and settled, and be not moved away from the hope of the Gospel" (1:23). Evidently the believers at Laodicea were having the same problem since Paul requested that this letter be read to them (4:16).

Colossians is linked to Ephesians, as Romans is to Galatians. Ephesians emphasizes the *oneness* of Christ (2:13–22). Colossians emphasizes the *completeness* of Christ (2:10). The theme of Ephesians is the church (5:25–27). The theme of Colossians is the *Head of the church* (1:18). Philippians portrays Christ as having emptied Himself to become a *Servant*, obedient unto death (2:5–8). Colossians portrays Christ as the *ascended Son* in His rightful place as the fullness of God (2:9).

Outline of Colossians

   I. The Supremacy of Christ (chaps. 1–2)
      A. Doctrine: Christ's Deity, sufficiency, preeminence, our All in all (chap. 1)
      B. Disputation: refuting arguments about Christ's adequacy and fullness and warning believers about being led astray by false teachers (chap. 2)
  II. Submission to Christ (chaps. 3–4)
      A. Spiritual matters: devoted, inward Christian living by all—families, masters, and servants (chap. 3)
      B. Consistent outward Christian living, walking circumspectly, praying one for another, always ready to give an answer for the hope we have in Christ (chap. 4)

Paul's Epistle to Philemon

In all probability, Philemon had been led to the Lord by Paul. He infers this in verse 19: "How thou owest unto me even thine own self besides." His desire to serve the Lord was such that he opened his home for believers to assemble in Colossae.

Judging from Paul's greeting to him in verse 1, Apphia was his wife and Archippus was his son. Philemon was a man full of faith, knowledgeable in the things of the Lord, and one who loved and comforted the brethren. He was also a man of forgiveness. His name means "friendly," "one who has compassion," "an affectionate one." Paul used many descriptive words indicating that his whole family made up a godly home: *dearly beloved, fellow laborer, fellow soldier, love, faith, encourager of the saints, brother, obedience,* and *prayer.*

Philemon was sufficiently wealthy to possess slaves, one of whom was Onesimus. A slave was the personal property of his owner, and most were treated worse than one would treat an enemy and were subject to every desire and whim of their masters. Onesimus had robbed Philemon and had run away. Unnoticed by the law, Onesimus found his way to Rome where he sought out the depraved of his own kind and lived among the dregs of society. Yet, from the depths, he was dragged forth by an unknown hand of Christian love.

The Lord engineered circumstances in such a way that he was taken to Paul's house. Perhaps some Asiatic Christian, who had formerly seen him at his master's house, recognized him in the streets of Rome, destitute and starving, and had compassion on him. Or, it is not impossible that he had known Paul at Ephesus, having met him on occasions when he accompanied his master to visit Paul during his three years in Ephesus. Nevertheless, under the providence of God, Onesimus met Paul in Rome, told him his story, and listened to this man of God tell him that Christ was the only One who could save him from sin and that he was the only One who could help him in his dilemma with his master. He was converted and no doubt immediately saw the need to make amends for his wrong doing. Like Zacchaeus, he was willing to restore what he had taken (Luke 19:8).

The apostle seems to have been unusually attracted by the character of Onesimus and he perceived in him the indications of a stalwart believer that would prepare him for a far more important position than he could hold as Philemon's slave. Paul wished to keep him as a fellow laborer in Rome (Colossians 4:9). However, he knew he would break the law and violate Philemon's rights if he did.

Runaway slaves were treated harshly by the government; no mercy was shown them and it was Paul's desire to get this converted slave back in the good graces of his master before his crime was found out. The very year Paul arrived in Rome the prefect (governor) of the city, Pendanius Secundus, had been murdered by one of his slaves. In accordance with Roman law, all of the slaves belonging to him, including women and children, were executed together, though only one was guilty. Paul wanted no such fate to befall Onesimus. He made arrangements immediately to send him back to Colossae. To help matters, he offered to reimburse the amount Philemon had lost.

An opportunity presented itself for Onesimus to return to Philemon in good company. Paul was sending Tychicus to Asia Minor with his epistle to the Colossian church. It would take much courage for this slave to face his master, but Christ made the difference in his life. He would be under the protective care of Tychicus, and if perchance they were stopped by any Roman soldiers, Paul's letter to Philemon would suffice under the circumstances.

The epistle to Philemon is not only a beautiful illustration of Paul's character but is a practical commentary on the relationship of a Christian master and his Christian slave, who was now his brother. Just as Philemon had been shown mercy by the grace of God, so he needed to forgive Onesimus as God for Christ's sake had forgiven him (Ephesians 4:32). He needed to recognize that God is no respecter of persons and that Onesimus was one with him in Christ. Paul expected the forgiving Philemon to accept his runaway slave, and he in no way denied Philemon's rights over his slave but asked of him the courtesy of offering to this slave the right hand of fellowship; the right hand of brotherhood. Onesimus may have left Philemon for a season, but according to Paul, Philemon now needed to receive him forever: "Not now as a servant, but above a servant, a brother beloved, specially to me, but now much more unto thee both in the flesh and in the Lord? If thou count me therefore a partner, received him as myself" (Philemon 15–17).

Scripture is silent as to how Philemon received Onesimus, but it could be, taking everything into consideration, that Onesimus was set free by his master (see illustration 52, where the master [right] touches the bowed slave with the "manumission" rod, indicating emancipation. The "faces" in the left hand of the freed slave indicate power, not subjection any more. Each freed slave wears a "pileus," or brimless conical hat to let all know he is a free man.)

Onesimus was Paul's "son" in the faith (Philemon 10). The Talmud says: "If one teach the son of his neighbor the Law, this is the same as if he had begotten him."[1] Paul no doubt had this Rabbinical saying in mind when he wrote to Philemon that even though Onesimus had been unprofitable or useless in the past, he was now profitable and useful both to me and you (v. 11). *Onesimus* means "useful." Paul is showing Philemon that to speak of brotherly love between master and slave will ultimately make

52—Freeing Roman slaves. *Courtesy of the American Bible Society, New York.*

slavery meaningless in Christ. Christ is portrayed to Philemon (and us) as "the Payer of our sin debt."

Outline of Philemon

This is the briefest, most personal, and most tender of all of Paul's epistles. It is a model of love for the unlovely and concern for forgiveness for one who otherwise would face the sentence of death. Onesimus, who sinned against his master, is a picture of a sinner who has run away from God—gone astray—and faces the wages of his sin—death. But in coming to know Christ as his Savior, he is brought back to his master, forgiven, and made a new creature, having become one with him in the body of Christ.

    I. Paul's Greetings; Giving Thanks for Philemon (vv. 1–7)
    II. Paul's Petition for Onesimus (vv. 8–18)
    III. Paul's Vow to Philemon (vv. 19–21)
    IV. Paul's Personal Request and Salutations (vv. 22–24)

Lessons from the Epistle of Philemon

There are several lessons to be learned from the epistle of Philemon. First, this letter shows Paul's great humility. In his office as an apostle he finds time to bring about the reconciliation of a master and a slave. No matter who or what we are, we should never be too busy to help individuals in need, irrespective of their station in life.

Second, it displays the riches of God's grace in the conversion of a vile sinner; the wonderful providence of God in overruling the determination of this slave to be free from slavery as well as an acceptance of freedom from sin.

Third, it shows that when one becomes a Christian he still has obligations to the law and that restitution, if necessary, must be made. Onesimus *must* return to Philemon.

Fourth, it shows the generosity of one Christian (Paul) to pay back what had been taken when the forgiven brother (Onesimus) had nothing. It is a display of sympathy for the lowly.

Fifth, it reveals the brotherhood of saints. There are no social or class distinctions in Christ. This is a practical solution to the age-old problem of capital and labor. Furthermore, God is *no* respecter of persons (Romans 2:11).

Sixth, as Paul pleaded Onesimus' case before Philemon, so Christ pleaded our case before His heavenly Father. As Onesimus now has standing before Philemon, so now we have standing before Jesus Christ. As Paul paid the debt for an unworthy slave, so Christ paid the debt for all unworthy sinners. Paul paid a debt he didn't owe, because Onesimus had a debt he couldn't pay. Christ paid a debt He didn't owe, because we had a debt we couldn't pay.

Seventh, it shows the need for an older Christian to "stand" for a younger Christian; for a mature believer to help a babe in Christ. Just as Barnabas had accepted Paul as a disciple of Christ and had commended him to the Jerusalem disciples (Acts 9:26–27), so Paul commends Onesimus to Philemon as Christ's servant.

PAUL AND THE EPISTLE TO THE HEBREWS? The writer of Hebrews chose to conceal his identity and as a result, it must be labeled "anonymous." Anyone inspired of God could have written it, and whoever did was well versed in the Law of Moses, the Psalms, and the Prophets, as well as the cardinal truths of Christianity. The origin and history of this epistle was a subject of controversy even in the second century. There is no portion of the New Testament whose authorship is so disputed, and none whose inspiration is more indisputable, but even the early church fathers themselves could not pinpoint the author. One essential feature of an epistle is that it be addressed to some named person or persons and acknowledged by the name of the writer. The fact that Timothy is mentioned shows the author was personally acquainted with him, as well as with others in Italy (Hebrews 13:23–24). This personal touch alone suggests it is a letter or an epistle rather than simply a treatise.

Paul, Barnabas, Apollos, Clement, and Luke have been suggested as authors. Since the Reformation, a greater diversity of opinion has existed. The church of Rome now maintains by its infallibility that Paul wrote it, while in the second, third, and fourth centuries, the same church, with the same infallibility, denied that he had! It is certain from internal evidence that it was written before the fall of Jerusalem in A.D. 70 when the temple was destroyed by Titus and all sacrifices ceased. It was received by the apostolic churches as authentic or canonical from the first and was read in the public services from the earliest times. Many scholars of our day attribute its authorship to Paul, among them Scofield,[2] primarily because the letter itself, in some instances, sounds like the apostle. Note the following phrases:

in bonds (10:34),

a desire to see them later (cf. 13:18–19 with Philemon 22),

a reference to Timothy (13:23),

an apostolic benediction (13:20–21), and

they of Italy salute you (13:24).

In 2 Peter we are told of Paul's having written things that are hard to understand and that those who are unlearned and unstable wrest the Scriptures to their own destruction (3:15–16). Some things in Hebrews do tend to give credence to Peter's statement as they relate to Paul.

Many in the primitive church attributed this letter to those other than Paul. His letters were written in *koine*, a common dialect of the Greek-speaking world of his day. Hebrews was written in *classical* Greek. For this reason four other saints were well qualified to pen this epistle in classical Greek.

First is Apollos, an influential, eloquent, well-educated Alexandrian; a man of boldness and courage (Acts 18:24–28). He was well versed in the Old Testament Scriptures, and having been shown the way of God more perfectly, he mightily convinced the Jews by publicly showing them from their Scriptures that Jesus was the Christ. The fact that he was with Paul toward the end of his ministry could well qualify him to be the author of this masterpiece of contrasting Christ with the "beggarly elements" of the Old Testament (Titus 3:13). Who knows but what Paul may have assisted him. In more recent times, Martin Luther is of the opinion that Apollos wrote Hebrews.

Second is Clement, a disciple of and laborer with Paul (Philippians 4:3). He later became bishop of the church at Rome. It is said that Clement, a brilliant writer, arranged Paul's thoughts as we find them in Hebrews, penned them in classical Greek under Paul's supervision and approval but did not use Paul's name since it was addressed primarily to Hebrews. As we have noticed throughout Paul's travels, he was very unpopular among unbelieving Jews and Judaizers everywhere, and lest they ignore it completely with Paul's name attached, his name was not used.

Third is Luke. He had been Paul's right-hand man—the historian of much of his travels. He sat under many sermons based on the Old Testament Scriptures, and was probably as well versed in Old Testament rituals as others who assisted Paul. He was also an educated physician who knew classical Greek. The same can be said about him that was said of Clement or Apollos.

Fourth, according to Tertullian, an early Latin church father, Barnabas wrote Hebrews. Others were also of this opinion because Barnabas, whose surname was Joseph, was a Levite and was well qualified to emphasize the Levitical priesthood and worship that is so prominent in this book. Also, Barnabas was a native of Cyprus, and Cyprus was closely tied to Alexandria. A Cypriot Levite would most probably receive his theological education in Alexandria since this city was well populated with Jews who considered Jerusalem to be their Holy City, though Alexandria was the "Metropolis of the Jews." It was here that the Jews had their Old Testament Hebrew Scriptures translated into *koine* Greek, which they called the Septuagint. Barnabas, being educated both in *koine* and classical Greek, was well qualified to pen this letter. In addition, the Hebrew meaning of Barnabas is "son of exhortation," which tells us he had the necessary gift for speaking as well as for writing this epistle.

As far as the authorship of Hebrews is concerned we are safe in saying that the Holy Spirit is the author of Hebrews. Beyond this fact, we can only speculate as to who the human author was. Like the ancestry of Melchizedek, the writer of Hebrews remains unknown, and it seems foolish to speculate on something that can't be proved and ridiculous to spend so much time arguing about a human writer when the epistle itself is designed to exalt Christ, the "author and finisher of our faith" (Hebrews 12:2).

Whoever wrote it, the author likely wrote it primarily to Hebrew Christians. Many of these Jewish believers had no doubt lived before the death of Christ—they were from the Old Testament side of the Cross. Sacrifices for sin had been made by them according to the Law of Moses. Now they were on the New Testament side of the Cross, and for them it was difficult to fully realize that everything they had believed and stood for had been "nailed to the Cross" (Colossians 2:14–15). Christ has been God's Lamb offered for sin once and for all. The veil of the temple had been torn in two, Jew and Gentile were brought to God by His Lamb's blood and Christ had become the great High Priest who alone made it possible for anyone to come boldly to God through the new and living way He had established. The Old Testament covenant had been done away with and the New Testament covenant was now in force.

The temple, however, was still standing, and unbelieving Jews were putting such pressure on believing Jews that they hardly knew what they should and should not do. If Jerusalem and the temple had been destroyed in fulfillment of Christ's prophecy (Matthew 24:1–2) before Hebrews was written, this, no doubt, would have been emphasized, pointing out that the Mosaic ceremonies and sacrifices were no more. The writer, however, in view of the fact that the temple was still standing, wrote to show that it made no difference whether they had a temple or not. The finished work of Christ made Him superior or better than all the shadows of the Mosaic covenant. He wrote to tell them that there remained no more sacrifice for sin—that Christ had by Himself purged our sins, and, unlike priests of old who had to stand because their work was never completed, Christ was now seated at the right hand of His Majesty on high, ever living to make intercession for all who come unto God by Him. What the writer was really trying to get across to the Hebrews was this: They had to quit acting like Hebrews and begin acting like Christians.

The **key verse**s of Hebrews are

> 1:3—Christ, "Who being in the brightness of his [God's] glory, and the express image of his person, and upholding all things by the word of his power, when he had by himself purged our sins, sat down on the right hand of the Majesty on high."

> 9:28—"So Christ was once offered to bear the sins of many; and unto them that look for him shall he appear the second time without sin unto salvation."

The **key words** are

> *Better*, used thirteen times, and showing Christ's superiority over angels, Moses, Aaron, the Levitical priesthood, and the beggarly elements of the Law.

> *Heaven*, used fifteen times, and showing that what the believer has in Christ is spiritual and heavenly while the ceremonies of the Law were natural, earthly, and physical (see 1 Corinthians 15:46). Some examples are as follows (N is for natural; S for spiritual):

1. Abraham's seed
   N: the children of Israel (Genesis 13:14–16)
   S: born again believers (Galatians 3:16, 29)

2. The Passover Lamb
   N: animal from the flock (Exodus 12:1–28)
   S: Christ, the Lamb of God, our Passover (John 1:29; 1 Corinthians 5:7)

3. The Aaronic/Levitical priesthood
   N: Aaron's sons (Exodus 28:1; Leviticus 8–9)
   S: all believers (1 Peter 2:5, 9; Revelation 1:6)

4. Solomon's Temple
   N: located at Jerusalem (1 Kings 5:1–7:51)
   S: the believer's body (1 Corinthians 3:16–17; 6:19–20)

5. Jerusalem
   N: the Holy City of the Jews (Psalm 122:3; Luke 2:41–42)
   S: in heaven, our New Jerusalem (Galatians 4:26; Hebrews 11:10; 12:22)

There are over thirty direct, and forty-one indirect, Old Testament references in the book of Hebrews.

Outline of the Epistle of Hebrews

I. Introduction: 1:1–3
   A. In Old Testament days God spoke through His prophets (v. 1)
   B. In early New Testament days God spoke through His Son (v. 2a)
   C. Jesus is the creator of all things (v. 2b)
   D. Jesus is the express image of His Father (v. 3a)
   E. Jesus is the finisher of man's redemption (v. 3b)

II. Christ Is Better than the Angels (1:4–2:18)
   A. By His Person and position with God (1:4–14)
   B. By His power (2:1–4)
   C. By His being salvation (2:5–18)

III. Christ Is Better than Moses (3:1–6)

IV. Christ Is Better to Deliver and Give Rest (3:7–4:16)

V. Christ Is a Better Priesthood (5:1–10:39)
   A. By His qualifications (5:1–10)
   B. By His being after the order of Melchizedek (7:1–8:13)

VI. Christ's Blood Is Better than the Blood of Bulls and Goats (chap. 10)

VII. Christ Is the Better Object of Faith (chap. 11)

VIII. Christ's Love Is Better to Empower His Saints (13:1–19)

IX. Benediction (13:20–25)

Christ, by His name, person, and character, is portrayed in at least forty-seven different ways in this book of the Bible. Some examples are

1. The Captain of our salvation (2:10)

2. The Apostle and High Priest of our profession (3:1)

3. The Sacrifice for our sins (10:12)

4. The New and Living Way to approach God (10:19–20)

5. The Object of our faith (12:2)

6. Our Intercessor (7:25)

7. The Deliverer of the tempted (2:18)

8. The Supplier of our need (4:14–16)

9. The Mediator of the New Covenant (12:24)

10. The Great Shepherd of the Sheep (13:20)

TEST YOURSELF ON CHAPTER TWELVE

1. Who was Paul's friendly Roman captor?

2. About how far was the journey from Jerusalem to Caesarea to Rome for his imprisonment? When did he arrive in Rome?

3. Who was the Roman emperor at that time?

4. Describe the situation in Rome at that time.

5. In whose home did the church of Rome meet?

6. With whom did Paul first meet after his arrival in Rome? Discuss his conversation.

7. Explain the result of this meeting with Paul.

8. What was Paul's reaction to those who did not believe his presentation of the kingdom of God and the Old Testament truths concerning Jesus as Messiah?

9. To whom did Paul preach after being rejected by unbelieving Jews?

10. How many epistles did Paul write during this Roman imprisonment?

11. Who was the runaway slave Paul led to the Lord? Why had this slave run away?

12. Who was Philemon?

13. What was the important message Paul wanted to get across to Philemon in his relationship with Onesimus, his slave?

14. What are some of the lessons to be learned from the epistle to Philemon?

15. Who are the five suggested writers of the epistle of Hebrews, and why have their names been suggested?

16. In your opinion, who was the human author of the epistle to the Hebrews? State why you accept the author of your choice.

17. To whom was the epistle written?

18. How does the author exalt Christ?

19. What are the key verses? These should be memorized.

20. How are the ceremonies of the Law contrasted with Christ? Name a few and list some of your own.

21. List how Christ is seen in this book.

Chapter 13

PAUL'S FOURTH MISSIONARY JOURNEY

I t is quite possible that the Jews, seeing that Felix, Festus, and Agrippa had declared Paul to be innocent, gave up on him because he had appealed to Caesar. They may have figured that their arguments would not stand up against the opinions of these Roman rulers, because they had sent no word to any of the Jewish leaders in Rome condemning him, though at the time, Paul may have thought the Romans had been tipped off about him (Acts 28:21). Luke made no mention of Jewish opposition or persecution against Paul during his imprisonment, though there could have been some since Paul denounced the Jews for not believing their own Scriptures (Acts 28:24–28).

PAUL'S RELEASE FROM PRISON The big question at this point is: Was Paul released at the end of his two-year imprisonment (see map 6, p. 452)? Luke, who was meticulous in giving minute details of Paul's journeys, was completely silent about this matter. Are there any answers to satisfy our minds one way or the other? I, as well as others, believe that he was released. "The amicable attitude of the Roman government favors his release, the Prison Epistles expect it, the Pastoral Epistles demand it, and tradition asserts it."

Attitude of Government

First, the attitude of the Roman government favors his being released. There was no more shameful, contemptible Caesar than Nero. It was not, however, until the great fire in Rome in A.D. 64 that his attitude toward Christians changed for the worse. Paul had been in bonds from the spring of A.D. 61 until the spring of A.D. 63, during which time Christians were free from tyranny and contempt. The atmosphere was in their favor, so there was really no good reason for Caesar to act harshly toward Paul because of his preaching and the favor he had among other Christians.

Verification of Scripture

Second, the Prison Epistles expect that he was released. There are some verses in his Prison Epistles that show Paul's expectations of being released. He had sent Timothy to Philippi and told the believers there "I trust in the Lord that I also myself shall come shortly" (Philippians 2:19–24). When the slave, Onesimus, was saved and Paul wrote to Philemon to receive Onesimus as a brother in Christ, he said, "Prepare me a lodging, for I trust that through your prayers I shall be given unto you [restored or granted the gracious privilege of coming to you]" (v. 22).

Third, the Pastoral Epistles demand that Paul was released. There are two verses in 2 Timothy that give us the best evidence of his release. When Paul wrote to Timothy after having been rearrested, he said:

> At my first answer [verbal defense], no man stood with me, but all men forsook me: I pray God that it may not be laid to their charge. Notwithstanding, the Lord stood with me and strengthened me; that by me the preaching might be fully known, and that all the Gentiles might hear: and I was delivered out of the mouth of the lion 4:16–17).

In analyzing these two verses, we note that he stood trial before Caesar and gave his own defense. On the basis of evidence, "at my first answer" must refer to his being before Caesar and not his first answer to the Jews in Jerusalem. His being before the imperial ruler was expected because an angel of the Lord had told him: "Fear not, Paul, thou must be brought before Caesar: and lo, God hath given thee all them that sail with thee" (see Acts 27:22–24). Proof that the angel did not lie about all being saved is that all 276 souls found refuge on the island of Melita (see Acts 27:37–28:1).

We note that no Christian friend was there to stand with him. Tacitus, in one of his accounts, had said that it was dangerous to appear in public with one who had appealed to Caesar, that no *procurator* (lawyer or advocate) would venture to plead a case like Paul's because of the severity of the sentence should there be a guilty verdict.

We note also that Paul had a more powerful Intercessor and a wiser Advocate, One who would never leave him nor forsake him. The Lord Jesus was always near him but now, He almost felt visibly present in this hour of Paul's need. It must have been mighty discouraging not to have a friend in his presence but what an encouragement to have this "friend who sticketh closer than a brother" (Proverbs 18:24). Paul knew that "greater is he who is in you than he who is in the world." Christ in him was his hope (see 1 John 4:4; Colossians 1:27). Christ knew what it was like to have all forsake Him, even His Father, he would never forsake one of His own.

Finally we note that the expression, "I was delivered out of the mouth of the lion," would seem to indicate a not-guilty verdict and his release. The word *lion* comes from the Greek word *leōn*, which is figurative of the imminent peril of death, as in Psalm 22:21. It is also used in speaking of Christ as the "Lion of the Tribe of Judah" (Revelation 5:5). Some Greek commentators regard the lion as Nero; others understand it to be Satan (1 Peter 5:8). Elsewhere in Scripture it has a literal meaning, such as is found in 1 Samuel 17:34–36 when David killed not only a lion but a bear; Daniel 6:20 when this prophet was cast into the lion's den; and Hebrews 11:33 when many early saints were devoured by them during times of persecution. There were times, however, that at many trials the guilty were, just for sport, thrown to wild beasts (lions) in the Circus Maximus and then delivered from their jaws before being devoured; thus being saved from the mouth of the lion only to be executed a short time later. In Paul's case, he was talking about his being set free. It would appear that there were no Jerusalem Jews present to testify against him and he won his freedom by default.

In addition to these verses, in Paul's second letter to Timothy and in Titus, we have additional evidence—statements and events that took place at a different time from those already mentioned by Luke. These letters give us an untold story of a part

PAUL'S RELEASE FROM PRISON

of his ministry not included in Acts, a story about two of Paul's trusted co-laborers in his ministry and a work that had to be done in the church at Ephesus and some churches on the island of Crete. These letters to these two pastors are vastly different from those to whom he wrote in various churches, which alone indicates a period of time after his two-year imprisonment. In these documents it is recorded that Paul, with Titus, was on the island of Crete as a free man and that he was going to Nicopolis, places not mentioned before. He stated in Titus 1:5, "For this cause I left thee on Crete." That he had not previously been to Crete on a missionary journey is clear from this passage. That he could not have made such an important visit and evangelize an island on a previous visit without its being mentioned by Luke means that his presence there must have been *after* the time in which Luke ends his history in Acts 28. It is even possible that he also went to Colossae to see Philemon, since he requested of him lodging before he was released from his house arrest (Philemon 22). Based on his epistle, we find him back in Ephesus, Macedonia, Miletus, and then afterward a second time in a Roman dungeon (1 Timothy 1:3; 2 Timothy 4:20; Titus 1:5).

Confirmation of Church History

Fourth, church history confirms Paul's release from prison. Not only do we have scriptural evidence that Paul was tried and set free to travel again, but we have the writings of several early church historians and fathers to substantiate his being released, and in particular of his going to Spain. One of Paul's disciples was Clement Romanus of Rome (Philippians 4:3), a prolific writer of the first century. Another early church father, Origen, identified Clement as the bishop of the church at Rome. Because the church at Corinth became more calloused in their loose living, Clement wrote a letter to them about A.D. 96. He had access to a copy of the letter we know as 1 Corinthians, for he quotes from it frequently, reminding those carnal saints that they should have paid more attention to what their founding apostle had taught forty years before. It is in Clement's writings that we find some information outside Scripture about Paul's fourth missionary journey. There are also scattered bits of evidence from other early church fathers that give us some insight about his years of freedom after his two-year prison ministry in Rome. Considering this evidence from church history as to his release and his whereabouts the next few years, we start with Clement.

In his letter to the Corinthians, Clement expressly asserts that Paul had preached the Gospel "in the East and in the West," that "he had instructed the [then known] whole world [which was the Roman Empire] in righteousness," and that "he had reached the extreme limits of the West before he passed out of this world."

To the Romans, the Pillars of Hercules (the Strait of Gibraltar) was the extreme West.[2] The expression, "the extreme limits of the West" was often used by Roman writers to designate Spain. Clement mentions that Paul's going to the "extreme limits of the West" was before his martyrdom, and that his original intention and ambition to go to Spain was fulfilled (Romans 15:24–28).

The next bit of church-history evidence is the Muratori Canon compiled by an unknown Christian about A.D. 170, and commonly called "Muratori's Canon." After giving its account of the Gospels, it has this to say about Acts: "Then the 'Acts of the Apostles' were written in one book. Luke tells the 'most excellent Theophilus' that the various incidents took place before our eyes, but omits . . . Paul's journey when he set out from Rome to Spain."[3]

The church fathers, also believed that Paul was released. Irenaeus, in A.D. 185, as bishop of Lyons (Gaul, or France), drew up a list of bishops to help make clear just how much expansion had taken place since the end of Paul's ministry in the West. His list said that, "The church's frontiers had pushed westward into Spain." By the end of the century, according to Tertullian, Christianity "had pushed upward to Cologne in the Rhine valley." [4] Eusebius (ca. A.D. 263–339) was bishop of Caesarea, and has been called the "father of church history." He tells us that "[Paul] after defending himself successfully, it is currently reported that the Apostle again went forth to proclaim the Gospel, and afterwards came to Rome a second time, and was martyred under Nero."[5] John Chrysostom (A.D. 345–407) was an eloquent orator and preacher, later becoming patriarch of Constantinople. He mentioned as an undoubted historical fact that "St. Paul, after his release in Rome, departed to Spain."[6] Jerome (ca. A.D. 340–420) was one of the four great Latin church fathers who translated the Bible into Latin from the Old Testament Greek Septuagint and the Greek New Testament. This Bible was called the Vulgate and is known today in Roman Catholic circles as the Douay Version. Jerome bears the same testimony as the others, saying, "Paul was dismissed by Nero, that he might preach the Gospel in the west."[7]

Here we have the unanimous testimony of the Bible itself and some early church fathers that Paul was released from prison and started on his fourth missionary journey. There is no evidence to refute his release. Those who doubt his liberation from his two-year imprisonment in Rome must rely on inconclusive arguments based on probability.

PAUL IN SPAIN?

We have no Biblical proof that Paul ever went to Spain (see map 6, p. 452). However, three of the six early church fathers and the unknown Christian who compiled the Muratori Canon made mention of Spain by name and of Paul's going there. Two in particular said he went there immediately after his release, and one attributed established churches to Paul's credit as a result of his having been there. With his dream of being in Rome fulfilled, even though not under desirable circumstances, his release in A.D. 63 was a golden opportunity to fulfill his dream of also going to Spain (see Romans 15:28).

By what route he went, whether by land or by sea, we do not know. Ships sailed freely and often between western Italy and Massilia (modern Marseilles) and daily communication was available from this port into various regions of Spain. We may suppose that he reached the fullest degree of the West at least by the fall of A.D. 63, and remained there possibly one-and-a-half or two years, which would have given him sufficient time to plant seeds of truth and Christian churches among Jews and proselytes who were found in many coastal cities as well as among many Gentiles inland. We have already noted that Irenaeus mentioned the expansion of the gospel and established churches in Spain at the end of Paul's ministry in that country.

PAUL BACK IN EPHESUS

Leaving Spain, probably in early A.D. 65, Paul evidently made his way back to Ephesus. He indicates that he was in this city before going again into Macedonia (1 Timothy 1:3). This verse, in the original, reads: "I urge you [Timothy] as I go to Macedonia that you stay here [in Ephesus]." When he was with the Ephesian elders in Miletus on his third missionary journey there was the feeling that they would not see his face again (Acts 20:38), but what a joy it must have been to welcome him back into their fellowship.

Upon his arrival he found that the predictions he had uttered to these church leaders several years before in Miletus were being fulfilled (Acts 20:28–32). Heretical teachers such as Hymenaeus and Philetus were sowing seeds that were destined in another generation or two to bear a ripe crop of error: "and their word will eat like a canker [gangrene]" (2 Timothy 2:17–18). We must remember that in Ephesus we have the "melting pot of the East and West, the Occidental and the Oriental."[8] Diana's magic was still the number-one influence in the city, and Satan was relentless in his efforts to infuse the truth with poison. There were profane and vain babblings that were steering people to indulge more and more in ungodliness. There were subtleties and contradictions in what was called the science of knowledge and spiritual illumination, all of which were causing many believers to err concerning the faith (1 Timothy 6:20–21; 2 Timothy 2:16). This combination of science of knowledge and spiritual illumination was a damning curse in Paul's day and was running rampant in Ephesus, making inroads into the church (see chapter 8). Something had to be done for these Ephesian saints, so Paul acted quickly in getting them a stable pastor—Timothy.

Paul's estimate of this young man (see chapter 7) is as follows:

> But I trust the Lord Jesus to send Timothy shortly unto you, that I also may be of good comfort, when I know your state. For I have no man likeminded, who will naturally care for your state. For all seek their own, not the things which are Jesus Christ's. But ye know the proof of him, that, as a son with the father, he hath served with me in the gospel (Philippians 2:19–22).

None of Paul's companions is mentioned as often and is with him any more than this young man. Paul's relationship with Timothy is made clear by Paul's desire to have Timothy with him during his last days on earth (2 Timothy 4:9, 21).

Although Timothy was shy and reserved, he was dependable and faithful to the fundamentals of the Gospel and to the preaching of the Word of God. At times he was weak physically (possibly with ulcers, 1 Timothy 5:23), but he was not a mama's boy and Paul could rely on him to stay put. He had been with Paul enough to know about trials and persecutions, which helped prepare him for the pastorate. With all these qualifications, Paul still felt the need to remind this young preacher in 2 Timothy, chapter 2, that he must be strong like a son (v. 1); a good fighter like a soldier (vv. 3–4); striving like a man (v. 5); laboring like a husbandman (farmer) (v. 6); victorious like one willing to suffer (v. 12a); separated unto the Potter like a vessel (v. 21); and gentle, patient, and teaching like a servant (v. 24). Timothy had also been in close contact with Paul during his imprisonment in Rome (Philippians 1:1; Colossians 1:1; Philemon 1). We know that when Paul wrote to the Philippians in Rome prior to his release he said he was going to send Timothy to them to assist in the work there.

Paul now sends for Timothy to come to Ephesus and assume pastoral responsibilities in the church. After the two met, Timothy was given sufficient advice on how he should "behave in the house of God." At the same time, Paul exhorted him to "give attendance to reading, to exhortation, and to doctrine" and for him not to be intimidated by his youth (1 Timothy 3:15; 4:11–12). After Paul left Timothy in Ephesus, he headed for Macedonia (see 1 Timothy 1:3). Where he went in this region is unknown, but we can within reason assume he visited as many of the churches that he had established as possible, especially the ones in Philippi, Macedonia, and Berea. Sensing that he had left much unsaid in instructing Timothy, he is moved by the Holy Spirit of God to write a letter to him, giving fuller details concerning the duties and responsibilities of a pastor not only relating to his personal life but also to church policy. Written somewhere in Macedonia and forwarded to Timothy, this first letter to him will be discussed later in this chapter.

TITUS AND PAUL AT CRETE It is impossible to tell where and when Paul met Titus again, but since Paul had often sent him to various places to check on the different churches, it is possible that they met somewhere in Macedonia (see map 6, p. 452), and from there set sail to a needy field—Crete (see map 6, p. 452). It is not known if they went to Ephesus first and sailed from there to Crete, or whether they sailed directly from Neapolis near Philippi to this island. We previously stated that Titus is not mentioned at all by Luke in Acts. Paul, however, made mention of him at least thirteen times in his epistles. He was Paul's "own son after the common faith" (Titus 1:4). Paul had used him as a test at the Jerusalem Council (Galatians 2:1–3) to show that a Gentile could be saved by faith apart from circumcision (see chapter 7 in connection with Timothy's circumcision). On Paul's third missionary journey Titus was with him in Corinth (2 Corinthians 7:6–7; 8:6, 16). Titus took Paul's second Corinthian letter to them to urge them to make good on their promise to give to the poor in Jerusalem as well as to check on these fickle Christians. Titus seemed more of a leader than did Timothy. There is some of the aggression in him that we find in Paul, yet he knew how to comfort others (2 Corinthians 2:7). He was able to instruct saints and help them grow; he cared for them. As Paul's partner and fellow helper, he had learned much about how to "care for the churches" (see 2 Corinthians 8:23; 11:28). Paul had also trusted him to go to the belligerent Dalmatians in Illyricum. Now we find "father and son" together on the island of Crete.

Historical Background of Crete

This island has an interesting history. It is mountainous; about 156 miles long and up to 30 miles wide. When the Greek mainland was semibarbarous (ca. 1,600 B.C.), there was a flourishing and peaceable civilization on this island, then known as Minoan, from the mythological founder, King Minos, the earth ruler. This king was the son of the legendary father-god, Zeus, head of the Greek pantheon. For the benefit of the Cretans, Zeus established maritime supremacy for them by defeating pirates who were ruining commercial trade. The Minoan civilization spread to the mainland, but by 1,400 B.C., after two hundred short years, it collapsed on Crete. Due to an earthquake or volcanic eruption, the island was invaded by a ruthless army from the mainland, who took advantage of the chaos and confusion brought about by the disaster. This instilled hatred in the hearts of the Cretans and down through the succeeding centuries and on into the first century A.D., they had become lawless, and were notorious for being "liars, evil beasts [ferocious, destructive, and brutes in their manner]; lazy [idle] gluttons" (Titus 1:12). Their big lie, which was probably told to appease Minos, was that the tomb of his father, Zeus, a nonexisting personage was located on their island.

Churches at Crete

Luke makes no mention of any missionary effort by Paul when his ship stopped at Fair Havens on this island (Acts 27:8–9), and this is understandable since he was a prisoner. They spent much time there, however, before sailing to Phenice, and we can be assured he witnessed at every opportunity. Whether or not he left a nucleus of believers there, we cannot say. He certainly did not have the time to penetrate the island and win enough to the Lord to establish churches. However, from Acts 2:11, we learn that some Cretans had been present at Pentecost, and since there were churches already established on this island when Paul returned, we can assume many had been saved under Peter's ministry and then went back home with their new-found faith to establish a gospel ministry.

Churches had been established long before Paul and Titus arrived, and it was evident to them that Jews on the island were the same as Jews elsewhere. They were "unruly and vain talkers and deceivers, especially they of the circumcision: whose mouths must be stopped, who subvert whole houses, teaching things which they ought not, for filthy lucre's sake" (Titus 1:10–11). Paul gave Titus instructions to go throughout the churches to help set things in order. Not only was there opposition from Jews and their myths, but many were denying the Lord, being abominable, detestable, lawless, and disobedient. They were defiled and un-believing because they held nothing to be pure or sacred (1:14–16).

Having visited parts of the island with Titus, Paul left, and apparently went to Miletus (see map 6, p. 452). With the same feeling he had toward Timothy when he left Ephesus for Mace-donia, Paul realized he had more to say to Titus. He felt a need to fill him in on certain details; thus this epistle to him. This letter, no doubt, was sent from Miletus.

Leaving from this city (see map 6, p. 452), Paul headed for Nicopolis (in Epirus, on the western coast of Achaia or Greece), to get there before winter set in (Titus 3:12). Paul had spent quite a bit of time in fellowship with his "sons in the faith." Both were responsible servants and he had designated a job for each—Timo-thy in Ephesus and Titus on the island of Crete. He had full confidence in each, and he knew that by following his instruc-tions, the believers under their ministry would be edified and strengthened and the testimony of the churches would be more effective.

THE PASTORAL EPISTLES   A comment or two is in order about the authenticity of these letters—two to Timothy and one to Titus. Critics have questioned whether Paul wrote them.

The church order that Paul set forth in them did not become common until the second century. This objection is easily re-futed, however, because as early as Paul's first missionary journey, he and Barnabas were ordaining elders in churches they had established throughout southern Galatia at least twenty years or more prior to the writing of these Pastoral Epistles (Acts

14:21–23). These elders had been appointed for the purpose of church order and government.

The authenticity is also questioned because Paul's vocabulary and style are vastly different from those of his other letters. Rightly so; he was writing to different people—pastors rather than members. A lawyer would not write the same type of letter to a personal friend that he would write to a judge about a case. Common sense rules out any argument here.

Another argument against Paul's authorship is that Luke does not describe any of the travels mentioned in these letters. The letters, however, do not fit into the history of Paul's ministry as described by Luke in Acts. There are many things that Luke does not mention, in particular Paul's second imprisonment in a Roman dungeon and his death. There is no valid argument here by the critics.

Finally, there is no other argument against Paul's authorship because he said he, himself, wrote them (1 and 2 Timothy 1:1; Titus 1:1).

The purpose of each letter revolves around church discipline, and sets forth church order and government at Ephesus and Crete. One would not expect to find in these letters as much "doctrine" (sin, faith, justification, grace, and so forth) as is found in Paul's epistles to churches and believers in general. Rather, in writing to pastors, one will find mainly pastoral duties and responsibilities. In his general epistles, Paul's salutation is two-fold: "grace and peace." In his letters to these two pastors, Timothy and Titus, his salutation has an extra component—"mercy." (1 and 2 Timothy 1:2; Titus 1:4). Only a pastor knows why mercy is added. After you read *The Pastor*, you will know why.

> If he is young, he lacks experience; if his hair is grey, he is too old.

> If he has seven or eight children, he has too many; if he has none, he is setting a bad example.

> If his wife sings in the choir, she is being forward; if she doesn't, she isn't interested in her husband's work.

> If he speaks from notes, he has canned sermons and is dry; if he is extemporaneous, he is not deep.

If he spends too much time in his study, he neglects his people; if he visits a lot, he is a gadabout.

If he is attentive to the poor, he is playing to the grandstand; if to the wealthy, he is trying to be an aristocrat.

If he suggests improvements for the church, he is a dictator; if he makes no suggestions, he is a figurehead.

If he uses too many illustrations in his sermons, he neglects the Bible; if not enough, he is not clear.

If he condemns wrong, he is cranky and meddlesome; if he does not, he is a compromiser.

If he preaches an hour, he is windy; if less, he is lazy and not fully prepared.

If he preaches the truth, he is offensive; if not, he is a hypocrite.

If he fails to please everyone, he is hurting the church; if he does please everyone, he has no conviction.

If he preaches tithing, he is a money-grubber; if he does not, he is failing to develop his members.

If he receives a large salary, he is mercenary; if a small salary, it proves he is not worth much.

If he preaches all the time, the people get tired of hearing one man; if he invites guest preachers, he is shirking his responsibility.[9]

So what! They say the preacher has an easy time. And I guess he does at that, but he'll have to wait until he gets to heaven to enjoy it all.

Now you know why he needs all three of these "helping hands," grace, mercy, and peace when he works with church members, especially mercy.

Paul's First Letter to Timothy

There is so much one wants to say when they are in the presence of a friend. Paul no doubt explained much to Timothy in Ephesus before leaving for Macedonia. Once on the European continent, however, he thought of many things he wished he had said. So he penned his first letter to Timothy around A.D. 65. Realizing that any dedicated Christian is in a constant battle with the forces of evil, he expressed a desire that Timothy might "fight a good fight" as he faces all odds (cf. 1 Timothy 1:18–19 with 7–10, 20).

The **theme** of the epistle revolves around behavior in the house of God (3:15).

The **key verse** is: 3:16—"And without controversy great is the mystery of godliness: God was manifested in the flesh, justified in the Spirit, seen of angels, preached unto the Gentiles, believed on in the world, received up into glory."

While mysticism was uppermost in the minds of the scientifically knowledgeable Ephesians, the difference between the "mystery of godliness" and the mysteries of Diana is that when one believes the gospel, which embraces the mystery of godliness, he becomes a new creation—his life is changed for the better. Old things of the world passed away; all things of the Lord became new to him. The worshipers of the mystery of Diana remained in gross sin, and became more ungodly.

The **outline** of 1 Timothy is as follows:

I. Salutation (1:1–2)
II. Timothy's instructions
    A. Be on Guard against False, Ungodly Teachers (1:3–11)
    B. Realize the Importance of Prayer (2:1–8)
    C. Outline the Manner of Dress and the Activity of Women (2:9–15)
    D. Place Qualified Bishops (Elders, Overseers) and Deacons (Servants) in Office (3:1–13)
    E. Beware of a Falling away of Saints in Perilous Times and Unnecessary Church Rituals and Traditions (4:1–5)
    F. Be a Good Minister (4:6–16)
    G. Work Together with Church Members (chap. 5)
    H. Help Masters Deal with Servants (6:1–2)
III. Have a Proper Evaluation of Money (6:3–21)

Timothy means "valuable, dear to God; honored by God." What a jewel the Ephesian saints had for a pastor.

Very little of the Old Testament is referred to in First Timothy.

1. cf. 5:18 with Deuteronomy 25:4: A working ox must not to be muzzled

2. cf. 2:13 with Genesis 2:7, 21–22: Adam's creation

3. cf. 2:14 with Genesis 3:12: Adam's sin

4. cf. 6:7 with Job 1:21: We brought nothing into this world

Paul portrays Christ to Timothy as the mystery of godliness (3:16); and the only Potentate, the King of Kings, and Lord of Lords (6:15).

Paul's Epistle to Titus

In his letter to Titus written about A.D. 66, Paul mentioned his going to Nicopolis to spend the winter (3:12). He had mentioned to Timothy that he had previously left Trophimus sick at Miletus (2 Timothy 4:20). Since this incident cannot be placed in Acts, it must have been on his journey from Crete to Nicopolis that Paul stopped in Miletus and penned this letter. The urgency of it suggests that it was written soon after he left Titus on Crete. It would seem that Artemas and Tychicus delivered the letter to Titus, and now that they were on Crete, Titus would be replaced by them so that he could go to meet Paul in Nicopolis.

The **outline** of Paul's letter to Titus is as follows:

I. Greetings to Titus (1:1–4)

II. Titus' Instructions
  A. Reprove them sharply so that they may be sound in the faith (1:13). *Sharply* is an interesting word. It means to severely rebuke them in a manner that cuts as with the sharp edge of a sword. No doubt Paul had in mind the metaphor used in Hebrews 4:12; he wanted Titus to so use the Word of God as he would a sharp "two-edged sword, piercing even to the dividing asunder of soul and spirit, and the joints and marrow," that it might be a "discerner of the thoughts and intents of their hearts." In our language, Titus was to "pull no punches" in trying to get these Cretans straightened out. They needed to learn how to engage in good deeds so that they would be able to meet pressing needs, overcome their circumstances, and be fruitful (2:1; 3:8, 14).
  B. In addition, Paul felt that certain Christians should be put in places of authority in their churches, "to set in order things that are wanting"; are destitute and lacking (1:5). As a result, he instructed Titus to appoint elders in every assembly as di-

rected. Before appointing them, they must meet certain standards (1:5–9).

C. Give standards for both the young and elderly, as well as slaves or servants (2:2–10). Since they were liars and lawless, Titus was instructed to teach them to respect those in authority (3:1–2).

D. Always be on guard so as not to become involved in their foolish contentions, genealogies, and entanglements about the Jewish laws and customs (3:9–10).

E. "These things speak and exhort, and rebuke with all authority. Let no man despise thee" (2:15). Titus was never to back down no matter what subject the Cretans brought up; he was to stand tall and never compromise his convictions, no matter how "brutish" these people might be.

F. There was ever the need to constantly remind these islanders, as sinful as they were, "that the grace of God that bringeth salvation hath appeared to all men [including them], teaching us that, denying ungodliness and worldly lusts, we should live soberly, righteously, and godly in this present world; looking for that blessed hope, and the glorious appearing of the great God and our Saviour Jesus Christ; who gave himself for us, that he might redeem us from all iniquity, and purify unto himself a peculiar people, zealous of good works." (2:11–14)

What a message of hope to help these "liars, evil beasts, and gluttons" to be conformed to the image of God's dear Son.

The **key verses** are

1:5—"For this cause I left thee in Crete, that thou shouldest set in order the things that are wanting, and ordain elders in every city, as I had appointed thee";

2:11–14; 3:5—"Not by works of righteousness which we have done, but according to his mercy he saved us, by the washing of regeneration, and renewing of the Holy Spirit";

3:8—"This is a faithful saying, and these things I will that thou affirm constantly, that they which have believed in God might be careful to maintain good works. These things are good and profitable unto men."

Paul portrayed Christ to Titus as "The Great God and our Saviour Jesus Christ" (2:10, 13; 3:4, 6).

Paul's second epistle to Timothy, which makes up the third letter of the Pastoral Epistles will be discussed in chapter 14.

NICOPOLIS AND TROAS   Beginning with Paul's release from his house arrest in the spring of A.D. 63, he spent a little over four years on his fourth missionary journey (see map 6, p.452). It is now early June, A.D. 67 and, on the basis of his remark that he wanted to winter in Nicopolis, we assume he had arrived in this western seacoast Achaian city (Titus 3:12; 2 Timothy 4:13). Nicopolis would serve as a spring board from which to penetrate Illyricum in Dalmatia and visit some churches that perhaps he established or helped to organize on his third missionary journey (Romans 15:19). It is quite likely that when Titus arrived, he helped Paul become acquainted with some in that area of Dalmatia where he had been and whom he had not met (2 Timothy 4:10b).

As we shall see in the next chapter, Paul, in all probability, left Nicopolis much sooner than expected, not staying there for the winter. Why, we do not know. He bade Titus and other believers goodbye, and went back, no doubt through Macedonia, and made his way on down to the home of Carpus in Troas (2 Timothy 4:13). *Carpus* means "fruit," possibly a fruit of Paul's labors in this city; someone in the assembly who knew him and welcomed him in his home as a guest. Little did Paul realize these would be his last days of freedom.

TOTAL MILEAGE OF PAUL'S TRAVELS   On this last missionary journey, Paul had traveled approximately 5,800 miles from Rome to Spain, Spain to Ephesus, Ephesus to Macedonia, Macedonia to Crete, Crete to Miletus, Miletus to Nicopolis, and Nicopolis to Troas. The total distance of his four journeys is roughly 13,950 miles. The mileage from Jerusalem to Caesarea to escape assassination from the Jews, plus the voyage to Rome, was approximately 2,050 miles. Then there was the mileage from Damascus to Arabia, Arabia back to Damascus, Damascus to Jerusalem, Jerusalem to Tarsus, Tarsus to Antioch, and two round trips from Antioch to Jerusalem of approximately 2,750 miles. Last was his journey from Troas to Rome (see map 6, p. 452) for his second imprisonment, about 1,050 miles, plus about 4 miles from his dungeon to the place of his execution. Paul traveled by foot approximately 9,500 miles and approximately 10,300 miles by sea in his service for the Lord, for a grand total of approximately 19,800 miles.

RESULT OF PAUL'S
FOURTH MISSIONARY JOURNEY

1. The climate in Rome was conducive to Paul's release from his two-year house arrest; the New Testament expected and demanded it; and tradition asserted it.

2. It is quite possible that Paul fulfilled his dream of going to Spain.

3. Paul placed Timothy and Titus as pastors in two needy fields—Ephesus and Crete.

4. Paul wrote two of his Pastoral Epistles during this time of freedom—1 Timothy and Titus.

5. Paul revisited Ephesus, Macedonia, and Crete.

6. Paul visited Nicopolis and possibly Illyricum again.

7. Paul's days in Troas were his last days of freedom before his second imprisonment in Rome.

TEST YOURSELF ON CHAPTER THIRTEEN

1. List four reasons why it is believed Paul was released after his two-year imprisonment. Discuss them.

2. How does church history confirm Paul's release and who were the church fathers who wrote about his release?

3. Do you believe there is any evidence to refute his release? If so, what is it?

4. Do you believe Paul visited Spain? Give reasons why you do or don't.

5. What was Paul's purpose in going back to Ephesus?

6. Who did Paul appoint as pastor of the church at Ephesus?

7. What was Paul's evaluation of Timothy? Elaborate.

8. What were some of the admonitions Paul listed for Timothy?

9. What letter did Paul write from Macedonia?

10. Who did Paul take to Crete with him?

11. Give the historical background of Crete and the Cretans.

12. Define the Pastoral Epistles.

13. How many were there? Name them.

14. How do these epistles differ from Paul's general epistles?

15. Why do you believe Paul added *mercy* in his salutation to Timothy and Titus?

16. What is the theme of 1 Timothy?

17. What is the key verse of 1 Timothy?

18. Why was it necessary to make known the truth of this verse to the Ephesians?

19. List the reasons Paul wrote to Timothy.

20. How does Paul portray Christ to Timothy?

21. What does the name *Timothy* mean?

22. From where do some believe that Paul wrote the epistle to Titus?

23. Who are the ones believed to have delivered this epistle to Titus?

24. Where did Paul request Titus to meet him?

25. How was Titus to preach and admonish the Cretans? List the instructions given to Titus.

26. What are the key verses of Titus?

27. How did Paul portray Christ to Titus?

28. What was the total mileage for Paul's fourth missionary journey?

29. What was the mileage grand total for all of Paul's travels as a servant of Jesus Christ?

Chapter Fourteen

PAUL'S REARREST, HIS TRIAL, AND HIS DEATH

With Roman law being what it was, we are assured that Paul came to the attention of Nero upon his arrival in Rome from Caesarea. Julius had presented the report from Festus, either to the emperor or some high-ranking official, who made known Paul's case. During his prior imprisonment in Rome, Paul's name must have been well-known in palace circles because there were those of Caesar's household who had come to know Christ as their Savior. His name must have been mentioned often under Nero's roof (Philippians 4:22). This Apostle to the Gentiles had not only made a great impact on the imperial city of the Romans but was also a great influence in royal circles. Nero could not have overlooked him.

NERO AND THE CHRISTIAN HOLOCAUST Nero (see illustration 53) was born Lucius Domitius Ahenobarbus in A.D. 37 of a family of ill repute. His father, a typical crooked Roman politician with several murder victims to his credit, died when Nero was three. Nero's mother remarried, and later murdered her second husband. Somewhere up the societal ladder she met Emperor Claudius and married him. Claudius adopted her son with the promise that Nero would be heir to the throne. At the age of fifteen Nero married his stepfather's thirteen-year-old daughter. When he was seventeen his mother murdered Claudius to keep him from changing his mind about his promise, and Nero

53—Left: Nero. *Courtesy of author.*
54—Below: Nero and his mother. *Courtesy of American Numismatic Society, New York.*

became the Roman emperor in A.D. 54 (see illustration 54). Much of the family's "blood-tainted hands" rubbed off on him. He had his first wife slain and he himself killed his second wife. He had the husband of his third wife killed in order to marry her. To keep Britannicus, son of Claudius, from making an attempt to claim the throne, Nero had him poisoned. He became a blood-thirsty, wild man, greedy for a sport that drove him to acts of violence. Chariot racing and bloody scenes with gladiators, wild beasts, and prisoners in the arena were his greatest delight. His conceit was second to none. It is said that when he sang, no one but the dead left the room; some women gave birth in his presence rather than leave and incur his wrath.

Nero's government as a whole was becoming weak. Soldiers and palace guards were defecting. Why he had tolerated Christians in Rome only the Lord knows. He knew that basically there were only two religions throughout the whole empire; emperor worship and the worship of Christ the Savior. To Nero the Jews' religion was too fanatical and repulsive (due to their blood sacrifices) for any but Jews and a few proselytes.

Tacitus, the noted Roman historian, gives us a bit of information that is very important at this point in time. About halfway during Paul's first imprisonment (A.D. 62), Nero married his adulterous mistress, Poppaea, who had become a proselyte to Judaism. This infamous woman, not content with inducing her lover to divorce his young wife, Octavia, and to marry her, demanded of Nero Octavia's death and gloated over the head of the victim, which she had requested be brought before her. Her power rose to its highest the following year when a daughter was born. She had temples and altars erected to herself and her infant, and divine honors were paid to both of them.[1] Josephus informs us that she exerted her influence over Nero in favor of the Jews and patronized their emissaries at Rome. No power on earth would prevent her from seconding any demand they

55—Poppaea, Nero's wife. *Courtesy of American Numismatic Society, New York.*

might make, even if it was the severe punishment and death of an enemy of theirs. Josephus also speaks of "Nero granting favors to the Jews to please Poppaea, who was a religious woman."[2] By A.D. 63, Nero had not yet turned against Christians. Evidently the Jews at Rome still had not heard anything about Paul's run-in with the Jerusalem Jews, so no complaint had been made to Poppaea about him; thus we can better understand why Paul was released when he was.

It was not long, however, as Nero listened to his wife that the situation became worse. At the same time, criticism against him by the senate was becoming all the more severe. During the middle of the night in mid-July, A.D. 64, while Paul was probably in Spain, a fire broke out in the Circus Maximus, the horseshoe-shaped colonnade of shops that surrounded the sports grounds. The fire raged for five days. Although Nero was in Antium (Anzio, on the coast near Appii) when the fire started, he rushed back to Rome to put relief measures into operation. His reputation for violence was such that he was soon blamed for igniting the inferno to make room for a new palace that his wife desired. Outraged, and probably with the help of his wife (Poppaea), Nero found his scapegoat in the Christians, and all the forces of hell broke loose against them. Nero charged them with arson and with being "haters of the human race." The holocaust among the Jews in World War II was almost incomparable, and so was this one—Nero's brutality against the Christians.

NERO AND THE CHRISTIAN HOLOCAUST

Many Roman historians have had much to say about Nero's atrocities. Suetonius, in his *Life of Nero*, said: "Punishment was inflicted on the Christians, a class of men addicted to a novel and mischievous superstition."[3] Tacitus gives a most vivid account:

> Therefore, to scotch the rumor, Nero put culprits who punished with the utmost refinements of cruelty, a class of people, loathed for their vices, whom the crowd styled 'Christians.' 'Christus,' from whom they got their name, had been executed by sentence of the procurator Pontius Pilate when Tiberius was Emperor; and the pernicious superstition was checked for a short time, only to break out afresh, not only in Judea, the home of the plague, but in Rome itself, where all the horrible and shameful things in the world collect and find a home. First of all, some who were arrested informed on others and a huge multitude was convicted, not so much on the ground of incendiarism as for hatred of the human race. Their execution was made a matter of sport: some were sewn up in the skins of wild beasts and savaged to death by dogs; others were fastened to crosses as living torches to serve as lights when daylight failed. Nero made his gardens available for the show and held games in the Circus, mingling with the crowd or standing in his chariot in charioteer's uniform. Hence, although the victims were criminals deserving the severest punishment, pity began to be felt for them because it seemed that they were being sacrificed to gratify one man's lust for cruelty, rather than for the sake of public weal [satisfaction]. . . ."[4]

Although the government, prior to the fire, had acted favorably toward Christians, it is likely that Christians were not looked on with any degree of approval by the public in general because of their nonparticipation in worldly events that the average citizen indulged in and because they worshiped Jesus rather than Caesar. The Romans misinterpreted Christians' separation from the world to mean they hated the human race. Oftentimes weak Christians succumbed to peer pressure, and it just could be that when Nero's soldiers raided their homes, in order to save their skin they confessed, as Tacitus mentioned, that their brethren had set fire to the city. This resulted in a vast multitude of Christians being convicted without trial.

Christians took refuge in the catacombs because superstition kept Roman soldiers from entering those burial grounds. Early New Testament saints left many paintings and carved symbols in

56—Colosseum (Flavin Amphitheater) statue of Nero. *Courtesy of author.*

these tunnels beneath Rome, proving their allegiance to Christ as their Savior and King. One such symbol was that of the fish (see chapter 10).

Cruel, barbarous acts continued in Rome throughout the rest of the first century, especially in the Colosseum (see illustration 56), also called the Flavin Amphitheater, built by Emperor Vespasian and his son, Titus, in A.D. 75–80. It was built on the grounds that Nero had used for his Golden House, and under its floor were the cages of the wild animals and the locker rooms for the gladiators (see illustration 57). The Arch of Titus is located nearby. A bronze colossus of Nero, 120 feet high, stood nearby at the vestibule of Nero's house; thus giving the Colosseum its name. It was one of the greatest buildings in the world up to that time, and seated over forty-five thousand people. It was dedicated by Titus in A.D. 80 during one hundred days of elaborate and gory games. Here many saints, who refused to deny their faith in Christ, forfeited their lives to the cheers of the Romans as wild beasts devoured their bodies (see illustration 58). The persistent persecution of Christians in Rome sparked by Nero became a flame that spread throughout the empire. Relatively few Christians were safe anywhere, and Christianity became taboo. Christians were stripped of freedom, and it was not safe to meet in

NERO AND THE CHRISTIAN HOLOCAUST   357

57—Gladiators fighting in Colosseum. *Courtesy of author.*

public. This is one reason why, especially in Rome, believers met in secret in the catacombs.

PROBABLE REASONS FOR PAUL'S REARREST   It is at this point that our sanctified imagination comes into play once again. With all that was going on in Rome against the Christians, we can well imagine that within the confines of the imperial palace, Nero and Poppaea were in constant conversation suggesting new methods with which to continue their destructive opposition against Christians. The name of one man, Paul, stood out in Christian circles. Since his name had become a byword among the converted soldiers in Caesar's household, it only stands to reason that sooner or later his name would be discussed in connection with their plots. No doubt Julius' report from Festus about Paul's appeal came to Nero's mind. Since Paul's case involved a confrontation he had had with the Asian Jews in Jerusalem, and since Poppaea favored the Jews, and was even willing to kill to appease them, it would be an easy matter for her, with the control she had over Nero, to see this record and find something she could pin on this popular and influential Christian. What she read about the fracas in the temple between Paul and these Jews, and possibly the charge of sedition by Tertullus before Festus (Acts 24:2, 5) was all the ammunition she needed to get Nero to reopen Paul's case. What better person, with his popularity among Christians, to indict than Paul?

Considering the animosity on the part of the Jews toward Christians, it would not surprise us that they were delighted with Nero's taking his spite out on the Christians instead of the Jews. Then, too, we can well imagine that many of the Jewish leaders were peeved with Paul. We must remember that when he had first came to Rome as a prisoner and had had his meeting with the Jews, he had read them the riot act when they rejected his message. Paul had also added fuel to the flame when he told them that God would turn to the Gentiles, who would accept the gospel (Acts 28:24–28).

Armed with information from Festus' report, Poppaea must have contacted the Jewish leaders. Considering what Paul had told them about the temple incident (Acts 28:17–20), it is probable that some of them felt they should make it their business to find out from the leaders in Jerusalem what had happened. After getting the Jerusalem Jews' point of view and discussing the matter with Poppaea, it was not difficult for the Roman Jews to assist her in persuading Nero to rearrest Paul. Paul had reasoned with the Jews about the kingdom of God, and the word *kingdom*, which to them was other than Rome's, meant sedition—a plot against the empire. Paul had said in his defense before Festus,

58—Christians praying before death. *Courtesy of author.*

PROBABLE REASONS FOR PAUL'S REARREST   359 "yet against Caesar, have I offended any thing at all" (cf. Acts 25:8 with 25:17), which had also been his answer to the charge of sedition by Tertullus (Acts 24:2, 5). This, coupled with the fact that Paul had been instrumental in helping some in Caesar's household turn from emperor worship to the true worship of God through Christ, made him a hunted man.

PAUL'S REARREST   Finding Paul would not be hard to do. Couriers were sent throughout the Empire with a message to be on the lookout for him. Paul was not an unknown nobody. He had left a trail in witnessing and establishing churches throughout the heart of the empire. There was hardly a place where he was not known. Word soon reached Troas that he was Rome's "number-one," most-wanted man, and his visit in the home of Carpus was cut short with his arrest in late summer (A.D. 67).

In the first century, when one was apprehended by Roman soldiers, regardless of where, he or she was arrested on the spot. There was no warning, no packing, no goodbys. He or she was bound by a chain, taken to the nearest dock, and shipped to Rome (that is, if the offense demanded the prisoner's presence in Rome, as was the case of Paul). He was taken to Rome to face the Caesar to whom he had made his original appeal—Nero. If someone says my sanctified-imagination theory might not stand up in court, the fact remains that Paul was rearrested and he was in Rome—here to spend his last days in prison in a far different setting than his house arrest had been (Acts 28:30–31).

TYPES OF   Paul was no longer given the privilege of
ROMAN PRISONS   *custodia militaris,* in which he was chained to a soldier and had the freedom of the barracks or his own private house. This time he was placed in *custodia publica,* the most severe kind of imprisonment (e.g., as was his imprisonment in Philippi, Acts 16:22–24, see chapter 7). He said in 2 Timothy, "I am suffering even to the point of being chained like a criminal" (2:9 NASV). Many scholars are of the opinion that he was placed in the *tullianum,* known today as the "Mamertine Prison" (see illustration 59).

A Roman prison usually had three distinctive parts: (1) The *communiora,* where the prisoner had light and fresh air; (2) The *inteniora,* shut off by iron gates with strong bars and locks; and (3)The *tullianum,* or dungeon. These were cells that bred pestilences; they were cold, damp, filthy, smelly, and dimly lit. Excrement piled up and the odor was stifling. One entered a dungeon with ropes tied under their arms (see illustration 60), via a hole through which they were lowered. There was absolutely no possibility of escape. Some prisoners were forgotten and stayed in so long their chains rusted. Many died before their trials. The only time fresh air came into the dungeon was when the door at the top of the hole was lifted to let a new prisoner in, take one out for trial, or take out a dead body; or when a breeze might pass through the iron bars and gates of the *inteniora*. It was through the inteniora that they received any light. (Note Jeremiah's, similar experience, Jeremiah 38:6.)

59—Mamertine Prison in Rome. Place of Paul's second imprisonment. *Courtesy of author.*

60—"Hole" entrance to Mamertine Prison. *Courtesy of author.*

Chapter Fourteen

CAESAR'S COURT The nature of Paul's rearrest and the
(OR JUDGMENT HALL) charges to be leveled against him
necessitated a quick hearing or trial. It was now autumn A.D. 67.
Having been released from his first imprisonment in Rome in
the spring of A.D. 63, Paul was free for a little over four years. The
wheels of so-called justice were turning in the courts and preparation was in the making to bring this "criminal" to trial.

What was it like to be tried as an enemy of Rome before
Caesar? Although Paul was still innocent, in the eyes of Rome he
had already been tried, found guilty, and condemned to die. The
only thing left was the formality of going through the motions
of a trial. Paul's case came up before the emperor himself. Usually
appeals from the provinces in civil cases were not heard by Caesar
but by delegates of consular rank. The original charge against
Paul had been of a religious nature. Now, however, because he
was a Christian, he was viewed as a criminal, and could easily be
charged with treason or sedition.

Trials conducted by the emperor were held in the imperial
palace. Conybeare gives us an excellent description of such a
court scene.

> At the end of the splendid hall, lined with the precious marbles
> of Egypt and of Libya, we must imagine the Caesar seated in the
> midst of his Assessors. Twenty in number, these men were of the
> highest rank and greatest influence. Among them were two
> consuls and selected representatives of each of the other great
> magistrates of Rome. The remainder consisted of Senators cho-
> sen by lot. Over the bench of judges presided the representative
> of the most powerful monarchy which has ever existed, the
> absolute ruler of the whole civilized world—Nero himself. But
> the reverential awe which his position naturally suggested was
> changed into contempt and loathing by the character of the
> Sovereign who now presided over that supreme tribunal, for
> Nero was a man who, having power equal to the gods, could
> not render a just verdict. The fear and excitement of his omnipo-
> tence and his cruelty were blended with contempt for his craving
> for ignoble lust of praise and licentiousness. He had plunged his
> reign into that extravagance of tyranny which exhausted the
> patience of his subjects and which would ultimately bring him
> to destruction. By the time he was twenty-five his hands were
> blood-stained with several murders. He had been responsible for
> countless believers being slaughtered in the Christian Holocaust.

His degrading want of dignity and insatiable appetite for vulgar applause drew tears from the counsellors and servants of his house, who could see him slaughter his nearest relative without a moment's hesitation and without remorse.[5]

PAUL'S TRIAL Before the tribunal of this blood-stained adulterer, Paul the apostle was now brought in fetters under the custody of his military guard. We may be sure that he who had so often stood undaunted before the delegates of the Imperial throne did not quail (falter or even lose heart) when he was brought before Caesar.[6]

Paul's life was not in Nero's hands. He knew that while his Lord had work for him to do on earth, he would be shielded from Caesar's sword. If his work was over, he would gladly depart to be with Christ because to live was Christ, and to die would be gain (see Philippians 1:21, 23). Just as the three Hebrew boys had stood in the strength of the Lord before Nebuchadnezzar, so Paul stood in the strength of the Lord, calm and collected, ready to answer the charges of his accusers, knowing that in this, his hour of need, God would give him words to speak. He knew that nothing could separate him from the love of God. It did not matter if he had no earthly sympathy. Although his Savior had been forsaken by all, even by the Father, Paul knew that Christ would not leave him nor forsake him.

The order of the proceedings was as follows: (1) the speech of the prosecutor, (2) examination and cross-examination of witnesses for the prosecution, (3) the speech of the prisoner, (4) examination and cross-examination of the witnesses for the defense. After the prosecutor's speech, he and his witnesses were called forward to support their accusation. Although the subject matter for decision was contained in a written deposition, Roman law required the personal presence of the accusers and witnesses whenever possible. In Paul's trial, the witnesses were probably the Jewish leaders of Rome who accused Paul of being the ringleader of the sect of the Nazarenes and of his preaching a different kingdom than Rome—the kingdom of God. The charge was most serious because the alleged crime amounted to *majestas*, or treason, and was punishable by death. We do not know if Festus' report concerning the charge that Tertullus had made in regard to Paul's being "a mover of sedition" (Acts 24:5) was brought up at this trial or not.

Then it was Paul's turn. We cannot suppose that he had

secured the services of any professional advocate to refute whatever false accusations were brought against him. Paul was well qualified with the help of the Lord to defend himself and put the truth clearly and squarely before his Roman judges. We know that he had not used any lawyers on former occasions. It would seem consistent with his character and his unwavering reliance on his God to present a plain and simple statement of facts, like he had done before Felix, Festus, and Agrippa. He could easily prove the falsehood of any charge of sacrilege by the testimony of any true witness. He would show that far from being a seditious agitator against the state, he taught his converts everywhere to honor the imperial government, and to submit to ordinances decreed by magistrates for conscience sake. We need only to look at Romans 13:1–7 to see his stand on this matter. Paul never made the government an issue. He never preached against the evils of Rome. He never announced a text and then became a rabble-rouser about current events. Although he admitted belonging to the sect of the Nazarenes, preaching nothing save Jesus and Him crucified, yet he would remind the court that Rome acknowledged a division of various sects, each equally entitled to protection by the law, and that his sect of Nazarenes had a right to the same toleration that had been extended to Pharisees and Sadducees. If he gave as full a defense before Nero as he had before others, he certainly made comments on the resurrection of the dead and on the reasoning of righteousness, temperance, and of judgment to come.

The Roman magistrates were ill-informed concerning the questions of religion at issue between Paul and his opponents, but when we consider how easily the Jews were excited by any leader who appealed to their nationality such as Poppaea must have been doing, it is understandable how the tables began to turn against Paul when it was brought up that Paul had really proclaimed the kingdom of Messiah—the kingdom of God. To the Romans this was interpreted to mean a temporal monarchy, one to be set up in opposition to the throne of Rome. This would not be tolerated.

When the parties on both sides had been heard and the witnesses had all been examined and cross-examined (a process that likely took several days), the court pronounced its judgment. Each of the assessors gave his opinion in writing to the emperor who never discussed the judgments, but, after reading them, gave sentence according to his own pleasure, without any reference to the judgment of the majority. No matter what Paul might have said in his defense, Nero would not have heard a word. He probably was thinking: *Don't confuse me with facts, my mind is already made up.* The Jews could easily have bribed Poppaea to encourage Nero to find the defendant guilty of treason.

PAUL SENTENCED TO DIE   Knowing Paul, we can be assured that he mentioned the resurrection from the dead, temperance, and judgment to come; and when he did, there was one in that courtroom who had more cause to tremble than had Felix. "Doubtless the seared conscience, and a universal frivolity of character, rendered Nero immune to emotions which for a moment must have shaken the nerves of all else in the judgment hall."[7] Since the emperor gave sentence according to his own pleasure, without any reference to the judgment of the majority, his sentence was, as might be expected, "guilty as charged." Paul must die. Nero set a date for his execution and the curtain was about to come down on the one man who probably did more to spread the Gospel than all the other disciples combined. "I labored more abundantly than they all" (1 Corinthians 15:10); Paul had fought a good fight, he had finished his course, and he had endured to the end by keeping the faith. He had resigned himself to the verdict by saying, "I am now ready to be offered, and the time of my departure is at hand" (2 Timothy 4:6). "To be offered" means "to be poured out as a libation," or to be sacrificed in death. He used this expression as a metaphor, comparing his own blood shed in martyrdom to the libation.

PAUL'S SECOND EPISTLE TO TIMOTHY   Stripped of all possessions when arrested, Paul managed, probably through visitors, to get writing material in order to write his second letter to his son in the faith, Timothy. This was to be his last letter and the third of his Pastoral Epistles. It was now the fall of A.D. 67. In his first epistle to this young man, Paul had expressed a desire to go back to Ephesus and see him (1 Timothy 3:14). In this second letter, he tells Timothy why he failed to return. Luke had stuck with him through thick and thin and was now the only one who was with him. Tychicus had been sent to Ephesus; probably taking Paul's letter to Timothy (2 Timothy 4:10–12).

However much he valued his friends, it appears that none could console him as much as Timothy could. Timothy had been a constant minister (servant) to Paul since they first met (Acts 16:1). Having left Timothy in Ephesus to help believers with their church problems, his spiritual father now requested him to come with all speed to Rome. Winter was fast approaching and Paul needed his cloak to keep warm and his books for meditation and study. Deep down inside Paul must have had a feeling that Timothy might arrive too late. He wondered if his "son" might shrink from the perils of Nero's city.

In this letter, Paul emphatically urged the necessity of Timothy's exercising boldness in Christ's cause, of steadfastness under pressure, and of his share in the sufferings of the Roman saints. Note some admonitions he gives him: God has not given us a spirit of fear but of power and of a sound mind; be not ashamed of the Lord or of me as a prisoner; hold fast to the Word preaching it in season and out of season; don't follow the example of those who have become drop-outs; be strong and endure hardness as a good soldier; if we suffer we shall also reign with Christ; shun the vain babblers; continue in what you have learned from the Scriptures. In these verses he urges Timothy to consider what he had said so that the Lord would give him understanding in all things. Christ was as the "righteous Judge" in contrast to Nero, who was the "unrighteous judge" (2 Timothy 4:8). Last, he impressed on this pastor the earnestness of a dying man, and the victory that was his both on earth and in glory. There is a note of sadness in this letter—he was cold, without his books and parchments (the Scriptures), friendless, and expecting at any time to be led to his death (4:6, 10–11, 13, 16). This letter is Paul's swan song, a song of triumph because he knew full well "there is laid up for me a crown of righteousness, which the Lord, the righteous judge, shall give me in that day: and not to me only, but unto all who also who love his appearing" (4:8).

The **outline** of 2 Timothy is as follows:

I. Greetings to Timothy (1:1–2)
II. Thankfulness for Timothy (1:3–7)
III. Encouragement to Be Strong and Faithful (1:8–2:26)
IV. Warning to Timothy about Apostasy (3:1–9)
V. Paul's Example to Timothy to Live Godly in Christ Jesus (3:10–13)
VI. Importance for Timothy to Preach the Word of God (3:14–4:5)
VII. Paul's Dying Words to Timothy (4:6–8)
VIII. Request for Timothy to Visit Him in Prison (4:9–18)

IX. Salutation to Saints in Ephesus (4:19–22)

The **key verses** of 2 Timothy are

1:13; 3:14—"Hold fast the form of sound words, which thou hast heard of me; continue thou in the things which thou hast learned."

2:1, 3—"Be strong in the grace that is in Christ Jesus. Endure hardness, as a good soldier of Jesus Christ."

2:15—"[Continue studying] to show thyself approved unto God, a workman who needeth not to be ashamed, rightly dividing the word of truth."

4:2—"Preach the word; be instant in season, out of season."

The **key word** of 2 Timothy is "endurance" or "perseverance."

There are no direct Old Testament references in this epistle, but two are alluded to:

1. cf. 2:19 with Numbers 16:5: "The Lord knoweth those that are his."

2. cf. 3:8 with Exodus 7:11: opposition to Moses.

Paul portrays Christ to Timothy as (1) the Abolisher of death and the Giver of life (1:10), (2) the Provider of salvation with eternal glory (2:10), (3) the One with whom we shall reign (2:12a), (4) the Righteous Judge (4:1, 8), (5) the One who is always with us in spirit (4:22).

Some scholars are of the opinion that this letter was penned soon after Paul's incarceration, because his apparel seems to be what was worn at a sunny, summer seashore such as Troas. With his sudden arrest, all his personal belongings had been left at the home of Carpus. Fall was fast fading, and winter would soon come. All Paul had when taken prisoner was what he had had on his back; thus it is no wonder he requested his cloak before cold weather set in (2 Timothy 4:13, 21). The dungeon was cold and damp. Most of all, however, he wanted his books, but especially his parchments—his own personal copies of the letters he had previously written. Even in prison he needed to constantly remind himself of what he had penned, particularly in his present circumstances. Timothy was in Ephesus and it would be an easy matter to swing up to Troas and pick up his belongings. He could just as easily set sail from Troas as he could from

Ephesus. Paul also wanted Timothy to bring Mark with him. There was a time when Paul had no use for this young man, but Mark had proved himself a good soldier of the Cross and Paul said, "he is useful to me for service" (4:11).

PAUL'S VISITOR IN PRISON It is quite apparent that Paul had a number of visitors during his early months of imprisonment. Onesiphorus left Ephesus on learning of Paul's arrest and after much searching, he found out which prison he was in and visited him. Paul said of him: "he often refreshed me and was not ashamed of my chains" (2 Timothy 1:16–18). Luke was with him and for a while Demas was also by his side—until the things of the world lured him (4:10). Tychicus, who had been with Paul on his third missionary journey, also saw Paul in prison. As mentioned, he was the one who probably took the second epistle to Timothy (Acts 20:4; 2 Timothy 4:12). Some close friends who lived in Rome had stuck by him; Luke, Eubulus, Pudens, Linus, and Claudia no doubt had made many visits (4:11, 21). Linus, mentioned by Irenaeus and Eusebius, afterward became bishop of Rome. Pudens was the son of a senator and his bride, Claudia, was perhaps the daughter of a British king. All we know about Eubulus is that he was a Christian disciple at Rome. While there were those who saw Paul as often as possible, there were other friends, even fellow workers, who turned their backs on him (Phygellus and Hermogenes, 1:15); Demas forsook him because he loved this present world more than he loved the Lord (4:10); and Alexander, the coppersmith, did him much evil (morally and ethically, 4:14). As time marched on, no doubt, fewer visitors came to see Paul. He mentioned that only Luke was with him (4:11).

Concerning Paul's prison visitors, there remains one question: Did Timothy ever arrive in Rome to see Paul? This is an unanswerable question. The only intimation we have that might throw some light on the subject is the statement in the epistle to the Hebrews that Timothy had been liberated from prison in Italy (Hebrews 13:23–24).

It has been mentioned (see chapter 12) that someone other than Paul probably wrote Hebrews. Clement, in A.D. 95, quoted from it, indicating it had been in use for a little over twenty-five years. There is no mention of the destruction of Jerusalem and the temple in A.D. 70. Had the destruction of Jerusalem and the temple already taken place (by Titus in A.D. 70), in fulfillment of

Christ's prophecy (Matthew 24:2), the writer of Hebrews would have capitalized on this event, but since this event is not mentioned, there is a strong argument that this epistle was written in the late sixties. It appears unlikely that Paul wrote this letter in the few remaining months of his imprisonment, and that it was written from Italy by a well-versed Old Testament scholar shortly after Paul's death. If this hypothesis is correct, Timothy must have visited Paul because due to his association with a "criminal," Paul, (2 Timothy 2:9 NIV), Timothy was probably placed in bonds with him. Having escaped Paul's fate, and with the death of Nero in June of A.D. 68, he was released. This leads us to think that Timothy must have answered Paul's request to visit him for otherwise there would have been no reason for his being arrested in Rome (or Italy, as the writer of Hebrews put it). If Timothy had come too late, he naturally would have returned to Ephesus without attracting the attention of any authorities. We may, therefore, surmise that Paul's last earthly wish was fulfilled.

PAUL'S PLACE OF EXECUTION It has been difficult to place the date of Paul's execution. Some say it was in late A.D. 67; others in the spring of A.D. 68. Two early writers who mention his death, Jerome and Eusebius, say it was early A.D. 68. The privilege of Roman citizenship exempted him from the ignominious death of lingering torture, such as crucifixion or being thrown to wild beasts to be eaten alive, which had been inflicted on so many of his Christian brothers and sisters. Paul was escorted to his "home going" by a number of soldiers whose responsibility it was to carry out the orders of the court. It was not uncommon to send prisoners, whose death might attract too much notice inside the city, to die on the Ostian Road (see illustration 61), which led to Rome's river port.

Running through Paul's mind, no doubt, was his Savior's trek as He bore the cross from Pilate's judgment hall to "suffer outside the gate [or city wall]" (Hebrews 12:13). As Paul passed through Rome's city gate, he probably lifted his eyes heavenward. He had first met Jesus by looking up at the light from heaven, which blinded him. Now he was looking up with the realization that in a matter of minutes he would be looking at Him in person, face to face—that soon he would be in His presence forever. He had been forgiven as the persecutor of the church; now he would be welcomed as the "defending establisher" of the church on two continents.

61—Roman wall and the Ostian Road. *Courtesy of author.*

As the condemned one and his executioners marched on the road that ran between the metropolis and its harbor, they found it crowded with a multitude of characters. There were merchants hurrying to receive their cargoes, sailors eager to enter the capital city and squander their pay in dissipation, officials of Caesar's government scurrying from place to place in their various duties, legionnaires coming home from foreign service, astrologers from the Far East, eunuchs from distant kingdoms, Syrian dancing girls with their painted turbans; priests from Egypt chanting prayers to Osiris, commercial agents in search of profit, philosophers, magicians, and so forth—Occidentals and Orientals from all walks. Each was probably saying: There goes another criminal to the chopping block! Unbeknown to this small band of soldiers, they were threading their way with their prisoner through the dust and commotion of an unconcerned throng; they were in a procession to perform an event that would be more triumphal than any they had ever witnessed—one that would be talked about for centuries to come. You can be sure that these soldiers had heard the story of Jesus and His love from the lips of this one who was determined to know nothing among men save Jesus

Christ and Him crucified. Paul was making his last few moments count for the Lord! If ever these soldiers had a vision of Christ, it had to have been when they saw His beauty on the face of this man they were about to execute.

PAUL'S LAST THOUGHTS   At last Paul and the soldiers arrived at the scene of his last earthly opportunity to reveal that he had something the world could not offer nor could take away from him. There were no tears, only a smile of confidence. Roman citizens were decapitated by the executioner's axe or sword. According to the Roman historian, Titus Livius, usually called Livy, the criminal was tied to a stake, cruelly scourged with rods, and then beheaded.[8] Of all the early church fathers who mentioned Paul's execution, none mentioned the scourging. We assume that he escaped this last-minute torture. Tacitus informs us that the military mode of execution was by the sword, especially under Nero.[9] The sword was more cruel in that oftentimes it took several strikes to complete the job.

As Paul awaited the executioner's blow, possibly the last thoughts that raced through his mind had to do with his readiness to die—his readiness to be offered. Looking back over a life of service for his Lord and Master, he knew that he had fought a good fight. He knew that he had been more than a conqueror through Christ who loved him. He knew that he had completed his course. He knew that his faith had not wavered (Romans 8:37; 2 Timothy 4:7).

Paul used three illustrations to testify of his dedication.

First, he compared himself to a fighter: "I have fought a good fight." In wrestling matches opponents pit their strength against each other. Paul had given every ounce of his strength in opposition to the forces of evil. Although it might have looked at times as though he was defeated, he had proved that one plus God makes a majority, and he had done all things through Christ who loved him (Romans 8:31; Philippians 4:13). Not even Satan, nor Paul's thorn, could pin him. In boxing matches a poorly trained fighter will "beat the air," trying hard to land a haymaker in the early rounds. The wise boxer knows this, and waits till his opponent is out of breath; then he lands the knock-out blow. Paul trained so that he could aim every blow well, thus winning the fight. He knew that if he didn't discipline himself and keep his body in subjection, he would become a castaway (one who was put on the shelf, only for someone else to take his place in service for the Lord, 1 Corinthians 9:26–27).

Second, he compared himself to an athlete—a runner, a hurdler: "I have finished my course." He had kept his body in subjection, running with certainty. He had been temperate in all things (1 Corinthians 9:24–26a). He was totally focused on the Lord, just as an athlete is focused on a corruptible crown (see illustration 62). To Paul, the Christian life was demanding and filled with obstacles over which he had to hurdle. Each hurdle was a victory that enabled him to cross the finish line a winner. His aim was to win an incorruptible crown—a victory cup (see illustration 63).

Third, he compared himself to a soldier who was willing to die for his country; a guard who stood at his post and would not let the enemy approach. Paul was able to say that he had kept the faith. As a sentry clothed in the whole armor of God, Paul had guarded his post well, even though at times the enemy had outnumbered him. To him, faith was the victory that overcame the world, and he had kept it to the end! (See illustration 40.)

As he thought of having kept the faith, no doubt Stephen's last words came to mind: "Behold, I see the heavens opened, and the son of man standing on the right hand of God." Stephen then fell asleep in Jesus (Acts 7:56, 60). Jesus stood up to welcome Stephen, and we can be assured He stood up to welcome Paul, for "precious in the sight of the LORD is the death of his saints" (Psalm 116:15). Paul had lived in expectation of going to heaven. Having received a foretaste of its glories when he was caught up into third heaven, it was the moment he had waited for. He had said to those at Philippi that for him to die was gain, that to be with Christ was far better (Philippians 2:21, 23). Whether by life or by death, he only wanted Christ to be magnified in his body. He knew that the sting of death had been removed, that his earthly tabernacle would soon be laid to rest, and that he would be absent from the body and present with the Lord in a place where he had a house not made with hands (see 1 Corinthians 15:55–57; 2 Corinthians 5:1–8).

PAUL'S EXECUTION With these thoughts hastily going through his mind, just then the *speculatores*, a chosen imperial bodyguard, under the command of the centurion, brought down the sword. Thus ended Paul's long course of preaching and suffering as his emaciated body crum-

62—A corruptible crown.
Courtesy of British Museum.

63—The cup of "victory."
*Courtesy of Metropolitan
Museum of Art.*

bled to the ground. Yet for him, it must have been a thrill to suddenly be absent from the body and present with the Lord—to leave this old world and his old vile body and suddenly find himself standing in heaven!

When a person forfeited his life, as Paul did, friends were permitted to accompany the condemned to claim the body. Whoever they were, possibly Eubulus, Pudens, Linus, Claudia, or other brethren (2 Timothy 4:21), these weeping friends tenderly took up his corpse and buried him in one of the many catacombs beneath the city of Rome (see illustration 64). The place where Paul was buried—a place where persecuted Christians not only lived but also buried their dead—was still visited in Eusebius' latter days (A.D. 95).[10]

Today, the great Basilica of St. Paul stands outside the old city walls of Rome on the road to Ostia in commemoration of Paul's martyrdom. It was built by Constantine, the first so-called Christian emperor of the Roman Empire in early A.D. 300. The nearby Porta Ostiensis (wall) is called the Gate of St. Paul. In front of this church, often referred to as St. Paul's Outside the Wall, stands a huge statue of the apostle, with an upright sword in his right hand and a copy of Scripture in his left hand (see illustration 65). This is symbolic of his wielding the Sword of the Spirit and his complete reliance on the Word of God: "They can bind me, but the word of God cannot be bound" (2 Timothy 2:9). It is estimated that Paul was 68 or 69 years old when he died.

PAUL'S WELL-DESERVED EULOGY "Thus died the Apostle, the Prophet, and the Martyr, bequeathing to the Church of the living God, in her government and her discipline, the legacy of his Apostolic labors; leaving his Prophetic words to be her living oracles; pouring forth his blood to be the seed of thousands of martyrdoms. Thenceforth, among the glorious company of the Apostolic family, among the goodly fellowship of Prophets of old, among the noble army of Martyrs his name has stood preeminent. And wheresoever the Church throughout the world doth acknowledge God the Father and Jesus, His Son, there Paul of Tarsus is revered as the great teacher of a universal redemption through Jesus Christ, his Lord and Saviour—the proclaimer of Glad-tidings to all mankind."[11]

He had forged a gospel-preaching ministry from Jerusalem to Spain. As far as we know, he had made known Christ throughout the whole Roman Empire. Numerous churches had been established on two continents. People from all walks of life—bond and free—had been witnessed to and many of them had been saved. There were ordinary Jews, Jewish leaders and chief priests (Pharisees and Sadducees), Roman proconsul, governors, kings, philosophers, pagan priests, idolaters, ungodly Gentiles, sorcerers, jailers, prisoners, ship owners, soldiers, and even Caesar, who had heard that Christ and, Christ alone, according to Moses and the Prophets, should suffer, die, and be raised to "open their eyes, to

64—An ancient Roman catacomb. *Courtesy of author.*

turn them from darkness to light and from the power of Satan unto God, that they may receive forgiveness of sins, an inheritance among them which are sanctified by faith." It mattered

not to Paul where he preached Jesus Christ and Him crucified. He had testified on highways, in synagogues, in prisons, on ships, in amphitheaters, by a river, in forums, in courthouses, on Mars' Hill, and in the marketplace. No matter where he went or under what circumstances, he preached Christ. Anyone who ever needs a spiritual shot in the heart, can look at the life of this persecuted, battered, suffering, yet vibrant and joyous servant of God and be inspired to go on to greater heights. There was only one Paul—there will never

65—Statue of St. Paul outside Basilica. *Courtesy of author.*

PAUL'S WELL-DESERVED EULOGY

be another, but his example of Christian living and witnessing is a challenge to every child of God, a challenge that can and must be met if one is to be an imitator of the one who said, "for to me to live is Christ" (Philippians 1:21; 2 Thessalonians 3:7, 9).

Ever since Paul's visit into the third heaven when he had been given a thorn in the flesh to buffet him, God's grace had been sufficient for him in every trial and circumstance.

TEST YOURSELF ON CHAPTER FOURTEEN

1. How well was Paul known in Rome and in Caesar's household?

2. Give the background of Nero and his family.

3. What type of person was Nero?

4. According to Tacitus, who did Nero finally marry?

5. What kind of a woman was she? Describe her.

6. What great event happened in Rome to turn Nero against Christians? Explain, giving reasons why.

7. Describe the Christian Holocaust.

8. To where were many Christians able to escape?

9. What one symbol did Christians carve and what did it symbolize?

10. Describe the probable reasons for Paul's rearrest.

11. What probable role did Nero's wife play in his rearrest?

12. What probable charge was brought against Paul?

13. How did Nero go about finding Paul in order to rearrest him?

14. What made it easy for him to be found?

15. Name and describe the three types of Roman prisons.

16. Into which type was Paul placed? Describe it.

17. How did Paul describe himself as a prisoner?

18. Describe Caesar's court.

19. Where was Paul's trial held?

20. Who sat and listened to the trial?

21. Give the order of the court's proceedings in the trial.

22. Who was Paul's defense attorney and how was he defended?

23. Who made the final decision of guilty or not guilty?

24. What was the outcome of the trial?

25. What statement did Paul make that gives evidence that he was sentenced to die?

26. What does "to be offered" mean? Explain.

27. To whom did Paul write during his second imprisonment?

28. Who was the one friend Paul wanted as a visitor?

29. Why did he write to this person?

30. What are the key verses in 2 Timothy?

31. How did Paul portray Christ to Timothy?

32. What were the three things Paul wanted Timothy to bring to him in Rome?

33. What was the most important of the three? Explain.

34. Who else did Paul request to come to Rome to see him?

35. Who might have been some of Paul's prison visitors?

36. In your opinion, did Timothy visit Paul in the Roman prison?

37. What method of capital punishment was inflicted on Roman citizens and non-Roman citizens?

38. What method of capital punishment was inflicted on Paul?

39. Where was Paul taken to be executed?

40. Describe the crowds who passed by as Paul was led to his place of execution.

41. What do you think might have gone through Paul's mind just before he was slain? List them.

42. When Paul said he was ready to be offered, what three illustrations did he use to describe himself?

43. Who executed Paul and what instrument was used?

44. Who possibly buried Paul and where?

45. What was built in honor of this apostle? By whom?

TEST YOURSELF ON CHAPTER FOURTEEN

46. What is the name(s) of this structure?

47. What was erected in front of this structure and what does it symbolize?

48. If you were called on to give Paul's eulogy, what would you say?

49. As you look back over the life of this man of God, do you think he had any regrets? If so, list them, and see how you can apply both his assets and any liabilities to your own life.

Chapter Fifteen

PAUL'S EPISTLES FROM HEAVEN TO SAINTS ON EARTH

If Paul could have written any epistles soon after his arrival in heaven, they would have been addressed and sent to his contemporaries and to us. His message would have been twofold: his new-found joy of being home in heaven because he had finished his course on earth and prophecy.

PAUL'S EPISTLE TO HIS FRIENDS IN CHRIST

¹I, Paul, a former apostle of Jesus Christ, to the saints who knew me personally and to those who knew of my ministry in the Gospel, both in Asia Minor and in Europe—from Jerusalem to Spain. Grace and peace to you all.

²In preaching Jesus Christ and Him crucified, I was ever mindful that as a pilgrim and a stranger on earth, my citizenship was where I am now, in heaven.

³I knew a day would come when I would cross the finish line and that life's race would be over.

⁴I was fully persuaded that in committing my soul to Him against that day that I would be kept eternally.

[5]When the time of my departure was at hand, I was ready to face God, having fought a good fight.

[6]I finished my course because I kept the faith.

[7]I am in my eternal home now. Although I had countless thrills in my service as an apostle, my greatest thrill came when I stood in the presence of Jesus and saw Him face to face.

[8]From the first time I met Him on the road to Damascus, I looked for His appearing, but I fell asleep in Him before He came to rapture me and all those who knew Him personally. Now I am absent from the body and present with the Lord.

[9]I was speechless for a time, but later I thanked Him for paying a debt He did not owe because I had a debt I could not pay.

[10]Heaven is absolutely magnificent. Human words cannot describe it.

[11]I am so free, so happy, and so perfectly content.

[12]There is no darkness here in this abode of God, for this place has no need of the sun, neither the moon to shine in it; for the glory of God lightens it, and the Lamb is the light thereof.

[13]I am so filled with ecstasy I could cry. That, however, is impossible, for He has wiped away all tears. I am so full of God's love I can hardly comprehend it.

[14]My mind is clear, all pain is gone, and my hopes and dreams were all satisfied the moment I left earth's shores and arrived here in heaven. I just woke up and found myself in glory—safe in the arms of Jesus. No longer am I plagued with my thorn in the flesh.

[15]Because I labored more abundantly than they all, having built on the foundation Jesus Christ, it was with excitement and gladness that I heard Jesus say unto me, "Paul, well done, thou good and faithful servant. Enter into the joy of the Lord!"

[16]There are no misunderstandings in this place. No anger, no harsh words, no hurt feelings, no selfish acts, no problems on my part or that of others. Bitterness, jealousy, envy, gossip, and hate are unknown here.

[17]On earth I saw through a glass darkly; but now I see plainly.

Although God's will was sometimes hard for me to understand on earth, here it is beautifully perceived.

[18]Yes, there were times while on earth that I questioned God. There were times that I looked at the footprints in the sands of time and saw His and mine together. Then there were times I saw only His. Now I know it was then that He was carrying me through some trial when I thought He had forgotten me.

[19]Promises in His Word while on earth had great meaning for me, but their fulfillment in the presence of the Living Word is so plain and simple. Faith has now been turned into sight.

[20]I am now getting a little taste of what is in store for me throughout the ages to come. I am beginning to see what the exceeding riches of His grace is in His kindness toward me through Jesus Christ.

[21]I am filled with God's glory, with His beauty, and with His radiance. Sorrow is foreign in this place. It is joy unspeakable and full of glory.

[22]When I had the experience on earth of being caught up to the third heaven, I saw things that were unbelievable; things that staggered the imagination. I heard words that were not lawful to be uttered on earth. Up here, the language is so sweet and understandable. There are no foreigners here, no language barrier. Everything has been made so plain. No one here is a stranger. We are all brothers and sisters in Christ. There will be no cliques in glory.

[23]What a blessing it has been to see many here in heaven that I had the privilege of leading to the Lord. Fellowship with them has been wonderful, incredible, and unprecedented.

[24]It was a thrill on earth to see them come to Christ; it is an even greater thrill to be with them here and to know we shall never part—our fellowship will continue throughout all eternity.

[25]I cannot get over the fact that the Lord used me to help others know Him. And to think that at one time I wanted all Christians annihilated!

[26]I have met some here I didn't expect to see, and some I had hoped to see are not here. Many hardened their hearts when I

preached the Gospel, and what rejoicing there will be here in the presence of angels if they do repent and believe in Christ.

[27]I well remember in some of our churches that we sang songs and made melody in our hearts to the Lord. The music of the heavenly choir is exuberant.

[28]But, the blood-washed saints are outsinging them with their new song, "worthy is the Lamb who was slain and redeemed us by His blood."

[29]You haven't heard singing until you hear us rejoice in the presence of angels over one sinner on earth who repents. There is no minor refrain in our singing.

[30]In parting let me say, don't ever pity me or shed bitter tears. I am better off now than in all my earthly years, even with all the rich blessings I had then in Christ. There is no anguish or poverty here.

[31]I have started my new life here in glory with my Savior, and whatever I went through on earth was worth it all.

[32]My labors are all over; no more tentmaking. Although I did not know what a home on earth was like in all my travels, now I know a home.

[33]The sufferings I had in various places are not worthy to be compared to what I now have in my new home, which my Lord just completed—the one He had been preparing for me for almost thirty-five years.

[34]I'm home now! Please come to see me sometime after you arrive.

[35]I do trust I will meet all of you someday here in this wonderful place. Just make sure you have made your peace with Him before He calls you. When your time comes, you will never regret having received Christ as your very own personal Lord and Savior.

[36]There is no disappointment in heaven. There is no hunger nor thirst here; no broken hearts; no graves on the hillsides of glory. All is life; abundant life, eternal life. Here the old will be young forever!

[37]The brothers and sisters who are here with me send their

greetings and love. The grace of God be with all of you who love and serve the Lord Jesus Christ in sincerity. Amen.

Paul

PAUL'S EPISTLE TO SAINTS OF THE TWENTIETH CENTURY

[1] I, Paul, greet you in our Savior's name with a burden on my heart, even though I am far removed from life's battles on earth.

[2] On earth, the Lord gave me insight and revelation as to what it would be like at the close of your century.

[3] You are now living in the closing days of this present dispensation, just prior to the Lord's return; in perilous times that surround you daily.

[4] You are in the midst of a people who are lovers of their own selves, coveteous, boasters, proud, blasphemous, disobedient to parents, unthankful, unholy, without natural affection (homosexuals, lesbians), truce breakers, false accusers, incontinent (lacking self-control), fierce (lawless, brutes), despisers of those who are good, traitors, heady, high minded, lovers of pleasures more than lovers of God, drunkards, murderers, dope peddlers and users, criminals, baby killers (abortionists), humanists, evolutionists, atheists—people who deny God and His power; who deny Jesus Christ and their need for a Savior.

[5] You are in the midst of wolves who are determined to stamp out Christianity.

[6] Organizations have been formed to deprive you of your God-given rights as believer. Christmas (manger scenes) can no longer be placed on government property.

[7] Your own government is forcing public schools to eliminate the use of the name of God. Christian boys and girls can no longer pray and read their Bibles in school.

[8] Schools are teaching "sex" and many are providing contraceptives, which encourages pupils to have premarital sex.

[9] Christian parents out of necessity must help establish and send their children to Christian schools, which has become an added financial burden to believers in the last days.

[10] I, along with brother apostles Jude and Peter, warned of a day

when there would be a failing away from the true faith, when ungodly (modernistic and liberal preachers) would sneak into pulpits and turn the grace of God into lasciviousness (give people a license to sin—permissiveness) as they denied the only Lord God and our Lord Jesus Christ; and that there would be false teachers among you who would bring in damnable heresies.

[11] Beloved, those days are now on you. Things will not get better; they will get worse.

[12] O foolish twentieth-century believers, who has bewitched you so that you have become so indifferent to the times in which you live?

[13] Instead of your standing and having done all to stand, there is a satisfied complacency in your churches. Prayer meetings have been dead and buried in the majority of assemblies throughout the land.

[14] Evening services are almost a thing of the past and Sunday school is no longer felt useful by many parents; thus depriving their youngsters of a much-needed background of Bible study and biblical history.

[15] Without such a background, young people become frustrated; they don't know where they have come from, where they are, or where they are going, and then say their parents don't understand them.

[16] Citing the Old Testament prophets Amos and Haggai, you are at "ease in your Christian walk" and are "living in the luxury of your beautiful homes." Material things have come between you and your Savior.

[17] I had to warn the elders of Ephesus to beware of grievous wolves who would come in and not spare the flock, who would draw many away from the church.

[18] I warn you to watch and be faithful and active continually in the things of the Lord, just as I warned Timothy that evil men and seducers would wax worse, and that he, too, must continue in the things he had learned.

[19] Yet, possibly thirty-five years after giving this admonition to the Ephesian elders, the saints there became indifferent to my

warnings and lost their first love. Not repenting and doing their first works again, they forfeited their light (testimony).

20 This must not happen to you. Remember the question our Lord Jesus Christ asked: "When I come will I find faith?"

21 So that you don't forget, He is ever living to make intercession for you, and He is praying that "your faith fail not."

22 I remind you—as you expect Him to answer your prayers because He is the only one who can, don't forget, you are the only one who can answer His.

23 Faltering faith tends to weaken the body of Christ. The church soon becomes worldly and the world becomes churchy.

24 I mentioned to Timothy that "those who live godly in Christ Jesus suffer." The world hated Christ; it will hate you if you live for Him and witness of His saving grace.

25 The world will never oppose you as long as you are silent about what great things God has done for you.

26 When King David was establishing his kingdom, "the children of Issachar were men who knew what to do because they had understanding of the times."

27 Only as you have understanding of the times in which you live will you know what to do.

28 This means you will first have to give yourselves to Christ as those at Thessalonica did. They understood the meaning of presenting their bodies as living sacrifices. If you do what they did, you, too, will live godly in Christ Jesus.

29 I urge you to answer Christ's prayer daily—keep your faith; don't let it fail!

30 Follow my example in keeping the faith; witness at every opportunity—in season and out of season.

31 Determine that you will not stand empty handed when it is your turn to meet the Lord face to face.

32 Never let it be said of you what the psalmist said: "I looked on my right hand, and beheld, but there was no man who would know me: refuge failed me; no man cared for my soul."

33 Do not be so self-centered that you forget there are believers

who are being persecuted elsewhere in the world; pray for them and find out how you can help them in their need.

[34]Fight the good fight; endure hardness as a good soldier of Christ Jesus.

[35]If you do this, as I told Timothy, you will be mature, furnished with good works. Do not be satisfied until you make this your experience.

[36]Just remember this throughout life's journey: If you have everything but Jesus, *you have nothing*. But if you have nothing but Him, *you have everything*!

[37]Resolve that you will hear your Savior say to you, "Well done, thou good and faithful servant. Enter thou into the joy of the Lord."

[38]Together then, when you arrive in heaven, our fellowship will be all the more precious because we will see people here that we have won to the Lord.

[39]Not only will our fellowship be sweet with each other, but together we will constantly be telling Jesus, "Thank You Lord for saving my soul."

[40]Now the God of peace, who brought again from the dead our Lord Jesus, that Great Shepherd of the sheep, through the blood of the everlasting covenant, make you perfect in every good work to do His will, working in you that which is well-pleasing in His sight, through Jesus Christ; to whom be glory forever and ever. Amen.

Surely His and truly yours,

Paul

Appendix One

PAUL THE SUFFERER AND FOLLOWER

aul was a *persecuted* man. The Lord told Ananias that He would show Paul what great things he would suffer for Christ's sake (Acts 9:16). Just as Paul had persecuted Christ and His church, so Paul would get a taste of his own medicine (see chapter 4); he would reap what he had sown (Galatians 6:7). Paul counted himself worthy to suffer shame for the Lord. He was one who gloried in all his infirmities (Acts 5:41; 1 Corinthians 4:9–13; 2 Corinthians 12:9). It was said of him that he hazarded his life for the name of the Lord Jesus (he did not count his life dear unto himself, Acts 15:26; 20:24). In this man we have one of the greatest possible examples of endurance. Note some of the things he encountered so that he might bear in his body the dying of the Lord Jesus (2 Corinthians 4:8–11; Philippians 3:7–10)

1. The Jews of Damascus sought his life (Acts 9:22–24).

2. He escaped arrest from the soldiers of Damascus and persecution by the Jews by being let down over the city wall in a basket (Acts 9:25; 2 Corinthian 11:32–33).

3. The Grecians threatened his life in Jerusalem, but the brethren helped him escape to Caesarea and Tarsus (Acts 9:26–30).

4. He was expelled from Antioch of Pisidia because of Jewish persecution (Acts 13:45, 50–51; 2 Timothy 3:11).

5. He was afflicted at Iconium (Acts 14:2, 5; 2 Timothy 3:11).

6. He was stoned at Lystra and left for dead (Acts 14:19).

7. He was beaten and imprisoned in the worst of Roman prisons in Philippi (Acts 16:22–24).

8. Jews at Thessalonica and Berea persecuted him (Acts 17:5–14).

9. He was charged with insurrection in Corinth (Acts 18:12–17).

10. The Jews and labor unions opposed him in Ephesus (Acts 19:8–9, 23–41), he fought with wild beasts (1 Corinthians 15:32) and was finally forced to leave the city (Acts 20:1).

11. He was made a spectacle, was despised, hungry, thirsty, naked, buffeted, homeless, reviled, persecuted, and defamed; was made the filth of the world and was the offscouring (garbage) of all things (1 Corinthians 4:9–13).

12. 2 Corinthians 11:23–33 summarizes his physical sufferings for about the first 22 or 23 years of his ministry. He went through enough physical torture to have killed him several times over, yet God preserved this saint, time and time again, to continue preaching Christ (see chapter 4).

13. Paul wrote to the Corinthians in A.D. 57 and gave the list of his sufferings. There is no list of his sufferings from A.D. 57 to his death in A.D. 68. However, he still had to contend with his thorn in the flesh, as well as great opposition, persecution, and suffering including threats of death from the Jews on his third visit to Corinth (Acts 20:3). Upon his arrival in Jerusalem for the last time, he was soon captured by the Jews and was nearly murdered (Acts 21:27–31). He was chained by Roman soldiers to be flogged but was soon released

(Acts 21:33–39). He was almost torn limb from limb (Acts 23:10). Two assassination plots were made against him (Acts 23:12; 25:1–3). He was placed under house arrest in Jerusalem, which continued for two years in Caesarea, then in sailing from Caesarea to Rome, as well as for two years in Rome (Acts 23:23–25; 24:27; 21:1–28:30). On the way to Rome he almost lost his life in a storm at sea but was assured of safety by an angel (Acts 27:14–25). His life was threatened by a poisonous snake but a miracle was performed and he was spared (Acts 28:3–6). During his second imprisonment he suffered as an evil doer in bonds—or as a criminal in chains (2 Timothy 2:9). His heart was broken by a dear friend and fellow laborer who deserted him (Philemon 24; 2 Timothy 4:10). Finally, he forfeited his life in defense of the gospel.

And you think you have troubles and problems. Paul was a *follower* of Jesus Christ. His testimony is summed up in the words "For to me to live is Christ" (Philippians 1:21). He told Timothy that God had saved him to be a "pattern" to those who were yet unsaved (1 Timothy 1:15–16). This apostle lived so Christlike that he could tell others he wished they were "such as I am" (Acts 26:29). He could say to weak Christians to "follow [or imitate] me" and do what they had seen in him (1 Corinthians 4:16; 11:1; Philippians 3:7; 4:9; 1 Thessalonians 3:7). This preacher was not one who would say, "Don't do as I do; do as I say." He lived what he preached. Yes, he was human, and there were times that he did what he knew he shouldn't have, and there were times he didn't do what he should have. However, he knew that victory was only in Christ and he sought by the grace of God to be "more than a conqueror through Him" (Romans 7:15–25; 8:37).

Appendix Two

PAUL'S
GODLY TRAITS

The characteristics of this man of God who was as human as the rest of us, are such that any honest Christian should seek to make them a part of his or her life. One of them, which is important in the lives of believers, was his prayer life. As busy as Paul was, as much as he traveled, and as much as he preached and suffered, he took time to pray. He did not preach the need to pray and not put it into practice. Paul defined prayer as taking the time to open up one's heart and mind to God by making requests known to Him according to His will by prayer and supplication with thanksgiving. To Paul, prayer was not only talking to God and getting answers, but getting a hold on God and letting God get a hold on him so that God could talk to him. He knew that prayer was reciprocal—God answered his prayers and he answered His. Jesus said "I have prayed for thee that thy faith fail not" (Luke 22:32). He is the only One who can answer our prayers; we are the only ones who can answer His (Philippians 4:6; Romans 8:26–27; 1 John 5:14–15).

PAUL'S PRAYERFULNESS

He prayed:

1. for himself as a "babe in Christ" (Acts 9:11);

2. and fasted (Acts 13:2–3; 14:23);

3. faithfully (Acts 16:13);

4. for those possessed by Satan (Acts 16:16);

5. in pain and song (Acts 16:25);

6. with friends (Acts 20:36; 25:5);

7. for the sick (Acts 28:8);

8. for his friends (Romans 1:9; Philippians 1:4; 2 Timothy 1:3; Philemon 4);

9. for lost souls (Romans 10:1);

10. continually, (always in an attitude of prayer) (cf. Colossians 1:9 with 1 Thessalonians 5:17; 2 Thessalonians 1:11);

11. for believers' spiritual welfare (2 Corinthians 13:7; 1 Thessalonians 5:23);

12. for believers' edification and power (Ephesians 1:15–19);

13. for believers' fellowship to be sweet, that they may abound more and more in knowledge of their Lord and Savior Jesus Christ; that they might be without offense and be filled with the fruits of righteousness (Philippians 1:1–11; 2 Thessalonians 1:3);

14. for believers to know the will of God for their lives and to walk worthy of the Lord to all pleasing with all patience and longsuffering with joyfulness (Romans 12:1–2; Colossians 1:9–11);

15. for believers' work of faith, labor of love and their patience of hope in the Lord Jesus Christ (1 Thessalonians 1:3);

16. for individual believers, such as Timothy, that he might stir up the gift of God in him (2 Timothy 1:3–6), and for Philemon to be faithful in sharing his faith (v. 1).

Paul knew that "prayer is a golden river at whose brink some die of thirst, while others kneel and drink."

PAUL'S CHARACTER TRAITS

Alertness: Keenly watchful; ready for sudden action (not unobservant or casual)

Elymas the sorcerer (Acts 13:6–11)

The lame man (Acts 14:8–10)

The "Unknown god" altar (Acts 17:22–23)

Attentiveness: Keeping one's mind on the subject at hand (not neglectful or uninterested)

The Macedonian Call (Acts 16:6–10)

The Philippian jailer (Acts 16:25–34)

Not disobedient (Acts 26:12–19)

Availability: Ability to adjust one's personal ambitions to the need or situation at hand; usable (not preoccupied with self-interests)

Willingness to serve (Acts 9:6)

Assisting Barnabas (Acts 11:25–26)

Becoming a missionary (cf. Acts 13:1–3 with Isaiah 6:8; Romans 1:14–16)

Boldness: Courage; fearlessness; daring (not faint-hearted or cowardly)

At Antioch before the Jews (Acts 13:44–45)

At Corinth (Acts 18:4–6)

Before Agrippa (Acts 26)

Before Jews in Jerusalem (Acts 22:1–24)

Compassion: Humane; considerate; concerned; caring (not indifferent to needs of others)

Toward fellow believers (1 Thessalonians 2:7)

As an ambassador (2 Corinthians 5:14, 20)

Witnessing night and day with tears (Acts 20:31; Romans 9:3)

Contentment: Peace of mind under every circumstance and thankful in it; completely satisfied; always thankful (not an ingrate or covetous)

"Thanks" was expressed many times. Paul knew that giving thanks was a course from which one never graduates. He even gloried in his infirmities (Acts 28:15; Philippians 4:11–13,19; Colossians 1:3, 12; 1 Thessalonians 5:18; 1 Timothy 6:6–8)

Decisiveness: Making a proper decision in an immediate or complicated situation (not indifferent or impassive)

Speaking in Hebrew to quiet the angry Pharisees (Acts 22:1–2)

Having Timothy circumcised (Acts 16:1–3)

Dependability: Honesty and loyalty in performing one's duty (not fickle or unreliable)

To the Ephesians (cf. Acts 18:19–21 with 19:1)

Truthful (2 Corinthians 11:31)

Steadfast, unmoveable (1 Corinthians 15:58)

Determination: Energetically doing his job—doing what should be done with enthusiasm (not apathetically)

To preach Christ only—anywhere, anytime (1 Corinthians 2:1–5; 2 Timothy 4:2)

To glory only in the Cross (Galatians 6:14)

To live only for Christ (Philippians 1:21)

To win others to the only Saviour (1 Corinthians 9:19–21; Galatians 4:19)

Endurance: Perseverance, to continue without yielding or compromising one's convictions (not quitting under pressure)

Pressing on (Philippians 3:14)

Enduring all things (2 Timothy 2:10; 2 Corinthians 4:8–12; 11:21–28)

Fighting a good fight, keeping the faith, finishing his course (2 Timothy 4:7)

Faith: Assurance; accepting the promises of God as one's title deed; taking God at His word (not distrust or unbelief)

Security in Christ (1 Timothy 1:12)

Trust in any circumstance or trial (Romans 8:28; 2 Corinthians 4:8–14; 12:8–9)

Rejoiced in hope of Christ's Second Coming (Romans 12:12; 1 Thessalonians 4:13–18)

Forgiveness: To show mercy by never bringing up the forgiven matter (not holding a grudge)

His forgiveness of John Mark (cf. Acts 13:13; 15: 36–4 1; with Colossians 4: 10 and 2 Timothy 4:11. See also Ephesians 4:32 and 2 Corinthians 2:7, 10)

Being Organized: Systematic; methodical; to put in order (not disarrayed)

Paul disciplined himself to do things right, following necessary rules and regulations in establishing churches; "straightening" out church matters (Acts 14:21–23; 1 Corinthians 5:1–5; 11:34b; 14:40)

In giving qualifications for church leaders (1 Timothy 3:1–13; Titus 1:4–9)

In redeeming the time (Ephesians 5:15–17)

In keeping his body in subjection (1 Corinthians 9:24–27)

Persuasiveness: To lovingly win over by reason; endeavoring to influence or convince (not insecure or with an inferior complex; not timid)

Paul had an uncanny ability to persuade others that he was telling the truth as he based it upon Scripture (Acts 13:48–49; 17:1–4; 19:10, 18–20; 2 Timothy 2:24–26)

Responsibility: Ability to meet one's obligation; accountability (not derelict)

Doing all that he did to the glory of God (1 Corinthians 10:31; Colossians 3:17)

Being answerable to God in all things (1 Corinthians 3:9–15; 2 Corinthians 5:10)

Reverence: An attitude of worship; consecration; veneration (not desecrating nor disrespectful)

Paul recognized that the Spirit indwelt his body; that he was always in the presence of a holy God, and that it was God's purpose to conform him to the image of His dear Son—Christ (2 Corinthians 6:16; Colossians 1:27; 1 Corinthians 3:16; Romans 8:29)

Sincerity: Freedom from hypocrisy; integrity (not an imposter or pretender)

Compassion for kinsmen (Romans 9:1–3; 10:1) or Compassion for Gentiles (Acts 13:46–49; 26:2, 28)

Compassion for fellow believers (Acts 20:17–38; 2 Corinthians 2:4)

Workmanship. Industrious; laborer; active; hustler (not slothful or shiftless)

From the time Paul was saved until he died, he labored night and day in traveling, preaching, praying, and writing; in labors more abundant than the rest of the apostles (Acts 20:24; 1 Corinthians 15:10; 2 Corinthians 11:23; Philemon 1)

PAUL'S DEDICATION

So much more could be said about the apostle Paul that it is difficult to enumerate all his characteristics and qualities. In summary, it could be said he was like a western cowboy: "He died with his boots on."

He was totally consecrated, having become a **bond servant** for his Master. He took the position that having been bought with a price he no longer belonged to himself, which resulted in his becoming a good example of what Luke had to say about a servant:

Which of you, having a servant plowing or feeding cattle, will say to him by and by, when he is come from the field, Go, and sit down to meat? And will not rather say unto him, make ready wherewith I may sup, and gird thyself, and afterward thou shalt eat and drink? Doth he thank that servant because he did the things that were commanded him? I trow not. So likewise ye, when ye shall have done all those things which are commanded of you, say, We are unprofitable servants: we have done that which was our duty to do (17:7–10).

Paul knew that God's "thanks" and rewards would be given at the judgment seat of Christ, where faithful bond servants would then hear Him say: "Well done, thou good and faithful servant." We notice Paul's total consecration in his willingness to count everything he was and had as refuse that he might win Christ, and his willingness to die for Christ that he might finish his course with joy (Philippians 3:7–14; Acts 20:24).

Paul was a **soldier** who knew how to endure hardness (2 Timothy 4:7a; Philemon 2).

Paul was a **burdened Christian**, noted for his concern for lost souls, for edifying, confirming, caring for, and encouraging fellow believers (Acts 14:21–23; 20:17–38; Romans 10:1; 2 Corinthians 5:20; 2 Corinthians 11:28).

Paul was a **praying saint**, not only teaching the importance of prayer, but practicing it as well (Colossians 1:9).

Paul was a **faithful witness** in giving his testimony of conversion as recorded in Acts 9:1–20 during his last visit to Jerusalem (Acts 22:1–21); before Agrippa and Festus (Acts 26:1–23); in part to Timothy (1 Timothy 1:12–16).

Paul was a **determined preacher**, preaching Christ only and glorying only in the Cross (1 Corinthians 2:2; Galatians 6:14). His recorded sermons give insight as to his approach to the Jews (Acts 13:14–44), to the Gentiles (Acts 13:46–49; 16:16–34), on Mars' Hill before Greek philosophers (Acts 17:15–34), and in "mini" sermons as part of his defense before Felix (Acts 24:10–26); and before the Jews at Rome (Acts 28:17–29).

Paul was a **man who had divine visions**: from a Macedonian to come to Europe and help them (Acts 16:9), from an angel to assure him and those on board of safety during a storm at sea (Acts 27:23), of heaven (2 Corinthians 12:1–4), from Christ. Paul was an apostle "born out of due time" (1 Corinthians 15:8). He was not an eyewitness to Christ's earthly ministry like the other apostles, but on several occasions during his ministry Christ did appear to him; thus assuring him he was a qualified apostle (see chapter 3). Christ appeared to Paul on the road to Damascus (Acts 9:3–6), on his first visit to Jerusalem (Acts 22:17–18), in Corinth (Acts 18:9–11), and on his last visit to Jerusalem (Acts 23:11).

Paul was a **man of miracles**. By God's power he blinded Elymas (Acts 13:6–11), worked signs and wonders in Iconium (Acts 14:3), healed a lame man in Lystra (Acts 14:8–10), cured a fortune teller in Philippi (Acts 16:18), performed special miracles in Ephesus (Acts 19:11–12), and performed special miracles on the isle of Malta (Acts 28:7–9).

PEOPLE IN PAUL'S LIFE

I n reading Paul's letters, we often come across many names he included in his travels. It is evident that he does not mention everyone he met. There is a tendency at times to skip over many of the names, thinking that they are unimportant, or it really doesn't matter who they were or because we cannot pronounce them. Names are important, however, and those that Paul listed were important people—some good and some bad. If they hadn't been of interest to him, he would not have recalled their association with him. In considering the names of these people, we want to single out just a few, giving some information about their relationship and usefulness to Paul, and, in listing the rest, giving just the meaning of their names and what part they played in his life.

You can tell much about people by the company they keep. When someone spends a lot of time with friends, they begin to reflect their behavior. If they associate with evil companions, it will not be long before their morals are corrupted (Proverbs 13:20; 28:7). If they are with good people, they behave themselves. Many a young Christian student has gone off to a secular college, only to falter when beliefs are questioned. Throughout the Old Testament, we see strict laws regarding purity. If the clean touched the unclean, the unclean did not become clean or pure; the clean became impure. The company we keep is a matter of choice—birds of a feather flock together.

As we approach Paul's letters, we get a good photograph of his friends. Had he lived in the twentieth century, no doubt a picture would accompany what he had to say about each. The best he could do was send a word picture of their personal lives. He mentioned over one hundred people in his epistles, mostly those who were his fellow helpers. One was a Roman captain; another a Roman guard. A few betrayed him; thankfully, the majority were true friends. He did not list them all, but all believers were included in his greetings. The fact that these friends were mentioned tells us a couple of things: (1) He knew that presenting Christ to a lost world was not a one-man show. Service to God is a team effort. Paul knew that the gospel would not progress unless others were involved. (2) Paul was never too big for people. He was always concerned about individuals, no matter how insignificant their work was in the eyes of men. He is telling us in his writings that his ministry would never have been possible if it had not been for help from others.

Helping others is a pattern that runs throughout the Bible. When Israel was fighting Amalek, they were winning as long as Moses held his hands up. When Moses' hands became heavy and he lowered them, Amalek prevailed. Finally, two friends held up Moses' hands and Israel defeated their enemy (Exodus 17:8–16). Moses could not hear all the Israelites' complaints in the wilderness, so God gave him seventy elders or friends to assist him (Numbers 11:16). Joshua had Caleb, Ruth had Naomi, David had Jonathan, Elijah had Elisha, Jeremiah had Baruch, Peter had John, Paul had Barnabas, and so forth. The Bible advocates team effort, always a group of people to do the job. "Iron sharpeneth iron; so a man sharpeneth the countenance of a friend" (Proverbs 27:17). "A friend loveth at all times; faithful are the wounds of a friend" (Proverbs 17:17; 27:6). All these illustrations show that we need friends if we are to make it in our pilgrim journey. There is no such thing as isolationism in Christianity (Acts 2:42–47; Hebrews 10:25). Paul recognized the truth that

> two are better than one; because they have a good reward [as they share] for their labor. For they fall, the one will lift up his fellow: but woe to him that is alone when he falleth; for he hath not another to help him up. If one prevail against him, two shall withstand him (Ecclesiastes 4:9–10; 12).

Paul has an attitude of thankfulness as well as an exhibition of love for his friends. As he wrote of his friends, he not only thanked the Lord for them but in expressing his love for them he was desirous that others love them also. Space does not permit us to go into detail, but as an example of his love for and devotion to them, we look at a few mentioned in Colossians. The rest are mentioned briefly, giving the meaning of their names and their relationship to Paul.

TYCHICUS

> All my state [in prison] shall Tychicus share with you, who is a much beloved brother and a faithful minister [servant] and fellow [bond] servant [with us] in the Lord, whom I have sent to you for this very purpose, that you may know how we are faring and that he may comfort and cheer and encourage your hearts. (Colossians 4:7–8)

Tychicus assisted Paul in taking the offering for the poor to Jerusalem and was with him during his second imprisonment. We learn that after several years of loyalty to Paul he was sent to Crete to be the interim pastor (elder) while Titus went to see Paul (Titus 3:12). Later, with full confidence in this bond servant, Paul sent him to Ephesus so that Timothy could visit him in prison (2 Timothy 4:12). The Ephesian church was probably third in importance to the churches at Antioch and Jerusalem. What a tremendous task this was for Tychicus. Having entrusted this beloved brother with taking the epistles of Ephesians and Colossians to the designated churches, Paul also placed in his care the runaway slave, Onesimus, who had been converted to Christ and was now taking the epistle to Philemon, his master. Paul could ask this servant to do anything and he would readily accept the responsibility. Tychicus never attained prominence; he just served. Whatever had to be done, he did it without question or argument. What a splendid example to illustrate that a ministry will never be fully accomplished unless there are people like him. Tychicus was known as a man one could depend upon. Someone has said that the greatest ability in the world is dependability. His name means "fortuitous" (accident or by chance). He was more than his name as a servant of the Lord.

ONESIMUS

Onesimus, the man with the sinful past, now a "faithful and beloved brother, who is one of you [or now one in Christ with you]" (Colossians 4:9). The path of this runaway slave had crossed that of Paul's in Rome while Paul was under house arrest. In time Onesimus was led to the Lord. The burden of guilt as a runaway slave, coupled with his theft from his master, weighed heavily on his mind. He knew that if he were caught, he would be put to death. Finally, he unburdened his heart to Paul. Asked where he was from, Onesimus said Colossae. Paul's eyes must have lit up because he knew a number of people in the church there. Upon learning that his master was Philemon, Paul leaped to his feet with joy, telling Onesimus that he had led Philemon to a saving knowledge of Christ. Here was the link Paul needed to really encourage this troubled brother.

Helping him become rooted and grounded in the Word of God, Paul told Onesimus that he would write a letter to his master. Philemon was requested to forgive his former slave, and to take him back not only in a slave relationship but also accept him as a brother in Christ equal with his master in the things of the Lord. Accompanied by Tychicus, who gave him the protection against any possibility of arrest, Onesimus returned to his master. He gave the letter to Philemon (see chapter 12). Since the church met in Philemon's house, no doubt on the Lord's day, Onesimus stood up before the congregation to give his testimony. He probably concluded by saying: "I am a man with a past, but now I have a past that is passed."

Onesimus is a good example of true conversion, one who was headed in the wrong direction, but through repentance had an about-face and headed in the other direction to make things right with those he had wronged. True repentance and conversion are based on a complete change. John the Baptist told the Pharisees to "bring forth fruits [evidence] in keeping with repentance" (Matthew 3:8). Zacchaeus said he would give the half of his goods to the poor, "and if I have taken anything from any man by false accusation [or by cheating him], I will restore unto him fourfold" (Luke 19:8). Only Christianity can enable anyone to do what Onesimus and countless other believers have done in similar circumstances. *Onesimus* means "profitable". After his conversion he truly lived up to his name. Tradition tells us he later became the pastor of the church at Colossae.

ARISTARCHUS

Aristarchus, "my fellow prisoner," a saint with a compassionate heart who was also Paul's companion in travels (Acts 19:29; Colossians 4:10). He helped Paul deliver the offering for the poor to Jerusalem. Along with Gaius, he was attacked in the riot at Ephesus where he risked his life for the sake of the gospel. He had joined Paul and the missionary team in Ephesus; was with him in the shipwreck; and was a fellow prisoner. The Roman system permitted a person to "sign in" as a prisoner so that they might be with a prisoner. He chose to associate with Paul in his bonds (chains). He became a burden bearer to encourage this man of God. One may not feel qualified or be able to do many things in God's service, but one is without excuse if he does not help bear another's burdens (Galatians 6:2). How precious this fellowship of Aristarchus must have been for Paul. It shows that he was one who stood by a man in need, not only as a friend, but as a fellow prisoner. His name means "best ruling." It is no wonder Paul used him so long and so much in the spreading of the gospel.

MARK

Mark, cousin to Barnabas (Colossians 4:10 NIV). He might be known as "the man with the second opportunity." He was also known as John Mark and Marcus. Marcus was his Roman name. He grew up in a godly home. His mother was Mary, in whose house prayer was held for Peter (Acts 12:5, 12), and he was Paul's minister (servant) on his first missionary journey. However, when the going got tough, Mark backed out. How typical of so many Christians today! He returned to Jerusalem and no doubt began to rethink his actions. Peter, Mark's good friend must have been a great help to him. After all, Peter knew something about a second chance. He denied the Lord three times, but he preached a mighty sermon on the Day of Pentecost and was bold in witnessing (Mark 14:66–72; Acts 2; 4:5–13; 5:29). Evidently, after the Jerusalem Council, Mark went to Antioch, but his prior desertion precipitated a split between Paul and Barnabas, which resulted in Paul's taking Silas as his partner and Barnabas taking Mark as his (see chapter 6). It is evident that after Mark's forsaking Paul and Barnabas he made a true about-face and became a useful servant of the Lord. He became one of Paul's fellow laborers (Philemon 24). Paul asked the church at Colossae to receive him. Several years later during Paul's second imprisonment, Mark had become profitable to Paul (2 Timothy 4:11). Second-chance Peter had taken a second-chance Mark under his wing and said this of him: "The church that is Babylon, elect together with you, salute you; and so does Mark [Marcus] my son" (1 Peter 5:13). It appears that Mark had become a servant with Peter.

There were three reasons that Mark got back into the service of the Lord. First, was the encouragement he received from his missionary partner, Barnabas. Second, was Paul's discipline. Mark began to realize that Paul was right, that the work of the Lord was a serious matter and one must be totally dedicated to Christ. Third, was Peter's acceptance as well as what Mark learned from Peter's experience. One's experience teaches great wisdom, and what a blessing Peter must have been to this young man at a turning point in his life. What a lesson for us—"Brethren, if a man be overtaken in a fault, ye which are spiritual, restore such an one in the spirit of meekness; considering thyself, lest thou also be tempted" (Galatians 6:1). Too often we are prone to write someone off who fails the Lord, when all they need is a smile, a word of encouragement, a pat on the back, and some healthy spiritual advice to get them going again.

Mark's name means "known by Jehovah." In spite of failure, he was still remembered by God, and He who had begun a good work in him took him up and continued it until his dying day (Philippians 1:6). God trusted him to write the second gospel account. What a great testimony for this prodigal son.

JUSTUS

Jesus, called Justus, "my fellow worker unto the kingdom of God, who has been a comfort unto me" (Colossians 4:11). Justus was a no-name circumcised Jew, but he worked with Paul and meant a lot to Paul. He comforted Paul and had a healing ministry in encouraging Paul in his trials. He never made the headlines but was a useful tool in God's kingdom. How typical of God's faithful servants today. The vast majority will never be in the limelight, but as each builds on the foundation of Christ Jesus and builds with gold, silver, and precious stones, they will not go unrewarded. They are steadfast, unmovable, always abounding in the work of the Lord. Their labor is not in vain in the Lord (1 Corinthians 15:58). Justus' name means "just" and fair to all; Jesus means "Joshua."

EPAPHRAS

Epaphras, "who is one of you, a servant of Christ, always laboring fervently [or agonizing in pain] for you in prayers, that ye may [be able to] stand perfect [or be mature] and complete [or fully assured] in all the will of God" (Colossians 4:12). Paul respected Epaphras as a man of prayer. He made time to pray for others, not just praying for those who had physical disorders, as important as those requests are, but praying for spiritual needs—the most important thing in the lives of believers. He wanted to get to the deeper needs of their Christian walk—that of doing God's will that they might fulfill Romans 12:1–2. The next time you go to prayer meeting in your church (if your church has one), count the number of physical and spiritual requests and you will find that the requests for physical needs far outweigh those for the spiritual needs. Epaphras was one of the three persons Paul referred to as a "servant of Christ" (or the Lord). He and Timothy were the other two (Romans 1:1; 2 Timothy 2:24). Not only was Epaphras Paul's fellow servant, he was also his fellow prisoner (Colossians 1:7). He was the founder and pastor of the church at Colossae; he was possibly the founder of the churches at Hierapolis and Laodicea. His name means "devoted," and what a devoted man he was to Christ.

LUKE

Luke, "the beloved physician" (Colossians 4:14) is mentioned only two other times in Scripture: as a faithful companion (one of the last to be with Paul during his second imprisonment, 2 Timothy 4:11), and a fellow laborer (Philemon 24). He was present as an unseen laborer in many situations, as we note by the use of the personal pronoun *we* (Acts 16:11). He was a man who used his talent as a medical doctor, spending much of his time attending to Paul's physical needs. He was dedicated and was willing to tackle any job for the cause of Christ. In giving his all to help the Apostle to the Gentiles spread the Good News of salvation, he ended up writing fifty-two chapters in the New Testament (the gospel account of Luke and the Acts of the Apostles). Luke was a man of education and culture, knowledge-able in seafaring as we note in his account of Paul's voyage from Caesarea to Italy (Acts 27:1–28:15). Yet, he was humble enough to sacrifice his talents that he might serve his Savior.

DEMAS

Demas, the man with a sad future. Mentioned three times by Paul, he was a loyal, faithful fellow laborer with Paul, especially during Paul's first imprisonment (Colossians 4:14; Philemon 24). He was involved in an intense ministry with Paul for possibly five years. Paul often dictated his letters and it could be that Demas was the secretary who penned the letter to the Colossians.

However, during Paul's second imprisonment, Demas became a spiritual drop-out and forsook Paul and his calling in Christ for the things of the world. Paul mentions this incident in 2 Timothy 4:10. Paul was hurt when this happened. Jesus had had a similar experience when Judas betrayed Him and through Demas' actions Paul experienced some of Christ's sufferings (Philippians 3:10). Many a child of God has been disappointed by a friend who turned his back on him and especially on the Lord. Paul, though, set a good example by keeping his eyes on the Lord and requesting a friend, Mark, who once left Paul but came back (2 Timothy 4:10–11). Christ never disappoints and we are without excuse if we do not keep looking to Him, "the author and finisher of our faith" (Hebrews 12:2). Demas means "popular". So often when a child of God becomes popular in the eyes of people, they soon fall by the wayside, disappointing countless numbers of people they have had a hand in helping. Popularity soon becomes a worldly trait to a Christian, and we see that such contributed to the downfall of Demas.

OTHER WORKERS

We have considered eight of the ten people Paul mentioned in his letter to the Colossians, giving the meaning of their names, their characteristics, and some spiritual applications for our benefit.[1] The following list of names gives only brief information about others associated with Paul. Oftentimes, however, Roman and Greek names had no specific meaning.

Achaicus

Achaicus, an Achain (1 Corinthians 16:17), was, with Fortunatus and Stephanas, a good contributor to Paul.

Agabas

Agabas, meaning "good"; "benefit"; "worthy" (Acts 11:27–28; 21:10), was a prophet from Jerusalem who warned of a famine in Judaea and of Paul's arrest in Jerusalem. Both prophecies came to pass, an indication that he was God's prophet (note Deuteronomy 13:1–5; 18:20–22).

Alexander

Alexander, meaning a "man defender" (1 Timothy 1:20; 2 Timothy 4:14–15), was a coppersmith. He became an enemy of Paul; was immoral, unethical, a blasphemer (defamer; speaking evil of others); and opposed Paul's preaching. He certainly did not live up to his name.

Ampliatus

Ampliatus (Amplias), meaning "enlarged" (Romans 16:8), was Paul's beloved in the Lord.

Ananias (1)

Ananias, meaning "Jehovah hath favored" (Acts 9:10–17; 22:12), was a devout man of God, having a good report of all the Jews who lived in Damascus. He was obedient and was used of God to welcome Paul (Saul) at his conversion, restoring his sight and baptizing him.

Ananias (2)

Ananias, meaning "Jehovah hath favored" (Acts 23:1–5), was the high priest who commanded those near Paul to smite him.

Andronicus

Andronicus, meaning a man of "victory" (Romans 16:7), was Paul's relative and fellow prisoner.

Apelles

Apelles (Romans 16:10) was approved in Christ.

Apollos

Apollos (Apollonius), named for a pagan deity (Acts 18:24–28; 1 Corinthians 3:3–8; 16:12), was eloquent and mighty in the use of the Scriptures. Aquila and Priscilla helped him to understand the way of God more thoroughly (perfectly). He became a helper of those who believed through grace, and had a following in the Corinthian church. Some believe he may have written the epistle to the Hebrews.

Apphia

Apphia (Philemon 2) was called beloved. She was Philemon's wife and Archippus's mother.

Aquila

Aquila, Latin meaning "eagle" (Acts 18:2, 24–28; Romans 16:3–5), was a Jewish convert, tentmaker, and Paul's helper. Used by the Lord, along with his wife Priscilla, to show Apollos the full revelation of Christ's finished work at Calvary, he had a church in his home. He was one who "laid down his neck" for the cause of Christ (or who, like Paul and Barnabas, risked his life in his stand for Christ). As his name implies he was able to soar above Old Testament Scripture and see its fulfillment in Christ.

Archippus

Archippus, meaning "ruler" (Colossians 4:17; Philemon 2), was Philemon's son, Paul's fellow soldier, and a champion of the gospel. Paul encouraged him to "keep on keeping on" in the ministry.

Aristobulus

Aristobulus, meaning "the best counselor" (Romans 16:10), was Paul's fellow laborer. Tradition says that he was one of the seventy disciples and that he preached in Britain.

Artemis

Artemas, meaning a "gift from Artemis" (goddess Diana) also means "ready"; mainsail of a vessel (Titus 3:12). He was Paul's companion and tradition says a Bishop at Lystra.

Asyncritus

Asyncritus, meaning "incomparable" (Romans 16:14), was one who was able to combine spiritual ideas with appropriate expressions.

Barnabas

Barnabas, meaning "son of exhortation"; "consolation" (Acts 4:36–37; 9:26–:27; 11:22–24; 15:25–26), was a Levite from Cyprus. Generous and a good man full of the Holy Spirit and of faith, Barnabas was the Bible teacher in Antioch (Syria) and Paul's companion on his first missionary journey. He risked his life for Christ (surrendered himself to any trial or circumstance; endangered his life for the gospel). Some have suggested that he wrote the epistle to the Hebrews (see chapter 3).

Carpus

Carpus, meaning "plucked fruit" (2 Timothy 4:13), was Paul's host in Troas.

Cephus

Cephus (Peter; Simon), meaning "rock or stone" (John 1:40–42: Acts 15:7; 1 Corinthians 1:2; Galatians 2:7–14), was the Apostle to the Jews and the writer of the two epistles that bear his name.

Chloe

Chloe, meaning "green"; "alive" (1 Corinthians 1:11), was a well-known Corinthian believer; informed Paul of the contention in the Corinthian church.

Claudius Lysias

Claudius Lysias (Acts 23:26) was a Roman captain who cooperated with Paul after his arrest in Jerusalem (Acts 21:31–40; 22:30; 23:1–30).

Claudia

Claudia (2 Timothy 4:21) was a Christian in Rome who no doubt visited Paul in prison.

Clement

Clement, meaning "merciful" (Philippians 4:3), was Paul's fellow laborer in Philippi. He later became bishop of Rome.

Crescens

Crescens, meaning "growing" (2 Timothy 4:10), was a companion of Paul in Rome and later went to Galatia.

Crispus

Crispus, meaning "crisp", "fresh" (Acts 18:8; 1 Corinthians 1: 14), was a converted chief ruler of the Jews who was baptized by Paul.

Epaenetus

Epaenetus, meaning "praised" (Romans 16:5) was an early convert of Paul, and was spoken of as his "well beloved, the firstfruits of Asia unto Christ."

Epaphroditus

Epaphroditus, meaning "devoted; lovely" (Philippians 2:25–30; 4:18), was highly esteemed as a "brother companion in labor and fellow soldier." He was a messenger of the Philippian church delegated to take gifts to Paul while he was imprisoned.

Erastus

Erastus, meaning "beloved" (Acts 19:22; Romans 16:23), was Paul's friend and a chamberlain (city treasurer of Corinth).

Eubulus

Eubulus, meaning "goodwill"; "well done" (2 Timothy 4:21), was a disciple in Rome.

Eunice

Eunice, meaning "victorious" (Acts 16:1; 2 Timothy 1:5; 3:15), was Lois' daughter and Timothy's mother. She was a wise mother who taught her son the Scriptures, which made him wise unto salvation.

Euodias

Euodias, meaning "fragrance" (Philippians 4:2), was a helper on the road (assisting travelers). A Philippian believer at odds with Syntyche.

Eutychus

Eutychus, meaning "fortunate" (Acts 20:9), was the young man who fell asleep during one of Paul's extra-long sermons at Troas. He fell from the third loft but was revived by Paul.

Fortunatus

Fortunatus, meaning "blessed"; "fortunate"; "one who like a ship carries cargo"; "burden-bearer" (1 Corinthians 16:17) helped Achaicus and Stephanas take supplies to Paul.

Gaius (1)

Gaius (Acts 19:29; Romans 16:23; 1 Corinthians 1:14) was a Macedonian and Paul's companion and host, Paul baptized this well-beloved man.

Gaius (2)

Gaius (Acts 20:4) was from Derbe, he accompanied Paul from Macedonia to Asia.

Hermas

Hermas, meaning "speaks"; "messenger" (Romans 16:14), was a disciple at Rome to whom Paul sent greetings.

Hermes

Hermes, meaning "speaks"; "messenger" (Romans 16:14), was a Roman disciple.

Hermogenes

Hermogenes, meaning "speaks"; "messenger" (2 Timothy 1:15; 4:16), was a professing Christian in Asia who deserted Paul.

Herodion

Herodion, meaning "hero" (Romans 16:11), was Paul's kinsman and a Roman believer.

Hymenaeus

Hymenaeus, (1 Timothy 1:19–20; 2 Timothy 2:16–18), was a professing Christian who became prey to heresies and tried to shipwreck the faith of believers. He opposed Christianity, was evil, and a character destroyer. He denied the resurrection and was excommunicated by Paul.

James

James, from Jacob, meaning "supplanter" (Acts 15:13; 21:18), was an apostle, believed to be Christ's half-brother (Matthew 13:55; Mark 6:3). He moderated the Jerusalem Council, and gave Paul wrong advice on his last visit to Jerusalem. He favored the Jews over the Gentiles and wrote the epistle that bears his name.

Jason

Jason, meaning "to make whole" (Acts 17:5–9; Romans 16:21), sheltered Paul and Silas in Thessalonica. He was greeted in Paul's letter to the Romans.

Judas

Judas, meaning "celebrated" (Acts 9:11), hosted Paul in his home in Damascus after Paul was converted.

Judas Barsabas

Judas Barsabas, meaning "celebrated"; Barsabas meaning

"son of" or "born on the Sabbath" "to please" (Acts 15:22, 27, 32). He was a prophet of the Jerusalem church.

Julia

Julia (Romans 16:15) was a Roman believer and Phiologus' wife.

Julius

Julius (Acts 27:1–3, 43) was a Roman guard the kind and courteous centurion who had charge of Paul on his voyage to Rome.

Junia

Junia (Romans 16:7) was a Roman believer and one of Paul's relatives.

Justus

Justus, meaning "just" (Acts 18:7) also surnamed Titus, had a home where Paul lodged for a time in Corinth.

Linus

Linus, meaning "unmovable"; "esteemed" (2 Timothy 4:21), befriended Paul during his second imprisonment. According to Irenaeus and Eusebius, he was the first bishop of Rome.

Lois

Lois, (2 Timothy 1:5) Timothy's maternal grandmother was commended for her faith and for helping her daughter, Eunice, bring Timothy up in the Scriptures (2 Timothy 3:15).

Lucius (1)

Lucius, meaning "illuminative" (Acts 13:1), was a Cyrenian who ministered to the church in Antioch (Syria).

Lucius (2)

Lucius, meaning "illuminative" (Romans 16:21), was Paul's kinsman in Rome who might have been with him in Corinth when he wrote to the Roman believers.

Lydia

Lydia, (Acts 16:14–15, 40) was hospitable and the first European convert. Some have suggested she was called Lydia because she was a seller of purple from Lydia in Asia. Some scholars believe her personal name was unknown; others that she might have been either Euodias or Syntyche of Philippians 4:2.

Manaen

Manaen, meaning "comforter" (Acts 13:1), was a leader in the Antioch church and a foster brother of Herod (Antipas) the tetrarch (called "that fox" by Christ Luke 13:31–32).

Mary (1)

Mary (Acts 12:12) was the mother of John Mark. She was hospitable and her home was a house of prayer.

Mary (2)

Mary (Romans 16:6) was a member of the church at Rome. A faithful laborer, she labored for Paul.

Mnason

Mnason (Acts 21:16) was a cypriot and a Christian of long standing who played host to Paul and his friends in Jerusalem at conclusion of third missionary journey.

Narcissus

Narcissus, meaning "flower" (Romans 16:11), was a Roman believer whose household received Paul's greeting.

Nereus

Nereus, meaning "to float" (Romans 16:15), was a Roman believer and servant of the emperor. It is not known if this is the one greeted by Paul. There were those in Caesar's household who knew Christ (Philippians 4:22).

Nymphas

Nymphas, meaning "togetherness" (Colossians 4:15), hosted the church of Colossae or Laodicea.

Olympas

Olympas, meaning "wine" (Romans 16:15), was a Roman believer.

Onesiphorus

Onesiphorus, meaning "profit bearer" (2 Timothy 1:16–18; 4:19), was devoted to Paul and ministered to him while in prison.

Patrobas

Patrobas, meaning "father" (parent) (Romans 16:14), was a Roman believer.

Persis

Persis (from Persia) (Romans 16:12) a beloved Roman woman who labored much in the Lord.

Peter

Peter (Simon; Cephas). See Cephas.

Philemon

Philemon, meaning "friendly"; "lovely" (Philemon 1, 19, 24), was Paul's convert. The church met in his house. He was a fellow laborer and the master of runaway slave, Onesimus.

Philetus

Philetus, meaning "amiable"; "worthy of love" (2 Timothy 2:17–18), was an evil person, character destroyer, and denier of the resurrection. He failed to live up to his name.

Philip

Philip, meaning "neighborly"; "friendly" (Acts 6:5; 21:8–9), was an evangelist at Samaria who won the Ethiopian eunuch to the Lord. He settled in Caesarea (Acts 8:16–40).

Philologus

Philologus, meaning "fond of learning"; "teachable" (Romans 16:15), was a Roman believer.

Phlegon

Phlegon, meaning "ignite"; "blazing or burning" (Romans 16:14), was a Roman believer to whom Paul sent a loving greeting.

Phoebe

Phoebe (Phebe) (Romans 16:1–2) was a servant (deaconess)

in the church in Cenchrea. She took the epistle of Romans to the believers in Rome.

Phygellus

Phygellus (2 Timothy 1:13–15; 4:16) deserted Paul and the Word of God.

Priscilla

Priscilla, meaning "little" (Acts 18:2; Romans 16:3–5a), was Paul's helper, a student of the Scriptures, a laborer in the faith, and the wife of Aquila. Both laid down their necks for Christ. The church at Rome met in their home.

Pudens

Pudens, meaning "modest" (2 Timothy 4:21), was a Roman believer and probably visited Paul during his last imprisonment.

Quartus

Quartus (Romans 16:23) was a laborer in the Corinthian church. Tradition says he was one of the original seventy disciples (Luke 10:1).

Rufus

Rufus (Romans 16:13) was chosen in the Lord. He was a Roman disciple, the brother of Alexander, and son of Simon the Cyrenian, who carried the cross (Mark 15:21).

Silas

Silas (Sylvanus), meaning "asked" (Acts 15:22, 32, 40; 2 Corinthians 1:19), was prominent in the Jerusalem church being the chief man, prophet, and colaborer. Paul chose him as his partner on the second missionary journey after Barnabas chose Mark. Silas later became Peter's secretary (1 Peter 5:12).

Simeon

Simeon (Niger), meaning "black" (Acts 13:1), was a prophet and teacher in the Antioch church.

Sopater

Sopater, meaning "safe" (Acts 20:4; Romans 16:21), was a Christian from the church in Berea. He accompanied Paul from Corinth to Jerusalem on Paul's third missionary journey.

Appendix Three

Sosipater

Sosipater, meaning "safe" (Romans 16:21), was Paul's kinsman.

Sosthenes

Sosthenes, meaning "safe"; "strength" (Acts 18:17; 1 Corinthians 1:1), succeeded Crispus as ruler of the synagogue at Corinth. He was beaten by the crowd when Gallio freed Paul but was later converted.

Stachys

Stachys, meaning "head of grain"; "outstanding" (Romans 16:9), was Paul's beloved and a Roman believer.

Stephanas

Stephanas, meaning "crowned" (1 Corinthians 1:16; 16:15–17), was baptized by Paul. He and his household were Paul's firstfruits of Achaia. He helped Archaicus and Fortunatus supply Paul's needs and was "addicted" to the ministry of the saints. He labored in the Corinthian church and probably, along with the above friends, went to Ephesus to give Paul the letter of questions from the Corinthians.

Stephen

Stephen, meaning "crown" (Acts 6:8; 7:59; 8:1; 22:20), was unselfish; full of faith and power. The first Christian martyr, his death was approved by Saul (Paul).

Syntyche

Syntyche, meaning "to reach together" (Philippians 4:2), was prominent in the Philippian church. She was at odds with Euodias. Paul encouraged her to be of the same mind as Euodias in the Lord—to live up to her name.

Tertius

Tertius (Romans 16:22) was one of Paul's secretaries who took dictation for the epistle to the Romans.

Timothy

Timothy, meaning "dear to God"; "honoring God" (Acts 16:1; 19:22; Romans 16:21; 1 Thessalonians 3:2; 1 Timothy 1:2;

2 Timothy 4:9–13), was Paul's "son in the faith; his dearly beloved son." Shy and reserved, he was a great follower as contrasted to "leader" Titus. Timothy was Paul's official representative. Referred to as youthful (anyone between the ages of twenty-two and forty was considered "a young man"), Paul loved him and desired Timothy's presence with him during his last days on earth.

Titus

Titus, a Greek (2 Corinthians 2:13; 7:6; 8:16, 23), was Paul's "son after the common faith." He was an aggressive leader, Paul's brother—comforting, caring partner and fellow helper. He was used in the council of Jerusalem to prove that one could be saved without being circumcised (keeping the Law, Galatians 2:3–5). Tenney, in the *Zondervan Pictorial Bible Dictionary*, says that Titus "was consecrated, courageous, resourceful. He knew how to handle the quarrelsome Corinthians, the mendacious Cretans, and the pugnacious Dalmatians."[2]

Trophimus

Trophimus, meaning "nourishing" (Acts 20:4–5; 21:27–29; 2 Timothy 4:20) was a Gentile Ephesian Christian and a fellow helper and companion to Paul. He helped Paul take the offering to the poor in Jerusalem. He was incorrectly identified by the Asian Jews as a Gentile taken by Paul into the temple in Jerusalem. He became ill and Paul left him at Miletus.

Tryphena

Tryphena, meaning "dainty"; "luxurious" (Romans 16:12), was a female believer in Rome; a laborer in the Lord. Tryphena was common name found on many inscriptions in burial places of royal household servants.

Tryphosa

Tryphosa, meaning "delicate" (Romans 16:12), was a laborer in the Lord. Tryphosa was another common name among servants of the royal household.

Urbanus

Urbanus (Urbane), meaning "polite" (Romans 16:9), was a Roman believer and helper in Christ.

Zenas

Zenas, meaning "gift" or "present" (Titus 3:13), was a Christian lawyer on Crete.

What a variety of people. Each had a niche in Paul's life and his ministry. God has always been pleased to use humans to do His work. In Christ Jesus each person is to be a colaborer with Him as we work together to accomplish His plan. It has always been God's method to use humanity. He does not use schemes, machinery, and so forth to get the job done. "There was a man sent from God whose name was John" (John 1:6). God so loved the world, but He did not send a committee—He sent a Man, the Man Christ Jesus. All through Scripture we find God choosing people to get the job done. Some fail, but He always raises up more. When Joshua came on the scene, God had just buried His worker, but not His work (Joshua 1:1–2). What a blessing it is to have fellowship with those of like faith and work together in the greatest job on earth, that of winning souls to Christ and edifying one another. These people, mentioned by Paul, being dead, yet speak, because their deeds follow them. Of course we only know of them because Paul mentioned them, and we (like they) do not serve the Lord for the praise of men. If so, we already have our reward. Although we might be forgotten by the world, God is keeping a book of remembrance of those who feared (obeyed and served) the Lord and thought on His name (Malachi 3:16–17).

OTHER WORKERS

Appendix Four

THE VACANT PULPIT

Achurch was in need of a pastor. One of the elders was interested in knowing just what kind of a minister they desired. He wrote the following letter as if he had received it from an applicant and read it to the pulpit committee. It read as follows:

Gentlemen:

Understanding that your pulpit is vacant, I should like to apply for the position. I have many qualifications that I think you would appreciate. I have been blessed to preach with power and have had some success as a writer. Some say I am a good organizer. I have been a leader in most places I have gone.

Some folks, however, have some things against me. In fact, I have some things against myself also. I am over fifty years old. I have never preached in one place for more than three years at a time. Although I am not a racist, one group in particular accused me of downing their religion and being a proselytist. That is because I left one religion of which I was a member for thirty-four years and joined a new group.

In a few instances I have had to leave town after my preaching and work caused disturbances. On one occasion I was the cause of a riot that lasted for two hours. It took the town clerk some time to quiet the people.

I have been in jail several times. At times I have argued with my helpers. Many times religious leaders have tried to kill me. Politicians have frowned on my actions. I have been to court several times. I must be frank and tell you that my health isn't the best.

All my churches have been small, although located in large cities. I have been classified as a world traveler because I have preached on two continents. You should know, however, that in some circles I have the reputation of being a long-winded preacher. On one occasion I preached until midnight. A young man fell from the balcony and got the wind knocked out of him. Did that ever disturb the service! I consider myself one who fights a good fight, although I realize that many churches do not like an agitator or squabbles.

I mentioned I am a writer. Once I wrote about a member who was having an affair with his own father's wife. You can imagine what a stir that caused. One of my churches was very disorderly.

I use only the Bible for sermon preparation. I confess I do not preach current events or politics or give book reviews or preach little sermons to cause people to remain comfortable in their sins. I do not hesitate to preach about judgment to come, that the wages of sin is death, and that Jesus Christ and His shed blood is the only cure for sin. I also preach separation from the world, the flesh and the devil, whether people like it or not.

You might as well know now that I haven't gotten along too well with the ministerial associations in the different churches where I have pastored. They all seem to preach a social gospel, a do-better religion of works rather than faith in the old time religion—the old, old story of Jesus and His love. They just don't like it when I attend their meetings. Some of them say I am "too sensational," like the time some of my "religious fanatics" helped me escape from enraged church members by helping me over the city wall in a basket. You should have seen the mob when they dragged me outside the city and stoned me, leaving me for dead!

I am not too good at keeping records. I have been known to forget those I baptized. However, if you can use me, I shall do my best for you, even if I have to work at my trade of tent making to support myself.

The elder, upon reading the letter, asked the pulpit committee if they were interested in the applicant. They replied that such a character would never do for their church. They said they were not interested in an unhealthy, contentious, trouble-making, absent-minded jailbird, and that they were insulted that his application had ever been submitted to them. When they inquired of the elder the name of the brazen applicant, he replied, "the apostle Paul."

Appendix Five

CHRONOLOGICAL TABLE
OF EVENTS IN
PAUL'S LIFE

I n 46 B.C. Julius Ceasar made calendar change that was a great improvement over the previous methods used for dating. In the sixth century A.D., a civil calendar was adopted for civil chronology. In A.D. 1582 the Gregorian calendar, after finding errors in the previously mentioned systems, was adopted. As a result, it is generally agreed that since time is dated by or from the birth of Christ, the beginning of the Christian era should be dated at least four, possibly five years earlier. Scripture confirms that Jesus was born during Herod the Great's reign. Josephus said that Herod died in the spring, 4 B.C. (according to the current calendar). Scholars accept the dates of 5/4 B.C. (some say 6 B.C.) as the time of Christ's birth, and about A.D. 29/30 as the date of His death.

To avoid confusion or complicate matters in the usage of dates in this chronological table of events in Paul's life, the starting point will begin with 0 B.C.–A.D. 1. It is generally assumed that Paul was born about a year after Christ's birth and that he died in late A.D. 67 or early A.D. 68.

DATE A.D. (CA.)	PAUL'S LIFE	CONTEMPORARY EVENTS	DATE A.D. (CA.)
BOOK CHAPTER ONE			
		Caesar Augustus (Luke 2:1)	B.C. 31–A.D. 14
2/32	Birth; hometown; education at home and in Jerusalem	Archelaus, Ethnarch of Judaea and Samaria (Matthew 2:19–22)	2–11/12
		Herod the Tetrarch of Galilee (Luke 3:1; 13:32; 23:6–12	2–39
		Emperor Tiberius (Luke 3:1)	14–37
		Caiaphas, high priest (Matthew 26:57)	18–36
33/34	In Tarsus	Pontius Pilate, Governor of Judaea (Matthew 27:1–2)	26–36
		Christ's crucifixion (Matthew 27:27–50)	33/34
BOOK CHAPTER TWO			
34/35	Persecution of the church (Acts 9:1–2; Galatians 1:13–14) Conversion (Acts 9:3–6)	Caiaphas, high priest (Acts 9:1–2) Emperor Tiberius	
BOOK CHAPTER THREE			
36	In Arabia (Galatians 1:17)	Ananias, high priest	36–?
37/40	Back to Damascus for three years (Galatians 1:17–18)	Emperior Caligula	37–40
40	First visit to Jerusalem; received commission— "Apostle to Gentile" (Galatians 1:11–18; 2:8–9; Acts 22:17–21; Romans 11:13)	King Agrippa I given jurisdiction over Galilee, Samaria and Judaea	39
BOOK CHAPTER FOUR			
40/44	In Tarsus (Acts 9:30; Galatians 1:18–21) Caught up to third heaven; received "thorn in the flesh" (2 Corinthians 12:1–10)	Emperor Claudius	41–54
		Rome's invasion of Britain	
		Death of Herod Agrippa I	44
		Cuspius Fadus appointed governor of Judaea	44

DATE A.D. (CA.)	PAUL'S LIFE	CONTEMPORARY EVENTS	DATE A.D. (CA.)

BOOK CHAPTER FIVE

DATE A.D. (CA.)	PAUL'S LIFE	CONTEMPORARY EVENTS	DATE A.D. (CA.)
45	From Tarsus to Antioch with Barnabas (Acts 11: 19–26)		
46	Took offering to poor in Jerusalem (Acts 11:27–30	Tiberius Alexander made procurator of Judaea	46
46/47– 49/50	First missionary journey: from Antioch to Cyprus, Pamphylia, Southern Galatia (stoned at Lystra), Derbe; retraced steps back to Antioch (Acts 13–14). Traveled approximately 1450 miles.	Agrippa II made king of Chalcis (Acts 25:13). Son of Herod Agrippa I (Acts 12) and great-grandson of Herod the Great	48
		Cumanus made Procurator of Judaea	49

BOOK CHAPTER SIX

DATE A.D. (CA.)	PAUL'S LIFE	CONTEMPORARY EVENTS	DATE A.D. (CA.)
50	Council at Jerusalem (Acts 15) Paul wrote Epistle to Galatians Dissolved partnership with Barnabas (Acts 15:36–41	Rome conquers Britain Cognidunus, father (?) of Claudia (2 Timothy 4:21), assists Romans in Britain; probably made king	50

BOOK CHAPTER SEVEN

DATE A.D. (CA.)	PAUL'S LIFE	CONTEMPORARY EVENTS	DATE A.D. (CA.)
51/54	Second Missionary journey; from Antioch through Asia Minor to Troas, Philippi (Macedonian call), Thessalonica, Berea, Athens, Corinth, Cenchrea, Ephesus, to Jerusalem and back to Antioch (Acts 15:40–18:22). Traveled approximately 2800 miles.	Claudius expels Jews from Rome (Acts 18:1–2)	52
		Gallio, Procounsel of Achaia	52
53	Wrote First Thessalonians in Corinth	Felix made Procurator of Judaea (Acts 23:23–24).	53
54	Second Thessalonians in Corinth	Emperor Nero	54–68

DATE A.D. (CA.)	PAUL'S LIFE	CONTEMPORARY EVENTS	DATE A.D. (CA.)

BOOK CHAPTER EIGHT

54/58	Third missionary journey: from Antioch through Asia Minor to Ephesus, Corinth, back to Ephesus, Macedonia, Corinth, Philippi, Miletus to Jerusalem (Acts 18:22b–21:17). Traveled approximately 3900 miles.		
55/56	Wrote First Corinthians in Ephesus		
57	Second Corinthians in Macedonia	Nero brutally murders different members of own family and others	56–62
57/58	Wrote Romans in Corinth		

BOOK CHAPTER NINE

58	Last visit to Jerusalem; visits brethren; in Temple to make vow; arrested; almost killed by Jews; rescued by Roman soldiers; defended self before Sanhedrin (Acts 21:15–23:22)	Feast of Pentecost	

BOOK CHAPTER TEN

58/60	Paul sent to Caesarea; under house arrest for two years; before Felix; Festus; appeal to Caesar; before Agrippa; must go to Rome (Acts 23:23–26:32).	Felix replaced by Festus	60

BOOK CHAPTER ELEVEN

60/61	Voyage September, A.D. 60 from Caesarea to Rome. Shipwrecked at Malta (winter A.D. 60/61) arrived in Rome, spring, A.D. 61 (Acts 27:11–28:16)		

DATE A.D. (CA.)	PAUL'S LIFE	CONTEMPORARY EVENTS	DATE A.D. (CA.)
BOOK CHAPTER TWELVE			
61/63	Arrived in Rome; under house arrest for two years' won both Jews and Gentiles to Christ, including some of Caesar's own household (Acts 28:16–31; Philippians 4:22)	Nero married Poppaea after murder of second wife, Octavia	62
61	Philemon		
62	Colossians		
62	Ephesians (see book chapter 8)		
63	Philippians (see book chapter seven)		
63	Luke concluded writing Acts in the spring of A.D. 63, covering a period of approximate 29/30 years of Paul's life.		
BOOK CHAPTER THIRTEEN			
63/67	Released from prison; fourth missionary journey from Rome to Spain, Ephesus, Macedonia, Crete, Miletus, Nicopolis (?), Troas (Philippians 2:19–24) with Timothy in Ephesus (1 Timothy 1:3) with Titus on Crete (Titus 1:5)	Great fire in Rome' Nero blamed, followed by severe persecution of Roman Christians; the "Christian Holocaust"	July 64
65	Wrote First Timothy in Macedonia		
66	Wrote Titus in Miletus (?)		
BOOK CHAPTER FOURTEEN			
67	Rearrested in Troas; taken to Rome; tried before Nero; death sentence		
67	Wrote Second Timothy in prison		
67/68	Decapitated on Ostian Road outside walls of Rome A.D. 68; buried by friends in catacomb	Nero died	June 68

DATE A.D. (CA.)	PAUL'S LIFE	CONTEMPORARY EVENTS	DATE A.D. (CA.)
BOOK CHAPTER FIFTEEN			
68	To die is gain; absent from the body, present with the Lord (Philippians 1:21b; 1 Corinthians 5:8) Paul's Epistles from heaven		

Appendix Six

HOW TO READ PAUL
TWO-THOUSAND
YEARS LATER

The following article appeared in *Newsweek*, 29 February 1988. It was written by Kenneth L. Woodward, and is used by permission. What a contrast we will see between modern-day Protestant and Catholic theologians and the apostle Paul of New Testament days.

After Jesus, the Apostle Paul is the most authoritative figure in the New Testament. In fact, long before the four Gospels were ever written, Paul was already traveling the Mediterranean, founding churches and writing letters that make up more than one-fourth of the New Testament. But unlike Jesus, who taught mainly in parables, Paul's letters are filled with abstract doctrines and dogmatic-sounding dictums that have earned him the reputation of being Christianity's "second founder"—and "first" theologian.

Now, however, a new generation of Scripture scholars are challenging many of the commonplace assumptions about who Paul was and what his teachings meant. Armed with a more precise information about the historical Paul and his times, these scholars offer an arresting view of Paul as he saw himself: a Jewish apostle to the Gentiles who did not envision the founding of a new religion, a pastor who was more concerned about communal behavior than individual salvation—and a counselor who never expected that his ad-hoc advice would become sacred Scripture.

"Because Christian theology has been shaped so largely by Pauline thought, the tendency has been to argue over every nuance, on the premise that Paul was a systematic theorist setting down doctrinal truth for all time," says Prof. Robert Jewitt of Garrett Evangelical Theological Seminary in Evanston, Ill. "In fact, his letters are highly situational responses to complex congregational problems." In the new scholarly consensus, Paul is a synthesizer and advocate, not a lonely and abrasive innovator—shedding an intriguing new light on 2,000 years of Christian theology. The key areas of scholarly revision are:

Paul and Judaism. The stereotype of Paul is that of a zealous rabbi who persecuted Christians until he himself was converted to Christ. After that experience, conventional opinion holds, Paul repudiated Judaism and became equally zealous in preaching faith in Jesus. But according to the new scholarly consensus, Paul did not reject Judaism. "As Paul himself understood it, his pivotal experience of the risen Christ on the road to Damascus was not a conversion from one religion to another," says Jesuit scholar Daniel J. Harrington of the Western School of Theology in Cambridge, Mass. "Rather, he regarded that experience as a calling by God to extend to Gentiles the religious aspirations of the Jews, which he now saw as available to everyone through faith in Jesus." For Paul, then, the Torah [Pentateuch-Law] was the path that led to Christ. And through Christ, he believed, Gentiles could join Jews as God's children.

Personal Salvation. Paul has long been regarded as Christianity's premier psychologist of religious experience. Through the commentaries of St. Augustine and, especially, Martin Luther, Paul's discourses on sin, grace, and "justification by faith" have achieved singular status as the classic explanation of how individuals achieve personal salvation through Christ. But many scholars now contend that both Augustine and Luther misinterpreted Paul as addressing personal rather than communal questions of faith.

"Paul's doctrine of justification by faith should not be understood primarily as an exposition of the individual's relation to God," says British scholar James Dunn of the University of Durham, England, but in the context of the problem he was trying to solve. That problem, scholars now believe, was to find a theological way to explain how Jews and Gentiles related to each other within the new Christian communities. Many Jewish Christians argued that Gentile converts should be circumcised and abide by dietary regulations. Paul insisted that these precepts of the Torah were not necessary for Gentiles because the source of righteousness for both groups is faith in Christ. In sum, Paul developed his doctrine of justification by faith to show that Jews and Gentiles are spiritual equals in Christ—not to explain how the individual sinner experiences God's forgiveness. Therefore, many scholars feel, Paul should not be used—as evangelists typically do—to preach a personal salvation apart from incorporation into the church [in a communal relationship—Jew and Gentile alike].

The Role of Women. Paul's attitudes toward women have also undergone a reassessment. Scholars now tend to de-emphasize Paul's admonition to women to "be silent" in the church (1 Corinthians 14:34), as a relic of his Jewish background. They cite ample evidence elsewhere in Paul's letters that he accepted and approved of women as co-workers in the church. New Testament scholar Jouette Bassler of Perkins School of Theology in Dallas points to passages in Paul's "Letter to the Romans," where seven of ten church workers he hails are women. One of these, called "Junia" or "Junias," is believed by some scholars to be an apostle like Paul himself. Moreover, Paul's use of the early Christian baptismal slogan "neither male nor female" (Galatians 3:28) offers weighty evidence that he was not the misogynist [woman hater] that fundamentalist Christians, especially, have made him out to be.

Church and State. In his "Letter to the Romans," Paul warns that "those who refuse to obey the laws of the land"—meaning the Roman Empire—"are refusing to obey God, and punishment will follow." From the Holy Roman Empire to modern South Africa, this has been a favorite passage of kings and governments. But according to Father Harrington and other scholars, Paul's remarks were merely practical exhortations to the Christians in Rome. Says he: "They were part of an on-going debate in those days about what attitude Christians should take toward

Roman rule, and should not be absolutized into a philosophical doctrine of church and state.

In sum, the new scholarly consensus presents Paul as primarily a pastor whose letters were designed to resolve congregational problems that the roving apostle could not attend to in person. Some of those problems are no longer important to Christians. But even if Paul's writings are not to be taken as immutable Holy Writ, today's scholars nonetheless insist that his teachings retain authority for Christians. "Paul addressed problems that are naggingly familiar to all religious people," says Biblical expert Paul J. Achtemeier of Union Theological Seminary in Richmond, Va. "He understood that sin is not just a nasty behavior but the condition of everyone who tries to make the world work without the necessary relationship to God."

—Kenneth L. Woodward, Religious Editor for Newsweek

The author thanks Mr. Woodward for permission to use his fine article in "exposing" the beliefs of some "modern" scholars who choose to pick out only the portions of Scripture that appeal to their "natural" reasoning.

To say that Paul was interested more about communal behavior than individual salvation is calling him a liar (see Acts 16:27–29 and Romans 10:1).

Paul's whole message was to reveal that justification is by faith, and that both Jew and Gentile were lost and needed to be saved—reconciled to God. Chapters two and three of Romans bear this out.

In appealing to *all* members of the human race, never once did He encourage Gentiles to embrace any of the Old Testament Jewish law, but since Christ was the end of the law to all who believe, had nailed all the handwriting of ordinances that were against them to the cross, and had put away all Jewish sacrifices by the offering of Himself once and for all, Paul's inspired argument was that "*All* have sinned and come short of the glory of God," and that a sinner is saved "by grace through faith," even as Augustine and Luther had taught (Romans 10:4; Colossians 2:14; Hebrews 10:4–10; Romans 3:23; Ephesians 2:8–9). Furthermore, if Paul, as Harrington said, regarded his Damascus experience as a calling by God to extend to Gentiles the religious aspiration of the Jews, and that Gentiles could join Jews as God's children, why did he receive so much opposition and persecution from Jews as he preached?

Yes, women played an important role in New Testament times, assisting Paul on occasions, as mentioned by Jouette Bassler, as well as the Lord Jesus (Luke 23:49; 24:10). Women were with the men praying in the Upper Room (Acts 1:14). There are many acts of service women can perform in a church by applying their "gifts of helps," but when it comes to authority in the church, Paul gave instructions *only* to men for this responsibility (1 Timothy 3:1–13; 5:17 with Hebrews 13:17). Not once did Paul, nor Christ for that matter, ever choose a woman for an authoritative position in their ministry. Fundamentalist Christians *do not* make Paul out to be a misogynist. They only follow Scripture in giving both man and woman their rightful place in God's divine order of service. True, there is "neither male nor female" in Christ. This has to do with our oneness in Him, which is vastly different from our being male and female in our respective positions. This may sound a bit ridiculous, but if one follows Jouette's argument to its logical conclusion, does this mean that a Christian lady can no longer have a baby since she is no longer a female in Christ? And, how can some scholars say that a female named Junia or Junias was an apostle like Paul when the New Testament names all apostles, all of whom were males? Junia was listed with Andronicus as Paul's *kinsmen*, not kinsperson.

If the powers that be are ordained of God, and if our sovereign God can pull down one nation and set up another, are we not obligated to follow the Scriptural injunction and "obey them that have the rule over us?" To follow the view of the scholars mentioned by Mr. Woodward, makes it sound like the philosophy of "civil disobedience" is legal.

Paul was more than "primarily a pastor." He was an apostle of Jesus Christ and his writings were addressed, not only to people of his day and many problems that they encountered, but problems of our day as well. While these scholars say that "some of these problems are no longer important to Christians," they had better look again at Paul's letters, for the answer to their "liberal" problem was given by Paul two thousand years ago!

One further word: True Bible scholars *do not* agree with the scholars mentioned in Mr. Woodward's article.

APPENDIX 7

JEWISH OPPOSITION TO THE APOSTLE PAUL

Once again we must ask the question: "Why was there such unholy opposition on the part of the Jews to the preaching of the Gospel by the apostle Paul?" Was he not proclaiming all about Messiah from *their* own Scripture—Moses, the Psalms, and the Prophets? Had not the prophets stated the *time* when Messiah would come and the *place* where He would be born (Daniel 9:24–27; Micah 5:2)? Had not God chosen them in Abraham with the promise that they would be a great nation with a land of their own; and had He not promised them a Prophet like unto Moses (Genesis 12:1–3; Deuteronomy 18:15, 18)? Had not God promised them a Redeemer who would be their sacrifice for sin (Isaiah 53)?

SPIRITUAL BLINDNESS Yet, having been chosen by God to be His peculiar people (Deuteronomy 7:1–6) and having been entrusted with His sacred oracles (the Scriptures) to be a testimony to heathen nations (Acts 7:38; Roman 3:1–2), they, at some point, began to believe and obey the traditions of their elders instead of the inspired, sacred Scripture (Matthew 15:3, 6). The traditions were oral laws that had been added to God's laws; they were the interpretations of God's laws as the elders viewed them. When this is done, man's opinions are accepted instead of "thus saith the Lord," and the Word of God becomes ineffective.

To answer our question as to why the Jews opposed Paul and

his scriptural presentation of Messiah, we must to go back to confirmed Jewish history as given in *their* Bible. In Deuteronomy God told Israel that He would bless them if they obeyed Him completely (28:1–14). He said:

> The LORD shall establish thee an holy people unto himself, as he hath sworn unto thee, if thou shalt keep the commandments of the LORD thy God, and walk in his ways. And all the people of the earth shall see that thou art called by the name of the LORD; and they shall be afraid of thee. And the LORD shall make thee plenteous in goods, in the fruit of thy body [healthy], and in the fruit of thy cattle, and in the fruit of the ground, in the land which the LORD sware unto thy fathers to give thee (vv. 9–11).

He promised to give sufficient rain for their crops, to have such an abundance that they could lend to other nations, and that they would be "the head, and not the tail;" that they would be "above only, and not be beneath" other nations or peoples, "if [they hearkened] unto the commandments of the LORD [their] God, which [He] command [them] this day, to observe and do them." What a high calling for this nation and what blessings would be theirs *only* through obedience to God.

He also told them in the same chapter of Deuteronomy (28:15–67) that they would be judged if they disobeyed Him. God spelled out for them just what these judgments would be, not only for that present generation in the wilderness for their sins of disobedience, but for future generations of Israelites (Jews) as well (v. 46). Note some of the judgments: sickness, famine, defeat by other nations; they would become an astonishment, a proverb, a byword, few in number (as contrasted with being as the sand of the sea, numberless, Genesis 32:12); they would serve other gods, be plucked off the land and scattered among nations; they would be the tail and not the head; they would have a trembling heart; their life would be in doubt; in the morning they would say, "would to God it were even," and at night say, "would to God it were morning" (v.67).

We face another dilemma. Did Israel obey God or disobey Him? It is ironic that God made a prophecy through Moses concerning their future disobedience:

> For when I shall have brought them into the land which I sware unto their fathers, that floweth with milk and honey; and they shall have eaten and filled themselves, and waxen fat [become

prosperous]; then will they turn unto other gods and serve them, and provoke me [to anger], and break my covenant (Deuteronomy 31:20).

This prophecy was literally fulfilled. After Joshua's death, biblical history shows that Israel disobeyed commands that God had given concerning their entrance into the Promised Land, as well as many, many more.

ISRAEL'S DISOBEDIENCE	
COMMANDMENTS GIVEN **Deuteronomy 7:1–5, 11**	**COMMANDMENTS DISOBEYED** **Judges 1–3**
Smite them; utterly destroy them.	She failed to drive out inhabitants of the land (v.1–2) , all the inhabitants (1:19,34).
Make no covenant with them (v.2).	A league (or covenant) was made to let some live (2:2–3; Joshua 9:14–21).
Do not intermarry (v. 3–4).	They intermarried (3:5–6).
Do not serve their gods (v.4).	They served other gods (2:11–13; 3:6).
Destroy their altars and idols (v.5).	They did not destroy their gods,altars, or groves (3:7).

Having forsaken the Lord God of their fathers who brought them out of the land of Egypt, and having begun to follow and serve other gods, they forgot the Lord their God, and every man did that which was right in his own eyes (Judges 2:11; 3:7; 17:6). They disobeyed Samuel when he asked them to retain God as their king by saying to him: "Nay, but we will have a [man] king over us that we may also be like all nations." They dethroned God as their king and were not the peculiar, holy people He had called them to be (I Samuel 8:19–20). During Solomon's latter reign and under his son, King Rehoboam, Israel hit the skids spiritually (1 Kings 11:1–11, 33; 14:21–24; 2 Chronicles 12:1, 13–14). Later King Manasseh seduced Israel to do more evil than all the nations round about (2 Kings 21:1–9; Psalm 106:34–43).

Tragically, this once mighty nation, which had been called to be holy, had become so blinded to God's goodness and His Word that their sin of disobedience caused God to liken them to the "rulers of Sodom and the people of Gomorrah" (Isaiah 1:1–15). Ezekiel called Israel the "sister" of Sodom (16:48–52). Jeremiah said:

I have seen also in the prophets of Jerusalem a horrible thing; they commit adultery and walk in lies: they strengthen also the hands of evildoers, that none doth return from his wickedness: They are all of them unto me as Sodom, and the inhabitants thereof as Gomorrah (23:13–14).

Isaiah accused Israel of calling evil good and good evil, of calling darkness light and light darkness, of calling bitter sweet and sweet bitter, of becoming wise in their own eyes and prudent in their own sight, and of justifying the wicked because they had cast away (or rejected) the law of the Lord of hosts and despised the Word of the Holy One of Israel (5:20-24). Had it not been for a faithful remnant, God would have done to His people what He had done to Sodom and Gomorrah over one thousand two hundred years before (Isaiah 1:9; Genesis 19:24–25). However, sooner or later their sin of disobedience would catch up with them. Nebuchadnezzar of Babylon, in 586 B.C., took them captive. Israel's disobedience had led to the Babylonian captivity. According to 2 Chronicles 36:14–21 Israel

1. had become the most sinful nation that ever existed, in spite of the gross, vulgar sins of other nations. Israel alone had light; she had the truth of God's Word. When one knows to do right and does it not, to him it is sin (Romans 14:23; James 4:17). Other nations had not been entrusted with God's Scriptures. Israel had, and her sin was greater because she knew better. She *rejected* His Word.

2. had dethroned God for a human king and worshiped the god Baal (Judges 2:11; 3:7; 1 Samuel 8:19–20.)

3. had, with her priests transgressed, after the abomination of the heathen nations and had polluted the house (temple) of the Lord, which He had hallowed in Jerusalem (2 Chronicles 36:14).

4. had "touched God's anointed, in spite of God's love and compassion for them (cf. vv. 15–16 with 1 Chronicles 16:22).

　SPIRITUAL BLINDNESS

5. had, for 490 years, failed to keep the Sabbatical year (cf. v. 21 with Leviticus 26:34–43).

With the fall of the nation, and after serving seventy years in captivity, a period of Gentile rule, called the "times of the Gentiles," began. (Daniel 2:36–45; Romans 11:26). When Israel returned from her Babylonian captivity, she was still Israel, the people of God, but she was not the same. Having been chosen by God to be His peculiar, holy people—a fruit-bearing vine that was to represent all that God stood for— Jeremiah said she had been "planted a noble vine, wholly a right seed" (2:21). Her disobedience, however, permitted her pastors to become unfaithful. They "destroyed God's vineyard" and made Israel a "desolate wilderness," or unfruitful land (Jeremiah 12:10). By this time she had become an "empty vine" (Hosea 10:1; Habakkuk 3:17).

Eventually, in fulfillment of her prophetic Scriptures, a child was born, a Son was given. His name was Immanuel, "God with us." He was the virgin-born Messiah (Isaiah 7:14; 9:6). This was God's solution to their sin problem. "He came unto his own [the Jews], and his own received him not" (John 1:11). As a result, God set them aside. They were "blinded in part until the fullness of the Gentiles be come in [or runs it's course]" (Romans 11:25).

In the meantime, in this dispensation of grace, God is calling out individual Jews and Gentiles for His name that they might be His new nation, a nation that will bring forth fruit for His glory (Matthew 21:33–46; Acts 15:14). No nation on earth ever had the opportunity that Israel had. She had the opportunity to obey God and enjoy His multiple blessings as the head of all nations (Deuteronomy 28:1–14). Whatever befell these people as a result of God's judgment due to her refusal to obey, cannot be charged to God or any other peoples. She deliberately chose not to be what God called her to be, a people known by His name.

Why did the Jews oppose Paul's preaching of the Gospel? The answer is obvious. Their eyes had become so blinded and their minds had become so hardened through disobedience to their own Scripture and their acceptance of their man-made theology (the traditions of their fathers) that anything contrary or in opposition to their beliefs would make them and their ancestors liars. They had resisted the Holy Spirit for centuries, as Stephen pointed out (Acts 7:51). To them, the Gospel was an infringement on their nation and religion (see chapter 1). The light that was once in them had become darkness, and that darkness was great

(Isaiah 6:10; Matthew 6:23). How sad, especially when we think of God's goodness to them throughout their Old Testament history in delivering them from Egyptian bondage (Psalm 106:7–11), in making every provision for them in their wilderness journey (cf. Deuteronomy 8:2–6 with 1 Corinthians 10:1–10), and in bringing them into the Promised Land (Joshua 1:2–3). The greatness of His goodness was shown in His sending Messiah in spite of their disbelief. Even though they tried Him, condemned Him, and demanded His crucifixion, they did so with the determinate counsel and foreknowledge of God (Acts 2:23). Although they had become enemies of the Cross (Romans 11:28; Philippians 3:18–19), technically, we cannot blame them fully for Christ's crucifixion. Humanity's sin is what really crucified the Lamb of God—your sin and my sin.

The Jews of Paul's day thought they had already established or attained their own righteousness (Romans 10:2–3), but Paul, knowing that they were, like all other human beings (Gentiles), lost sinners, sought to make it known that they, too, needed a sacrifice for their sins. This is another reason why they opposed Paul. In spite of their opposition, the apostle continued to preach Christ, hoping and praying that many of his kinsmen would have their blinded eyes and minds opened to truth. If anyone ever knew the "why" of such opposition, Paul did, for he had once done the same thing. Now that his eyes were open, he was all the more burdened for them and determined to reach them with the Gospel (Romans 9:1–3; 10:1; 1 Corinthians 9:16).

APPENDIX 8

MAPS OF PAUL'S
LIFE AND JOURNEYS

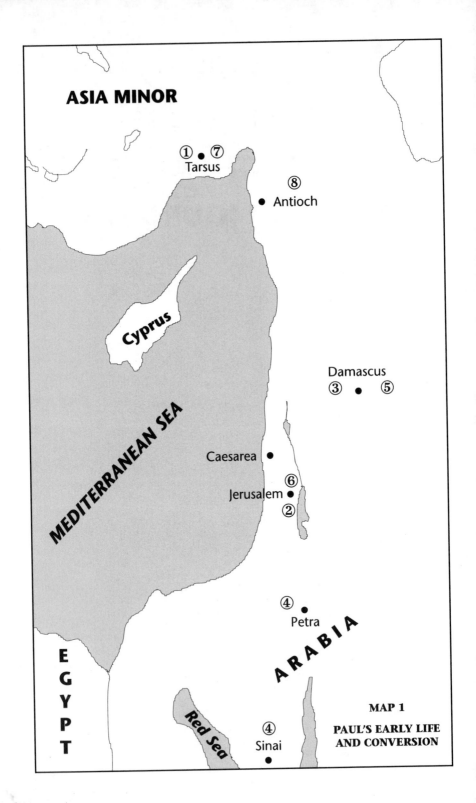

ASIA MINOR

① ● ⑦
Tarsus

⑧
● Antioch

Cyprus

MEDITERRANEAN SEA

Damascus
③ ● ⑤

Caesarea ●

⑥
Jerusalem ●
②

④
● Petra

ARABIA

EGYPT

Red Sea

④
Sinai ●

MAP 1

PAUL'S EARLY LIFE
AND CONVERSION

MAP 1
PAUL'S EARLY LIFE
AND CONVERSION

1. Tarsus, Paul's birthplace: Acts 21:39. See page 27.

2. Paul studied in Jerusalem under Gamaliel: Acts 22:3. See page 32.

3. From Jerusalem to persecute Christians in Damascus; kicking against the pricks; his salvation and preaching in Damascus: Acts 8:1–3; Galatians 1:13–14; Acts 9:1–21. See pages 44ff.

4. Paul went to Arabia—Petra and Mount Sinai: Galatians 1:15–17. See page 68.

5. From Arabia back to Damascus: Galatians 1:17b; Acts 9:22–25. See page 72.

6. After three years in Damascus, back for first visit to Jerusalem: Galatians 1:17b, 18; Acts 9:26–27; 22:1–21; Romans 11:13. See page 73.

7. Back to Tarsus via Caesarea and Syria: Acts 9:30; Galatians 1:21. See page 81 and chapter 4.

8. Left Tarsus with Barnabas for Antioch: Acts 11:25–26. See page 106. Took an offering to Jerusalem and returned to Antioch: Acts 11:27–30; 12:25. See page 107.

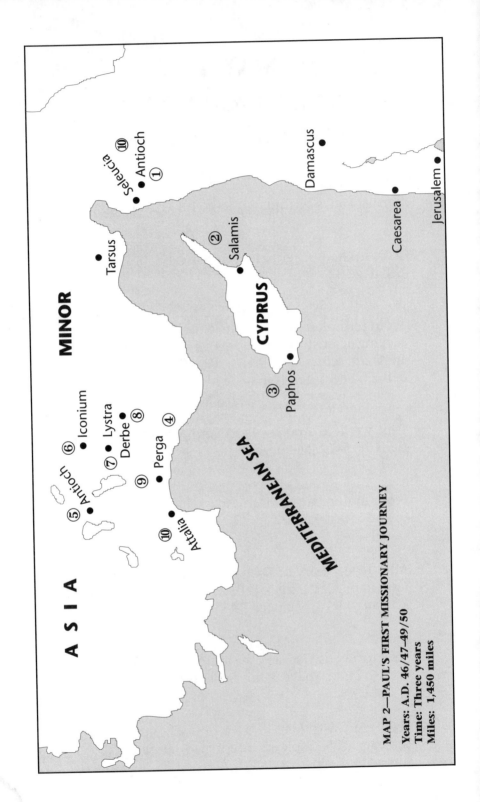

MAP 2—PAUL'S FIRST MISSIONARY JOURNEY

Years: A.D. 46/47–49/50
Time: Three years
Miles: 1,450 miles

ASIA

MINOR

Tarsus

⑤ Antioch
⑥ • Iconium
⑦ • Lystra
Derbe •
⑧
⑨ • Perga
⑩ Attalia
④

Seleucia
⑩ • Antioch
① •

② Salamis

CYPRUS

③ Paphos

MEDITERRANEAN SEA

Damascus •

Caesarea •

Jerusalem •

MAP 2
PAUL'S FIRST
MISSIONARY JOURNEY

A. D. 46/47–49/50

Traveled 1,450 miles

1. Paul and Barnabas ordained in Antioch: Acts 13:1–2. See page 111.

2. From Antioch to Seleucia to Salamis on the island of Cyprus: Acts 13:3–5. See page 114.

3. From Salamis through the island to Paphos: Acts 13:6–12. See page 114.

4. From Paphos to Perga in Pamphylia: Acts 13:13. See page 116.

5. From Perga to Antioch of Pisidia: Acts 13:14–50. See page 117.

6. From Antioch to Iconium: Acts 13:51–14:5. See page 120.

7. From Iconium to Lystra: Acts 14:6–20a. See pages 121.

8. From Lystra to Derbe: Acts 14:20b–21a. See page 123.

9. Paul and Barnabas retrace their steps from Derbe back to Perga: Acts 14:21b–25a. See page 124.

10. Paul and Barnabas sail from Attalia back to Seleucia and thence to Antioch of Syria: Acts 14:25–28. See page 124.

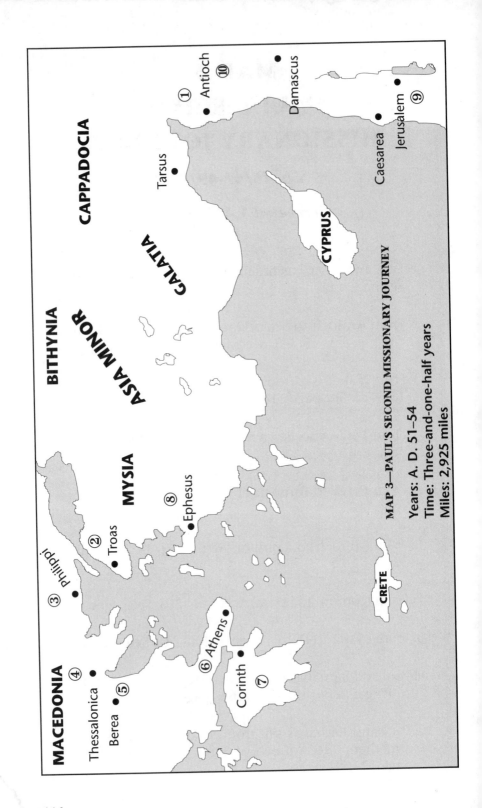

MAP 3—PAUL'S SECOND MISSIONARY JOURNEY

Years: A. D. 51–54
Time: Three-and-one-half years
Miles: 2,925 miles

BITHYNIA

ASIA MINOR

CAPPADOCIA

GALATIA

MYSIA

MACEDONIA

CRETE

CYPRUS

Thessalonica
Berea ⑤
④
Philippi ③
② Troas
⑧ Ephesus
Athens
⑥
Corinth ⑦
Tarsus
① Antioch ⑩
Damascus
Caesarea
Jerusalem ⑨

MAP 3
PAUL'S SECOND
MISSIONARY JOURNEY

A. D. 51–54

Traveled 2,800 miles

1. Left Antioch for Asia Minor to Troas: Acts 15:40–16:8. See page 148.

2. At Troas, the "Macedonian Call": Acts 16:9–10. See page 155.

3. From Troas to Samothracia , Neapolis, to Philippi: Acts 16:11–40. See page 156.

4. From Philippi to Thessalonica: Acts 17:1–9. See page 170.

5. From Thessalonica to Berea: Acts 17:10–14. See page 178.

6. From Berea to Athens: Acts 17:15–34. See page 179.

7. From Athens to Corinth: Acts 18:1–18. See page 193.

8. From Corinth to Ephesus: Acts 18:21. See page 208.

9. From Ephesus to Jerusalem: Acts 18:22a. See page 208.

10. From Jerusalem back to Antioch: Acts 18:22b. See page 208.

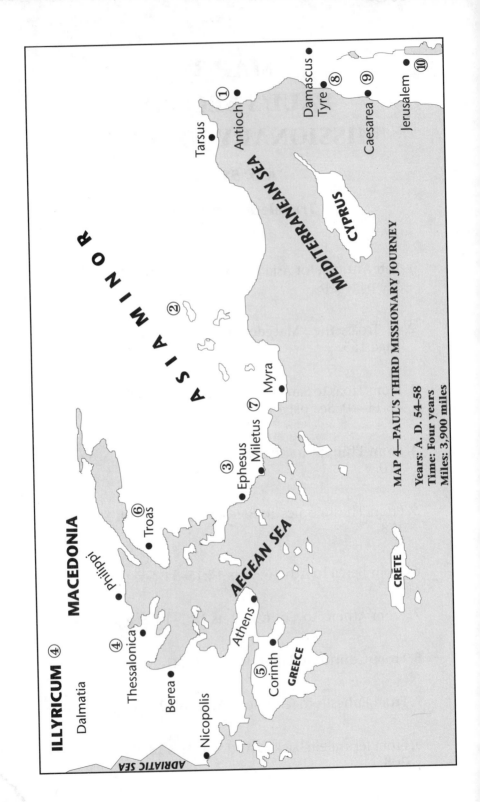

MAP 4—PAUL'S THIRD MISSIONARY JOURNEY

Years: A. D. 54–58
Time: Four years
Miles: 3,900 miles

ILLYRICUM ④

MACEDONIA

Dalmatia

Thessalonica ④

Berea

Nicopolis

Philippi

Troas ⑥

AEGEAN SEA

Athens

Corinth ⑤

GREECE

ASIA MINOR

②

Ephesus ③

Miletus

Myra

⑦

CRETE

MEDITERRANEAN SEA

Tarsus

Antioch ①

CYPRUS

Damascus

Tyre ⑧

Caesarea ⑨

Jerusalem ⑩

ADRIATIC SEA

448

MAP 4
PAUL'S THIRD
MISSIONARY JOURNEY

A. D. 54–58

Traveled 3,900 miles

1. Left Antioch for his third missionary journey: Acts 22–23a. See page 216.

2. Went all over the country of Galatia and Phrygia (Asia Minor): Acts 18:23. See page 216.

3. Arrived in Ephesus: Acts 19:1. See page 219. While in Ephesus he made a second visit to Corinth. See page 229.

4. To Macedonia and Illyricum: Acts 20:1–2a; Romans 15:19. See page 239.

5. To Greece—Athens and Corinth: Acts 20:2b–6. See page 240.

6. From Greece back to Troas: Acts 20:3b–12. See page 248.

7. To Miletus: met with Ephesian elders: Acts 20:13–38. See page 269.

8. To Tyre: Acts 21:3–6. See page 251.

9. To Ptolemais and Caesarea: Acts 21:7–14. See page 254.

10. Paul's final visit to Jerusalem: Acts 21:14–17. See page 256.

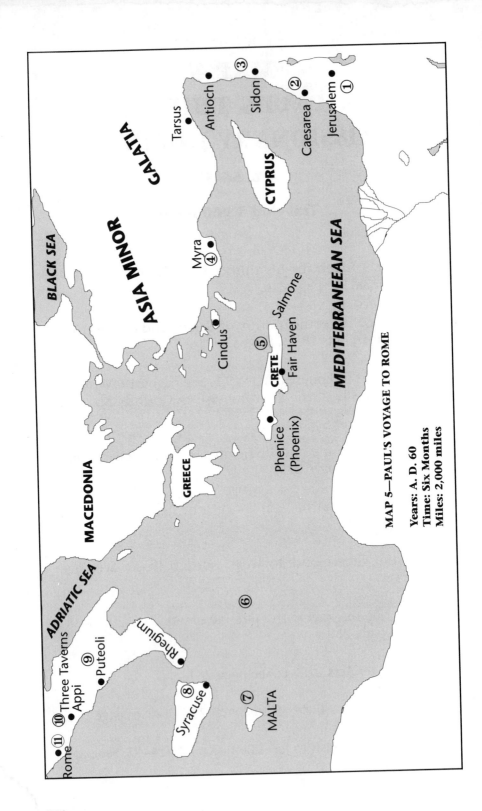

MAP 5—PAUL'S VOYAGE TO ROME

Years: A. D. 60
Time: Six Months
Miles: 2,000 miles

BLACK SEA

ASIA MINOR

GALATIA

MACEDONIA

ADRIATIC SEA

GREECE

Tarsus

Antioch

Sidon

Caesarea

Jerusalem

① ② ③

CYPRUS

Myra
④

Cindus

Salmone

Fair Haven
CRETE ⑤

Phenice
(Phoenix)

MEDITERRANEEAN SEA

Rhegium

Puteoli
⑨

Three Taverns
Appi
⑩

Rome
⑪

Syracuse
⑧

MALTA
⑦

⑥

450

MAP 5
PAUL'S VOYAGE
TO ROME

A. D. 60

Traveled 2,000 miles

1. Paul's last visit to Jerusalem; arrested in the temple: Acts 21:17–31. See page 261.

2. To Caesarea for two years: Acts 23:23–26:32. See pages 280, 285 ff..

3. Sailed from Caesarea to Sidon: Acts 27:3. See page 304.

4. From Sidon under and above Cyprus to Myra: Acts 27:3–6. See p. 305.

5. From Myra to Fair Havens on Crete: Acts 27:7–13. See page 305.

6. The Storm and Shipwreck: Acts 27:13–44. See page 306.

7. Arrival at Malta: Acts 28:1–11. See page 308.

8. From Malta to Italy—Syracuse and Rhegium: Acts 28:11–13a. See page 309.

9. Landed at Puteoli for seven days: Acts 18:31b. See page 309.

10. To Rome via Appii and the Three Taverns: Acts 28:14–15. See page 310.

11. Arrival in Rome: Acts 28:16–31. See page 333.

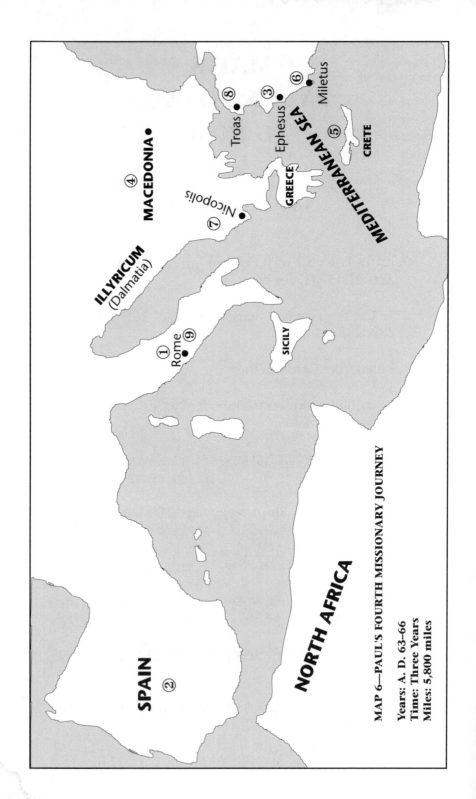

MAP 6—PAUL'S FOURTH MISSIONARY JOURNEY

Years: A. D. 63–66
Time: Three Years
Miles: 5,800 miles

SPAIN

②

NORTH AFRICA

ILLYRICUM
(Dalmatia)

MACEDONIA ●

④

Nicopolis

⑦ ●

GREECE

Troas

⑧ ●

Ephesus

③ ●

MEDITERRANEAN SEA

Miletus

⑥ ●

⑤

CRETE

SICILY

Rome

① ● ⑨

MAP 6
PAUL'S FOURTH
MISSIONARY JOURNEY

A. D. 63–66

Traveled about 5,800 miles

1. Paul released from first imprisonment. See page 333.

2. Paul's journey from Rome to Spain. See page 338.

3. From Spain to Ephesus. See page 338.

4. From Ephesus into Macedonia. See page 340.

5. To Crete with Titus. See page 340.

6. From Crete to Miletus. See page 342.

7. From Miletus to Nicopolis: Titus 3:12. See page 375.

8. From Nicopolis to Troas and his arrest. See page 348.

9. Paul taken back to Rome to face trial. His second imprisonment and execution: 2 Tim. 4:2, 9a; 4:6. See page 360. The journey from Troas to Rome was about 1,025 miles. See page 348

NOTES

Introduction

1. James Stalker, *The Life of St. Paul* (Old Tappan, N.J.: Fleming H. Revell, 1940).
2. William M. Ramsay, *Paul and Other Studies* (London: Hodder & Stoughton, 1906).

Chapter One

1. Flavius Josephus, *Antiquities* in *The Works of Josephus* (New York : A. L. Burt Co., n.d.), I, XVII, 3.
2. Conybeare and Howson, *The Life and Epistles of Saint Paul* (New York: Scribner & Sons, 1890).

Chapter Two

1. Stalker.
2. Ramsay.
3. Conybeare and Howson.
4. Copied, Newspaper Article
5. Ibid.
6. Ibid.
7. Goivani Papini, *Life of Christ*.

Chapter Three

1. Copied.
2. Papini.

Chapter Four

1. Stalker.
2. Ramsay.

Chapter Five

1. Josephus.
2. Stalker.
3. Merrill C. Tenney, *Zondervan Pictorial Bible Dictionary* (Grand Rapids, Mich.: Zondervan, 1987).
4. Adam Clarke, *Clarke's Commentary*, vols. 4–5 (Nashville: Abindgon-Cokesbury, n.d.).
5. Ibid.

Chapter Six

1. Conybeare and Howson.
2. *New International Version* (NIV) (Grand Rapids, Mich.: Zondervan, 1978; Clarke; Roland Knox, *The Holy Bible* (London: Burns and Oates, 1954).
3. Conybeare and Howson.
4. Matthew Henry, *Commentary on the Whole Bible*, 6 vols. (Old Tappan, N.J.: Revell, n.d.).

Chapter Seven

1. Clarke.
2. Tacitus, *The Annals of Imperial Rome*.
3. Ibid.
4. Robert T. Boyd, *World's Bible Handbook* (Iowa City, Iowa: World Bible Publishers, 1991).

5. Gouvoussis, C. *Greece*, (Athens: K. Gouvoussis Press, n.d.).
6. Ibid.

Chapter Eight

1. Andres Telford, *Studies in Ephesians* (Boca Raton, Fla.: n.p. n.d.).
2. Conybeare and Howson.

Chapter Nine

1. Josephus, *Antiquities*, XIX. 6, 1.
2. Charles C. Ryrie, Acts 21:24, *The Ryrie Study Bible* (NASB) (Chicago: Moody Press, n.d.).
3. Josephus, *War*, VI, 2, 24, V 5, 2.
4. Josephus, *War*, ii. 17, 9.
5. Josephus, *Antiquities*, XV. 8, 3, 4.
6. Ibid., *War*, ii. 17, 9.

Chapter Ten

1. Josephus, *Antiquities*, XIX. 354, XX. 139–143.
2. Ibid., XX. 143.
3. Ibid., XX. 8, 5, *War* ii 14, 1.

Chapter Eleven

1. Josephus, *Life*, c. 3.

Chapter Twelve

1. Boyd.
2. *The old Scofield Reference Bible* (New York: Oxford, 1917), 1291.

Chapter Thirteen

1. Tenney.
2. Clement Romanus, *Letter to the Corinthian Church*, sec. 5.
3. Muratori's Canon, "Routh's Riliquiae Sacrae," vol. iv.
4. *Atlas of the Bible* (Pleasantville, N.Y.: Reader's Digest, 1981).
5. Eusebius, *Ecclesiastical History* (Cambridge, Mass.: Harvard, n.d.), ii, 22.
6. Conybeare and Howson, *The Life and Epistles of Saint Paul.*
7. Ibid., no. 6.
8. Ibid.
9. Boyd, "Clip 'n Save."

Chapter Fourteen

1. Tacitus, *The Annals of Imperial Rome* (Cambridge, Mass.: Harvard, n.d.), XIV. 64, XV. 23.
2. Josephus, *Antiquities*, XX. 8, 11.
3. Tacitus, VI. 44. 3–8.
4. Conybeare and Howson.
5. Ibid.
6. Livy (Titus Livius), *Roman History* (Cambridge, Mass.: Harvard, n.d.), ii 6; Juvenal (London: Penguin, n.d.), 8.
7. Tacitus, VI. 67.
8. Eusebius, ii, 25.
9. Ibid., 4.
10. Ibid.
11. Ibid.

Appendix 3

1. Reverend William Boulet, Pastor, Grace Bible Church, Dunmore, Penn.

BIBLIOGRAPHY

Atlas of the Bible. Pleasantville, N.Y.: Reader's Digest, 1981.

Ball, Charles Ferguson. *The Life and Journeys of Paul.* Chicago, Ill.: Moody Press, 1951.

Boyd, Robert T. *World's Bible Handbook,* Iowa Falls, Ia.: World Bible Pub., 1991.

_____. *A Pictorial Guide to Bible Archaeology.* Grand Rapids: Baker, 1969.

_____. *Light from Biblical Customs.* Lancaster, Pa.: Vernon Martin Associates, 1971.

_____. *Clip 'n Save.* Lancaster, Pa.: Vernon Martin Associates, 1983.

Bruce, F. F. *Paul, Apostle of the Heart Set Free.* Grand Rapids: Eerdmans, 1977.

Byrk, Felix. *Circumcision in Man and Woman.* New York: American Ethnological Society, 1934.

Chadwick, Henry. *The Early Church.* New York: Dorset Press, 1986.

Chappell, Glovis G. *When the Church was Young.* New York: Abingdon, 1940.

Cicero. *Murder Trials in Rome: The Civil War.* New York: Dorset Press, 1985.

Clarke, Adam. *Clark's Commentary.* Vols. 4–5. Nashville: Abingdon-Cokesbury, n.d.

Conybeare, W. J., and Howson, J. S., *The Life and Epistles of Saint Paul.* New York: Scribner & Sons, 1890.

Early Christian Writings by the Apostolic Fathers. New York: Dorset Press, 1968.

Edersheim, A. *The Temple: Its Ministries and Services.* Boston: A. I. Bradley Co., 1874.

Encylopaedia Britannica. Vols. 8, 17. Chicago, 1955.

Eusebius., *The History of the Church.* New York: Dorset Press, 1965.

Everyday Life in Bible Times. Washington, D.C.: National Geographic Society, 1967.

Fagan, Brian M. *The Adventure of Archaeology.* Washington, D.C.: National Geographic, 1985.

Gouvoussis, C. *Greece.* Athens, Greece: K. Gouvoussis Press, 1970.

Great People of the Bible and How They Lived. Pleasantville, N.Y.: Reader's Digest, 1974.

Guest, W. J. *Unveiled Mysteries: Matthew 13.* Worcester, N.Y.: Worcester Press, 1904.

Ham, Kenneth A. *Creation Evangelism Impact #163*. El Cajon, Calif.: Institute for Creation Research, 1987.

Havner, Vance. *Blood, Bread, and Fire*. Grand Rapids: Zondervan, 1939.

Hislop, Alexander. *The Two Babylons*. 1916. Reprint. Neptune, N.J.: Loizeaux, 1959.

Josephus, Flavius. *The Works of Josephus Flavius*. New York: A. L. Burt Co., n.d.). *The Jewish Wars*. New York: Dorset Press, 1985..

Keiper, Ralph. *The Power of Biblical Thinking*. Old Tappin, N.J.: Fleming H. Revell, 1977.

Keskin, Naci. *Ephesus*. Istanbul, Turkey: Keskin Printing House, n.d.

Master, John R. *Lessons for Living; The Sermon on the Mount*. Schaumburg, Ill.: Regular Baptist Press, 1983.

Mauro, Philip. *The Hope of Israel*. Boston: Hamilton Bros., 1929.

Moody, Dwight L. *Secret Power*. Chicago: Moody Press, n.d.

Morton, H. V. *Through Lands of the Bible*. New York: Dodd, Meade & Co., 1938.

Mundell, George A. *The Pathway of Faith*. Philadelphia: Continental Press, 1951.

Owens, G.Frederick. *Jerusalem*. Grand Rapids: Baker 1972.

Patrick, Richard. *Greek Mythology*. New York: Crown, 1972.

Ramsay, Wm. M. *Pauline and Other Studies*. London: Hodder & Stoughton, 1906.

Rouse, William T. *God and the Jew*. Dallas: Helms Printing Co., 1946.

Ryrie, Charles C. "Especially the Parchments." *Bibliotheca Sacra* 117, no. 467 (July–Sept., 1960): 242.

Shanks, Hershel. *The City of David*. Washington, D.C.: Biblical Archaeology Society, 1975.

Stalker, James. *The Life of St. Paul*. Old Tappin, N.J.: Fleming Revell, 1940.

Story, Cullen I. K. "What Kind of Messiah Did the Jews Expect?" 104, no. 416 *Bibliotheca Sacra* (Oct.–Dec., 1947): 483.

Stover, Gerald. Acts, *The Church at Work*. Denver: Accent, 1968.

Tacitus. *The Annals of Imperial Rome*. New York: Dorset Press, 1984.

Telford, Andrew. *Studies in Ephesians*. Boca Raton, Fla.

Tenney, Merrill C. *The New International Dictionary of the Bible*. Grand Rapids: Zondervan, 1987.

Unger, Merrill F. "Archaeology and Paul's Tour of Cyprus." 117, no. 467 *Bibliotheca Sacra* (July-Sept., 1960): 229.

_____. "Historical Research and the Church at Thessalonica." 119, no. 473 *Bibliotheca Sacra* (Jan.–Mar., 1962): 38.

_____. "Pisidian Antioch and Gospel Penetration." 118, no. 469 *Bibliotheca Sacra* (Jan.–Mar., 1961): 46.

Unstead, R. J. *Inside A Roman Town*. New York: Barnes & Noble, 1977.

_____. *Inside an Ancient Greek Town*. New York: Barnes & Noble, 1977.

_____. *A Roman Galleon*. New York: Barnes & Noble, 1977.

Vine, W. E. *The Expanded Vines Expository Dictionary of New Testament Words*. Edited by John R. Kohlenberger III. Minneapolis: Bethany House, 1984.

Wilkinson, Samuel H. *The Israel Promises and Their Fulfillment*. London: John Bade & Danielson Ltd., 1936.

Wilson, William. *Wilson's Old Testament Word Studies*. McLean, Va.: MacDonald Publishing, n.d.

Woodward, Kenneth L. "How to Read Paul After 2,000 Years." *Newsweek*, 29 February 1988.

Wuest, Kenneth S. *An Expanded Translation of the New Testament*. Grand Rapids: Eerdmans, 1956.

SUBJECT INDEX

Subject Index

Scripture Index